Blackfoot Fur Trade on the Upper Missouri

J.M. Hutton

Fort Benton 1860

by

John G. Lepley

Printed in the United States of America
First Printing 2004

Library of Congress Number: 2004091100
ISBN: 1-57510-106-8

Published for John G. Lepley by
Pictorial Histories Publishing Company
713 South Third Street West; Missoula, Montana 59801
php@montana. com

Cover Painting by David Parchen
"The Booshway" Alexander Harvey at Fort Campbell, 1852

Dedication

For Duane and Ken and the Boys' Club: Larry, Bob, Parch and John and to many more nights of discussion and history

Maps

Table of Contents

Introduction

There have been many pages written about the fur trade from the return of Lewis and Clark in 1806 until 1840 at the end of the rendezvous system. Very little has been printed about the period of 1840 to 1865 when trade focused on the buffalo. This trade was concentrated along the Upper Missouri River where the heavy hides and robes could be shipped to market. Because transportation in Canada was by wagon and canoe to eastern markets, steamboats on the Missouri cut Canadian profits from pounds to shillings. American traders and companies had a tremendous advantage over the Hudson Bay Co., so the vast majority of the robe trade centered in the Blackfoot posts on the Upper Missouri. The Blackfoot robe trade began at Fort Union. The immense herds of buffalo soon moved further west and the trade shifted from beaver to buffalo. Fort Union lost its primacy to Fort Benton. When more reliable transportation on the upper river became a necessity, steamboats finally reached all the way up river to Fort Benton in 1860 and sealed Fort Union's fate. Fort Benton was established as the center of buffalo trade in the Northwest until they were nearly gone by the 1880's.

The Blackfoot were special people and although they got the horse late, they became the best buffalo hunters on the plains. An aggressive people, they were very protective of their lands and realized that those with furs and robes to trade were the rich ones. From the beginning it was a very different kind of trade, one founded on greed, whiskey and respect for violence. Both parties exercised a great deal of all three. As long as they both were isolated together in the wilderness, things remained in an uneasy peace. The Blackfoot knew that profit in furs and robes was from being the trapper or hunter. Both white and native alike coveted the high plains the Blackfoot called home for it was the continent's richest supply of beaver and buffalo. After the exploration of Lewis and Clark, the land of the Blackfoot became an obsession for exploitation by America's first big business in the West, the fur trade.

Although savvy about most of the aspects of the trade, the Blackfoot had a decided weakness for alcohol and it didn't take the English or the Americans long to exploit it. The American Fur Company and all subsidiaries and opposition companies that traded on the upper river were driven by greed just as big business is today. The cheapest trade item by far was alcohol; when diluted many times with water, it made poor men rich beyond belief. Regardless of the effects on their culture, "Give'm what they want and turn the biggest profit you can."

The Blackfoot tolerated the trader and allowed him to live in his country, but only as a trader . . . never as a trapper. Trade goods made their living better and improved their culture with firearms, clothing, iron and steel. The native culture was the source of wealth for trade, so non-violence was the watchword of the trader. With cross-cultural family ties, tension decreased and harmony existed with only a few isolated incidents marring the trade.

The alcohol sprees only occurred a couple of times a year and did not destroy their culture until free traders whose only motives were greed and a quick profit stepped on to the stage. Big companies were forced to leave and the native culture was decimated beyond repair. These once proud people of the high plains, independent and free nomadic hunters, became a reservation society dependent upon governmental support for their living.

Prologue: An Unspoiled Land

The canoe nosed out into the current as the first fingers of light brought the new dawn to the high bluffs surrounding the river. Barely visible on the bank is the State Memorial of the larger-than-life silhouettes of the two explorers, the Shoshoni woman and her son who had brought a new culture to this unspoiled land. They forged a trail that would be followed by the fur traders to the Upper Missouri.

A hundred yards down river is the only remaining vestige of this trade. Fort Benton with its high gray bastion standing lonely among the cottonwoods was the last fur post of the Blackfoot trade. Imagine a brightly colored company banner fluttering gently from the flagpole in the morning breeze. The ghosts of voyageurs and traders peer out of the narrow rifle slits and look with shaded eyes for the arrival of the summer's first keelboat from Fort Union. Those days are gone forever, but were once a colorful era of our wonderful past.

The canoe slipped silently around the conical base of Signal Point and then passed the mouth of the Shonkin where once was a chantier that built most of the boats for the fort. In the past along the stretches of brush and tree-lined banks several log structures were hastily erected to capture the high profits of the fur and robe trade for only a season or two. Appearing in the new light of the gray dawn was the rim of the river bluffs with the long saddle ridge of the Crocondunez. One can almost see the Piikani trekking along the ridge from their camp on the Tansey (Teton, 1) to trade at the fort. Just across the "bridge of the nose" lies the Tansey. Some of her waters trickle under the ridge and bubble up in the valley of the big river creating "Grog Springs" (2) of the Lewis and Clark Journals.

As the canoe moved through the gray waters of the river, the first rays of the morning sun danced along the crest of the far bluff, bathing it with an orange glow and bringing morning to the Upper Missouri. The hoarse throaty call of the ring-neck broke the silence of the new June day. Downstream the white-tail buck drinking at the bank lifted his head and stared for a moment, then with several quick ballet-like steps disappeared into the thicket of rose and chokecherry bushes held in the arms of the big cottonwoods. It was Blackfoot country, but glaciers had shaped the country before them. Their effects could be seen everywhere while drifting in the river.

The morning light slowly moved down the bluff and tan layers of glacial till, sometimes forty feet thick, brightened into yellow bands. The soil had been picked up by the glaciers from lands to the far north around Hudson Bay and deposited here, producing the rich farmlands of today and the vast grasslands of the past that provided a home for massive herds of bison and other plains animals of North America.

The Wisconsin Glacier had slowly rolled down from the Canadian North, pushing a wall of ice thousands of feet thick that shaped this land. It smoothed the island mountains that dot the high plains country. These isolated peaks, called the Sweetgrass, Bear's Paw, Little Rockies and Highwoods, had been extruded up from an earlier epoch when volcanoes spouted lava and spread ash while shaking and disrupting the land with plugs, dikes and sills of grey granite called Shonkinite. Today these signs of violence appear as the river cuts deeper and deeper into its valley and the wind exposes more of these rugged natural formations that have been named Le Citadel, Cathedral, the Grand Natural Wall and Haystack Butte.

The river of the plains had been a north-flowing river, carrying the water of the Rocky Mountains into distant Hudson Bay. As the glacier moved south, it blocked the river's northern flow so it gradually cut a new channel to the east along the face of the ice sheet. Glacial lakes formed as other rivers from the mountains to the south joined the new channel. The Judith, Mussellshell and Yellowstone all added their waters to this new and mighty river. Like all things on these timeless plains, they come and they go. The glacier gradually retreated back into the north from whence it came and the river was changed forever. Its channel now flowed to the east and south to the Gulf of Mexico, never again in our time to return to the Bay.

However, the region of Hudson's Bay had provided the soils that turned this short grass prairie into the world's best buffalo country and its streams into prime beaver habitat. The Bay also gave up a people with the Algonquin dialect who were as strong and resilient as the land itself. They migrated to the east slopes of the Rockies and to the Upper Missouri, changing and adapting their culture to life on the plains as had the animals before them. Unlike the first people, these were aggressive individuals who made a place for themselves in the new lands of the prairie, leaving their woodland homes forever. They became a buffalo culture and formed the large and powerful Blackfoot Confederacy composed of the Piikani, Kainaa and Siksika tribes.

By now the sun had reached the valley floor and the dark layers of Colorado shales absorbed its rays. These layers held the ancient fossils from the Silurian Seas and the giant creatures from the Mesozoic Era that today excite the public and have caused a fossil hysteria in books, toys and movies.

When the sun peeked over the southwest rim and the waters of the river took on the new colors of greens and blues, the canoe was rounding the corner where three giant cottonwoods marked the landing at Fort MacKenzie. As with most mornings, when daylight touches the valley floor the soft whisper of the gentle river breeze touches one's cheek. It twists and turns the long slender petioles of the shimmering leaves, making a hushed sound as it passes quickly through the foliage and reaches down to touch the rolling river. The canoe nosed onto the gravel bar landing near the stately trees that looked so much like royalty with their bright green crowns. Shimmering flashes of the morning sun reflected off the waxy surfaces of their leaves. This was the site of the premier post of the early Blackfoot trade. On the terrace above the landing once stood the wooden palisades of the fort, its log buildings and sod roofs. The large tree-lined bottom appeared much as it did in the early paintings of Karl Bodmer; the only noticeable change was the cultivated field.

Imagine hundreds of tipis spread along the river bottom; early morning smoke and sounds drifted up from the huge Piikani encampment. As the new day began, the barking of camp dogs and children's laughter echoed off the rugged bluffs that lined the bank across the river. A sharp report of the fort's cannon echoing off the bluffs signaled that trade was to begin. No visible signs of the fort remain, but look closely at the furrows in the field. Here and there are pieces of broken pottery, a single light blue trade bead or a splinter of bone peeking out from among the rich particles of dark soil.

The valley closed back in as the canoe drifted along. One cannot help but think about Hudson Bay and the Canadian lands where fur companies had been established by the French and English over a hundred years before those along the Upper Missouri. The one man who comes to mind is David Thompson. His adventures in the north as a cartographer, explorer and trader for over twenty-eight years are legendary. They provide a picture of the vast changes that occurred when the cultures of Europeans and Native Americans clashed on the fur frontier. His experiences with the Blackfoot people were among the first that were recorded and give a glimpse of their way of life during the first days of the Blackfoot fur trade. At age 16 Thompson came to the east slopes of the Rockies and spent a year in a Piikani camp along the Bow River. He lived with them, hunted and traded before returning to the fur posts on the Saskatchewan. The Hudson Bay Company had sent him to learn the language since they were interested in establishing trade with the buffalo hunters of the plains. In addition to learning the language, he also was a careful observer of their daily life: hunting buffalo, their ceremonies and lodge tales of the elders. Thompson lived with an old adopted Cree who taught him the language and told him many stories of the past. He mentioned the coming of the "Big Dog," leading Thompson to estimate that horses arrived in the Blackfoot villages around 1730. For twenty years they had been trading with their neighbors, the Cree and Assiniboine, for trade goods and muskets from the white man. This contact with the English and French gave the Blackfoot the trade gun long before their neighbors to the south and west. With the gun, the horse and their aggressive nature, the Blackfoot soon controlled the east slopes of the Rockies from the North Saskatchewan to the headwaters of the Missouri before the Americans arrived on the Upper Missouri.

Thompson's narrative discussed many Piikani who had pockmarked faces. His old mentor told of their plans to attack a Snake village. When they arrived, all were dead. The Piikani pillaged the village and within a few days smallpox broke out among the Blackfoot. 1781 was the first epidemic of the dreaded disease. The Blackfoot were never driven into submission by war; several epidemics of smallpox accomplished what armed conflict could not.

The canoe reached its destination at the mouth of Maria's River. A beautiful bluff loomed off to the left. From its crest the entire valley loomed into view, bathed in the afternoon sun. Where the Tansey flows into Maria's River is still a glorious site. Their waters then flow into the Missouri. Today it is obvious which is the main stream, but when the explorers stood here in early June 1805 it took several days of exploring both forks before they decided to proceed up the south fork, over the protests of all their men. It was not until Lewis reached the falls of the Missouri several days later that he knew they were traveling on the true Missouri.

Halfway across the valley floor the river flows around a sharp bend off to the east. Through time its current has cut deeper and deeper into the north bank and moved closer to the old channel of Maria's River, destroying the site of the first Blackfoot fur post on the Upper Missouri. In 1831 Fort Piegan was the beginning of American trade in Blackfoot country. The first furs and robes were exchanged for goods and whiskey to American Fur Company traders who came in peace to the land of the Blackfoot. Even if it only lasted one season, it was a beginning.

Text Note 1: Munikis Isisakta - Lewis and Clark spoke of it in the journals as the "Little River" and officially named it Rose River. If they were naming it for the large patches of wild roses along its banks, then this is appropriate. The traders called it the Tansey and the Blackfoot called it the Breast River and from this probably came the present French name of Teton.

Text Note 2: Lewis's camp of June 11, 1805 where he became deathly sick with stomach pains. He treated himself with a concoction of boiled chokecherry bark and was feeling much better the next morning.

Part I

Blackfoot Trade

The Sun

Fur Trade Chronology 1806-1830

August 15, 1806: John Colter left the Lewis and Clark Expedition at the Mandan Villages, and took up with two partners and returned to the mountains to hunt beaver.

Winter 1806: Manuel Lisa organized a company to tap the beaver trade on the Upper Missouri after hearing in St. Louis of the rich beaver country when Lewis and Clark returned.

Spring 1807: Lisa, headed up river, met John Colter at the mouth of the Platte River.

Summer 1807: Trouble with the Arikaras and the Assiniboine on the upper river.

Fall 1807: Lisa and his party changed their course and went up the Yellowstone because it was late in the season. They arrived at the mouth of the Bighorn in November and built Fort Ramon.

Winter 1807-08: Lisa sent two former Lewis and Clark men out to bring in the Crow and others to trade. Colter, Drouillard and Rose spent the winter looking for Indians.

Spring 1808: Spring hunt and the first trading

Summer 1808: Lisa and Drouillard returned to St. Louis, sending Colter out to bring in the Indians for trade. He found the Flatheads and was taking them to the fort when they were attacked by the Blackfoot. Colter fought notably well but was wounded. They were saved when the Crow entered the fight. Colter returned to Fort Ramon to recuperate.

Fall 1808: Fall hunt in the Three Forks area, Colter with John Potts. Potts was killed and Colter ran for his life from the Blackfoot. Other parties from the fort were trapping to the south.

Winter 1808-09: Colter returned to Three Forks to retrieve his traps near Bozeman Pass and was again almost killed by the Blackfoot. Lisa organized a new company called the St. Louis Missouri Fur Company in St. Louis with many partners including Chouteau, Menard and Henry.

Spring 1809: Completely discouraged, Benito Vasquez closed Fort Ramon and sent a party of trappers down the Yellowstone and to the Missouri with a very meager catch.

Fall 1809: At the Mandan Villages on September 22 Vasquez met Lisa coming up river with the new company and 150 men. Lisa returned to St. Louis for the next season's outfitting. From the villages Henry took 40 men on horseback and went overland to reopen the fort. Menard brought the boats on up the Missouri and the Yellowstone to the mouth of the Bighorn.

Winter 1809-10: Lisa's company on the Yellowstone traded with the Crow.

Spring 1810: April 3, began building a fort at the Three Forks. April 1, a large trapping party was attacked by Blackfoot, two dead and three missing. Colter was with this party. After four attacks by the Blackfoot he vowed he would leave the Upper Missouri for good and never return. Menard and the rest of the men hung on at the Three Forks. By May there were no more incidents so they began trapping in a large party for protection. After a short time they again split into small parties. Geo. Drouillard started out by himself; he was successful the first two days, but the third day out with two scouts he did not return. They were found butchered. The fort at the Three Forks was abandoned according to Menard's letter to Chouteau.

Mid-summer 1810: Andrew Henry, Reuben Lewis and a party of men had a fierce battle with the Blackfoot.

Fall 1810: Menard took the furs and headed back to St. Louis. Henry went with sixty men up the Madison River across the divide to Henry's Fork (north fork of the Snake) and built Henry's Fort where they stayed for the winter.

Winter 1810-11: Extremely cold and deep snow all winter. No game available, Henry's party almost perished.

Spring 1811: Henry's spring hunt west of the divide was cold and wet but profitable. On May 26 Robinson, Hoback and Reznor returned to Kentucky after spending the summer and winter with Henry's party. Met the Astorians on the Missouri and agreed to guide them to the Snake River on their trek to the Pacific. They persuaded Willson Price Hunt, leader of the Astorians, to go overland by horseback to avoid the Blackfoot on the Missouri. Trapper penetration into Blackfoot Country ended until 1830-31.

Summer 1811: Badly in need of supplies the trappers divided up. Many stayed in the mountains of the Central Rockies. Henry returned with 40 packs of furs down the Yellowstone to the Missouri. At the Mandan Villages he met Lisa coming up the river at the Mandan Villages with his third reorganized company, the Missouri Fur Company.

1813: Colter died of jaundice on a farm in Missouri, not yet 40 years old.

1814: Drouillard and Colter's knowledge of the Upper Missouri country incorporated into William Clark's big map in Biddle's publication of the Lewis and Clark Journals.

1821: The Hudson Bay Co. and Northwest Fur Co. were combined into a single company by royal decree.

1823: Immel and Jones were members of a trading/trapping party killed at Hell's Gate by the Blackfoot.

1825: First rendezvous on Henry's Fork up from the Green River.

1827: Kenneth MacKenzie joined the American Fur Company after the Columbia Fur Company was purchased by the American Fur Company.

1828: Fort Union was constructed at the mouth of the Yellowstone on the Missouri.

1830: MacKenzie sent Berger to make peace with the Blackfoot, first treaty at Fort Union. MacKenzie signed treaty for the Indians. Blackfoot agreed to a trading post in their territory.

BLACKFOOT LODGES

Lodge cover removed to show the 15 to 18 poles. Dew cloth on the inside was held down by rocks that left tepee rings on the landscape.

Blackfoot used four poles in their basic tepee structure; other tribes like the Sioux used a tripod.

1700 - 1800

Origins

Dog Days, Elk Dogs and Firesticks

Real People of the Prairie

In the Beginning

In the cultural origins of the Blackfoot, Napi, the Old Man, created the world. He produced water and earth, and all the animals and plants. From a lump of clay he made himself a wife. Old Man and Old Woman then fashioned the people of the earth and taught them how to live. The same creator appears in legends of the Arapaho, Atsina and Cree. In prehistoric times grandparents were probably telling their grandchildren wonderful stories of Napi long before their migration.

The ancient lodge tale of their origin came from Old Man. Napi had three married sons who with their families were near starvation in the woods of the north. They set out across the mountains to find better game and discovered a great treeless country. Upon the vast grasslands were countless numbers of giant brown beasts they had never seen before. The three sons tried to kill the shaggy-haired buffalo but failed because the animals always outran them.

Napi had a vision. He made a black-colored medicine and rubbed some on the eldest son's feet enabling him to run swiftly, and to

Artist David Parchen

Old Man or Napi with his pipe and friends

overtake and kill the huge beasts. Thus Old Man said his son should be called Siksika (Blackfoot).

The other two sons were very jealous of their brother and demanded some of the black medicine for themselves. Old Man refused. In his vision he had been told that the medicine was to be given only to his oldest son. His other sons would have new names also, but first they must earn them. The brothers set out on their adventures. When they returned, Old Man would bestow new names upon them according to what they had done during their quest.

Having traveled great distances during many winters, the youngest son came home. From the south he brought many tanned and painted buffalo robes for which he had traded with the friendly people he met on his journey. For his efforts, he was given the name Piikani (Far-Off Robes). The remaining son had traveled to the east and brought back scalps from enemies he had killed. He was named Kainaa (Many Chiefs). The legend of the three tribes of the Blackfoot Nation was born.

And So . . .

They called themselves Nitsitapi - the One, or the Only, or the Real People. The Confederacy was composed of three tribes: Piikani, Kainaa and Siksika. Their cousins were the Atsina (Gros Ventres of the Prairie) who were also cousins of the Arapahoe and the Sarcee (or Sarsi) who lived to the north and east.

Artist Rudolf Kurz

With a dog travois, the amount of goods a family could move was limited and curtailed their cultural progress.

Language as a Clue

The most valuable clue to the origin of the Blackfoot is their language and its Algonkian dialect. Algonkian-speaking people are the most numerous in the Native American Tribes; their disputed origins were in the forests of eastern North America. Some historians believe that these people were here before the ice ages and had migrated eastward. The theory is also based on language since the most ancient dialects are definitely among the western tribes. Before 1830, six peoples were on the Great Plains. The older resident tribes were Blackfoot, Arapahoe and Atsina. Plains Cree, Ojibwa and the Cheyenne were late-comers; their migration occurred within the historic period. The Atsina and Arapahoe were separated from one another in more recent times. As close cousins, they made long journeys to visit and trade well after the invasion of white trappers and traders early in the 19th century.

High Plains Migration

The Blackfoot were probably the earliest Algonkian-speaking residents on the plains. Although their language provides a clue to their origin, it should be noted that the Blackfoot dialect differs more from the parent tongue than do any other dialects spoken by Algonkian people. According to linguists, the longer the isolation of a language from its roots, the greater the differences in the dialect.

The adventurous migration from the Blackfoot homelands to the east may have begun in prehistoric times, and is comparable to pioneers from many countries that sought new opportunities when growing populations crowded existing space and/or threatened the food supply. Under those conditions men searched new horizons and became pilgrims of their people, braving dangers of the unknown and creating a vibrant independent people who fiercely protected their lands.

BLACKFOOT NATION
During Historic Times

Dog Days

By the 18th century the Blackfoot occupied lands of the mountain tributaries of the Saskatchewan and Missouri Rivers. Sometime during pre-history they were divided into three tribes that became politically independent from one another. They still spoke a common language, shared the same customs, intermarried and made war on mutual enemies. It is believed that their name came from their enemies the Cree. Whether their moccasins were intentionally dyed black or were stained from the dark earth or fire ashes of the prairie, no one knows, but the literal translation of the native name Siksikauw is black-footed people. For centuries the three tribes were known by separate names: Piikani or Piegan, Kainaa or Blood and Siksika or Northern Blackfoot.

It is certain that during prehistoric times the Blackfoot accompanied by their dogs were on the plains on foot and became isolated from their cousins. How long they were along the eastern frontier is up to conjecture. It is known that when they had their first contact with white traders, they were accustomed to life on the

Artist Karl Bodmer

An early Blackfoot camp during the "Dog Days" after they had come to the prairie and were hunting buffalo. Notice the stacked travois as the women get ready to break camp.

plains and had hunted buffalo on the short grass prairies since long before European settlement on the eastern shores of North America.

Before the traders came, the Blackfoot were a hardy people who shared their buffalo kills among families of the band. All prospered when buffalo were plentiful and starved together when the animals and other food were scarce.

Their culture was limited by transportation. People and their dogs could carry only limited burdens. There were few luxuries. Accumulation of anything, including food, was limited to the transportation available. They lived on what the land provided by becoming self-reliant hunters who defended their lands against neighbors to the south and west. Because of their isolation, those early times of the Blackfoot, called the dog days, were virtually unrecorded except for tales told by the old people to the first white men when they visited in the 18th century.

Three "Gifts"

White traders entered Blackfoot country by paddling up the Saskatchewan River in canoes, bringing an assortment of metal utensils and other items unknown to the Blackfoot culture. Such useful objects were exchanged

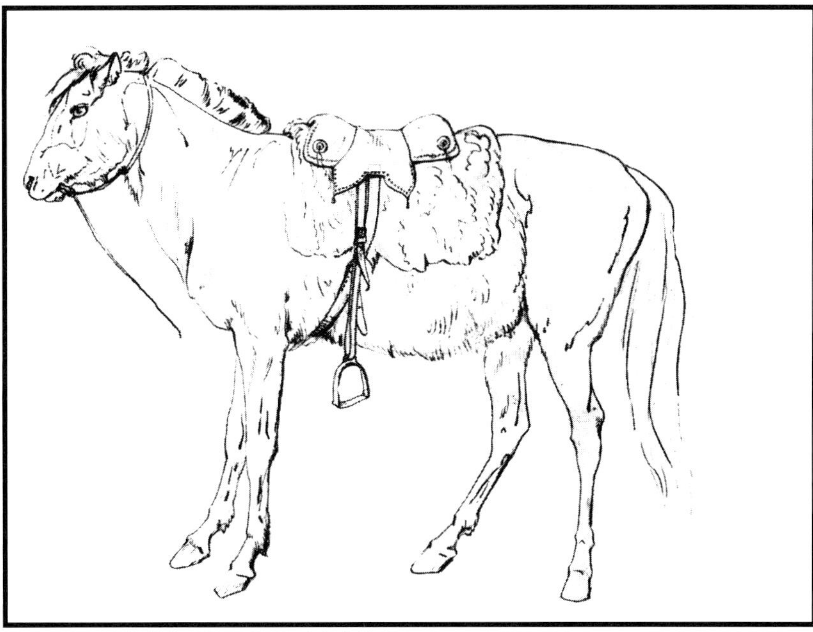

Artist Rudolph Kurz

Blackfoot horse with a native saddle and bridle but iron stirrups from the trade store. Note the short mane, perhaps is a Spanish Barb breed.

for furs and food and often made life easier. The strange bearded people, called Napikwan meaning old man person, were appropriately named for the miracles they brought to the native people.

Traders introduced hundreds of new articles that changed the native way of life. Trade items allowed the Blackfoot to more readily accomplish tasks that they had been doing for hundreds of years or added comfort to their daily lives. Metal pots provided unbreakable cookware; blankets became lightweight bedding and clothing. Metal tools held their edge better and were more durable than their stone counterparts. Two things in particular – firearms and horses - had the greatest impact by creating extensive modifications to their culture. The acquisitions of horses and weapons were miraculous events in native history, rivaling even the mysteries of Napi.

Communicable disease was the third great agent of change brought by white traders. The grimmest reaper was smallpox. It struck with a deadly, silent ferocity that wiped out entire bands at a time. Not understood at first, smallpox plied some tribes with so much death that they never recovered.

The Blackfoot, and most plains people along the east front of the Rockies, were introduced to firearms long before they saw their first horses. Firearms greatly increased the distance between enemies, making the bow and arrow obsolete for warfare.

Before firearms, a traditional Indian battle was fought along two lines of warriors about a distant arrow's flight apart. New weapons called rifles provided a tremendous advantage; from much farther away than an arrow's flight a rifleman could kill an enemy with almost every shot when a bowman exposed himself to shoot an arrow. Rifles fired a projectile so swiftly that one could not see its flight; they made a frightening noise and could kill man or animal at a great distance.

The Blackfoot first saw firearms in the Assiniboine and Cree villages. Through trade, using these tribes as middlemen, they obtained ten guns for hunting and war. When they first

Hudson Bay Co. peace medal with profile of King George III

took guns into battle with the Shoshoni, the invisible killer, the noise and the clouds of smoke so terrified the Shoshoni that they fled in panic with the Blackfoot in hot pursuit.

Artist George Catlin

Eagle Ribs, a Piikani warrior at Fort Union

A Change in Life Style

During the last years of the "dog days," the Shoshoni were the greatest threat to the security of the Blackfoot when they introduced a new four-footed living weapon into their battles. Many years later, the Piikani described their first experience with the weapon to David Thompson: "a large animal as swift as a deer being ridden by their enemy and dashing in and knocked them in the head with war clubs." Though they had never seen a horse before, they immediately recognized their need to acquire the beasts. Through trade, in battle, and by stealing from their enemies, the Blackfoot acquired the horse, first called "Big Dog," later "Elk Dog." By the 1730's the Piikanis' acquisition of both rifle and horse gave them a tremendous advantage over their enemies to the

Artist Karl Bodmer

With the horse, Indian culture changed, and the pishkin was no longer necessary to hunt the buffalo. From horseback the hunters could seek out the herds and with bow and arrow or gun could kill them on the run. Horses allowed them to move more freely on the plains and carry many more goods than they could with dogs.

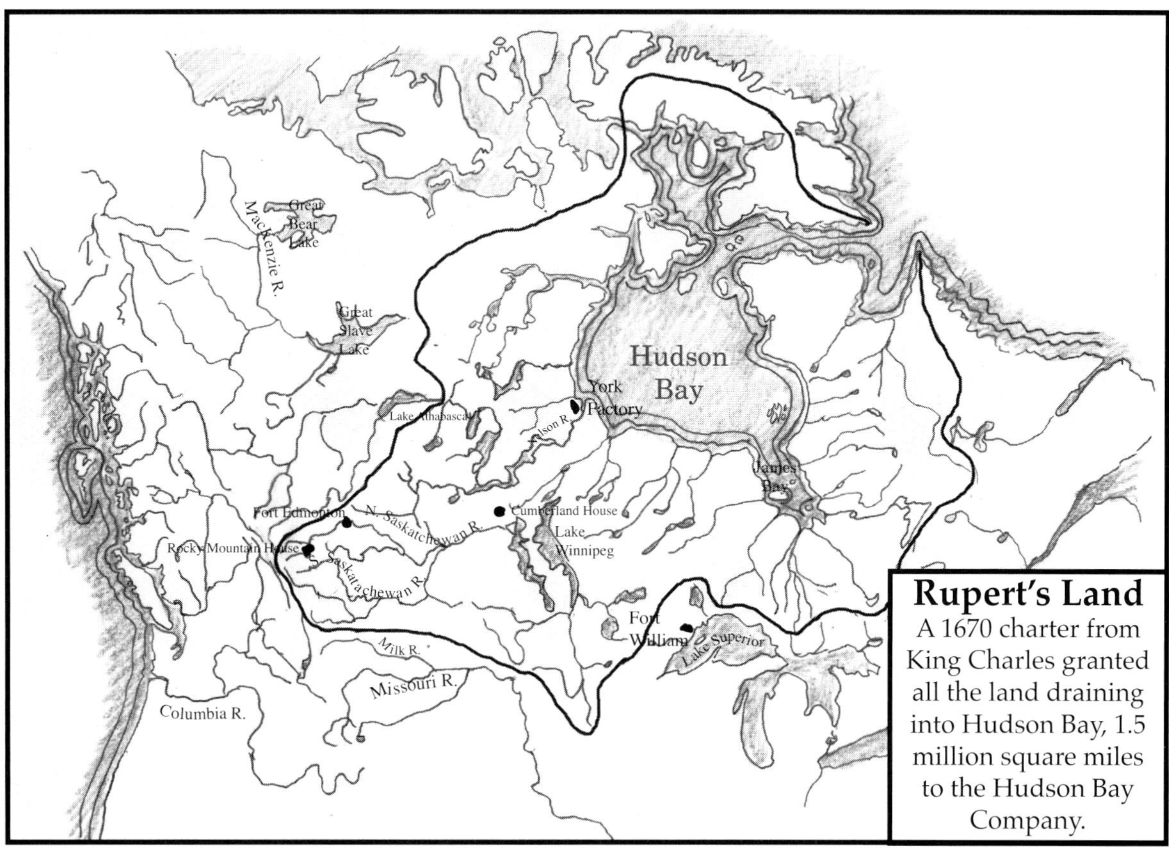

A map of the Canadian north showing the territory of Rupert's Land to be administered by the Hudson Bay Co. from 1670 to 1869. It contained all the land drained by the waters that ran into Hudson Bay and was granted by Royal Charter of the King.

south and west. The Shoshoni and other western tribes with no trade access to guns or other metal weapons were continually intimidated and gradually forced out of the Upper Missouri. The Kutenai, Salish and Nez Perce were driven into mountain valleys to the west away from buffalo country.

Elk Dog brought great changes to the Piikani culture. Like the buffalo, his food came from the lush prairie grasses. Unlike the dog he did not compete with people for food. Unlike the rifle, the horse was primarily a means of hunting and a beast of burden. It gave mobility to the warrior hunters who no longer had to stoop to scavenge among the victims of a pishkin. They could catch and kill game wherever it was found. A short bow could deliver several arrows as the hunter rode near the bison's side for the fatal shot. In that instance a bow was more effective than a rifle that fired only one shot before reloading. At best the hunt was a slow and difficult task on the ground, let alone on a galloping steed in the middle of a herd of stampeding buffalo.

The two important new items gained through trade occupied quite different niches in the Blackfoot culture, one for war and one for peace. The horse probably initiated the greatest change in their life style. Warriors began to acquire wealth via their herds of horses and attained a certain degree of freedom with perhaps a little leisure time. Mobility of the horse made it possible to range farther and faster than ever before; the Blackfoot could trade in regions never available to them on foot. The horse also changed the style of warfare in native culture as it had centuries before in other cultures around the world. Mounted warriors

Artist Karl Bodmer

The reason white traders came from the East was the beaver. Beaver felt was the basis of the hat industry in North America and Europe. Seeking the beaver plew brought traders and trappers into the West to trade with the natives, forever changing their culture.

always dominated those on foot, raiding deep into enemy country without the immediate threat of retaliation.

Coming of the Traders

As the decades passed, traders from the French and English colonies along the Atlantic seaboard penetrated deeper and deeper into the West. Adventure-bound businessmen were always on the alert for new country bearing the beaver. They continued to move westward in advance of trading posts and settlements.

The beginning of the fur trade dates back to 1535 and the French navigator, Jacques Cartier. During his exploration of the St. Lawrence River, he became stalled at the great rapids so he stopped and traded with some Indians, metal goods for beaver skins. The furs made ideal felt for hats of all types, and were a sensation with hatmakers in Europe. By the early 17th century the demand for beaver pushed the hunt farther into the West. By 1650 Montreal traders had opened up the Great Lakes region, seeking furs from Indians in the region rather than waiting for them to come to the settlements to trade. Encouraged by Samuel de Champlain, those canoe-paddling traders became known as French voyageurs. From their Montreal headquarters on the St. Lawrence, French traders and explorers went beyond the Great Lakes and into the Mississippi Valley during the 17th century.

The Hudson Bay Company

Henry Hudson's explorations to the north turned another vast territory into a trade region. He claimed an immense bay (Hudson Bay) and the area surrounding it for the Dutch, but the English Crown almost immediately confiscated the lands. In 1670 King Charles II issued a charter for the first English commercial enterprise in North America, the Hudson Bay Company, which eventually became the most powerful company in the new world. The king's charter gave the company all lands drained by any river flowing into Hudson Bay. The gigantic area, 1.5 million square miles, was named Rupert's Land for a royal prince who

This flag flew over hundreds of posts and forts that were built and operated by the Hudson Bay Company. Rival traders stated the letters stood for "Here Before Christ."

was a powerful supporter of the company. The great scope of territory was unknown at the time; it encompassed land all the way to the eastern slopes of the Rocky Mountains including Blackfoot Country.

The company started with Fort Charles at the south end of Hudson Bay and built several more "factories" (fortified posts) at the mouths of rivers along the bay. The ultra-conservative company then waited for Indians to come trade at their posts.

Westward movement by the French encouraged construction of trading posts on the Assiniboine River by the 1730's. In the next decade the Hudson Bay Company built its first post on the Saskatchewan, bringing them ever closer to the Blackfoot. At that time Hudson Bay Company trade items began to appear in Blackfoot camps, but came from middleman tribes who traded on the Bay and then with their neighbors, the Blackfoot.

Peace in Europe

After several decades of wars fought on two continents between the British and the French, the Treaty of Paris supposedly settled the fate of the fur trade in North America in 1763. With decisive victories at Montreal and Quebec, the British thought their troubles in Canada were over when the French ceded their Canadian territories to Great Britain. Owners of the Hudson Bay Company expected that their troubles with the French in the fur trade would vanish and that they would easily monopolize the trade. However the results were far different than they anticipated, and trade actually became much tougher for the HB Company.

By the 1750's the English had been spooked by French competition. Fear of losing their new trade motivated the Company to send a trading party to the new tribes. Anthony

Schwinden Library Fort Benton

The premier Hudson Bay Company post and headquarters in the new world was York Factory on the Nelson River at the edge of Hudson Bay. From here explorers and traders moved west finding new territory for trading and trapping.

Henday led a group that wintered on the plains with the Blackfoot, returning to posts on the Bay the next spring. He had no luck convincing the Blackfoot to bring their furs to the Bay to trade. Meanwhile, independent traders from Montreal with Scottish and French connections ventured onto the plains with superior, English-produced trade goods and competed successfully with the Hudson Bay Company. Throughout the next decade they gave the Company fierce competition in Rupert's Land (western Canada).

In 1772, after Henday's failure to engage the Blackfoot in trade, the Company sent Mathew Cocking from York Factory on the same mission. In December, Cocking found a Blackfoot winter village where warriors were hunting buffalo in a pound. He spent several weeks trying to persuade them to go to the Bay with him to trade but without success. With his Cree guides, Cocking returned to York Factory empty-handed, but had learned a great deal about the tribes. He could identify the three members of the Blackfoot Nation and their two allies, the Atsina and the Sarcee. After reading Cocking's report, Company officials realized that to compete with the so-called Scottish-French "peddlers," they needed to expand their posts southwestward.

In 1774 the Hudson Bay Company moved into the upper Saskatchewan River area and established Cumberland House. They gradually moved up the river, hoping to initiate a brisk trade with those long-sought customers. As Americans to the south later realized, the English also recognized that the richest fur country in the continent lay in the homelands of the Blackfoot and their allies.

A Deadly Killer

Shortly after the traders arrived, the first smallpox epidemic struck in Blackfoot Country, carried by Shoshoni from traders in the south. In 1781 on the Red Deer River the Piikani had found a Shoshoni village of dead and dying. Not realizing the disease's extremely contagious nature, they collected the spoils from the village and in a short time smallpox broke out among the Blackfoot. Before it was over, the disease destroyed over half of the Piikani population. Helpless against the strange new killer, the medicine men could not cure it nor did sacrificial rites to the spirits relieve their distress.

For the first time the Blackfoot met an enemy they could not understand or defeat. It would not be their last encounter with smallpox. With each succeeding attack of the plague, the power of the most successful Indian nation on the plains was diminished until only half of their population remained. The Shoshoni also were so badly weakened by the dread disease that they moved south, abandoning the Bow River country to the Blackfoot.

Traders not Trappers

Despite decimation of the Piikani, traders still enjoyed excellent trade and their invasion of the plains continued. Early in the trading period, the Blackfoot and their allies realized the worth of their furs. Perhaps their awareness occurred as a result of how the French and English did business, depending upon the Indians to bring in furs rather than trapping for themselves. Regardless, in Blackfoot Country it soon became known that it was all right for traders to come, but trappers were forbidden. Loss of life was payment for trapping in the land of the Blackfoot.

The area enjoyed peace for several years while the tribes recuperated from smallpox. However, any incident could trigger another confrontation between the Piikani and their neighbors. Such an incident occurred when

To make trade easier, the Hudson Bay Co. had its own currency in token coins that were used by both trader and native.

Schwinden Library, Fort Benton

Perched high on a bluff overlooking the North Saskatchewan River, Fort Edmonton was one of the major Hudson Bay Co. trade forts in northern Canada. The fort was on the edge of Blackfoot Country, much closer to their lands than York Factory on Hudson Bay.

the Shoshoni abandoned a small camp of their dead from smallpox. The Piikani took offense to such an act and were back on the warpath. In an unrelenting war against the Shoshoni and their allies, the Salish and the Kutenai, trade guns and horses drastically tipped the scales in favor of the Piikani. With a ready supply of powder and shot, they drove the Shoshoni, who had only bows and arrows, south of the Missouri headwaters. The Piikani chased the Salish and the Kutenai out of buffalo country across the Divide into the western valleys of the Rockies. Attacks were so successful that the Shoshoni eventually retreated into the western mountains to escape annihilation by their fearsome enemies.

New Competitor

With the fall of the French government, Scots who had immigrated to Canada's Maritime Provinces descended upon Montreal and became attracted to the fur trade. Independent by nature, the Scots established many small companies and adopted the French system of going after the furs. Being good businessmen, the Scots improved the system by actually leading their brigades of hired voyageurs into the western wilderness. They subsequently became rich in the fur trade. So competitive were the Scots among themselves that the Hudson Bay Company did not experience any real threat, derisively calling them the "peddlers." However the enterprising Scots soon realized they could compete only if they unified their companies for the common good. Consequently, the North West Fur Company was organized in Montreal in 1783.

Mutual Protection

During 1784 and the following years the North West Fur Company cut deeply into the Hudson Bay Co.'s beaver trade profits with the Kainaa and Siksika. In 1799 when the Bay Company built Rocky Mountain House at the mouth of the Clearwater, they finally had a permanent post to trade with the Piikani. They had tried to monopolize trade with the Piikani since 1787 when David Thompson spent the winter with the Piikani on the Bow River.

There was great rivalry between the two

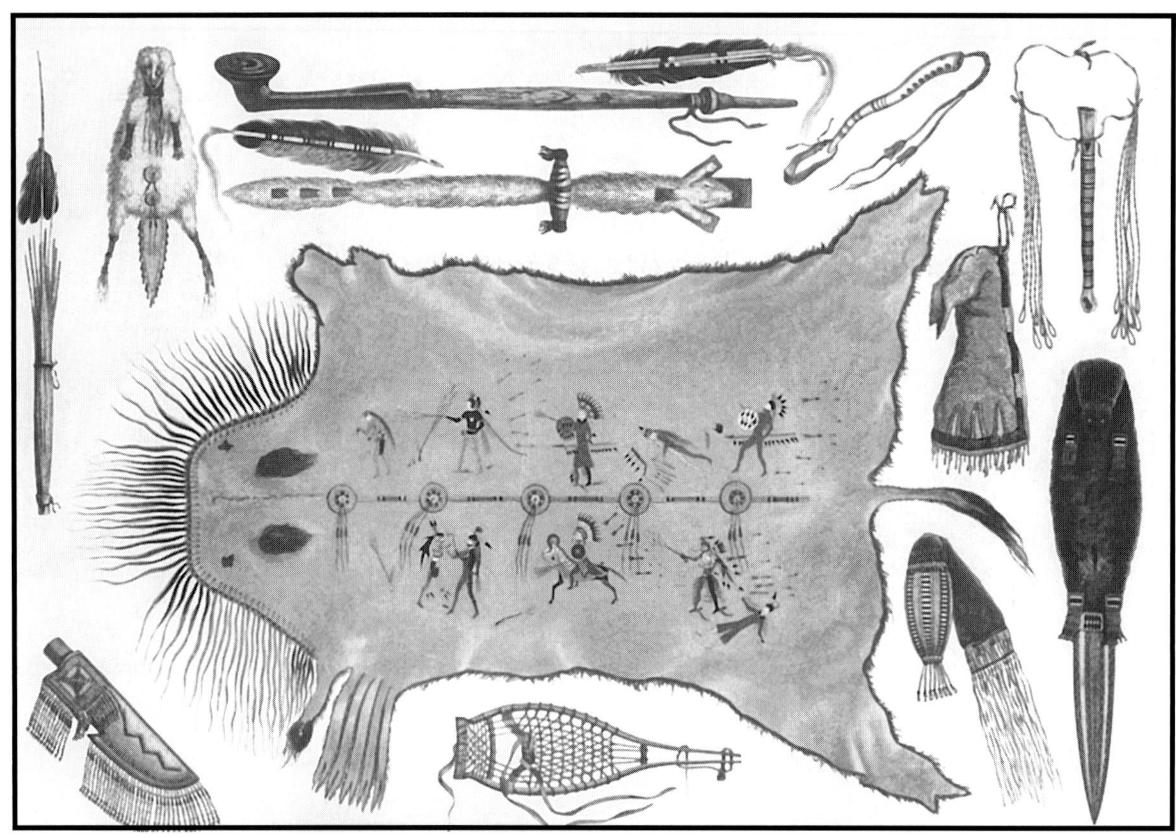

Artist Karl Bodmer

Notice the trade goods in these Blackfoot artifacts that were in use at Fort MacKenzie early in the fur trade era on the American side of the border.

companies; both were competing in Blackfoot Country. Rival posts were often built within sight of one another, for mutual protection and also perhaps to keep an eye on each other's trade. Fort Vermilion was one of the more interesting twin trading posts. Each company built a Masters House within a single stockade. Trade was very competitive, but the protection was greatly appreciated by both parties. From Cumberland House, the Hudson Bay Company advanced up the North Saskatchewan River 550 miles. Manchester House was built on an island in the center of the river at the edge of Blackfoot Country in 1786. The North West Fur Co. followed and built Pine Island House nearby.

The first white trader to reach the southern Alberta plains was Henry Kelsey from the Bay Company. He spent the winter of 1691 with the Assiniboine and Cree who told him of the war-like Blackfoot living to the west along the foothills of the mountains.

The next advance up the river occurred when the Bay Company built Buckingham House and Fort George was put up by their rival. In 1795 came Fort Edmonton and Fort Augustus. Rival forts were relocated several times, each time farther up river. The last sites are now within the present city of Edmonton; the Bay Company's Fort Edmonton site is part of the state house lawn.

Trouble

Most Blackfoot posts in Canada were under duress by the natives, just as they were on the American side of the border in later years. In the fall of 1793 the Piikani, or more likely their Atsina cousins, came to both Pine Island and Manchester House under the pretense of trade. Both posts were undermanned at that time of

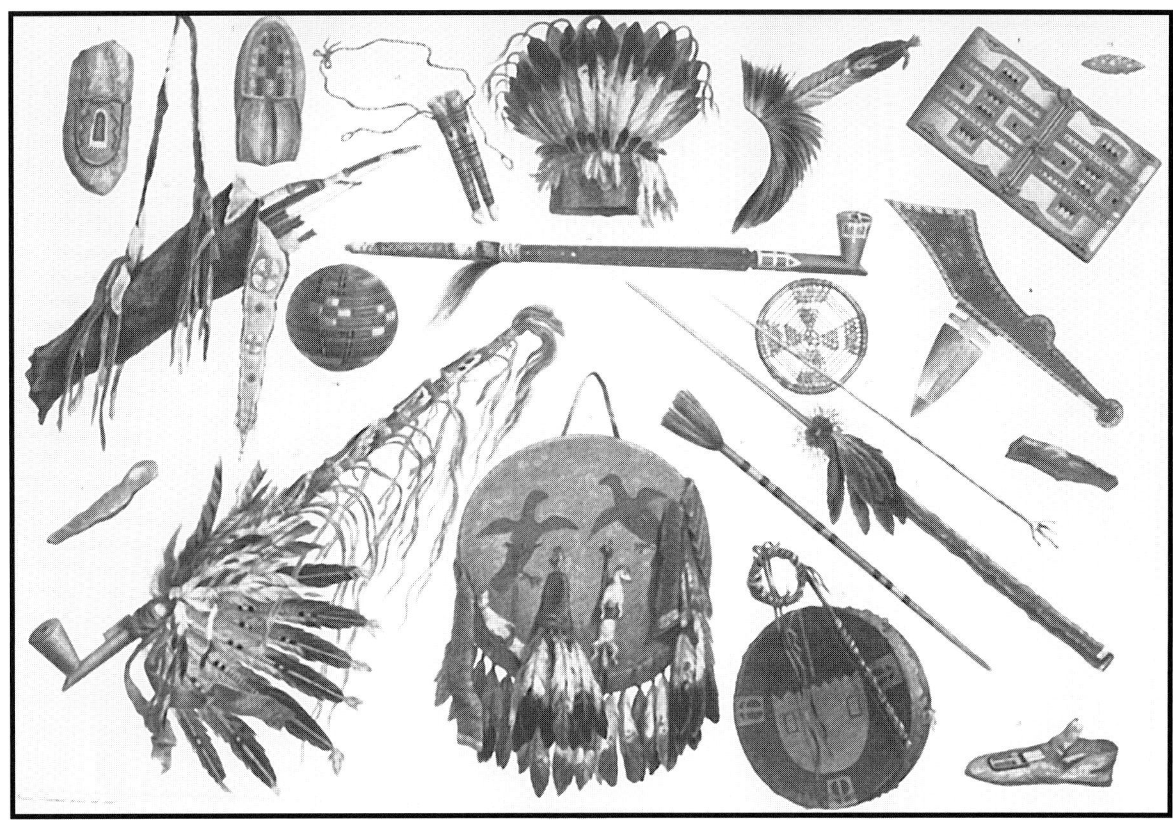

Artist Karl Bodmer

Blackfoot cultural items made without the white man's trade goods with the exception of the warclub with a dagger blade embedded in the wooden handle

year. Once the Indians gained access inside the walls, fighting began. Many traders were killed; the Indians drove off the horses and carried away the stores. As a result of attacks such as this, the trading houses were abandoned and burned by the natives shortly thereafter. In the summer of 1794 the Indians attacked houses on the south fork of the river with stunning success; those forts were also abandoned and burned.

Two posts under the most pressure during the early years were Fort Edmonton and Fort Augustus. The entire Blackfoot Nation and their cousins the Atsina and Sarsi, as well as their hated enemies the Assiniboine and Cree, traded there. The powder keg was ready to explode at any time. Thanks to their level-headed traders, both companies controlled the situation and there were never any serious incidents.

Tremendous competition between the Hudson Bay Company and the North West Fur Company led to heavy losses for both, to costly lawsuits in London, and to armed clashes in the wilderness. The rivalry continued until finally the Crown stepped in and forced a unification to save the Canadian fur trade. Hudson Bay Co. absorbed North West Fur Co. in 1821. Those associated with the Canadian trade said that the old company initials HBC meant "Here Before Christ" and again the royal company remained supreme. The Hudson Bay Company dominated fur trade with the Blackfoot north of the border until 1869, when all chartered land was turned over to the Dominion of Canada. The territory was then open to everyone.

Rocky Mountain House

1799 - 1821

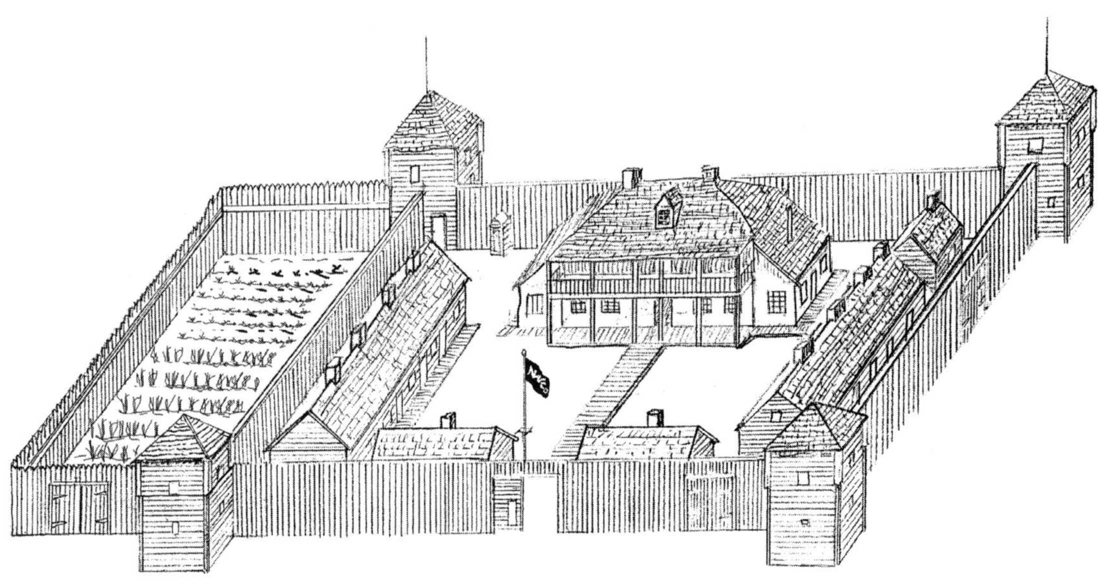

Rocky Mountain House was a Canadian fur post for Blackfoot trade along the eastern slopes of the Rocky Mountain Front. Founded by the Nor'Westers, it was taken over by the Hudson Bay Company when they merged in 1821. It was far enough to the south that all three tribes traded here. Rocky Mountain House was one of the posts that had an Opening of the Fur Trade Ceremony every fall.

1790 - 1800

Nor'Westers

A Company of Great Traders

The Beginning of the Trade Ceremonies

The Nor'Westers

At the end of the American Revolution, a young, shrewd, aggressive group of Scottish-French traders built a commercial empire that spanned the continent and defied the Royal Charter of the King. They organized two companies but in 1804 the XY Fur Company was absorbed into the North West Fur Company. So was born the North West Fur Company or the Nor'Westers as they called themselves. The company reached its zenith at the turn of the eighteenth century, with 2000 traders and clerks spread across the Canadian West. It made an estimated 15-year profit of 1,185,000 British pounds sterling.

In 1775 the first partnerships were formed. An American, Peter Pond, found a partner and backer in Simon McTavish, a rising star among the Scottish companies. Pond became his explorer and trader in the West. Pond first opened trade on the Saskatchewan River, then headed north, crossing the divide between the Hudson Bay drainage and the Arctic Ocean watershed. He opened trade on Lake Athabaska and the MacKenzie River drainage.

In 1790 Peter Pond returned to the United States after two episodes involving the deaths of rival traders. Before he left he

Artist Dave Parchen

Loading up at Montreal for the summer rendezvous at the Grand Portage

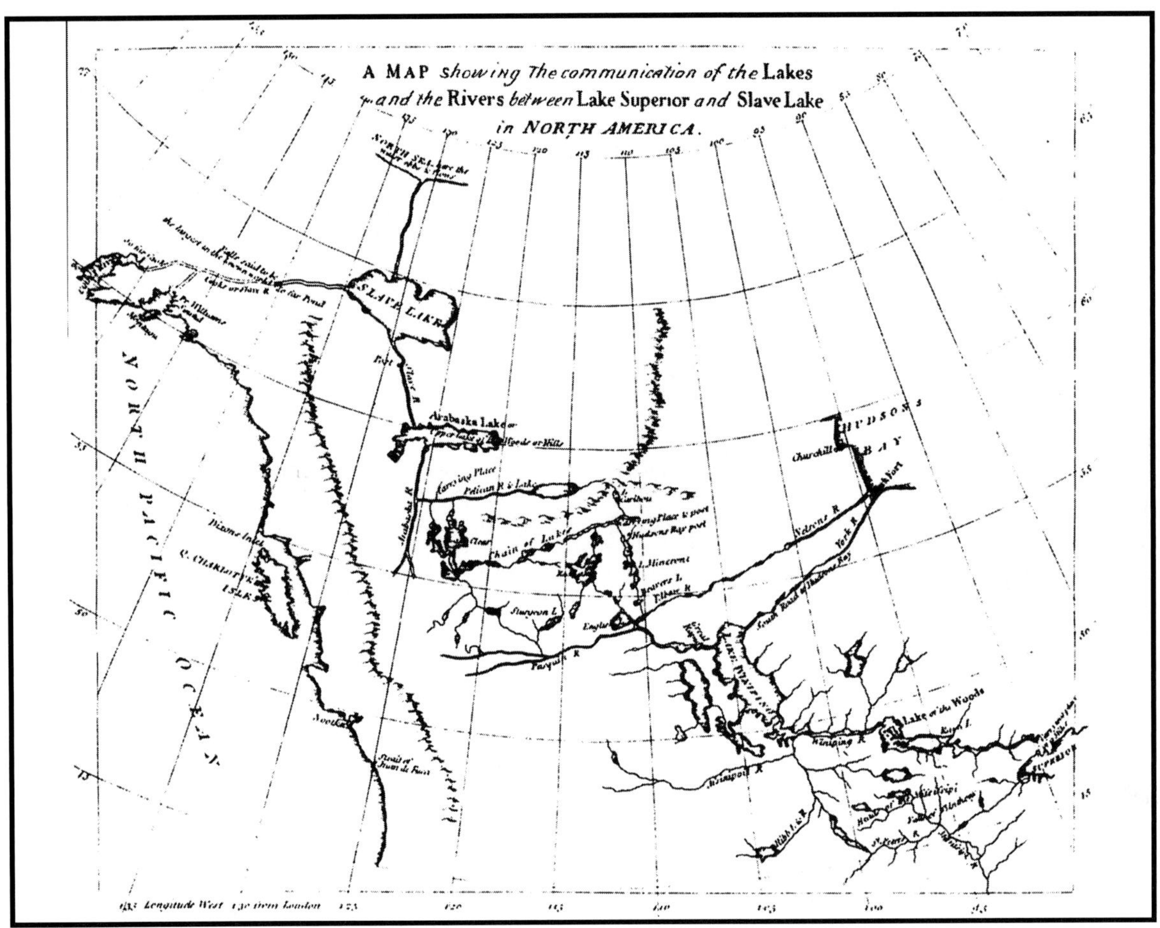

Peter Pond's map of 1789 shows the route between the Grand Portage on Lake Superior and the Great Slave Lake in the Canadian North. The route was followed by many Nor'Westers into the beaver trade and eventually to Blackfoot Country.

trained an able replacement in a young Scot, Alexander Mackenzie, who was destined to become the premier Canadian explorer and master trader. By that time Simon McTavish had risen to power as the head of the North West Company; the company dominated the fur trade north of the border, even spilling over onto the American side.

Large profits were the nemesis of the company. They were shared among the partners leaving little capital for investment. Their conservative rival, the HB Company, paid few dividends to the owners and used large amounts for investment capital to build a greater and stronger business. Tremendous competition between the two companies led to heavy losses. They joined ranks in 1821.

The most disgruntled traders headed south and joined the American trade on the Mississippi and Missouri Rivers. Practices brought with the North West Fur Company deserters included the ritual of the opening of the trade with the various bands of Blackfoot. The fanfare, gifts, uniforms, smoking the pipe and the drunken spree were all part of the ceremonies before actual trade began.

North West Company Rendezvous

In the 1790's, the great years of the North West Fur Company, the seasons dictated the routine operations of the trade. The season

Schwinden Library, Fort Benton

Alexander Mackenzie, the great explorer of the North West Fur Company, left the company after losing the feud with McTavish over company policy.

began and ended with the summer rendezvous at Grand Portage, a large depot on the north shore of Lake Superior. With the ice breakup in May, the partners started their thousand-mile journey from Montreal west to Grand Portage. Crews of 10 voyageurs handled brightly painted, 40-foot birch bark highbrow canoes loaded with 4 tons of freight. A brigade of up to thirty canoes was under the command of a clerk or partner called the bourgeois. The brigades headed out across the lakes and rivers with their red-bladed paddles dipping rhythmically to the songs of the voyageurs, which drifted across the waters.

When they approached the rendezvous, the men broke out their best attire - red tasseled knit caps, blue jackets and bright sashes - while the bourgeois dressed in the status symbols of his position, a beaver felt top hat and a long-tailed coat. With flags flying and much singing and shouting, they raced into the cozy harbor of Grand Portage amid the shouts and greetings of all on shore. It was a gala month of labor first, then drinking, dancing, parties and girls. The arrival of Simon McTavish's private canoe brought more cheers when he stepped onto the dock and surveyed his capitol in the wilderness. It had been completed in 1784 with high palisades and bastions on the corners; in the center of the enclosure stood the Great Hall, the place for business meetings, dining and the grand banquet and ball. Around the Great Hall were other buildings - warehouses, shops, a powder magazine and quarters for the voyageurs.

Spring Breakup

The wintering partners, those who stayed in the mountains and on the prairies trading for furs all winter, started south and east at spring break-up loaded with packs of furs. By early July they began arriving at the Pigeon River Depot from the many posts scattered through the north and west. Those traders arrived in smaller craft, only 25 feet long and each carrying a ton and a half of pelts. The buckskin-clad voyageurs who called themselves the Men of the North, were the elite. They were paid more than the Montrealers for their daring and dangerous life among the savages. Men

Schwinden Library, Fort Benton

Called the Marquis by his partners, Simon McTavish was the autocratic head of the Nor'Westers and had a running feud with Alexander Mackenzie on how the company should be run.

of the North never missed a chance to lord it over the Montrealers, calling them "manguers du lard" in reference to their diet of pork and lard. When passing each other along the portage trail, neither could resist sarcasm which sometimes produced deadly fights where one might lose his life. Fortunately a gouged eye, an ear bitten off, or a knife wound were the result of these "passage" encounters.

Physically the voyageurs were usually of a size, as if they had been stamped from the same mold. Short, deep-chested, with muscular arms and shoulders, they were built for carrying large loads, tireless walking or paddling for hours without rest. Yet they were small enough to fit in the bottom of their canoes. Those tireless French or mixed-bloods were the real men of the trade. Without their love of the wilderness and their hard work, the partners could never have made their millions selling beaver in the European and American markets.

Portage

From the fort on Lake Superior to the depot on the river was a distance of nine miles. The trail traversed a hilly, winding, rocky divide and crossed swampy flats. The men complained, "It was harder to cross the portage than it was to get into heaven." Before the voyageurs were allowed to begin carousing and drinking, they had to carry their cargo across the portage. The Montrealers usually arrived ahead of the fur brigades and started their trek over the portage with two ninety-pound sacks or pieces slung on their backs. With a leather forehead band to ease the load on their lower back, each was required to carry four loads across the portage. If a porter exceeded the eight-sack quota, he received

Leslie's Weekly

The river depot across the divide from the Grand Portage. The packs of furs weighed 180 pounds and were carried nine miles on the backs of voyageurs before they were loaded in canoes for the trip to Montreal.

Artist Dave Parchen

Anthony Henday, a Hudson Bay employee, entered a Blackfoot camp in October 1754, the first white trader to make contact with people along the eastern front of the Rockies.

extra compensation. Since the pay was by the piece, many carried more than two at a time and others made more than four trips. Each load weighed more than the voyageur, but with a shuffling trot he started up the trail to the first rest called a poses. The Grand Portage had sixteen poses from 600 yards to a half-mile apart. On their return, the Men of the North carried heavy bundles of furs back across the portage to be loaded into the great canoes and carried back to the warehouses in Montreal. The punishing work herniated many and was the second cause of death among the voyageurs, surpassed only by drowning.

With their work all done, the voyageurs had a couple of weeks to rest and be lazy around the fort. Many paid their bills, signed up for the next year, repaired their gear or bought new items from the trade store.

The beaver felt hat was the symbol of authority for all bourgeois on the frontier and the major millinery business in Europe and the Americas.

Schwinden Library, Fort Benton

A replica of the Great House at Grand Portage where McTavish reigned over the Nor'Westers. The Grand Ball was held at the end of the fur trading season before their return to Montreal and outlying fur posts in the north.

Most of their time was spent in the canteen, eating, drinking and enjoying the Cree and Chippewa girls. Meanwhile, the partners and traders met with Simon McTavish in the Great Hall. Last year's business was reviewed and prospects for the next season were discussed. When all decisions were made, McTavish gave the order to prepare for the Annual Banquet and Ball.

Schwinden Library, Fort Benton

After the year's business was completed, Simon McTavish presided at the Grand Ball in the Great Hall before taking the returns to Montreal.

A Party

After a week of preparation the big day arrived. Around the campfires outside the fort, voyageurs were dressing in their brightest and finest clothes in preparation for a boisterous evening of eating and dancing. The Great Hall, all in candle light, admitted the partners led by McTavish. They were decked out in bright silk vests, gray long-tailed coats, and of course, their swords. Everyone was seated according to rank. McTavish sat at the center of the head table in front of the fireplace with the rest of the partners seated around him. The officers, traders, clerks, interpreters and guides seated themselves at long wooden tables facing the front. The feast was on. The bill of fare included meats of all kinds - ham, venison, beef, fish and buffalo - along with vegetables from the fort's garden. All was washed down with Port and Madeira; kegs of rum and other spirits were also available. After many rounds of toasts to first the company and its leaders then to everything and everyone that could be remembered, the banquet hall became a site of rollicking, shouting and laughing men.

When everyone had eaten and drunk their fill, the tables were pushed back for dancing. The doors were flung open to admit the voyageurs and Indians who had been dining outside. McTavish led the local chief's daughter onto the floor for the Highland reel that started the ball. Other Scottish Highland dances to bag pipes, violin and flute followed. When the Scots tired, the voyageurs seized their partners and stomped and whirled until early morning. By then, the drinking had taken its toll and merrymakers stumbled and staggered out of the Great Hall. Met by the sunrise, they finished the celebration in small drunken groups along the edge of the lake.

Despite many hangovers, the next day was all business and started while the morning was still young. The Northerners headed wearily across the portage to the Pigeon River toward the wilderness. The Montrealers climbed into their giant canoes loaded with furs and headed across the lake to civilization.

Leslie's Weekly

When the voyageurs returned to the wilderness outposts on the rivers of the north, there was also a gala party. The next year's goods were examined, "high wine" had been made for the celebration, and gifts were given to wives and children. The celebration became a ritual at American posts in the fall of each year.

The fox-in-circle, an inspector's symbol on guns for the Indian trade, was first used in the Great Lakes region about 1800.

Return of the Voyageurs

The late summer or early fall return of the fur brigades was a joyous occasion at the faraway posts tucked into the wilderness of both the Canadian and American West. The traditions and customs established at Canadian fur forts by the Nor'Westers and the Hudson Bay Company were similar in Montana. However, the Missouri River provided a super-highway to the Montana fur forts compared to the long arduous return trips in canoes, across portages, and navigating the lakes and rivers in Canada. On the Missouri the return trips were made in large keelboats that were reloaded in St. Louis with the next year's trade goods and supplies.

The two-month-long trip up the Big Muddy to the Blackfoot fur posts in Montana

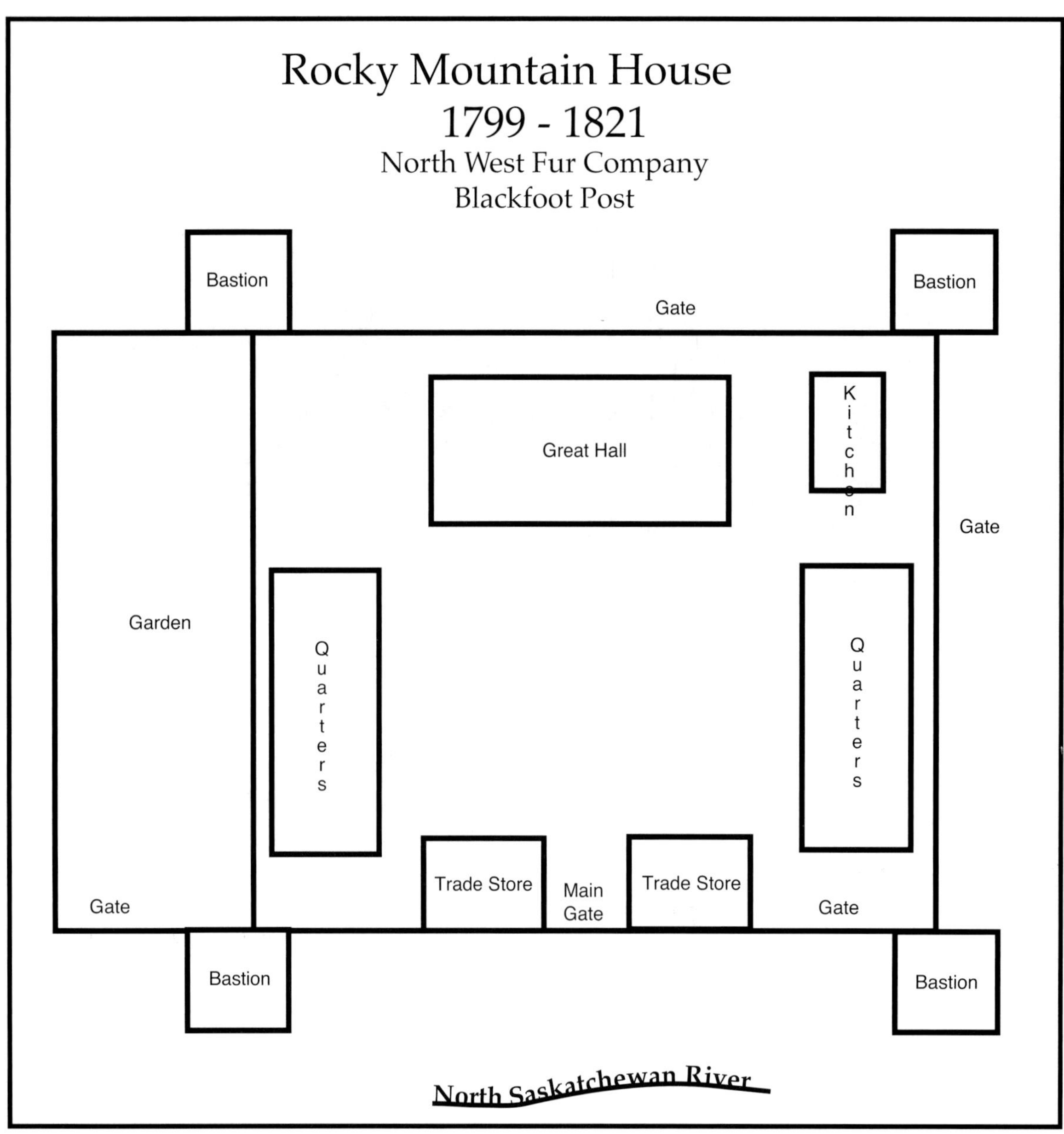

Rocky Mountain House was a large post near the mountains in Blackfoot Country in the Canadian West. It was the main trading post for the Blackfoot before any American posts were built on the Upper Missouri.

often involved towing the keelboats by sheer manpower by a rope called a cordelle. Infrequently favorable winds and a sail made the work easier. In a slow current the river allowed either poling or oars. In any case, it was a tough assignment for the voyageurs. Arrival of the steamboat on the Upper Missouri, first at Fort Union and later at Fort Benton, made the return seem a pleasure cruise compared to other means of water transportation. The only real labor then was loading wood to feed the smoking giants.

Upon their arrival at home, families and friends swarmed around the voyageurs exchanging hugs and kisses. After all the greetings, gifts brought back from civilization

The Fur Trade

Trading as seen through white eyes of the plight of an Indian woman

Schwinden Library, Fort Benton

Trading at the post store. The goods most cherished by native male traders were whiskey, trade guns and knives in that order. Women eyed pots, blankets, beads, metal tools and trade cloth. All of the goods made life easier and were adopted into their culture.

A North West Fur Company trade token dated 1820 was drilled to make a pendant for a necklace. It has the profile of a Roman Caesar on one side and a beaver, the symbol of the trade, on the other side.

were opened followed by a feast and dance. The natives closely monitored the voyageurs' return trip home because their arrival meant the opening of the annual fur trade with its elaborate ceremonies. To the Indian it meant gifts but most of all - whiskey!

Opening the Trade

When the bands of Indians arrived, they approached the main gate firing their rifles into the air in salute. Before entering the trade house, they were disarmed and treated to a few drams of rum before the pipe was brought out. The proceedings were described by Duncan McGillivary at Fort George, "...after the pipe has been plied about for sometime they relate the news with great deliberation and ceremony relaxing from their usual taciturnity in proportion to the quantity of Rum they swallowed, till at length their voices are drowned in a general clamor. When the women erect their lodges they receive a present of Rum

North Saskatchewan Trading House
Hudson Bay Company

Defender's walk 3 1/2 ft. below top of the wall
Bastion
Ice House
The Masters House
Men's Quarters
Trade Room
Quarters
Indian Hall
Shop
Men's Quarters
120 ft. by 140 ft.
Walk
Bastion
Main Gate
Stockade 15 feet

This is a typical floor plan of trading posts used by fur companies in Canada. Two rival companies, Hudson Bay Company and the North West Fur Company, were merged in 1821 when many Nor'Westers went to the American fur trade on the Missouri rather than work for the hated Hudson Bay Co.

and the whole Band drink during 24 hours and sometimes much longer. When the drinking match has subsided they begin to trade." The celebration was over when all the liquor was consumed or they had passed out in a drunken stupor.

Some trading was done on credit where the goods were given to the Indian at once and they promised to pay with returns from their winter trap line. Trading occurred not in coin but in beaver skins called "plus," most generally spelled and pronounced "plews." Flintlock trade guns cost 14 plews and were the most expensive. Blankets varied in weight and

Coins of the Canadian trade

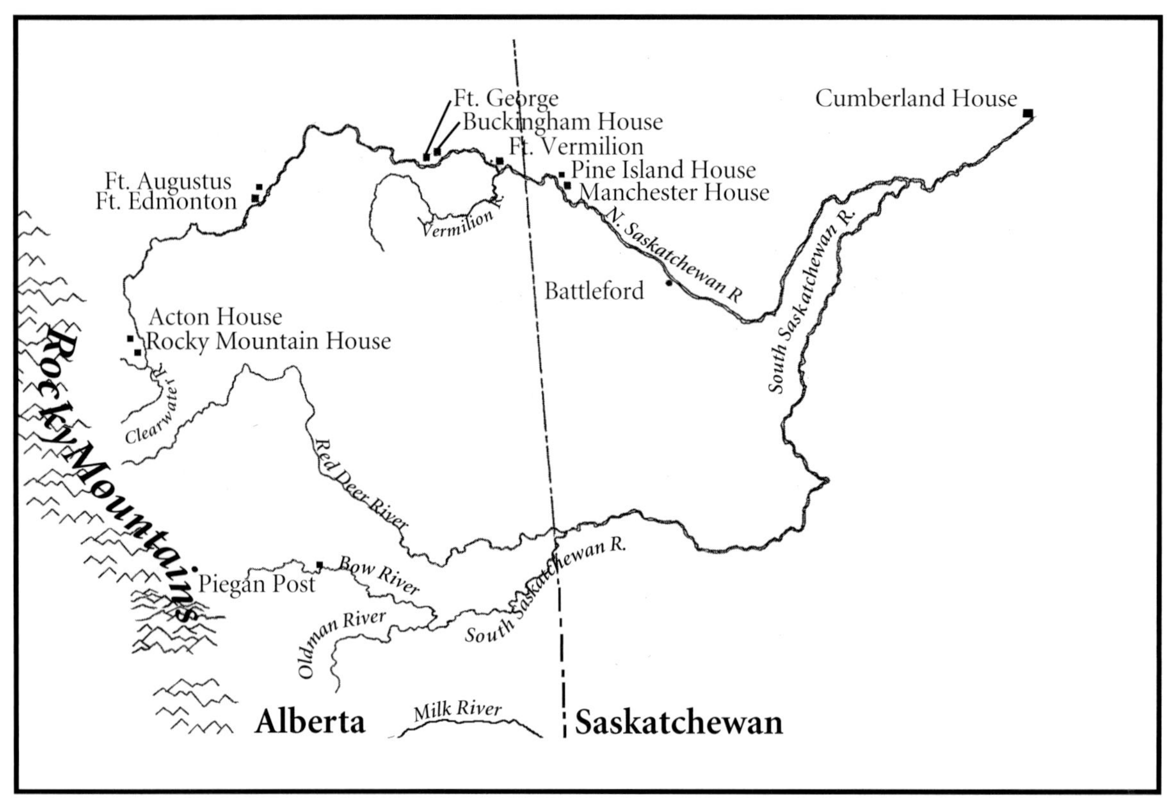

Map of early fur forts in the Canadian North where the Blackfoot traded before rival American trade moved into the Upper Missouri.

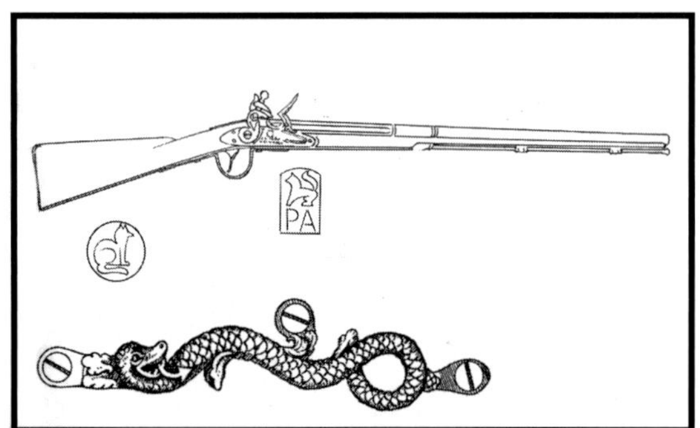

The most expensive trade item was the flintlock. It was a smooth bore with a large caliber barrel; it had to bear the dragon and sitting fox imprint for the natives to accept it as genuine.

size and were marked along the sides with bars called points; each point represented one plew. Smaller items traded for one or two plews. Trading even got as fine as a 1/2 plew on some items.

Guns, blankets, kettles, knives and axes were coveted items but none were as prized or bartered more than "high wine." Concentrated distilled spirits in small kegs were resold after they were diluted and doctored by the trader. Usually from 150 to 180 proof alcohol "wine" was diluted with water and other concoctions, depending upon whether the recipients were veterans or newcomers to the trade. The proportions varied from 4 to 9 quarts of alcohol to the nine-gallon keg of Indian whiskey. What a trade item! It was transported in concentrated form, then diluted at the site and traded for valuable furs with very little outlay or expense. A keg of "Blackfoot rum" as they called it traded for 30 plews. In the dark days of 1869 to 1874, Fort Benton traders became overnight buffalo-robe millionaires in the trade north of the border.

The effects of liquor on the Indians never seemed to change. It drove them to fighting and killing among themselves,

Schwinden Library, Fort Benton

Fort William on the Great Lakes was the North West Fur Company's largest and most lavish post in Canada. From here they challenged not only Canadian rival the Hudson Bay Company but also the American Fur Company in the United States.

destroyed their dignity and created havoc in their culture. But neither side was willing to stop. Surprisingly the situation never affected the relationship between the traders and the Indians. Mutual need was so fundamental that antagonisms never developed in either camp. In most instances every precaution was taken to prevent violent confrontations.

It was not until settlers, soldiers and miners invaded Blackfoot Country south of the border that trouble broke out between the Blackfoot Nation and the United States. These confrontations were not part of the Canadian West since the Mounted Police arrived before the settlers. No Indian wars were caused by lawless settlers or natives trying to defend their land.

The amicable relationship between white trader and Indian trapper and hunter went on for generations on both sides of the border. Customs, traditions, cultures and families of traders, voyageurs and natives blended until the passing of the beaver and the buffalo.

As they came out of the mist of the Great Lakes, adventurous traders brought the first impressions of white civilization to natives of the northern plains. They remained on the scene only a short time before big companies and big government swallowed up their part of the fur trade. The independent traders disappeared back into the mist and became legends of the times.

Fort Ramon

1807 - 1813

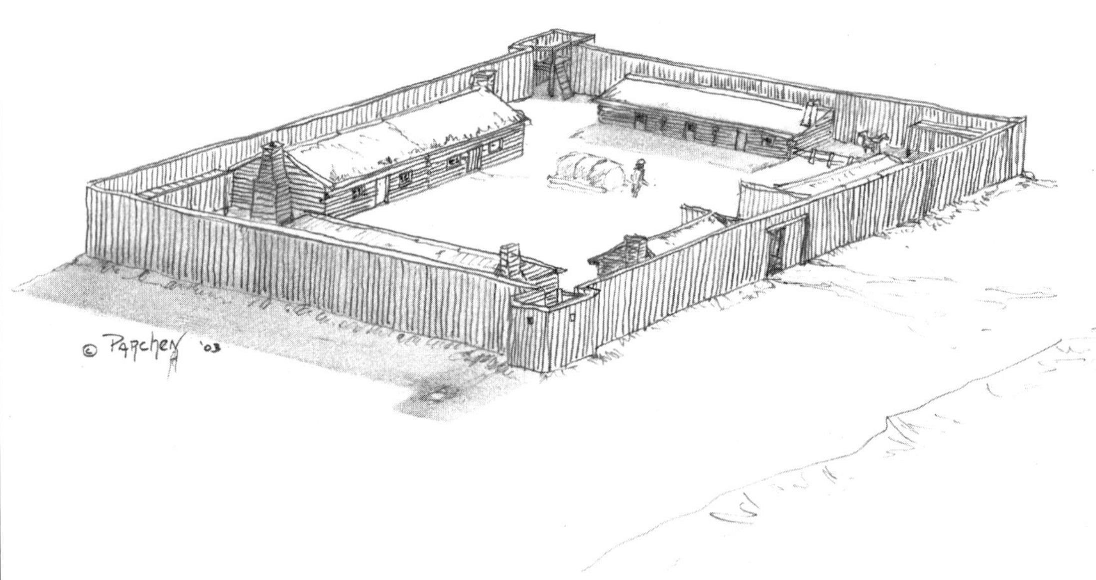

First fur fort erected in the Upper Missouri drainage at the mouth of the Bighorn River on a neck of land on the south side between the Bighorn and the Yellowstone. Built by Manuel Lisa for the Missouri Fur Co. and named for his son, Fort Ramon was the first fur trading post in Montana. It was also called Fort Lisa, Fort Manuel or Fort Raymond.

First Encounters

Dazzling Reports and Great Expectations

Manuel Lisa's Missouri Fur Company on the Yellowstone

The Two Medicine Prelude

The first meeting of the Blackfoot and the Americans occurred beside a small mountain stream flowing out of the eastern front of the Northern Rockies in present day Montana. There Lewis, on his return trip with the two Field brothers and George Drouillard, had a chance encounter with the Blackfoot people. They camped overnight together beside Two Medicine Creek. At daybreak a dozing guard thwarted an attempt by one of the Indians to steal a rifle. In the ensuing melee two Blackfoot were killed. The Indians also tried to drive off the horses, but Lewis and his men recaptured some of them including a few Indian ponies. Lewis and his companions made a hasty twenty-four hour dash back through Blackfoot Country to the Missouri. They arrived at the Fort Benton bottom in time to meet the rest of their party under Sergeant Ordway who were coming down the Missouri. The entire party made a hurried exit out of Blackfoot Country and had no further contact

Artist David Parchen

Killing the first Blackfoot on the Two Medicine in 1806 by Lewis and his party.

Artist David Parchen

Lewis with Drouillard and the Field brothers arriving at the Fort Benton bottom after their all-night ride to find Ordway and his party who were coming down river in dugouts.

with the Blackfoot.

This incident gave the Blackfoot a poor first impression of the Americans and may have contributed to hostile relations between the two parties over the next two decades. If that were the primary reason for the hostilities, it would be based strictly upon conjecture. Several other incidents occurred which added to the conflict. For instance, John Colter's and George Drouillard's terrifying experiences with the Blackfoot helped perpetuate the animosity that became a deep burning hatred.

The Hudson Bay Company traders continued to prod the Blackfoot into action against the Americans, whose greatest transgression was probably building trading posts in the country of the Blackfoot's most hated enemy, the Crow. Those posts meant that rifles, powder and ball were readily available for the Crow to use against the Blackfoot.

Whatever the reasons, the antagonism grew with each encounter. Coupled with their dislike of all who invaded Blackfoot territory, living in Blackfoot Country was indeed a hair-raising experience. During later encounters, revenge against the Americans was so swift and so final that it put an end to virtually all trading and trapping of beaver in their country for the next 25 years.

Lisa's First Try in 1807

From the onset of the fur trade west of the Mississippi and after the return of Lewis and Clark, the Upper Missouri was the most sought-after prize in the trade. As a coveted precious jewel, this region had many pitfalls and dangers that had to be overcome before its wealth could be realized.

On their return to St. Louis Lewis and Clark brought reports of the rich beaver country at the headwaters of the Missouri. The reports so excited entrepreneurs in this frontier town that twelve separate companies were formed in 1807 to exploit the newfound source of wealth.

One of the leaders was a Spaniard, Manuel Lisa, who was not very well liked by the French community in St. Louis. Consequently, he had to go outside the city to finance his first trapping and trading venture on the Upper Missouri. Prior to 1807 Lisa had been involved in trading on the lower river with the Osage, and even participated in a venture to trade in Santa Fe. However, he sensed that his future in trading was on the Upper Missouri.

A New Company

Manuel Lisa went down river to Kaskaskia, Illinois to find financial aid. He enlisted two partners, Pierre Menard and William Morrison, whom he had known from other business dealings. They formed the Missouri Fur Company. Lisa agreed to lead the party up river; the two partners appointed George Drouillard as their representative and agreed to remain in St. Louis to look after the business of the new company. Drouillard was the expert hunter whom Lewis had learned to trust in their years together in the wilderness.

In late winter and early spring Lisa put together an outfit valued at $16,000 and purchased two keelboats for the journey. He recruited 50 to 60 young, adventurous men to help him tap the riches of the upper river. Some of Drouillard's companions from the Expedition, among them John Potts and Peter Weiser, signed on for three years. Another group of inseparable companions, Edward Robinson, John Hoback and Jacob Reznor, were probably along. Those three stayed in the mountains after coming up river with Lisa in 1807.

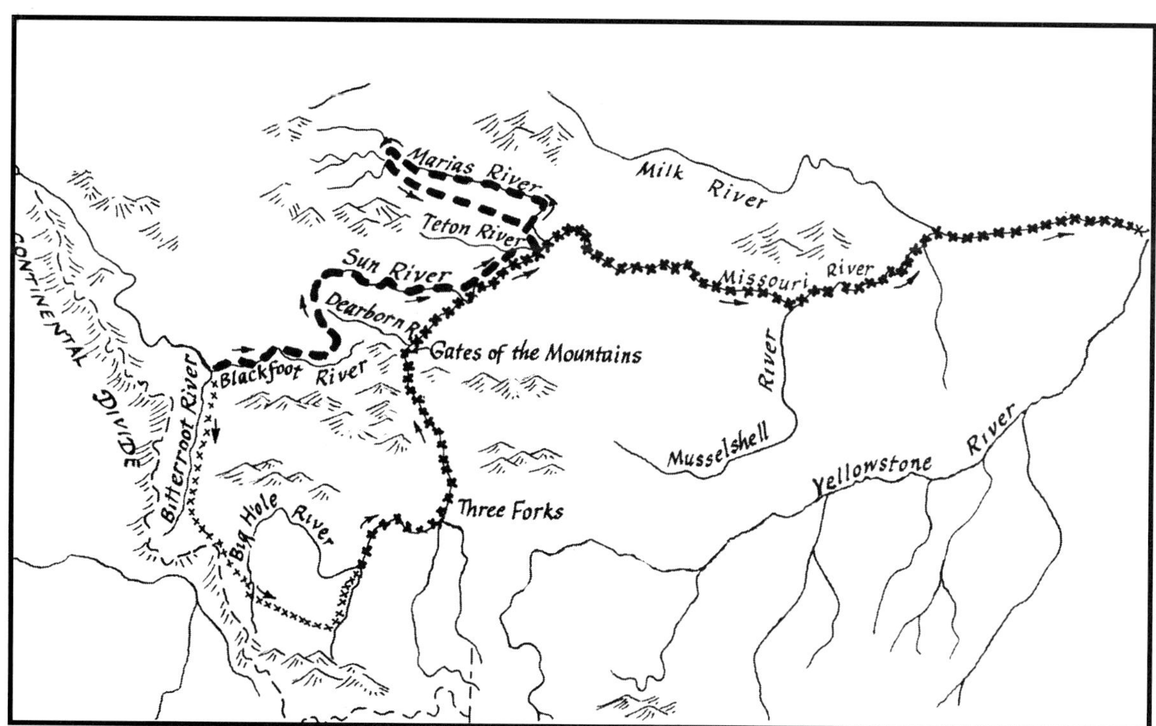

Lewis and his party journeyed across Blackfoot Country in Northcentral Montana. The map shows Sgt. Ordway's trail down the Jefferson and Missouri to meet with Lewis, the two Field brothers and Drouillard near the site of Fort Benton in 1806.

Schwinden Library, Fort Benton

Manuel Lisa, head of the Missouri Fur Co., built the first fur fort in Montana on the Yellowstone in 1807.

Slow Trip Upriver

In the spring of 1807 Lisa and his company of trappers and traders swung their keelboats into the muddy, turbulent waters of the Missouri, surely a different river from the easy flowing Mississippi. Some said the Missouri was too thin to plow and too thick to drink. Its swift four-mile-an-hour current made it impossible to navigate the cumbersome keelboats in its main current and required that the poling and cordelling be done in its backwaters and sheltered curves.

That tough grueling work soon separated the men from the boys; consequently, desertion reared its ugly head. Lisa immediately took a tough stance on desertion and sent Drouillard back down river after Antoine Bissonette who was wounded in the encounter and died on his return to St. Louis.

Progress was much slower than had been anticipated. Even with hunters supplying fresh meat to the company, food stores were being depleted at an alarming rate. By late April the party had traveled only as far as the mouth of the Platte.

John Colter's Return

Lisa's boats were tied up at the Platte when a lone canoe bearing a single trapper rounded the bend and came across the river to investigate. It was John Colter who was headed down the Missouri after spending the winter of

The stick out of the bank was scented with castorum. It attracted the beaver who stepped into the trap on the platform below the water. The chain on the trap was held by the stake, and the trap held the beaver under until it usually drowned.

Artist David Parchen

A likeness of John Colter, storied mountain man who had several encounters with the Blackfoot. One was his naked run for life.

1806 -1807 on the Upper Yellowstone. Captain Clark had given Colter an early release on August 15, 1806 at the Mandan Villages so he could join two trappers from Illinois and return to the mountains to trap beaver. In his journals, Lewis described his up-river meeting with the two trappers on August 12, 1806 before he caught up with Clark's party.

On August 17 Lewis and Clark left the Mandan Villages together; Colter joined his two new partners, Joseph Dixon and Forrest Hancock, and headed back up river. The addition of Colter to the partnership gave them an experienced hand and someone who was familiar with the river route and with the country. Since Colter had been with Clark's party on the Yellowstone, he convinced his partners to go up the Yellowstone River as it was the quickest way to the headwaters of the Missouri.

They entered Yellowstone country and traded with the Crow that fall. Not much is known of Colter's year in the mountains but it is believed they spent the winter in a lean-to cabin and a cave on the Clarks Fork of the Yellowstone. Bored during the winter, Colter explored Sunlight Basin by himself and waited for the spring breakup. The partnership was short lived. When the ice went out in the spring, Colter headed down river to civilization. However the lure of the mountains, the adventure, solitude and wonder once again put its captivating touch on Colter's shoulders and he agreed that spring of 1807 to return up river with his old friends from the Expedition. Lisa had just recruited a man who knew more about the upper river than any other living person.

Indian Trouble

Soon after Lisa left the Platte, game along the river became scarce. Even with expert hunters, the party was reduced to a quarter pound of meat per man per day. Luckily they passed through Sioux Country without encountering the Lakota tribes. Their first near encounter came at the Arikara village at the mouth of the Grand River. The Rees, as the traders called them, had settled in a village of earthen mound lodges and their village had become an important trade center on the Missouri for both eastern and western tribes. They still hunted buffalo but had also taken up agrarian pursuits like their neighbors the Mandans.

The Rees had volatile temperaments and were a problem for many years to all Americans traveling up and down the river. Lisa's party soon experienced their treacherous nature when they fired on the keelboats and ordered them to land. When accosted on shore

Hand forged square-jawed beaver trap used by both mountain men and Indians.

Artist Karl Bodmer

Hidatsa village of earthen mounds. These sedentary people raised agricultural crops but still hunted buffalo like the plains people. With their neighbors the Arikara, they were sometimes volatile and caused problems with the traders, one of the reasons that development of fur trade on the Upper Missouri was slow.

with their hostile mood, Lisa took strong-armed measures, leveling the swivel cannons and calling his company to arms. This show of force so startled the Rees that they returned with the peace pipe and offered a council with their chiefs.

After the council Lisa distributed gifts and the traders left the Arikara village in peace. The next confrontation occurred at the Mandan Villages over trading for gunpowder. Lisa was able to run the same bluff again and the problem was quickly settled. Lisa's boats continued up river without incident until they reached the Assiniboine Indians. Their third encounter with the natives, by far the most serious, involved several hundred warriors who demanded that they land their boats. Lisa again used a bold approach by firing his cannon into the air as he came to shore. The amazed Assiniboines scattered into the foothills. Only a few returned to council and received presents from the traders.

Trouble Followed

In 1807 the parties that followed Lisa's rather peaceful but stressful trip up river were not nearly that serene. One, under the command of Ensign Pryor who had been a sergeant in the Lewis and Clark Expedition, was a special mission for the federal government, the safe return of Chief Shahaka and his party to the Mandan Villages. They had come down river with Lewis and Clark and had visited Washington D.C. The chief's safe passage back home had been promised by the government. Along with Pryor and his 14 soldiers were Pierre Chouteau Jr. and a trading party of twenty-three men. When they arrived at the Arikara village, a fight broke out. The Indians killed three men and wounded several more. Immediately the whole party including the wounded retreated to St. Louis. Pryor blamed Manuel Lisa for his misfortunes, claiming that Lisa had turned the Indians

Shahaka, Mandan chief who went with Lewis and Clark, was returned to the Mandan Villages by Pierre Chouteau's party of traders in 1809.

against other parties that followed him up river.

Several other groups were headed up river, but because of the violence to Pryor's and Chouteau's party they chose to remain on the lower river. Another group, a partnership with Robert McCellan and Ramsey Crooks as its leaders, encountered Pryor's mangled command as it was returning to St. Louis. Discouraged and disenchanted, they dropped back down river and spent the winter at Council Bluffs. During the season of 1807 only Manuel Lisa and his trapping party reached the mountains and beaver country.

The First Fort

After three dicey encounters, Lisa's entire party had come through unscathed due to his dominating and bold actions. The rest of the journey was uneventful, but time was growing short to find and build winter quarters in the mountains. At the mouth of the Yellowstone they left the Missouri, probably at the insistence of veterans of the Lewis and Clark Expedition. From the time he left St. Louis Lisa had been determined to go to the headwaters of the Missouri, reported to be the richest beaver country on the continent. However, the Lewis and Clark veterans knew the quickest route to the Three Forks was up the Yellowstone and across the pass to the headwaters. They convinced Lisa to alter his plans to travel up the Missouri through Blackfoot Country.

When they arrived at the confluence of the Yellowstone and Bighorn Rivers, it was already November so they decided not to press on to the headwaters. Between the two rivers

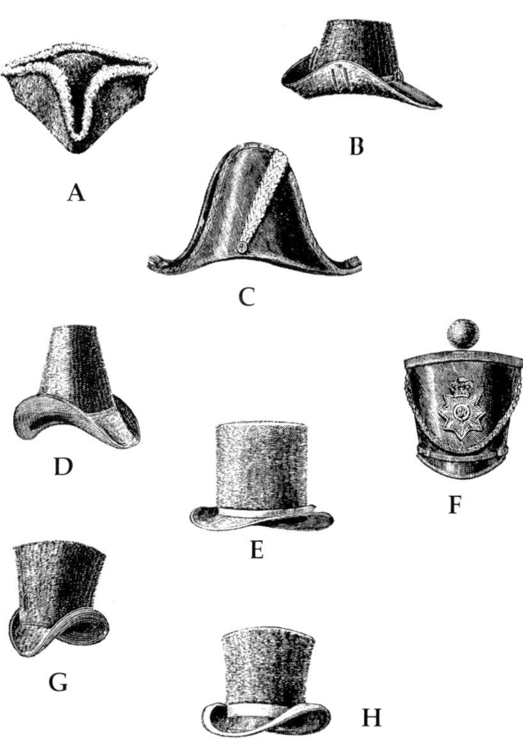

Beaver felt hats for all occasions: A. Tricorn, B. Clerical, C. Cocked or Napoleon, D. Paris Beau, E. Regent, F. Military Helmet, G. Beau Brummell or Wellington, H. The D'Orsay

they built a trading post called Fort Ramon (Raymond) after Lisa's son. Their move to the Three Forks would wait until spring. The post was in the heart of Crow Country but most of the Indians had gone to winter camps in the valleys upstream. Their arrival was much too late for the fall hunt and pushed the party into hurried construction of the fort before winter set in. Lisa immediately sent George Drouillard, John Colter and Edward Rose to find the Crow and bring them back. He was ready to trade.

Although he left no account of his trip in the mountains, Colter's winter journey was a memorable one. The story was pieced together from what he told others.

Winter Trips for Trade

Colter's journey of over five hundred miles took him through the Bighorn Basin to the Wind River Range, always spreading Lisa's message to come in and trade. He visited Jackson's and Pierre's Hole, traveled around Jackson and Yellowstone Lakes and into the canyon of the Yellowstone. He came out of the mountains along the Shoshone River, seeing the geyser basin later called Colter's Hell. Colter arrived back at Fort Ramon in the spring after that amazing solitary trek through the Rocky Mountains in the dead of winter, an incredible feat that must have tested his endurance every step of the way.

In contrast Edward Rose found a Crow village, took up residence in a tepee and stayed the winter. By the time spring arrived, he had given away all his goods and returned to the fort - to a very angry Manuel Lisa. Drouillard's winter trips to the south and east through the valleys of the prairie rivers did not take nearly as long nor were they as arduous as Colter's.

Lisa and Drouillard decided to return to St. Louis in the spring of 1808 to refinance and prepare for the next trading season. Before Lisa left, he put Benito Vasquez in charge of the fort and sent Colter out once again to bring in the tribes to trade.

Blackfoot Trouble

Colter headed up the Yellowstone and crossed Bozeman Pass where he found a party of Flatheads who had come east for the spring buffalo hunt. Colter convinced them to return to Fort Ramon with him. Near Bozeman Pass they were attacked by a large party of Blackfoot. Outnumbered, the Flatheads fought

"MAD AS A HATTER"

Lewis Carroll's Mad Hatter was a victim of the beaver hat's popularity. In the early nineteenth century, hat makers, looking for a way to use cheaper furs than the popular beaver, developed a way of turning rabbit fur into a relatively good quality hat-making felt. They used salts of mercury diluted in nitric acid, referred to as a "mercury carrot," to break down the keratin coating on rabbit fur that prevented it from felting properly. The finished rabbit hats were close in quality to beaver, and much cheaper. But there was a drawback: inhaling the fumes of this mixture led to a condition known as "hatter's shakes," an uncontrollable palsy that also affected the eyes and speech. In the final stages of hatter's shakes, the afflicted hatters went mad, the victims of a mercury-induced psychosis.

Schwinden Library, Fort Benton

Mammoth Hot Springs and Geyser Basin, later called "Colter's Hell, were sites seen by John Colter during his winter trip in 1807-1808.

courageously with Colter playing a prominent role in their defense. He was wounded in the thigh but continued fighting from a thicket and took his toll on the enemy. As the Flatheads were about to be overrun, the hated Crow jumped into the foray and helped drive off the Blackfoot. Colter's role did not go unnoticed. It was the first of several encounters in the Three Forks area that fueled the hatred of the Blackfoot for the Americans.

Colter returned to Fort Ramon, spent the summer recuperating, and in the fall of 1808 returned to the Three Forks with John Potts. Again crossing Bozeman Pass, they put their two canoes in the water and headed up the Jefferson River with their traps and equipment for the fall beaver hunt. Suddenly the Blackfoot appeared along the bank and demanded that they come to shore. Colter, not wanting to lose his traps, dropped them over the side and paddled to shore. He was immediately subdued and stripped of everything including his clothes. In the meantime, John Potts refused to submit and one of the warriors shot him in the hip. Potts returned fire and killed the Indian but the Blackfoot returned a volley and killed him. The Indians waded into the river and retrieved the canoe and Pott's equipment. In their rage at losing one of their members, they dismembered and mutilated Pott's body and flung his entrails into Colter's face. After a short council, they decided to let Colter "run for his life." The chase was chronicled many times. Colter escaped across Bozeman Pass to the fort and a second recovery from Blackfoot hostility.

Colter Makes a Vow

Early that winter Colter, who expected the Indians were in their winter camps in the north, headed back to the Jefferson to retrieve his valuable traps. A few days out he had just setup his night camp back in Blackfoot Country and was about to have his evening meal when he heard rustling in the bushes. He dove into the darkness surrounding his camp seconds before it was riddled with musket fire. He hid in the undergrowth waiting and watching, and finally decided during the night that after three near fatal encounters his time was running out. He vowed to the Almighty that if he got safely out of this scrape, he would never return to Blackfoot Country. The next morning he sneaked away from his camp and trekked over the mountains to Fort Ramon where he spent the winter before heading home to Missouri.

The spring of 1809 found a completely discouraged Benito Vasquez with only 15 beaver plews and 10 robes. He sent his trappers to the rivers to the south and closed Fort Ramon. Then he too headed down river to the Mandan Villages to spend the summer. On September 22, 1809 he greeted Manuel Lisa and a new company force of 150 men and 13 boats. Brimming with confidence the new men were positive that they were destined to make a fortune on the Upper Missouri.

The Second Season

Lisa's new entourage got a late start but was underway May 17, 1809. It was made up of two groups, a militia detachment and a trapping and trading party. The militia detachment under Pierre Chouteau was assigned to escort Mandan Chief Shahaka to his home in the Mandan Villages. The assignment was to rectify the debacle of Lt. Pryor's trip earlier, and to earn the company seven thousand dollars.

Artist Karl Bodmer

Mandan Villages on the Missouri where the Lewis and Clark Expedition spent the winter of 1804-05 before entering Blackfoot Country the next spring.

The trading and trapping party under Lisa headed north a month later with 190 men. Traveling was exasperatingly slow, and Lisa continually lost his patience with the Americans who were lazy, complained constantly and wasted their rations. Food was running out long before it should have. The hard work and drudgery of moving keelboats up the Missouri with new men produced the same problem, desertion. By the time they reached Fort Osage they had lost 18 men; the number grew to 32 by the time they reached the Mandan Villages.

At the mouth of the James River they met a large tribe of Lakota Sioux who demanded that a trading post be built for them. The new post was built on Cedar Island and Auguste Pierre Chouteau was left in charge.

With a show of force and their cannon threatening the Indians, the Arikara villages were passed without incident. The groups, then traveling together, soon reached the Mandan Villages. Pierre Chouteau Jr. delivered the chief safely to his home for the federal government. Nearby they built Fort Mandan with Sylvestre Labbadie left in charge. It was to serve both the Hidatsa and Mandans. A council was held with Vasquez who had remained with the Mandans; even after the talks none of the partners were a bit discouraged.

The company sent Andrew Henry, Reuben Lewis and William Morrison, guided by John Colter, and forty men on horseback overland to reopen Fort Ramon and get ready for the fall trade. Pierre Menard and the rest of the force brought the boats on up the Missouri and the Yellowstone to the fort. Pierre Chouteau and Manuel Lisa returned to St. Louis to get ready for the next year's trade.

Colter Breaks his Vow

After almost losing his life three times, Colter broke his promise to the Almighty by agreeing to return upriver "one more time" to face the "Terrible Blackfeet" at the headwaters of the Missouri. When Henry arrived, the fort was reopened and parties sent out for the fall hunt in Crow Country. The primary mission of the fur company was to establish a fur post at the Three Forks in the richest beaver country on the continent, and to open trade with the Blackfoot if possible. Menard arrived with the boats, supplies and the rest of the men in the late fall so they decided to wait until spring to move to the Three Forks.

One of the routine jobs of the trappers was skinning and stretching raw hides of the beaver laced on a willow round until they dried; then the plews were packed into bundles of sixty.

In early spring Menard, Lewis and Henry, again guided by Colter, took a trapping party of eighty men, including George Drouillard, over Bozeman Pass to the headwaters of the Missouri. On a neck of land at the confluence of the Jefferson and Gallatin, they started construction of a fort on April 3, 1810. Under duress created by the constant Blackfoot threat, the stockade was erected in a week. The first trapping party of 18 men went up the Jefferson on the spring hunt. On April 12 only a few miles up the river the Blackfoot attacked the trappers. When help finally arrived, two trappers were dead and mutilated and three were missing. Traps, furs, horses and ammunition were stolen. John Colter had again escaped unharmed. When they returned to the fort, he begged forgiveness from his Maker and vowed, "I will leave this country . . . and be damned if I ever come into it again." That time he kept his promise and the next day Colter left the Upper Missouri, never to return.

Artist Karl Bodmer

Winter on the Upper Missouri and Yellowstone was a tough time for trappers and Indians, but it was the best time to collect hides and furs.

Terrible Blackfoot

Colter carried messages from Menard about the situation at the Three Forks down river to the partners. Menard said beaver were there and plentiful, but so were the Blackfoot. If the Blackfoot could not be controlled, the location was untenable. Menard told the partners he planned to encourage the Nez Perce and Flatheads to make war on the Blackfoot thereby forcing them to sue for peace or totally destroying them. However, neither alternative was practical. There was a deep-seated fear in all tribes that dealt with the Blackfoot.

State Historical Society of Missouri, Columbia

Pierre Menard, one of the early leaders in the fur trade on the Upper Missouri, was in charge of the unsuccessful venture at the Three Forks.

Although very dejected Menard decided to stay. The mass assault on beaver meadows by large parties of thirty or more proved unwieldy; groups were soon reduced to parties of four. When there were no Indian signs along the streams, the men grew bolder, particularly George Drouillard who began to trap alone with excellent success. On his third solo trip, he was followed by two Shawnee hunters. By nightfall no one had returned. The next day they found the two hunters riddled with arrows and bullets. Further up the trail lay the remains of George Drouillard; nothing that looked at all human was left of him.

Everyone Leaves

The killings completely demoralized the company and wrote "finis" to beaver trapping in Blackfoot Country of the headwaters. By mid-summer the men had given up. They were tired of spending days behind the palisades under the ever-present threat of a major attack by an overwhelming number of Indians. In July Menard took the accumulated furs and the men who wanted out via the Yellowstone down river to St. Louis.

Henry experienced one last battle before he was convinced to leave. Abandoning the fort, he and sixty men headed up the Madison and crossed over the divide. They left eight dead comrades and much of their equipment and furs was stolen or lost. As a final parting gesture from the country that had defeated them, a Crow raiding party stole some of their horses. On the west side of the Continental Divide they came to a stream they named Henry's Fork. On that tributary of the Snake they built Henry's Fort, the first American post west of the divide. It became the headquarters for the fall hunt and the beginning of a new era for trapping beaver in the Rocky Mountains.

The behavior of the trappers and traders during those years was a personal affront to the Blackfoot. Having a post in their country at the Three Forks was unthinkable. Along with Colter's encounters, the fact that Lisa had a post and was trading with the Crow contributed to the insult.

The major cause of hostility was the fact that the Blackfoot had realized the value of furs early in the Canadian trade. They violently opposed the presence of any white trappers, English or American, in their territory. They were willing to trade the furs they trapped themselves, but would permit no trappers in their country under the penalty of death.

The first attempt by Americans to enter the Upper Missouri and trade with the Blackfoot was a disaster; no new attempts were made for a decade. A burned out fort and many dead men were the only remnants of Lisa and his partners. They were the first to find that the Upper Missouri made strong men weep, and rich men poor.

No one incident created the hostility of the Blackfoot. An accumulation of meetings, coincidental or planned, confrontations and suspicions triggered the troubles experienced by American trappers and traders on the Upper Missouri.

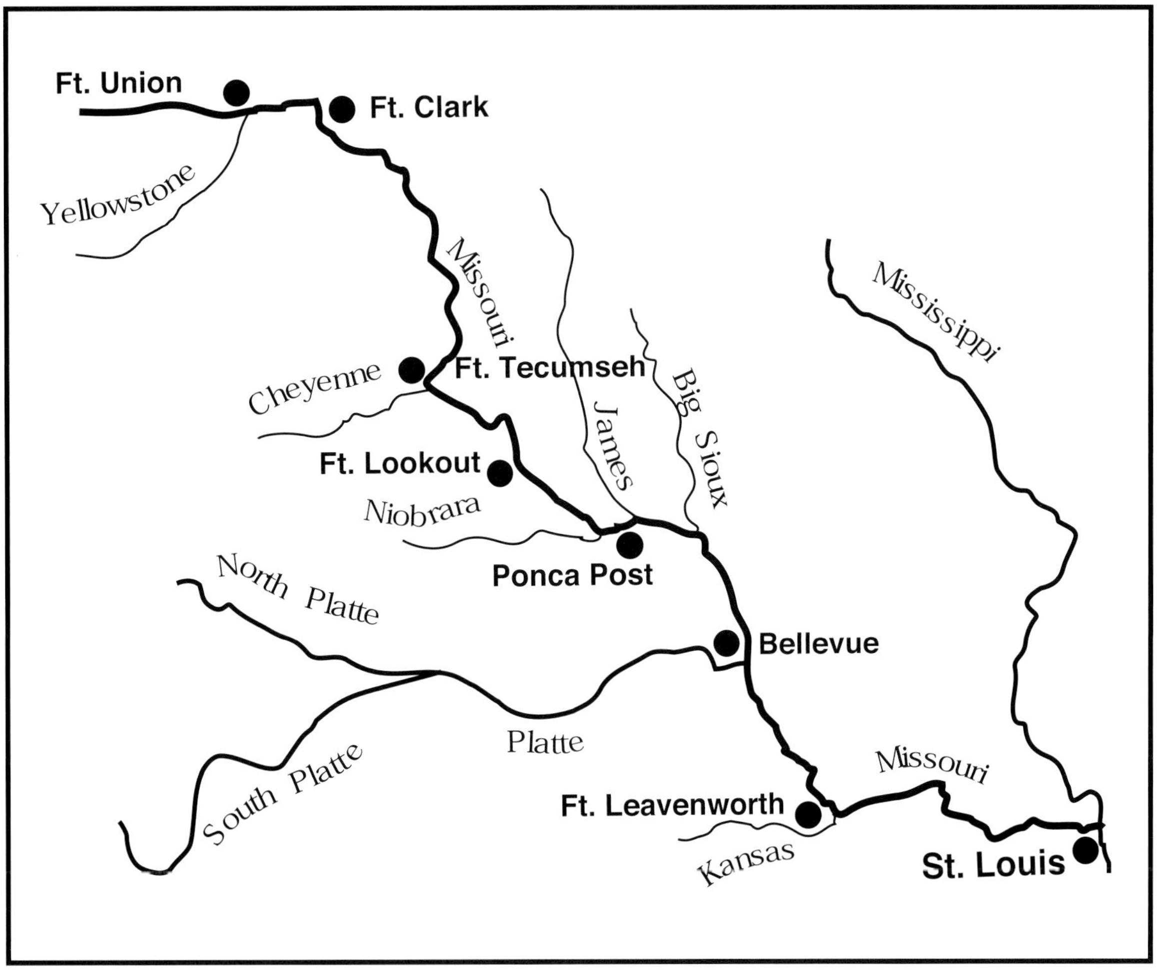

Trading posts in 1832 that served the various tribes on the Missouri River between Fort Union and St. Louis. Blackfoot trade finally began after the MacKenzie Treaty and construction of Fort MacKenzie above the mouth of Maria's River.

Schwinden Library, Fort Benton

The River became the highway to the beaver

Investigation reveals some, but surely not all of the causes:

1. Lewis's encounter on the Two Medicine
2. John Colter's fighting with the Flatheads and Crow against the Blackfoot
3. George Drouillard and trappers at the fort on the Three Forks
4. Blackfoot dislike of anyone - American, British or other tribes - who entered their territory to hunt or trap
5. Americans building trading posts in Crow Country and trading with their bitter enemies
6. Promotion of hostilities by the Hudson Bay Company so they could retain exclusive Blackfoot trade

Fort at the Three Forks 1810

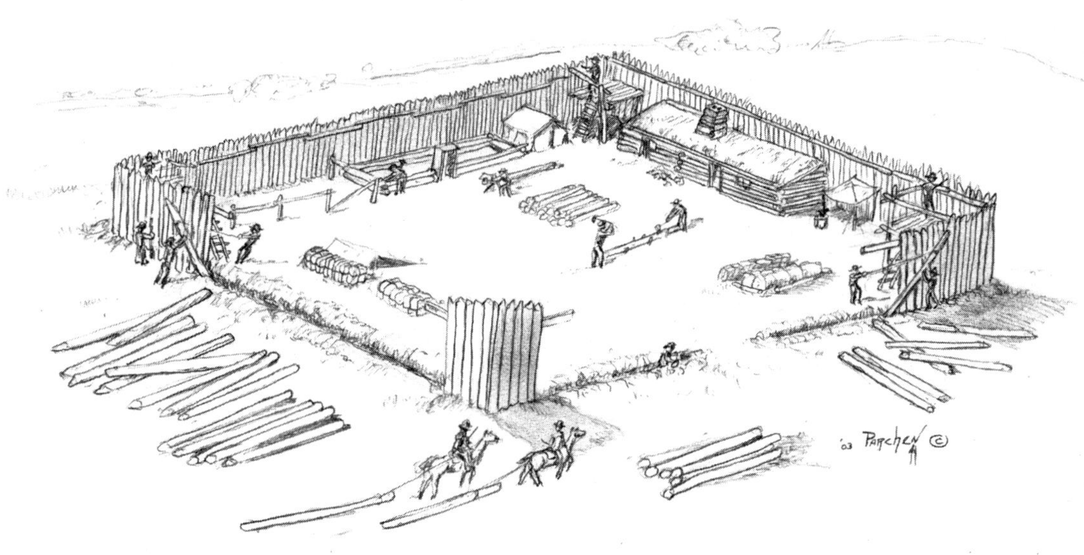

Pierre Menard with 80 men came to the Three Forks in the spring of 1810 and constructed a fort between the forks of the Madison and Gallatin. Under siege almost immediately by the Blackfoot, it was abandoned before winter. Andrew Henry and his party went across the Continental Divide and the rest of the trappers returned to the fort on the Yellowstone.

4

1825 - 1840

Free Trappers

Caravans, Rendezvous and Trouble

Atsina Visits to Their Cousins the Arapahoe

Trapping to the South

Three factors curtailed early Upper Missouri River trade in the early years: hostility of the Blackfoot, the presence of the Hudson Bay Company in the north and the antagonistic Arikara in the vicinity of the Mandan Villages. Sixty million beaver were in the Rocky Mountains in 1807; by the end of the trade in 1840 they were almost extinct. Free trappers spent every spring and fall trapping when pelts were in their prime, then spent their summers at rendezvous and winters with the Indians. The first rendezvous was held in 1825 and the last one in 1840; the era was short and overlapped the Blackfoot trade in its beginning years.

From 1807 to 1811 the Blackfoot had thwarted American traders and trappers in their attempts to invade beaver country at the Three Forks. The interlopers turned south to

Beaver (Castor canadensis) Initially there were over 60 millon in the mountains; as their numbers declined the trade turned to buffalo robes.

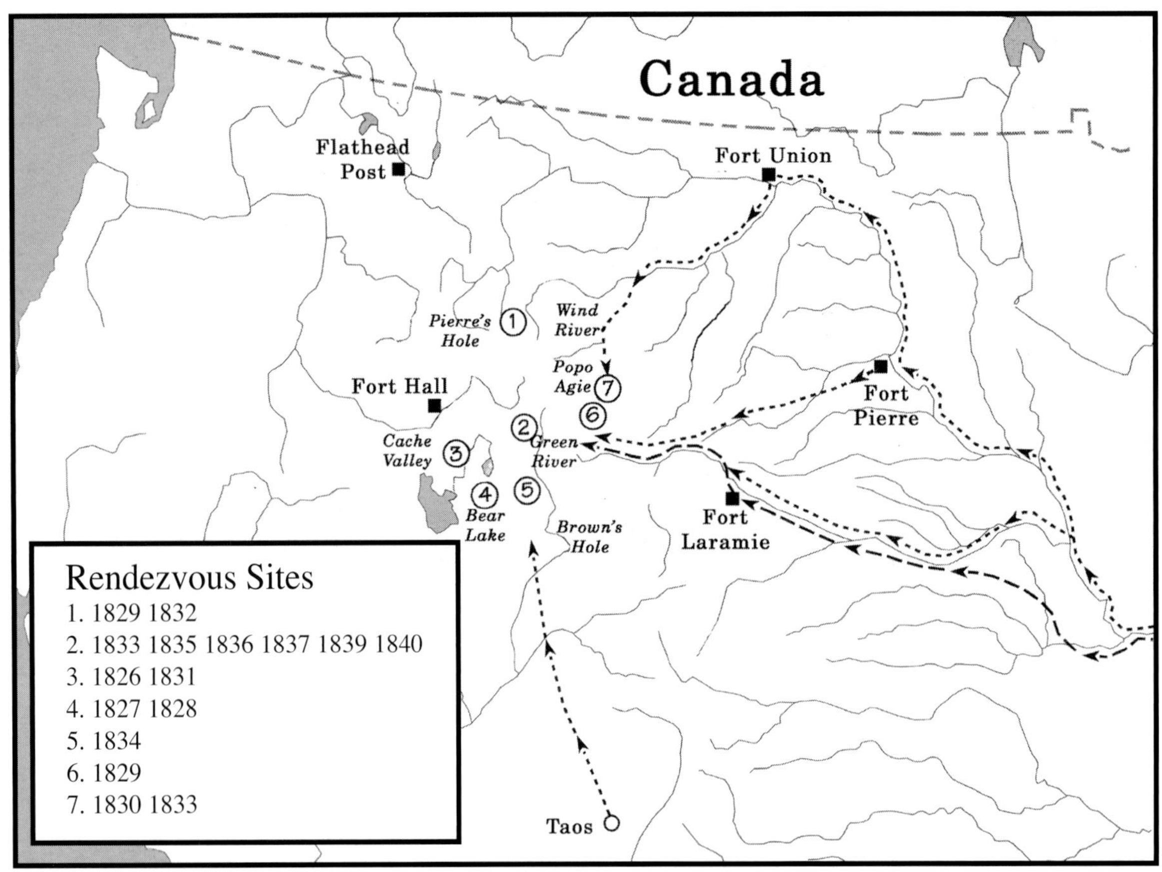

The Rocky Mountain fur trade was in the region south of the Three Forks and Blackfoot Country. Mountain men trapped with little interruption and held their annual rendezvous, where they resupplied for the next trapping season and sold their beaver to traders from St. Louis.

exploit beaver trapping in the central Rockies, ushering in the rendezvous period of 1825-1840.

Getting away from the aggressive Blackfoot was not possible. Harassment by the Blackfoot and Atsina continued in several chance meetings far outside their home territories when the Indians traveled to visit relatives in the south. Neither would trappers give up trying to invade Blackfoot Country, the richest beaver country in the Rockies. In the years following Andrew Henry's departure from the Three Forks, other groups tried to penetrate this country. Some wisely turned away, others met with the same catastrophes experienced by the first wave of traders and trappers.

Avoiding Trouble

One of the groups was the Astorians sent by John Jacob Astor on a mission to the Pacific Coast in 1811-12. Leading the group was Wilson Price Hunt who planned on following the route of Lewis and Clark on the Upper Missouri. While the Astorians were camped at the mouth of the Niobrara River, the three inseparable companions - Robinson, Hoback and Reznor - visited them. The three were returning to Kentucky after their harrowing experiences with Pierre Menard and Andrew Henry at the Three Forks, and a year of trapping in the mountains at Henry's Fort. Wishing to avoid going back into the country of the Blackfoot, they found a new route from the

State Historical Society of Missouri, Columbia

Wilson Price Hunt in 1811-1812 led the Astorians along the route of Lewis and Clark. While camped on the lower river, he was warned of the Blackfoot and changed his route from the Missouri to one further south.

Snake to the Wind River, through the Bighorns and across the prairie to the Arikara village on the Missouri.

After talking with his three visitors, Hunt changed his route to go across country to the Snake. He asked the three men to guide his party through the mountains; in return he would set them up with trapping outfits and ammunition. They agreed to go as far as the Snake with him. After a horrendous trip down the Snake River, the Astorians finally reached Fort Astoria on the Columbia. Edward Robinson, John Hoback and Jacob Reznor stayed in the region and explored and trapped the Bear and Green Rivers until 1814. They never again saw their Kentucky home. On a wintry January day they were surprised by the Indians and died as they had lived - together.

No matter how tragic were the results of the past, some trappers still sneaked in, setting a line of traps for a while then hurriedly leaving with their furs. Each time they were caught the results were the same - loss of horses, traps, furs and death. New entrepreneurs continued to head the fur companies in St. Louis. A game of musical chairs within the companies produced additional catastrophes in Blackfoot Country. New managers were challenged where others had failed and thought their plans would be successful. They well may have thought like Drouillard, "It can't happen to me."

The Quiet Years

The Missouri Fur Company's expansion west of the mountains suffered three fatal blows: abandonment, fire and meager returns. Abandonment of the forts in 1810-11 on the Bighorn, at the Three Forks and at Henry's post west of the divide left the company with no trading posts on the upper river. When the company storehouse on Cedar Island burned and Henry had returns of only forty packs of furs, the company's conquest of the upper river ended.

Reorganizations occurred in 1812, 1814, 1817 and 1819, when company trading was restricted to areas below the Mandan

Fort Astoria on the Columbia River was one of the first posts where Americans competed with Hudson Bay Co. in the fur trade.

Villages. Capital became more available as the effects of the panic began to wear off. With rising fur prices in the East and in Europe, things were looking up in the fur business. With new partners Andrew Drips, Robert Jones and Joshua Pilcher, the company's vision again shifted to the upper river and Blackfoot Country.

New Companies Invade Beaver Country

In 1821 the Mexicans threw off the Spanish yoke and Americans were again welcomed in Santa Fe. The change opened new markets to St. Louis merchants who pioneered the Santa Fe Trail, one of three main routes to the West. At first it was a fur trade route into the Southwest.

Four companies, all well financed by affluent merchants of St. Louis, took up the challenge to trap in the upper river. Two were willing to exploit only the more peaceable stretches of the river below the Mandan Villages. The "French Block" of Bartholomew Berthold, Bernard Pratte and Pierre Chouteau had operated successfully on the lower river below the Mandan Villages; they extended themselves up river to Fort Kiowa.

The Columbia Fur Company, which had come overland from the Mississippi, established itself on the Missouri near the Mandan Villages. It brought Kenneth MacKenzie (1) who had come south to enter the American trade and in a very few years became a dominant figure in the fur trade on the Upper Missouri. MacKenzie learned his lessons well from the Hudson Bay Co. and the other Nor'Westers. He took inexperienced American partners to deal with the citizenship issue of foreign-owned companies operating in the U.S. who were poised to be giants in the Missouri River trade.

The End of Manuel Lisa

After the death of Manuel Lisa, the Missouri Fur Company reorganized in 1821 under the leadership of Joshua Pilcher. Their dynamic leader planned a new assault on

Schwinden Library, Fort Benton

Andrew Drips was one of the new partners in the Missouri Fur Co. in 1819 when the company started to expand their up river business.

Yellowstone Country and the Three Forks, with two well-established posts on the river. In 1822 the company sent a party led by Robert Jones and Michael Immel up the Missouri and the Yellowstone, where they established Fort Benton near Lisa's first fort on the Yellowstone at the mouth of the Bighorn.

The Missouri Fur Company never really gave up their quest for the jewel of the upper river. Late the next spring the Immel and Jones party were trapping on the Jefferson when the Blackfoot appeared. Even though they escaped over the mountains into Crow Country, they were still not convinced. On May 17 near where Pryor Creek runs into the Yellowstone, the Blackfoot ambushed their trapping party of twenty-nine. Immel and Jones were killed instantly along with five others; four more were wounded. The rest of the trappers dove into the Yellowstone to save themselves. They abandoned everything - furs, traps and equipment - a loss estimated at $12,000. That was the finale. The Missouri Fur Company was dissolved in 1824.

State Historical Society of Missouri, Columbia

William Ashley's grand entry at the rendezvous on the Green River with his company of men and supply train. They were ready to open trade with the trappers and Indians.

Ashley and Henry on the Upper River

Organized in 1822, the fourth company was a partnership of William Ashley and Andrew Henry called the Rocky Mountain Fur Company. The partnership was built on Ashley's financing and Henry's know-how. (This is the same Henry who was chased out of the Three Forks country by the Blackfoot a decade before). The partnership advertised for "100 enterprising young men" to take part in an expedition to the sources of the Missouri River. They found more men than they needed. The company enlisted some of the most potentially prominent trappers to take part in the fur trade of the Central Rockies for the next twenty years. One was Jedediah Smith; other legendary mountain men included Mike Fink, Jim Bridger and David Jackson.

After a series of disastrous mishaps, Ashley, Henry and the company of men finally arrived at the Arikara village in September 1822. After purchasing horses, Henry took a party up the river to the mouth of the Yellowstone where on a narrow neck of land between the two rivers, they constructed a crude log fort. When Ashley arrived with the keelboat, the partners held a council at Fort Henry and decided after unloading the supplies that Ashley would return down river to St. Louis. Ashley's mission was to return the next spring with more men and goods.

Their venture into Blackfoot Country occurred by going up the Missouri rather than the Yellowstone, and across Bozeman Pass to the Three Forks. Shortly after Ashley's departure, Henry split his forces. John Weber went up the Yellowstone and Powder Rivers into Crow Country. Henry and his men advanced up the Missouri to the mouth of the Musselshell, where he left Jedediah Smith in charge for the winter, and returned to his fort at the mouth of the Yellowstone. Penetrating to the edge of Blackfoot Country should have

Artist Karl Bodmer

Iron Shield or Iron Shirt, Piikani Chief. He and his war party attacked Immel and Jones on the Yellowstone in the spring of 1822, killing many.

reminded Henry of the price they paid for entering Blackfoot Country in 1810-11.

The next spring a trapping party of eleven from the Musselshell post advanced without incident beyond the falls of the Missouri near the mouth of Smith River where the Blackfoot suddenly attacked. With four dead in the melee, the survivors buried some traps, leaving others still set along the banks of the river, and scrambled back to Fort Henry.

On his return to Fort Henry that spring, Ashley suffered a disastrous confrontation with the Arikara. The Arikara menace and the Blackfoot calamity dulled the luster of "the lure of the Three Forks" for the St. Louis companies.

Arrival of the American Fur Co.

The Columbia Fur Company and Bernard Pratte and Company were also trading on the lower river as far up as the Mandan Villages. Only a few venturesome trappers were willing to risk penetrating the upper river during those years. Losing their lives, equipment and furs to the Blackfoot was certainly a deterrent.

In 1821 Astor's American Fur Company attempted to get a foothold west of the Mississippi and gain control of the Upper Missouri. Ramsey Crooks was Astor's chief agent and the force behind the throne in the expansion of the Astor Empire into the West. By 1822 Astor, with the help of a few congressional friends, had eliminated the factory system set up by the federal government. The system had sponsored trading houses in Indian country since 1795. With those government houses gone, the American Fur Company created a Western Department in 1822 which absorbed the company of Stone and Bostwick and thus secured a foothold in St. Louis.

Two companies stood in the way of the American Fur Company's plan to expand to the upper river. Bernard Pratte and Company was

State Historical Society of Missouri, Columbia

Bernard Pratte of St. Louis was the principal owner of Bernard Pratte and Co. They joined forces with the American Fur Co. to control the Upper Missouri.

an organization of St. Louis traders who had been in the fur trade for years. Bartholomew Berthold, Pierre Chouteau Jr., Bernard Pratte and J.P. Carbonné organized the company in 1820 to trade up the Missouri and Platte Rivers. By 1824 Pratte and Company had created some real problems for the American Fur Company. The Columbia Fur Company came into existence after the merger of the North West Fur Company and Hudson Bay Company in 1821. Many of the unemployed Nor'Westers came south and joined a company first called Tilton and Company. The main power was Kenneth MacKenzie. Tilton was one of the few Americans in the company, so he was listed as owner to comply with the law of 1816 that barred foreign trading companies in U.S. Territory. Other people who came south to join the company were James Kipp, an excellent trader and fort builder; William Laidlaw and Daniel Lamont. All were invaluable to the group in their expansion into the Upper Missouri.

For years the American Fur Company had used two methods of ridding themselves of competition in the fur trade. They either absorbed competitors into their company or forced them out of business by cutting prices. After two years of negotiations, in 1826 they finally merged with Bernard Pratte and Company. Pratte was immediately put in charge of the Western Department of the American Fur Company with Pierre Chouteau Jr. as the Officer in Charge of developing fur trade on the Upper Missouri. The next year Kenneth MacKenzie and his associates from the Columbia Fur Company also joined the American Fur Company and a monopoly was setup to control the entire Missouri River fur trade. MacKenzie's portion of the new company was renamed the Upper Missouri Outfit that took charge of trade on the upper river above the mouth of the Big Sioux River. Throughout the next three decades the Upper Missouri Outfit was frequently challenged, but always maintained a monopoly on the upper river. Still referred to as the American Fur Company, it was usually just called "The Company." Its competition, whether an individual or a company, was called "the opposition." (2)

Schwinden Library, Fort Benton

Pratte's partner, Pierre Chouteau Jr., was put in charge of the Western Department of the American Fur Company which merged with the Columbia Fur Co. to become the Upper Missouri Outfit.

The Shifting Trade

With Chouteau's agents handling the trade down river, the American Fur Company was in a position to assault the Upper Missouri and invade Blackfoot Country, as well as compete in the mountain trade. Mergers provided an organization capable of tapping the most lucrative fur trade in the West.

The William Ashley and Andrew Henry partnership that had been put together in 1822-23, sometimes referred to as the Rocky Mountain Fur Co., came to the upper river and also moved into the mountain trade. After two more years in the mountains, Henry wanted to retire to an easier life. In 1825 Ashley took on

Schwinden Library, Fort Benton

Jedediah Smith was left in charge of the post at the Musselshell in 1822 while Henry returned to the post at the mouth of the Yellowstone.

a new partner, Jedediah Smith. The next year Ashley also wanted out. In a complex deal he turned his share over to Smith, Wm. Sublette and David Jackson. Sublette, the driving force in the partnership, became the master of the mountain and rendezvous trade.

Because attempts to trade on the Upper Missouri seemed futile, in the ensuing years the fur trade moved to the Central Rockies. Ashley and Henry's Rocky Mountain fur trapping system set up a new generation of free trappers who lived and trapped in the mountains the year round. A dream of William Ashley's, the plan was launched in 1822. A caravan from St. Louis brought yearly supplies. Furs were bought at designated mountain sites called the "rendezvous" during the summer.

Enemies in the Mountains

Although the Blackfoot and their cousins the Atsina had no part in trade in the Central Rockies, their wide-ranging bands and war parties adversely affected the fur trade in the rendezvous years 1825 to 1840. During the first years the Blackfoot and Atsina roamed far to the south of their home land. The Atsina were distant relatives of the Arapahoe and on occasion traveled into the Southwest to visit and trade with their cousins. Chance meetings were not rare since everyone used the same trails. Those coincidental encounters often ended in violence.

In May 1825, trappers from all directions in the Central Rockies headed to the first rendezvous on the lower Green River at the edge of the Unita Mountains. John Clyman and his party in a trapper's camp on the upper Green, invited seventeen Atsina into their camp. Before morning the Atsina had buried a tomahawk in the skull of LaBarge, the night guard, and tried to steal firearms. After exchanges of gunfire the engagement was broken off; Clyman and his party reached the rendezvous much wiser for having tried to befriend the northern savages.

After the first rendezvous on July 1, 1825 John Ashley and fifty men headed for the Bighorn River to return to St. Louis by water. They had one hundred packs of beaver plews valued at from seventy to one hundred thousand dollars. They crossed South Pass, went up the Sweetwater, through the Wind River Canyon and on to the Bighorn where it was navigable.

On the way Ashley and twenty men took a detour to pick up a cache of furs left by Fitzpatrick the previous summer. The rest of his party stayed on the direct route to the Bighorn. While catching up with the rest of the party, Ashley was attacked at daybreak by sixty Blackfoot who drove off all of their horses but two. One man was seriously wounded before the Indians were eventually driven off. The next day Ashley sent for help from the rest of the party, who returned with horses in two days. They were again attacked the next day, that time by a Crow war party, and again lost horses before arriving at the embarkation point on the Bighorn.

Ashley and his men hurriedly constructed boats and headed to the mouth of the Yellowstone. They hoped to make contact

Artist Alfred Jacob Miller

No matter where the Atsina or Blackfoot caught trappers, they were always at risk especially when caught in their homelands. No quarter was given and no questions were asked. Pursuit and death were usually the results.

with General Henry W. Atkinson and the treaty commission, which had been up river to negotiate a series of treaties with the tribes of the Upper Missouri.

After a few days the treaty party returned to the river. Ashley's men loaded their valuable furs onto the government keelboats for protection. On the entire expedition General Atkinson never located any Blackfoot tribes with whom he could negotiate. The one nation that every fur company wanted to pacify so they could trade and trap on the Upper Missouri was not to be found.

Consolidation of Companies

With the merger of the three companies in 1827, the American Fur Company acquired a string of fur posts up the Missouri to the Mandan and Arikara Villages. They also acquired an experienced and talented group of traders. As a result the organization existed into the 1860's when the fur trade came to a close. The Company inherited posts up to the White Earth River from the Columbia Fur Company. James Kipp had built a post there in 1825-26 to trade with the Assiniboine. Kipp's post at the Mandan and Hidatsa villages, built in 1822, also became part of the expanding empire.

The biggest prize was Fort Tecumseh, built in 1822 near Pierre, South Dakota at the mouth of the Teton River. It was a fort which had cut deeply into the Company's trade on that stretch of the river. The Upper Missouri Outfit also gained possession of all forts that were part of Bernard Pratte and Company. Fort Kiowa and the other posts above the Big Sioux all became part of the outfit. The posts

Artist George Catlin

A Hidatsa mound village on the Missouri. The Hidatsa were friendly traders among the Native Americans; they were engaged in agriculture as well as hunting buffalo.

at Council Bluffs and on down river to St. Louis fell under the jurisdiction of the Western Department directed by Pierre Chouteau Jr.

During the first year MacKenzie consolidated the Upper Missouri Outfit. In 1828 he directed Kipp to go to the mouth of the Yellowstone and build a post for trade with the free trappers and Indians on the Upper Missouri. That spring MacKenzie headed down river from Fort Tecumseh where he had spent the winter. He met the Company's keelboat coming up river but continued on to St. Louis, where he had an important conference with Chouteau on management of the river trade. After the meeting with Chouteau, MacKenzie started back up river to catch Kipp's party who was headed for the Yellowstone. After several delays at Fort Tecumseh, he resumed his journey up river. By then it was early winter of 1828-29 and he had to travel the last 600 miles by sled. When he finally reached the mouth of the Yellowstone, MacKenzie found his builders three miles up the Missouri. Kipp had picked a location on a broad plain on the north side of the river where they constructed a stockade 220 feet by 240 feet of squared cottonwood logs. One hundred feet back from the river's edge, the fort had two stone bastions on opposite corners and a large house for quarters for the bourgeois. Within the walls were storehouses, engages' quarters, trade stores and shops. MacKenzie was well pleased and probably christened it Fort Floyd at that time.

At Fort Tecumseh MacKenzie had talked with Hugh Glass, William Vanderburg and William Gordon who had trapped on the Bighorn in 1828-29. He realized that the logical supply route for free trappers to the mountains in the south was up the Yellowstone, so Fort Floyd became the base for unifying the river and the mountain trade. Fort Floyd was renamed Fort Union and was the main base of operations for the American Fur Company until the establishment of Fort Benton in 1846.

Artist Alfred Jacob Miller

Fort William on the Platte was one of three major depots to supply trappers in the Central Rockies. Also referred to as Fort Laramie, it later became a major stopping point along the Oregon Trail.

In less than a decade, Fort Union became the principal and handsomest trading post on the Missouri. On its payroll the post had 12 clerks and 129 men including a tailor, tinner, blacksmith, carpenter, cooper and gunsmith.

Fort Union, Fort Tecumseh and Fort William (called Fort Laramie) were the major depots for supplying the fur trade for the American Fur Company. For the next dozen years Fort Union was the center of civilization at the edge of the wilderness. From that post MacKenzie moved westward up the Missouri and the Yellowstone to consolidate the Company's monopoly of the last great region of the fur trade.

Berger to the Rescue

In 1829 MacKenzie attempted a trip up river near the mouth of the Milk River to trade with the Blackfoot but was unsuccessful. The reasons for failure were never recorded; perhaps the Blackfoot drove him off or the site for the trading post was not well chosen. MacKenzie, the "King of the Upper Missouri," never admitted to mistakes. At that point their Upper Missouri trade was a two-pronged plan: to capture the trade of the Blackfoot who would not allow trappers in their territory, and to build a post easily accessible to free trappers who were ranging south in the headwaters of the Yellowstone and the mountains of the Central Rockies.

While Fort Floyd was being finished in 1829, a free trader, Jacob Berger joined the company. He had been in the employ of the Hudson Bay Company for eighteen years before drifting south as a free trader. Berger had worked at Blackfoot posts in Canada and spoke the language fluently. He had even lived with the Blackfoot and had a Blackfoot wife. MacKenzie hoped that through Berger, he had found a way to enter Blackfoot Country.

Artist Granville Stuart

Fort Union, first named Fort Floyd, was located at the confluence of the Missouri and Yellowstone Rivers. MacKenzie sent James Kipp up river in 1828 to build a fort that became the premier fur post on the Upper Missouri and major supply depot for trappers south in the Bighorn Mts.

He wanted to send Berger up river to bring Blackfoot chiefs to Fort Union to sign a treaty for trade and peace, a treaty that would also allow the American Fur Company to establish a post for trade on the upper river.

After long persuasive conversations with Berger, MacKenzie convinced him to undertake the perilous journey into Blackfoot Country. In the fall of 1830 Berger and four other traders, who had traded with the Blackfoot at Canadian posts of the Hudson Bay Company, set out on foot up the Missouri. After four weeks they met a small party of Piikani somewhere on the headwaters of Maria's River. They unfurled the American flag over their camp, an act which the Piikani took as a sign of peace. Fortunately, Berger recognized one of the braves as they approached their camp and made peace by speaking to him in their language. They parlayed an agreement and were taken to the Blackfoot encampment for conversations with the chiefs. They stayed twenty days at the Indian camp. After presenting gifts, Berger convinced a group of men and women to return to Fort Union with him to negotiate a treaty with Kenneth MacKenzie.

A Blackfoot Treaty

A group of about forty including several chiefs set out on the long trek to Fort Union. Along the way the Indians complained that it was too far and too difficult. With winter approaching, they wanted to return home. Berger begged them to travel just one more day since they were very near the fort. By making concessions, such as being willing to give up his scalp (this might have been hard for him to do), he finally convinced them to continue. By mid-afternoon the next day they arrived at Fort Union. MacKenzie and the rest of the residents of the fort greeted them and Berger became a hero . . . still wearing his scalp.

Negotiations began with gifts, alcohol and promises. To the satisfaction of the Blackfoot, the outcome was a trading post near their villages. As with the British, no trappers only traders would be allowed in their territory. To show good faith, MacKenzie sent a small

From Fr N Point

Jacob Berger, one of the many Nor'Westers who came south after the amalgamation, was sent by MacKenzie to make peace with the Blackfoot.

trading party back with the Blackfoot to trade during the winter. He promised that a trading post would be built the next summer near the mouth of Maria's River.

The next year, in 1831, MacKenzie consummated a treaty between the Blackfoot and their enemies the Assiniboine who lived in the region of Fort Union. Hopefully the treaty would insure peace and permit the Company to carry on the fur trade without interruption from intertribal warfare.

Transportation of goods and the return of furs became problems for the American Fur Company as their trading posts were established further and further up the river. Keelboats and mackinaws were too slow and unreliable in the treacherous Missouri and were limited by how much they could carry. In 1832 at the insistence of MacKenzie, Fort Union was finally served by steamboats. As trade turned from beaver plews to buffalo robes, the demand for transportation was even greater and pushed steamboat navigation up the river to Fort Benton by 1860.

Blackfoot Raiding Parties to the South

Before the rendezvous in 1827, the Blackfoot and Atsina attacked the Shoshoni at Bear Lake, harassed Jed Smith and killed Old Pierre. The next year the Atsina attacked the Milton Sublette and Robert Campbell caravan within 18 miles of the rendezvous.

In 1828 the partnership of Smith, Jackson and Sublette went from one disaster to another. Led by Samuel Tulloch and Robert Campbell, detachments of men from the partnership were camped with Peter Ogden and the Hudson Bay traders. After leaving the English traders, the Tulloch-Campbell men were attacked by thirty to forty Blackfoot; three

Schwinden Library, Fort Benton

After leaving Canada, Kenneth MacKenzie became a leader of the Columbia Fur Co. When they joined the American Fur Co., he became its chief trader on the Upper Missouri.

were killed in the ensuing fight. They also lost forty thousand dollars in furs, forty-four horses and a considerable amount of trade goods. In 1830 after the rendezvous on the Popo Agie, Wm. Sublette and his main party awaited his long-absent partner Jedediah Smith. When Jed arrived, he assumed command of the party. After a brief hunt the group crossed over into the Madison and Gallatin valleys in Blackfoot Country. Before they could even set a trap, the Blackfoot jumped them. Two were killed and the rest scattered into the mountains. The men finally got back together without further loss of life on the Stinking Water of the Bighorn.

After wintering in the Wind River Valley, Sublette returned in the fall of 1831 to St. Louis. Jackson went to his old haunts on the Snake, but Jed Smith had not given up even after two encounters with the Blackfoot. With half the men he went back into Blackfoot Country. They moved north of the Yellowstone on the Judith and Musselshell. Before long they ran into a Blackfoot camp but were never attacked. The Blackfoot harassed them daily, stole their traps and were always nearby while the trappers worked. After weeks of daily stress Jedediah finally gave the command to move back to the Wind River. The brief hunt had been rewarding, and was one of the few encounters with the Blackfoot without loss of possessions or lives.

After the rendezvous on the Wind River in 1830, the three partners broke up the partnership and sold out to Milton Sublette, Tom Fitzpatrick, Jim Bridger, Henry Fraeb and Jean Baptiste Gervais. The group called itself the Rocky Mountain Fur Company. They sold out to the American Fur Company after the rendezvous in 1834 held at Ham's Fork on the Green River.

In 1831 the three former partners turned to trade in the south since Santa Fe was open to Americans. They formed a caravan and

National Park Service, Fort Union Association, Artist Robert Back

Fort Union became the head of navigation on the Missouri in 1832, making trade much easier and faster from St. Louis to the mountains. Here the Assiniboin is leaving with furs and robes after bringing up next year's trade goods and supplies.

Artist Karl Bodmer

Halfway to beaver country were the sedentary villages of the Mandan, Hidatsa and Arikara. For many years the villages had been a major trade center for the Native Americans. When trappers and traders came to the Upper Missouri, their villages became a jumping off place for fur companies.

headed down the Santa Fe Trail. After crossing the Cimarron they ran into a large party of Atsina and Blackfoot far south of their normal wanderings. Sublette escaped without a fight. Jedediah Smith, who left the caravan to scout ahead and had been missing since they reached the Cimarron, was killed by a war party of Comanche.

American Fur Co. Comes to the Mountains

Because Kenneth MacKenzie had such a powerful personality, the Upper Missouri Outfit operated almost independently of the American Fur Co. and its Western Department. Even before MacKenzie had completed Fort Union in 1828, he was looking for the opportunity to get a foothold in the mountain beaver trade. The catalyst was Hugh Glass of grizzly encounter fame. He came to MacKenzie on behalf the free trappers who wanted someone to challenge the high prices charged at the rendezvous by the three partners. MacKenzie not only agreed to a caravan, but also wanted to organize a brigade of his own to compete with the Rocky Mountain Fur Company.

In 1830 Ramsey Crooks, acting for Astor, urged the conservative Pierre Chouteau Jr. and the Western Department to send a caravan to the rendezvous. Lucien Fontenelle and Andrew Drips were chosen to lead it. They were veterans of trade on the river but were utter greenhorns in the mountains.

At the same time the Upper Missouri Outfit was organizing its own caravan, to be sent from Fort Union under the leadership of a river man William H. Vanderburgh. The battle to control the mountain fur trade was ultimately between very experienced partners of the new Rocky Mountain Fur Co. and the double-edged competition of the American Fur Company. The challengers could not even find the rendezvous site in 1830. After wandering about the mountains, Drips and Fontenelle finally cached their goods on the Green River and spent the winter trapping in Cache Valley, and not very successfully.

Vanderburgh's luck was no better

than the Western Department. He too turned to trapping in the headwaters of the Missouri at the Three Forks. The Blackfoot caught them on the Madison and after a daylong battle the whites drove them off, claiming they killed forty or fifty savages. Vanderburgh's party had one dead and two wounded, but the Indians had shot ten horses and injured fifty more. They retreated into Crow Country and set up a winter camp on the Powder River. By spring Vanderburgh's group was in desperate shape for mounts. MacKenzie sent Provost overland from Fort Tecumseh with mounts to rescue the beleaguered party.

After the rout of his caravan, MacKenzie got out of the mountain trade and went back to the river trade entirely. He successfully gained the confidence of the Blackfoot on the Upper Missouri in 1831 and turned the mountain trade over to Chouteau's Western Department of the American Fur Company.

A Wild and Woolly Season
Pierre's Hole 1832

The season of 1832 brought on more conflict and competition between the two companies and with their old nemesis the Blackfoot. In St. Louis that season beaver furs were worth $8 a pound in fifty to sixty pound bales. The rendezvous at Pierre's Hole not only intensified the rivalry between the two companies, it was also full of excitement. The site was named for Old Pierre, an Iroquois killed by the Blackfoot in 1827.

MacKenzie had supplies for his caravan brought up river to Fort Union on the steamer *Yellow Stone* on its first trip up river. The boat's arrival opened the Upper Missouri to steamboat trade which eventually changed the entire picture of the fur trade. From Fort Union, Fontenelle and Provost took supplies up the Yellowstone and overland to the rendezvous. Slow progress up the Missouri gave the American Fur Company caravan a late start and again they did not arrive until the rendezvous was over.

Schwinden Library, Fort Benton

Ramsey Crooks of the American Fur Co. was Astor's chief administrator in the West and pushed the company into rendezvous trade in the Central Rockies.

Fitzpatrick's Chase and Escape

The Rocky Mountain Fur Company's men and its heavily armed pack train also headed to Pierre's Hole. They had several fights with the Atsina who were returning from a visit with their Arapaho cousins. One of their men, Tom Fitzpatrick, ran into a band as he crossed South Pass. He tried to escape by hiding in a cave and managed to elude them until nightfall. After leaving his hiding place in the dark, he unfortunately stumbled into their camp but escaped back to the cave. The Atsina searched all day for him, finally gave up and

Artist Alfred Jacob Miller

A supply train arriving at the rendezvous in the mountains. Like most business ventures of the American Fur Co., once they formed a supply train and started bartering for furs they eventually crowded out their competitors.

rode off with his horses. Fitzpatrick headed to Pierre's Hole on foot. After days and days of living off roots and berries and repulsing an assault by wolves, he finally stumbled near death into the rendezvous camp.

At the breakup in 1832, Sublette with his party of trappers agreed to escort Nathaniel Wyeth and his men through Indian country to Oregon. The first night they camped at the south edge of Pierre's Hole, and awoke the next morning to see 200 Atsina at Teton Pass. The Indians had their families and were not looking for a fight; they advanced with the sign of peace to the camp. Two men from the camp rode out to meet them; one of them, a trapper whose father had been killed by the Blackfoot, was bent on revenge. He instructed his partner to be ready to shoot; as they rode up to shake hands he shouted "fire" and the chief fell dead. The Indians retreated into a wooded thicket of downed timber and prepared for a fight. Word was sent to the rendezvous for reinforcements. By the time they arrived and got organized for an assault, the Atsina were well fortified and ready for the attack. In the foray, led by Sublette and Robert Campbell, two men were killed; no one even got close to the Indian positions. After two more half-hearted attacks, the trappers returned to their camp for the night. Under cover of darkness, the Indians slipped away. The next morning they found ten dead Indians, the horses that had been stolen on the way to the rendezvous and the two Fitzpatrick mounts.

The Last Encounters

The two companies left for the fall hunt in 1832 with the American Fur Company dogging the trail of Fitzpatrick, Jim Bridger

Schwinden Library, Fort Benton

Nathaniel Wyeth with his party bound for Oregon encountered the Atsina at Pierre's Hole.

and their Rocky Mountain Brigade. They traveled north to the Three Forks, up to the Great Falls and back again, one trying to lose the other and both trying to trap with little success at either. In Blackfoot Country, one will eventually find them or they will find you, and both groups did. Bridger and Fitzpatrick met about 100 Blackfoot on the Madison in October. With white flags flying and the peace pipe in hand, all went well until Jim Bridger cocked his rifle. An Indian seized the barrel and the gun discharged into the ground. The Indian pulled Bridger off his horse, grabbed the rifle and rode off as Bridger took two arrows in his back. Rifle and arrow fire was exchanged until dark when, in the still of the night, the Indians withdrew. Bridger survived but his counterpart Vanderburgh was not so lucky.

While camped on the Ruby River, the American Fur Company Brigade, with Andrew Drips and William H. Vanderburgh in charge, found Indian signs. Vanderburgh and seven men went out to scout, and rode into a Blackfoot ambush. Vanderburgh's horse went down in the first volley of rifle fire. He pulled himself clear, shot the first Indian he saw and began shouting to his men not to run. The second volley caught him square and as Warren Ferris put it, "... a noble spirit of good and a brave man had passed away forever." Another trapper died in the skirmish and the rest galloped away; two were wounded during the retreat. Ferris was shot in the shoulder but recovered. Vanderburgh died and the Indians stripped his body of flesh and threw his bones in the Ruby. Both brigades packed up and headed out of Blackfoot Country.

The mountain men were never convinced that they could not trap in Blackfoot Country, and came back time after time only to lose again and again. Even after Kenneth MacKenzie's Blackfoot treaty in 1830, trappers made the attempt and lost their lives trying to get rich at the headwaters of the Missouri.

Montana Historical Society

Jim Bridger was one of the extraordinary mountain men who trapped and traded in Blackfoot Country and was able to keep his hair.

Artist Alfred Jacob Miller

The Rocky Mountain Rendezvous occurred every summer from 1825 to 1840 most often on the Green River in Wyoming.

Artist C.M. Russell

Trappers continued to be harrassed in Blackfoot Country

Text Notes

1. Kenneth MacKenzie was a Scotsman who spelled his name for years like he was an Irishman. After returning to his native Scotland and retiring to St. Louis, he began spelling his name as a Scot, Mackenzie. The author has chosen to correct the spelling throughout. The author has also chosen to correct the spelling of the Upper Missouri Outfit's fort on the Missouri that was named for him. After all, he was of Scottish heritage.
2. Throughout the text, when referring to John Jacob Astor's American Fur Company it will be often be referred to simply as the Company, as people on the river referred to the American Fur Company. When Astor left the business, the name of the American Fur Company carried on, even if it referred to the Upper Missouri Outfit, Pratte, Chouteau and Company and just Chouteau and Company. "The Company" was used despite changes in ownership.

Opening the Trade

1831-1865

C. M. Russell's pen sketch shows the Blackfoot coming down into the valley to trade at Fort Benton, opening the fall trade before the buffalo hunt for winter meat. The ceremony occurred every fall with great pomp and circumstance - a whiskey party, gift exchange, smoking the pipe and trading. After the hunt they returned to their winter camps.

5

1830 - 1865

Only with the Blackfoot

Fur Trade Cycle and Ceremony

Pageantry and Whiskey

Annual Cycle

The trading post was a social center where news, ideas, and customs were diffused among the Indians and between them and the traders. A fixed routine developed based upon the habits of the Indians who traded there, and on the supply and demand of the fur business.

Although the cycle was similar for traders and Indians in all posts on the Missouri, it varied slightly from place to place. On the Upper Missouri the Blackfoot and the river itself were the controlling factors. The nomadic nature of the three tribes of the confederation made Blackfoot posts different from those of the Indians down river. There were four distinct seasons with a site associated with each in the nomadic year of the Blackfoot. Their winter camp was from November to early April; a short spring hunting season lasted until late May when they were particularly nomadic. The Sun Dance occurred when all the camps gathered from June to September, and the last fall hunting season was to obtain food before the cold winter returned to the Northern Plains.

The Big Muddy dictated the trader's cycle on the Upper Missouri. It depended upon the rising, falling, freezing and thawing

Schwinden Library, Fort Benton

The trading cycle was always based upon the ecology of the buffalo and his wanderings.

Artist David Parchen

The winter express was a lone rider who carried Company letters between the posts and to the lower river. It was a perilous journey with Indians about and frostbite taking its toll.

of the river. Most years the river froze in late November which isolated posts up river from Fort Union until spring break-up in early April. There was minimal communication between the up river posts and Fort Union on the severely cold days of a Montana winter. A monthly carrier traveling by horse or sled brought communications through the snow and sub-zero weather. Only a few hardy traders were willing to tackle a winter journey on the high plains.

In most years the navigation season began on the lower river in mid-March and lasted until late June. The early spring rise came at break-up time; it was caused by snowmelt on the prairies and early rains. By mid-April the water was receding. A second rise followed caused by the usual June rains, when the Northern Plains get half of their annual rainfall for the year, and by snowmelt from the Rocky Mountains. After mid-July the river drops rapidly and makes navigation difficult for most boats no matter how shallow their draft.

Steamboats with the year's trade goods went up river to Fort Union on the early spring rise. They off loaded to keelboats that used the June rise to get up river to the Blackfoot posts. Arrival of the trade goods usually coincided with the end of the Sun Dance, so the tribes gathered at the fur post before the fall hunt for the ceremonial opening of the fur trade for another season. During those gatherings, hunting and trapping equipment were given to the Indians on credit. The debt was payable at the end of the season and was calculated in so many robes or furs owed to the Company by individual Indians.

Traders were interested only in buffalo robes from young bulls and cows taken between November and early March. Pelts of beaver and other animals were of value only if they were winter pelts. Denig, the factor at Fort Union, estimated that only one-fourth of the annual bison robes came to the traders.

The Blackfoot set up their winter camps in broad wooded river valleys that provided shelter from the weather and hay for their horses. The non-migratory bison frequented the same refuges in winter for forage and thus gave the hunters easy access to meat and robes through the winter. The Piikani usually set up their winter camps on the Teton or Maria's River and the Atsina on Arrow Creek or the Judith River. The Kainaa and Siksika usually wintered further north on the Milk, Oldman and Saskatchewan Rivers.

Winter

During the winter, traders in small groups visited camps close to the trading post and brought back robes and furs to the storerooms of the fort. The system evolved to where the traders built small trading houses for their families near the Indian encampment and traded all winter.

The number of animals killed was based upon the number the women could process during the season. According to Denig,

National Park Service, Ft. Union Assoc., Artist Robert Back

Steamboats arrived at Fort Union on the early spring rise, bringing goods for the next year's trading season. Keelboats took the merchandise from Fort Union to the up river posts.

one woman could dress and tan 25 to 35 robes in a season. The robe trade was exclusively with Indians; free trappers had no stomach for the laborious task of preparing a bison robe. Besides, no non-Blackfoot trappers survived very long in Blackfoot Country.

Life at a trading post during the winter was strenuous at best and survival was a continuous challenge. Daily activities centered around procurement of furs, food and fuel. At most posts by late winter both men and animals were always on the verge of starvation. Hunters provided only about fifty per cent of the necessary meat, the rest had to be obtained from the Indians.

Gardens and planting crops at a Blackfoot post are never mentioned in the journals, so they probably were minimal contributors to the food supply. The meat diet was seldom supplemented with food produced at the fort. Vegetarian supplements were brought by boat or traded with the tribes. The lack of gardens was probably due to the warlike conditions in Blackfoot Country. It would have been difficult to cultivate a garden outside the protective walls of the fort.

Winter feed for horses and other livestock was a real challenge. Hay gathered in the fall in meadows near the fort never seemed to be enough to last the winter. With hay gone the horses were turned out to forage for themselves. Hopefully they would be recovered in the spring, but some were lost to the Indians and others to severe spring storms.

Wood was in continual demand so men gathered wood every possible day. The longer a post existed, the further residents had to go to find wood and the longer the haul. By 1843 timber was so scarce at Fort MacKenzie that it was stored behind locked doors and rationed. Most of the early quarters in up river posts were built with stockade timbers serving as the rear wall. It was impossible to keep chinking in the vertical cracks and cold northerly winds made each room almost as cold as the outdoors. No one wanted to be far from the fire that burned 24 hours a day to keep the men and women from freezing.

Spring Comes at Last

With the spring thaw and break up of the river came a flurry of activity at the fort. There was considerable anticipation of the trip down river. Bundling the winter robes and pelts for the annual shipment down river was a necessary task.

By late March the robes were pressed into packs and readied for shipment. In the chantier (boat yard) mackinaws were constructed for a single trip down river. Soon after the ice disappeared and during the early spring rise, the boats were loaded and headed down river to Fort Union where the keelboat and some of the mackinaws were off-loaded to steamboats. In the late 1830's so many packs of robes were shipped to St. Louis that many mackinaws traveled to the lower river before they could off-load to steamboats.

Trade Goods

The annual cycle began in late fall or early winter when the St. Louis office placed orders with their suppliers in the eastern U. S. and Europe. The list of trade items was long. Major items included bolts of cotton, woolen goods and blankets. Those were some of the most expensive and came from England. Weapons were next in importance. Knives, lance and arrow points came from a variety of manufacturers in the northeastern United States. Guns, powder, flints and lead were ordered from both English and American companies. For many years the Northwest Trade Gun made in England was the favored firearm. Many American companies copied the golden dragon on the backside of the receiver and the "fox in the house" stamped on the plate to satisfy the Indians.

Less costly goods included glass beads mainly from Venice, tobacco, clay and catlinite pipes, kettles and brass bracelets. By the 1830's trade goods were mostly standardized so many were kept on hand in the warehouses of St. Louis. Indians were particular traders and demanded their preferences for many items. On the Upper Missouri small white and blue embroidery seed beads were items of choice. The Indians preferred white multi-colored striped "point" blankets that came in a variety of colors. However traders of other nationalities

Artist Karl Bodmer

The Yellow Stone was the first steamboat to open the Missouri River to the Montana border at Fort Union. A side-wheel and a six-foot draft made her impractical on the upper river. She was soon retired to the lower river and replaced with boats having a shallower draft and stern wheels.

Artist Karl Bodmer

Forts of the American Fur Co. further down river such as Fort Pierre were not burdened with the traditional opening of trade and gift-giving as were the ones in Blackfoot Country.

wanted other colors that were available such as red and blue.

Inventory

An inventory of goods valued at $20,000 at the beginning of the trade period was taken at Fort Union in 1831: awls, half axes, beads, hawk bells, blankets, combs, flannel shirts, pantaloons, kettles, lead, powder, gunworms, bar iron, rifle balls, gun flints, vermilion, and coat buttons.

An 1850's inventory of trade goods when Fort Benton was the premier post listed the following: blankets in all sizes and colors, calico, prints, cotton, ticking, blue and scarlet cloth, lindsay, blue ducking, guns fuses, revolvers, rifles, bullets, shot, powder, gun flints, percussion caps, powder horns, gun worms, awls, beads, hawk bells, gilt buttons, gold and silver lace, sewings, ribbons, fancy caps, combs, butcher knives, files, shears, vermilion, chrome yellow conchinical, brass tacks, Jew harps, brass kettles, iron kettles, tin cups, dippers, copper pots, small trunks, coffee mills, tin pans, crockery, bowls, mugs, sugar, coffee and tea.

Transport of Goods

At first trade goods arrived in New Orleans on three-masted schooners and were shipped to St. Louis by steamboat. Later they were shipped by railroad from eastern seaports to St. Louis and other ports on the Missouri. From there the goods went up river by keelboat until the *Yellow Stone* opened the upper river to steamboat navigation. The laborious trips often took the entire navigation season, and sometimes even longer. The Missouri always tested the steel of the men who lived and worked on her.

Regardless of the conveyance, the river with its high and low water seasons and its "freeze up" during the tough Great Plains winters dictated navigation patterns. Going up river beyond Fort Union was always a challenge for every engagé and even the most knowledgeable river pilot. Above Cow Island

Artist George Catlin

Earthen mound lodges of three tribes on the upper river, Arikara, Hidatsa and Mandan, made a permanent site for nomadic tribes of the plains to trade with one another.

the rock-river was dreadful, one forgetful moment could cost lives and / or boat. Across the Cow Island bar were a series of rapids followed by Dauphin's Rapids and its rocky shoots, Deadman's and Kipp's Rapids and then the snags and sandbars above Maria's River all the way to Fort Benton. It was a magnificently beautiful and enjoyable trip for the cabin passengers who could swim if necessary.

Because whiskey or inexpensive goods were traded for most of the furs, profits of the fur companies were enormous, making millionaires of owners and some very rich traders. William Gordon said that in his experience, a profit of from 200 to 2000 per cent on primary costs of goods was possible. Edwin T. Denig at Fort Union agreed, but he added in the overhead of operating the trading post so profits would not appear so enormous.

Beginnings of the Trade Ceremony

Gift-giving and ceremonial exchange were an important part of the native culture even before the white traders came. For centuries intertribal trading was carried out among various nations. Tribes and bands traveled great distances to trade with each other; certain sites along the river where tribes lived in permanent villages were recognized by the tribes as trade centers. The Mandan, Hidatsa and Arikara mound villages were examples on the Missouri River. Some trading ceremonies were part of the Blackfoot culture before the beginning of the Canadian trade. The Hudson Bay Company and the North West Fur Company strictly observed the ceremonies when they began trading with the Blackfoot in the Canadian West. When traders were unwilling to participate, the natives quickly deserted them for others who would. After 1821 and the amalgamation of the two companies under the Hudson Bay banner, George Simpson tried to do away with the costly practice of gift-giving.

In the south American traders were about to enter the trade scene with the Blackfoot. From the beginning in 1807 they had trouble with the Blackfoot but finally signed a treaty with them in 1830. It was then very unwise on Hudson Bay's part to stop the ceremonies when the natives traded at both Canadian forts and American forts. Gift-giving was not reduced at all but became more lavish

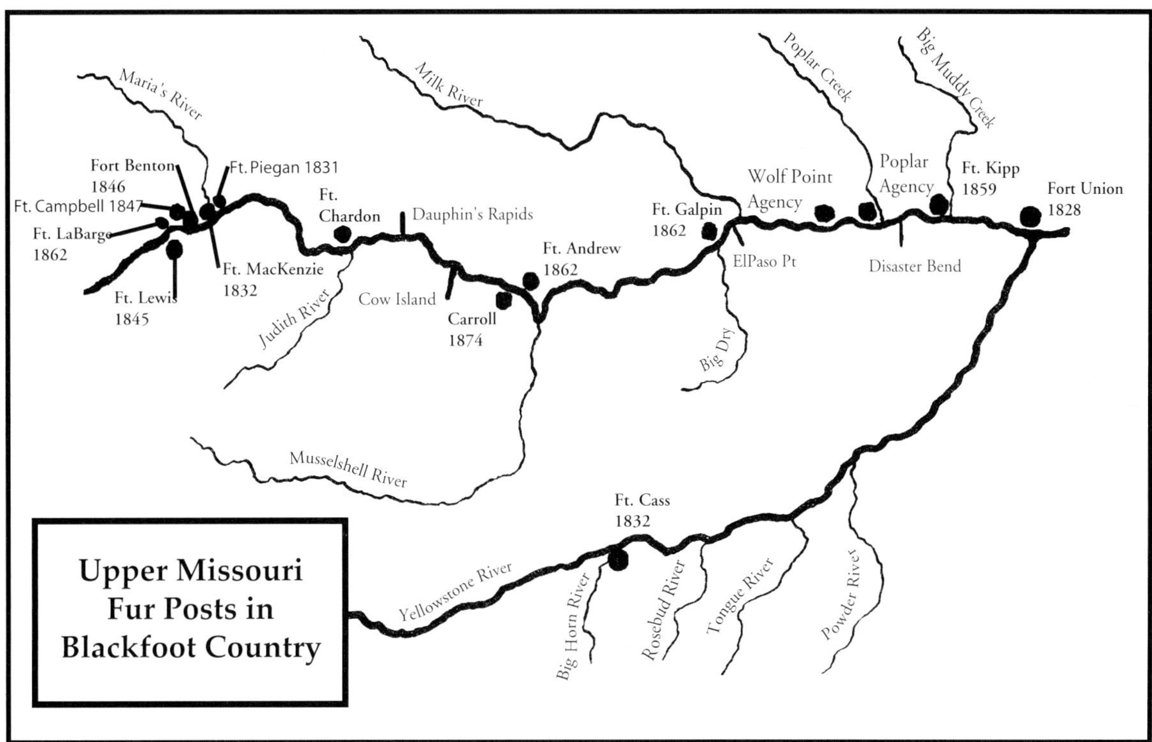

as the two forces vied with each other for the Blackfoot trade.

When the American Fur Company entered the Blackfoot trade, they knew full well that they must adopt the British system or they would never be able to hold their trade. Kenneth MacKenzie at Fort Union clearly understood that. He grew up in the fur trade with the North West Fur Company along with many of his traders who were now part of the Upper Missouri Outfit. In his first year at Fort MacKenzie, David Mitchell tried in vain to dispense with the ceremony. Being an American trader from St. Louis, he was not familiar with the ceremony and was unwilling to participate until the Indians became very hostile and began to depart without transacting any trade. Mitchell quickly amended his ways after listening to the more experienced traders who were familiar with the Canadian system.

In 1835 Kenneth MacKenzie even attempted to put an end to the costly practice: "I never was an advocate for large and indiscriminate distribution of presents: a good and industrious Indian may be encouraged to greater exertions by a well-timed gratuity, but when all receive alike, every good effect is destroyed and the nation claims a right what was intended as a boon. " Signed: Kenneth MacKenzie. With competition from the Hudson Bay Company, it was only his dream and was never put into practice with the Blackfoot.

Due to competition for the Blackfoot trade, traders on both sides of the border continued the ceremony regardless of cost and principle. Hudson Bay Company officials complained that the Indians were better dressed than ever before after receiving presents from the Americans each year. One of the major changes in Indian culture that came from the trading ceremonies was the idea that the individual had his own possessions rather than the earlier feeling of communal property within the tribe. Traders awarded more lavish gifts to individuals who produced greater numbers of furs and robes and showed the greatest loyalty to the Company. Those individuals then had more status within their culture.

The fur trade had shifted from beaver plews to buffalo robes by 1840. The bulky bison robes created a major transportation problem for Hudson Bay. The Americans with the Missouri River and the steamboat handled

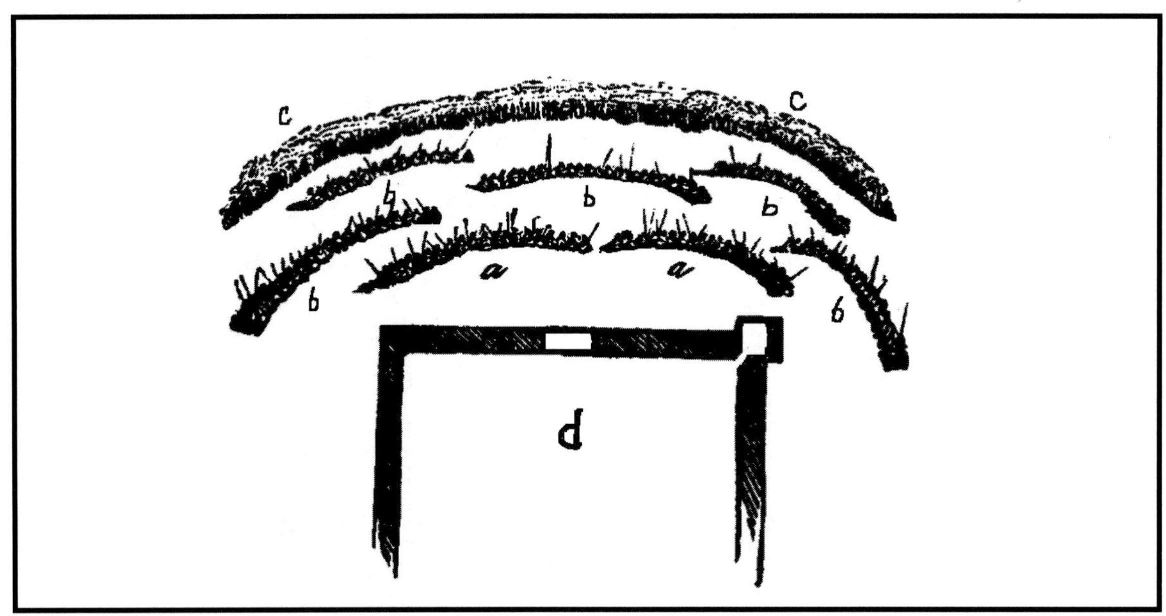

Prince Maximilian's drawing of the Blackfoot at Fort MacKenzie during the opening ceremonies: a. Chiefs b. Warriors c. Women and Children d. Fort.

them more cheaply and gained a tremendous advantage in the trade.

The use of alcohol changed. Early in the trade all fur companies used it in limited quantity as part of the trading ceremony; later it became a trading commodity throughout the remainder of the period. A drunken party lasted a day or two, but later whiskey created a continuing orgy that lasted until the entire trade was finished and all the robes were taken. Because trade in whiskey was illegal, not many written accounts exist from the later period.

Throughout the 1850's and early 1860's when Fort Benton reigned as the premier Blackfoot post, the trading ceremony was still observed by the fur company. A description of the salutatory greetings on arrival of a small party in September 1855 appeared in the Fort Benton Journals 1854-56: "In the evening the party of Bloods seen by Mr. Jackson (consisting of three men & three women) arrived at the Fort. When on the hill back of the fort they called a halt - commenced firing their guns and raised their colors and spread them to the breeze. Mr. Monroe went forth to meet them and to extend to them the hospitality of the fort."

Later Ceremonies

In later years at Fort Benton, food became part of the ceremonies. Tea, coffee, flour and molasses were either taken to the camps to induce trading or presented during the ceremony. After the treaty in 1855 the annuity system (an annual allotment of goods from the federal government) came to the Blackfoot. Annuities were a negotiated right of the native people and not a gift.

With the close association of Indian agents with the companies, annuities were often treated as "gifts" when incoming bands arrived at the fort and served the traders without cost to the company. The annuity system was full of considerable graft. Indian agencies were usually located at the trading company's fort so it was easy to disguise the transactions. Fort Benton was an example; it became the Blackfoot Agency in 1855 and continued until Chouteau and Company left in 1865.

Individualization within the bands of Blackfoot and the demise of the Upper Missouri Outfit (Chouteau and Company) in 1865 led to greater and greater changes until the ceremony disappeared completely. During the last trade period, smaller and smaller groups came to the fort, even down to a family group where an individual participated in trade for himself and not for the group. Trade occurred across the counter in the store. Then the "tail" was thrown in, the gift at the end of trade to encourage the individual's return. The gift was of material goods; by then whiskey had disappeared from the trade scene.

The Ceremony Begins

A day or two before the main encampment arrived at the environs of the fort, an advance party came for tobacco. They may be the principal chiefs or their representatives who delivered the tobacco back to the main camp.

When the main party arrived, the large flag was run up the center staff and salute cannons fired in their honor. If it was a return engagement by a band that had recently been there, the ceremonies were not performed.

The Opening Trade Ceremonies commenced by dispensing "high wine" or Indian rum, one pint per important personage. If the opposition was close at hand in a neighboring fort, more was given to hold the trade. The Chiefs were invited into the trading room of the fort where many of the principals might receive an outfit called the Captain's Suit and other gifts for distribution to his people. An important part of the ceremony was smoking the pipe. Speeches were made and the pipe was passed. Trading usually began the following day and continued as long as there were robes and furs available from the band.

Prince Max's Account

At Fort MacKenzie, Prince Maximilan of Wied and Neu Wied wrote one of the most complete accounts of the opening trade ceremonies conducted in August and September 1833. The Prince and his artist Karl Bodmer recorded the Blackfoot culture before smallpox and invasion of the Upper Missouri Outfit altered their way of life. The following is through the eyes of an observer who was completely unfamiliar with the trade ceremonies: (1)

Artist Karl Bodmer

Prince Maximilian of Wied and Neu Wied observed the ceremonies and recorded them in 1833.

"In preparation for the trade ceremony, the flag was hoisted on the main mast in the center of the courtyard, and two cannons were also wheeled into the yard and readied for firing to salute the opening of the trade. When both were fired this signaled to the Indians that the fort was ready to trade. It was nearly one half hour after this that the singing could be heard from the Indian camp, along with rifle shots into the air. Finally Spotted Elk arrived at the front gate, it was opened and he and three or four others entered the fort and were saluted by the cannon reports. They then were greeted by Mitchell with handshakes and led to (dining room) trading or chiefs hall. After buffalo robes were placed, the chiefs were seated on the floor. As more headmen arrived they too were greeted with cannon shots and a handshake from David Mitchell. Each was bearing gifts for the Factor; usually of 2 or more beaver skins or horse. After the greeting they to were taken to the trade room and seated with the rest. Eventually there were thirty to forty chiefs

Artist Karl Bodmer

Blackfoot brave with his horse and gun that made him the most feared mounted warrior on the plains. The Blackfoot were great buffalo hunters that made for lucrative trade in robes for the fur companies on the Upper Missouri.

seated together. The lesser men of the tribe then arrived and were invited in and seated on robes in the courtyard in front of the dwelling house. Many of the chiefs were clad in military like uniforms and round hats that had been adorned with feather tufts and metal bands. These had been given to them previously by the traders for being loyal to the company and trading here rather than with the British.

Spotted Elk wore his old overcoat made from a blanket with red lapels and collar added. He also wore a round hat and had his face painted with vermilion, along with other chiefs with blue or red uniform and even one half red and green gave the whole scene a carnival atmosphere. La Chemise de Fer with his unusual painted face entirely coal black with eyes, mouth and cheeks with two vertical stripes from the temples and jaws downward of vermilion.

Other bands arrived other than the Piikani; one of Kainaa that presented gifts and the chief entered the fort. Several bands of Atsina number as many as 80 braves presented themselves at the gate they too presented gifts and the most important chiefs were admitted to the fort. All of them received with cannon shots and they had British flags on long staffs as they entered. These preliminary ceremonies were the ones that Mitchell wanted to do away with last season and from it he almost lost the trade of the Blackfoot.

After all the chiefs had been seated in the hall probably about thirty in number, whiskey was passed among them and the pipe was passed and smoke by all as well as by the traders. While this was being done Mr. Mitchell led Spotted Elk to his quarters and presented him with a half red and green uniform with wide lapels and cuffs that were decorated with silver tresses. Also a red felt hat with feather bushes and a double-barreled shotgun. This was his reward for always being faithful to trade with the company and never with the British. After dressing in his new clothes he was led back into the hall in his new dress that was worth 150 dollars. Here Mitchell told the rest this is how the company treats its loyal friends and the others that take their beaver to the English could not be given these big gifts. If in the future these chiefs acted as did Spotted Elk they too could receive these gifts.

Spotted Elk then mounted his gray horse and rode out among the seated Indians outside of the fort. As he rode among the semicircular lines making a long speech animosity broke out and violent talk started among the chiefs. Spotted Elk was not popular and to avoid a confrontation Mitchell took him back to his quarters.

The whiskey was having its effect and chiefs stood giving long speeches, Spotted Elk was advise by his brother in law to go home as the Kainaa talked of killing him.

The mass of Indians all seated in semicircular rows around the main gate, with the men in front and the women and children in the rear sang endlessly. They periodically fired their rifles into the air and finally Indian whiskey was passed among them. These ceremonies continued until 6 P.M. The chiefs left but returned soon all carrying a whiskey barrel that was filled for them as a gift. Trade then started. They brought beaver skins and

Artist Rudolph Kurz

Indian council room at Fort Union. In all Blackfoot posts these chambers were where the traders "wined and dined" important men of the tribe, exchanged gifts, smoked the pipe and served drinks. Following the festive celebrations, trade began in earnest.

Artist David Parchen

After months of absence taking returns down to the Great Lakes, the homecoming of men to their wilderness trading post was a grand occasion for all of their families.

buffalo robes and the main trade item was whiskey. After a time, a tumultuous scene had developed where the drunken engages' began fighting with each other. Alexander Harvey the clerk, after getting into the fight used his tomahawk on the head of another and the Prince remarked as the brawling continued, " They were setting a bad example for the Indians, who were behaving much better and were standing there as quiet onlookers."

"As the fighting was quelled, the Indians who had been trading and drinking became quite tender handshaking over and over again and embracing the traders and kissing them, and the bartering continued for whiskey and when they had nothing else left they begged

Artist Karl Bodmer

Prince Maximilian of Wied and Neu Wied and Artist Karl Bodmer meeting the Indians at Fort Clark

Artist David Parchen

Greeting the chiefs at the gate of Fort Benton to begin the opening of the fur trade ceremonies. The ceremony occurred every fall with all Blackfoot and Atsina bands before their fall hunt.

for more and more whiskey. This continued into the evening until the drunken Indians returned to their lodges." (2)

The ceremonies continued almost daily with other bands arriving and all seeking whiskey in trade. The Indians also traded for other goods but the illegal whiskey was always part of the barter. As each group finished trading, they left the proximity of the fort for the fall hunt. They returned to their winter camps which were usually near the fort so trading continued throughout the winter.

A Long Tradition

From the very beginning the ceremonies coincided with the return of the voyageurs from the Grand Portage on the Great Lakes. The traditions and customs established at the fur forts by the Nor'Westers and Hudson Bay Company were similar on the Upper Missouri.

The return of the traders with goods for the next year's trade prompted the ceremonies and celebrations throughout the years of trade on both sides of the border. They were unique to the Blackfoot trade and were part of the history of the fur trade in Montana.

The Missouri provided easy passage to the fur forts compared to the Canadians' long arduous journeys in canoes. On the Missouri the return trips were in large keelboats loaded with supplies in St. Louis. The two-month trip up the Big Muddy involved towing or cordelling the keelboats; it was a tough assignment for the voyageurs. The arrival of the steamboat on the Missouri, first to Fort Union then all the way to Fort Benton, was an easy excursion compared to the earlier means of water transportation.

Text Notes

1. From Thwaites edition of the Maximilan Journals 1832-34.
2. 1965 translation of Maximilan Journals to English by Joslyn Art Museum of Omaha.

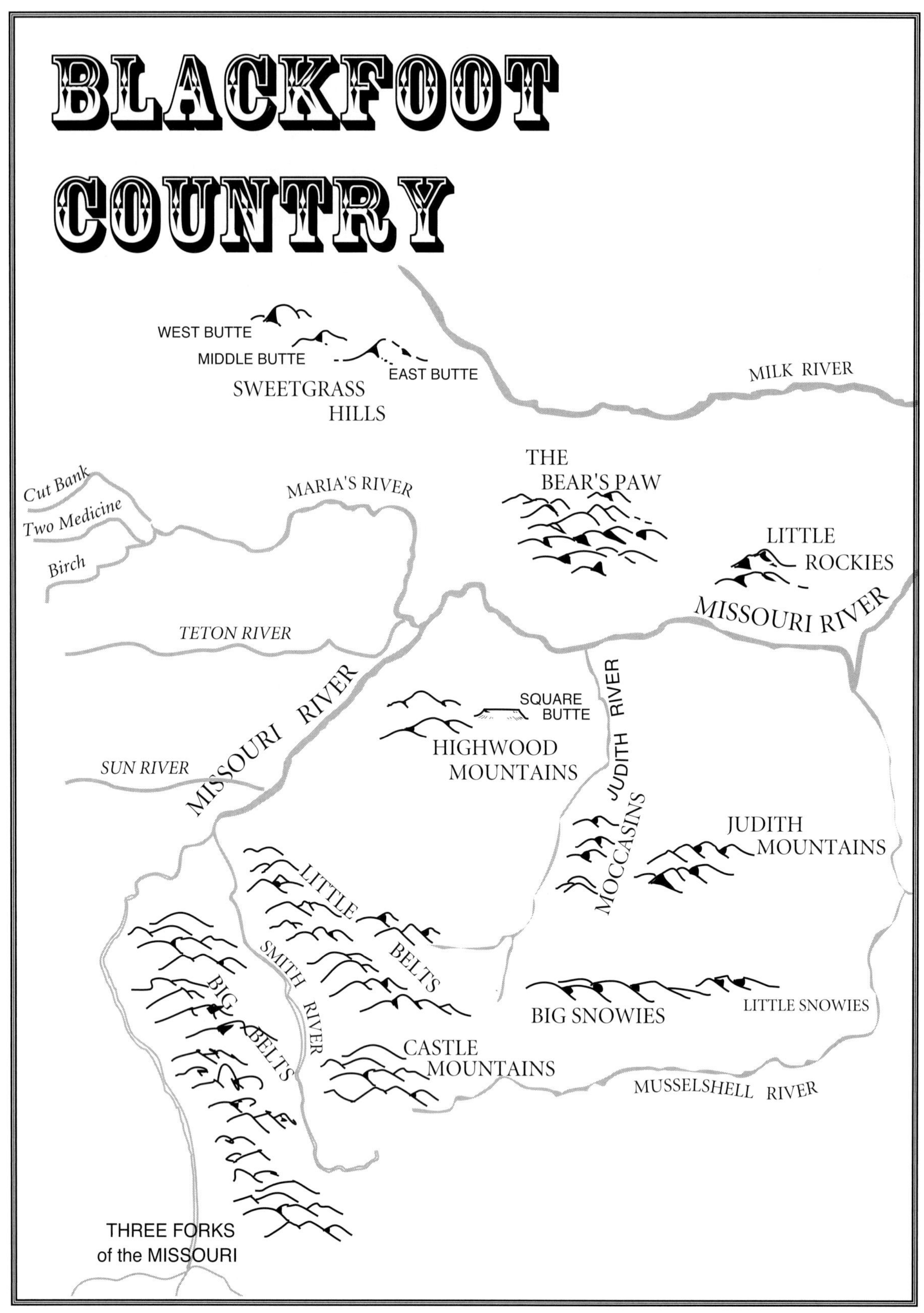
BLACKFOOT COUNTRY
WEST BUTTE
MIDDLE BUTTE
EAST BUTTE
SWEETGRASS HILLS
MILK RIVER
THE BEAR'S PAW
Cut Bank
Two Medicine
Birch
MARIA'S RIVER
LITTLE ROCKIES
MISSOURI RIVER
TETON RIVER
SQUARE BUTTE
HIGHWOOD MOUNTAINS
JUDITH RIVER
MISSOURI RIVER
SUN RIVER
MOCCASINS
JUDITH MOUNTAINS
LITTLE BELTS
SMITH RIVER
BIG BELTS
BIG SNOWIES
LITTLE SNOWIES
CASTLE MOUNTAINS
MUSSELSHELL RIVER
THREE FORKS of the MISSOURI

Part II

Upper Missouri Trade

Morning Star

Fur Trade Chronology 1831 to 1845

Fall 1831: James Kipp constructed Fort Piegan at the mouth of Maria's River on the Missouri, the first Blackfoot trading post.

Late Summer 1832: David Mitchell built Fort MacKenzie up the Missouri River about 5 miles from the Fort Piegan site.

Summer 1832: Rendezvous at Pierre's Hole

Winter 1832-33: In February Alexander Culbertson signed his first three-year contract with Chouteau and Company.

Spring 1833: Mitchell brought returns from Fort MacKenzie to Fort Union.

Summer 1833: Culbertson came up river for the first time with Mitchell. Alexander Harvey was a new employee of the company in the party. Prince Maximilan and Karl Bodmer were guests of the company at Fort MacKenzie that summer. Culbertson took a Piikani wife.

Fall 1833: Maxmilian and Bodmer returned to Fort Clark in September for the winter.

Spring 1834: Mitchell brought returns down river, went to St. Louis and did not return to Fort MacKenzie. Against his wishes, Culbertson was left in charge. He requested a new factor and James Kipp came to replace Mitchell at Fort MacKenzie.

1834: Astor sold out, American Fur Company broke up and Upper Missouri Outfit and Pierre Chouteau Jr. took over.

1834: American Fur Co. (Pierre Chouteau) bought out the Rocky Mountain Fur Co. of Wm. Sublette.

Spring 1834-35: Kenneth MacKenzie went to Europe after whiskey trouble at Fort Union.

Spring 1835: Before his departure, MacKenzie rehired Harvey and sent him to Fort MacKenzie to help Culbertson. A. Hamilton in charge at Fort Union. Kipp brought returns from Fort MacKenzie to Fort Union; did not return up river.

1835-36: Culbertson became factor in charge at Fort MacKenzie.

Spring 1836: Culbertson brought returns to Fort Union.

Spring 1837: Harvey took returns to Fort Union and brought smallpox back with him. MacKenzie left upper river for good. Smallpox killed almost half of Blackfoot population.

Summer 1837: Honore' Picotte in charge of upper river after MacKenzie left.

Spring 1838: Culbertson took returns to Fort Union.

Spring 1839: Culbertson brought down returns and went on to St. Louis. Mitchell left the river.

Winter 1839: Culbertson brought Malcolm Clarke up river for the first time.

Winter 1839-40: Harvey's winter trip to St. Louis, returned in summer with Larpenteur.

Summer 1840: Last rendezvous. Culbertson became a partner in firm and married Natawista.

1841: Culbertson took charge of both Fort Union and Fort MacKenzie.

Spring 1841: New opposition was Union Fur Co. established up river. Harvey killed Sandoval at Fort Union.

Fall and Winter 1841-42: DeSmet at Fort Union

Spring 1842: Fort Alexander was built on the Yellowstone.

Fall 1842: Clarke and Harvey killed Atsina. Union Fur Co. (Fox-Livingston) established Fort Cotton and Fort Mortimer.

Summer 1843: Culbertson at Fort Union; Little Dog's Buttons Without Eyes (Spanish gold) near Fort Hall.

Summer 1843: Audubon spent summer at Fort Union; Culbertson left for Fort Laramie in August.

Fall 1843: Chardon became factor at Fort MacKenzie. Audubon left Fort Union and went back down river.

Winter 1844: In February Harvey and Chardon killed Siksika with cannon blast and sealed the fate of Fort MacKenzie. They moved the fort March 19 to mouth of Judith and named it Fort Chardon or Fort FAC.

Spring 1844: Chardon came down river with few returns and was sent back to Fort Chardon.

Spring 1845: Chardon brought limited returns down river and was sent to Fort Clark. Harvey was left in charge at Fort Chardon.

Fall 1845: Culbertson returned with Clarke. Harvey was banished to Fort Pierre but quit and continued down river to start opposition company in St. Louis.

Late Fall 1845: Culbertson built Fort Lewis, completed in January 1846.

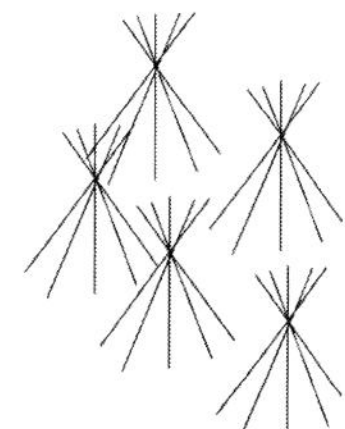

Fort Piegan

1831 - 1832

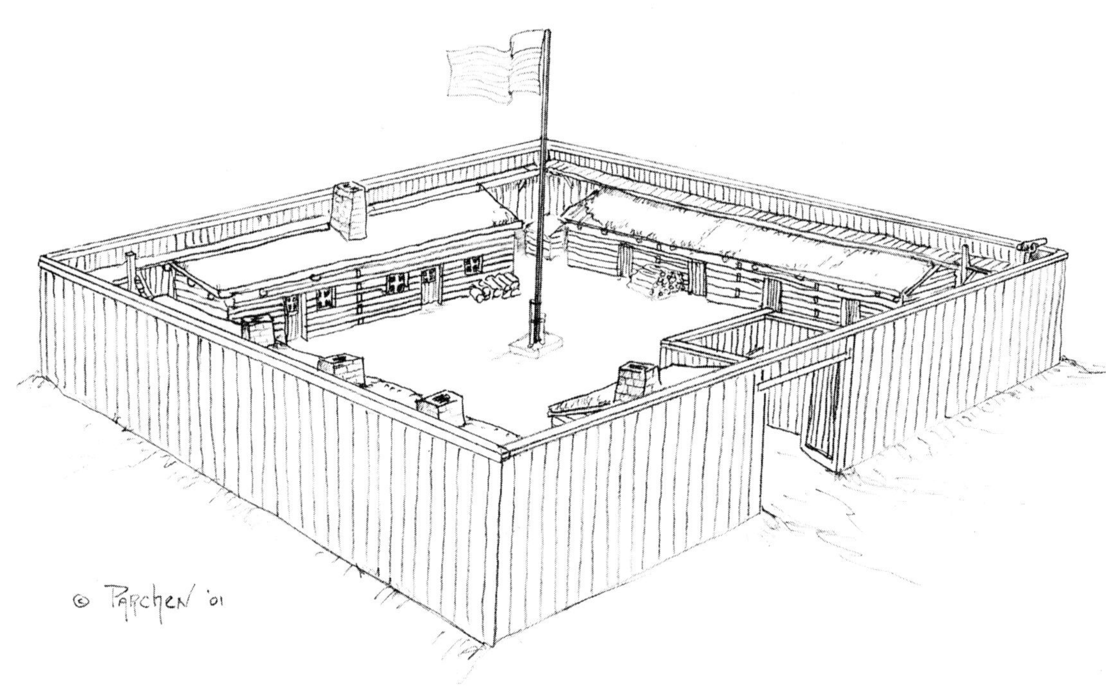

The first Blackfoot post at the mouth of Maria's River was built by James Kipp in 75 days during the fall of 1831. It survived only one trading season. When it was time to return to Fort Union, no one would stay. Indians burned it after everyone left.

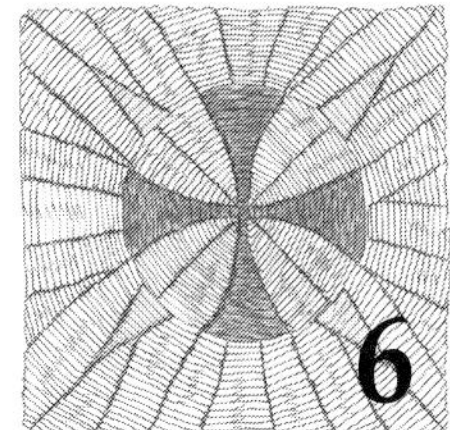

1831 - 1832

The First Post

James Kipp Builds Fort Piegan

The Company Starts a Monopoly

First Treaty at Fort Union 1830-31

The first treaty between the American Fur Co., the Assiniboine and the Blackfoot opened trade into Blackfoot Country for the first time. Trade continued until 1865 when the last trading post of the American Fur Co. closed its doors and the Company men returned down river to St. Louis.

Text of the treaty:

> "We send greeting to all mankind! Be it known unto all nations, that the most ancient, most illustrious and most numerous tribes of the red skins, lord of the soil from the banks of the great waters unto the tops of the mountains, upon which the heavens rest, have entered into solemn league and covenant, to make preserve and cherish a firm lasting peace, that so long as the water runs, or the grass grows, they may hail each other as brethren and smoke the calumet in friendship and security
>
> On the vigil of the feast of St. Andrew in the year eighteen hundred and thirty one, the powerful and distinguished nation of Blackfeet, Piegan- and Blood- Indians, by their ambassadors -----------------appeared at Fort Union near the spot where the Yellowstone River unites its current with the Missouri, and in the council-chamber of the governor Kenneth McKenzie met, the principal chief of all the Assiniboin-Nation, the man that holds the knife, attended by his chiefs of council, le Brechu, le Borgne, the

Artist Karl Bodmer

Fort Union at the mouth of the Yellowstone was where the first Blackfoot treaty was signed by Kenneth MacKenzie, chief trader for the Upper Missouri Outfit.

Sparrow, the Bears Arm, la Terre qui trembe, and l'Enfent de medecine - - when conforming to all ancient customs and ceremonies - and observing the due mystical signs enjoined by the grand medecine-lodges, a treaty of peace and friendship was entered into between the said high contracting parties, and is testified by their hands and seals hereunto annexed, hereafter and for ever to live as brethern of one large united happy family, and may the great spirit, who watchet over us all approve our conduct and teach us to love one another."

Done, executed, ratified and confirmed at Fort Union on the day and year first within, written in the presence of Jas Archdale Hamilton.

H. Chardon

signed

The Man that holds the knife.
The Young Gaucher.
Le Brechu or le fils du gros francais.
The Bears Arm or the man that lives alone.
Le Borgne.
The Sparrow.
La Terre qui tremble.
L'Enfant de medecine

on behalf of the Piegans and Blackfeet

K. MacKenzie.

After the treaty was signed, MacKenzie sent James Kipp and a party of traders to build the first trading post in Blackfoot Country. August was a late start from Fort Union. With very low water in the Missouri they were delayed even more as they cordelled

Schwinden Library, Fort Benton

Kipp and his party of traders and builders on their way to the mouth of Maria's River to trade for the first time in Blackfoot Country. Before the steamboat, supplies and materials came up river by keelboat, cordelled up the wild Missouri.

the keelboat upstream. Kipp and his party of seventy-five men (1) crept slowly upstream and did not reach the Musselshell, only about half-way to the mouth of Maria's River, until late September. Some days they made less than a mile a day as they pulled the heavy-laden keelboat across one sandbar after another and dodged the boulders of the upper river.

Give Us Seventy-Five Days

They finally reached the mouth of Maria's River in mid-October. The Piikani were nearby along the Missouri and Maria's Rivers; news had spread from band to band that the keelboat with Kipp's party was slowly coming up river to trade. That summer MacKenzie had wisely decided to send a party of his traders back with the Blackfoot after their treaty signing at Fort Union. His action thwarted the Hudson Bay Company's last desperate effort that fall to lure the Piikani back north for the opening of trade. Since the advance party paid double dividends, American Fur Company's traders persuaded the Piikani to wait on the Missouri to trade with the Americans.

The day after Kipp's keelboat tied up to the bank with a tired contingent of voyageurs, Piikani from a hundred lodges descended upon the traders ready to trade. Fear of the hostile Blackfoot was apparent among the outnumbered Americans. With only the keelboat for protection Kipp realized that construction of a fort would be impossible with the Indians camped so near. Kipp parlayed with the chiefs and convinced them to withdraw until the fort was constructed. It would take seventy-five days. When the Piikani disappeared, construction began

From Rudolph Kurz

James Kipp welcoming the Indians to trade at Fort Piegan

on a point of ground between the two rivers along the north bank of the Missouri.

Literally building for their lives, the party constructed quarters, storerooms and a trade room surrounded by cottonwood pickets twenty-five feet tall for protection. A small cannon was installed on a platform in one corner of the stockade. As promised the Indians arrived on time, just as the newly constructed fort was completed and named Fort Piegan. The Piikani were surprised at how quickly the new fort had been built, but they were ready to celebrate and to trade immediately.

The First Days of Trade

The Piikani, the best beaver trappers of the three Blackfoot tribes, came loaded with furs. The first event was a giant celebration, dedicated to the new fort and to the American's first trade with the Blackfoot. To open the festivities Kipp mixed up two hundred gallons of Indian whiskey made from a small barrel of almost pure alcohol. Called "high wine" by the traders, the concoction was made of whiskey diluted by Missouri River water with ginger, pepper and molasses added. It tasted somewhat like the rum used by the Hudson Bay Company, a favorite of the Blackfoot. The next ten days of hilarity, drunkenness and trading brought in over two thousand beaver plews, robes and other furs.

The Blackfoot began to like those Americans. They were more generous with their "Blackfoot rum" than traders in the north and the natives received more goods for their furs. Trade went smoothly with the Piikani until a few weeks later when a band of Kainaa arrived. Then the scene changed.

The Kainaa Trade

The Kainaa were more aggressive and unruly, and did not want Americans in their territory, an attitude probably instilled by British traders to the north. Incited to a fight, they immediately laid siege to the fort. The friendly Piikani had warned Kipp and his traders and they had laid up supplies. The river was freezing so they put up ice in the fort as

Schwinden Library, Fort Benton

Confluence of the Missouri River and Maria's River where in 1831 the first Blackfoot trading post was built for the Upper Missouri Outfit (American Fur Company). The site was to the right center of the picture, now probably in the river since the river has cut the bank for many years.

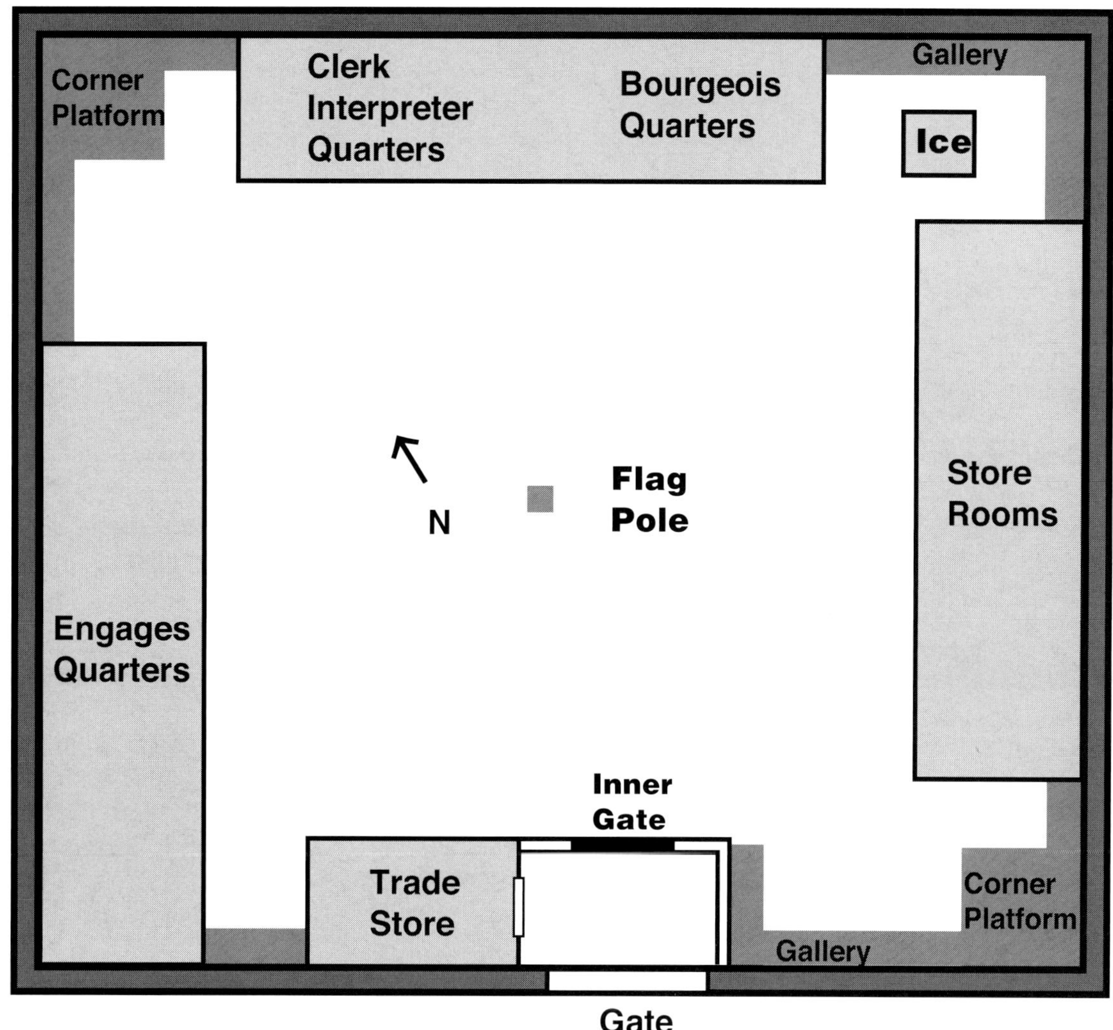

Fort Piegan floor plan 1831 - 1832

a source of water in case of an emergency and had killed extra game.

When the siege had lasted ten days and supplies were getting low, Kipp made his move. Not wanting to start a war and lose the Blackfoot trade, he fired his lone cannon at a large cottonwood tree outside the walls, shattering it into many pieces. It so stunned the Kainaa that they immediately brought their leaders to parlay with Kipp. The traders organized another celebration and used the rest of the whiskey to pacify and loosen up the Kainaa. Those inducements persuaded the Kainaa to trade and the Hudson Bay Company lost another customer, the first but not the last. Kenneth MacKenzie was determined to move his enterprises into Blackfoot Country, to stay there, and to dominate the trade thereby outdoing his bitter rivals in the Hudson Bay Company.

Abandonment

Kipp and his traders, huddled in

Schwinden Library, Fort Benton

Kenneth MacKenzie, "King of the Upper Missouri," expanded the fur trade into Blackfoot Country in 1831.

the first American post deep in the heart of Blackfoot Country, had a very successful winter season by taking over 6,450 pounds of beaver plews. In the spring of 1832 Kipp needed to take his returns down river to Fort Union and to resupply his depleted store of trade goods. The Indians wanted the traders to remain at the fort, but the men who were to stay behind refused. (2) They were in the country of the hostile Blackfoot and did not want stay over the summer. With no alternative, Kipp packed up his furs and other possessions, loaded them on board the keelboat and headed down river with his whole party. He promised the Indians that the Americans would return the next season. Soon after they left the fort, the Indians burned it. (3)

The first chapter of Blackfoot trade with the Americans was closed. A successful venture for MacKenzie and the Upper Missouri Outfit, it was only a harbinger of what was to come.

Steamboats in the Trade

The Company was about to solve another nagging problem, transporting robes and furs to St. Louis. A growing demand in the markets for buffalo robes presented quite a challenge since they were more difficult to transport than small furs. Keelboats and mackinaws could not carry many 200-pound packs; they were too slow and unreliable in the treacherous Missouri. Bigger, faster and more powerful boats were needed. At the insistence of Kenneth MacKenzie, steamboats began serving Fort Union at the edge of beaver country in 1832. By the 1840's trade was primarily in buffalo robes, a situation which pushed the steamboat to new navigational ports on the river until they finally reached Fort Benton in 1860.

In 1807 on the Hudson River Robert Fulton's *Clermont* was the first steamboat to move goods and people along any river. In 1811 one of the first steamboats on the Mississippi River, the packet *New Orleans* that was built in Pittsburgh, came down the Ohio River and reached its namesake in January 1812. In 1819 the *Independence* ventured up the Missouri River to the outposts of Franklin and Clariton. In the same year the dragon-designed *Western Engineer* came 660 miles up the Missouri to Council Bluffs, Iowa in support of a military campaign under Major S.H. Long

The American Fur Company initiated building a steamboat for the Missouri in the winter of 1830-31. Named the *Yellow Stone,* it was built on the upper Ohio at Louisville. Pierre Chouteau Jr. brought it down the Ohio and up the Missouri to Fort Tecumseh. He arrived just in time to have a new post three miles upriver named Fort Pierre in his honor. He returned to St. Louis in a boat loaded with furs and robes. An impatient MacKenzie came down river where he was met by John Sanford, agent for the Mandans at Fort Tecumseh. MacKenzie off-loaded the cargo of the next season's trade goods onto two keelboats for the Upper Missouri Outfit.

The next season Chouteau kept his promise to start early. After a short delay at Fort Pierre, the *Yellow Stone* reached Fort Union on the Montana border on June 17, 1832. Fort

Artist Gary Lucy

In 1832 the Yellow Stone was the first steamboat to reach Fort Union, bringing supplies to the upper river and taking the furs back to St. Louis. The first returns from the new Blackfoot post at Fort Piegan were carried down river on her decks.

Union remained the head of navigation on the river for the next 28 years. In 1833 two boats, the *Yellow Stone* and *Assiniboin*, came to Fort Union. It was the last trip for the *Yellow Stone* whose six-foot draft was too deep for the Upper Missouri.

Experience led to design changes; the new steamboats were called "mountain boats." After 1832, returns of the trade were transported by keelboat and mackinaw boats only from up river Blackfoot posts to Fort Union where they off-loaded to the steamboats. The keelboats were reloaded with supplies for the trip back to the wilderness fur posts.

In 1835 the *Assiniboin* came about 100 miles up the Missouri beyond Fort Union to the mouth of the Poplar River to retrieve a cargo of robes. Deeper penetration of the upper river continued until finally the hired company boats *Chippewa* and *Key West* reached Fort Benton on July 2, 1860 with Charles Chouteau on board. Fort Benton was established as the head of navigation on the Missouri River, the world's innermost port.

Text Notes

1. Various historians dispute the number of men taken up river to build the fort. Most accounts say that the average compliment was 70 to 75 men but others say only 40. The larger number seems to be the number usually at upper river posts during the trading season and is probably more accurate.
2. Over half of the men were used in transporting furs down river and to cordelle the keelboat back up river with the season's trade goods. During early spring and summer the number of men around the posts was approximately thirty, a marginal number to maintain security. The relative shortage of manpower was probably one of the reasons no one wanted to remain in Blackfoot Country during the first year, especially after they had survived a siege of the fort.
3. Some accounts say the traders burned the fort, others say the Kainaa did. Traders usually left abandoned forts alone to be used again if necessary. Logs from an abandoned fort were often used to build a new one if they could be easily transported to the new site. Even before steamboats, wood at up river posts was a valuable commodity.

Fort MacKenzie

1832 - 1836

Fort MacKenzie, the second Blackfoot post, was built by David Mitchell and 70 company employees in the spring of 1832. Mitchell and James Kipp had charge in the early years and left the fort in the capable hands of Alexander Culbertson during its most productive years. Meanwhile, the trade shifted from beaver plews to buffalo robes.

7

1832 - 1836

Trade and Strife

Mitchell and Kipp at Fort MacKenzie

Prince Maximilian and Bodmer Visit the Blackfoot

Years of Change and Expansion

MacKenzie's first success in Blackfoot Country strengthened his resolve to expand his empire on the upper river. He arranged for Berger to make the first peaceful contact, then consummated a treaty between the Assiniboine who lived near Fort Union and their hated enemies, the Blackfoot. A very strange treaty it was; no one is sure the Blackfoot knew anything about signing it. Several Assiniboine chiefs signed the treaty, but MacKenzie himself had signed for the Blackfoot. The king was king and anything was possible in his realm.

A Transportation Problem

MacKenzie's next formidable task was to develop a better supply system between Fort Union and St. Louis. Steamboats were supplying the lower posts, but none had ventured onto the upper river with its dangers to navigation and shallow, sandbar-choked channels. MacKenzie convinced Chouteau and other company members that the steamboat would be practical and an asset in the fur

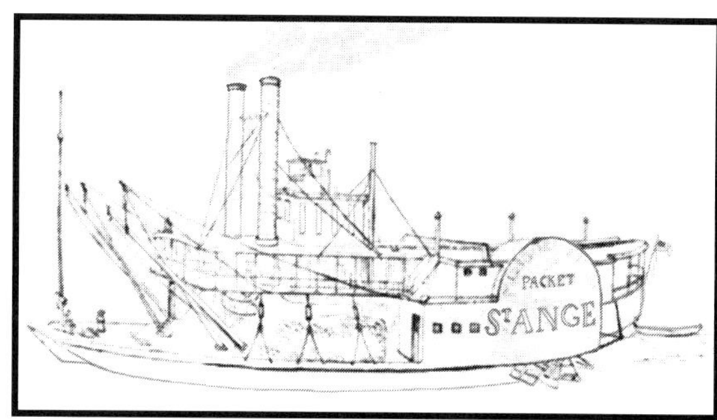

Artist Rudolph Kurz

The St. Ange was the first steamboat built by the American Fur Co. that was designed especially for the Upper Missouri.

Artist Karl Bodmer

Fort Clark was built by James Kipp near the Mandan, Arikara and Hidatsa villages. Built on a high bluff overlooking the Missouri, it was a supply point for the American Fur Co. on the upper river and the center of trade for the Dakota Territory.

trade on the upper river. Crooks, who was in charge of the Western Department, questioned the practicality and thought MacKenzie was too liberal and a troublesome partner. In 1832 the *Yellow Stone* arrived at Fort Union and MacKenzie had his way. Until the railroads arrived, steamboats were an indispensable part of transportation and frontier life on the Upper Missouri. Sunder said: "Steam unsealed the upper river; unsealed isolation kept the seal broken, and strengthened through improved communications the Company's hand in the upper valley." (1)

Invasion up the Yellowstone

The Company became involved in the Rocky Mountain trapping system designed for free traders, but was usually outdone by the opposition. MacKenzie reasoned that a post up the Yellowstone might serve some of the free traders rather than for them to go to the rendezvous. The Crow were demanding a post in their country to make trade easier for them. Chouteau wrote to Astor upon his return to St. Louis aboard the *Yellow Stone* that when he had been in Fort Union in June 1832 MacKenzie was "preparing an outfit for the Yellowstone in order to establish a post at the mouth of the Big Horn." MacKenzie equipped a party under Samuel Tulloch in the fall of 1832 to go up the Yellowstone and establish a fur post at the mouth of the Bighorn which was called Fort Cass.

The last problem MacKenzie addressed was the Company's return for a second year to the Upper Missouri and the Blackfoot. MacKenzie needed to find a replacement for James Kipp who had been sent down river to build a fort near the Mandan and Hidatsa villages to replace old Fort Kipp. The new fort was named Fort Clark in honor of the Indian Commissioner and early explorer, William Clark. It was one of the most important American Fur Co. posts on the upper river and served many tribes who came overland to the river.

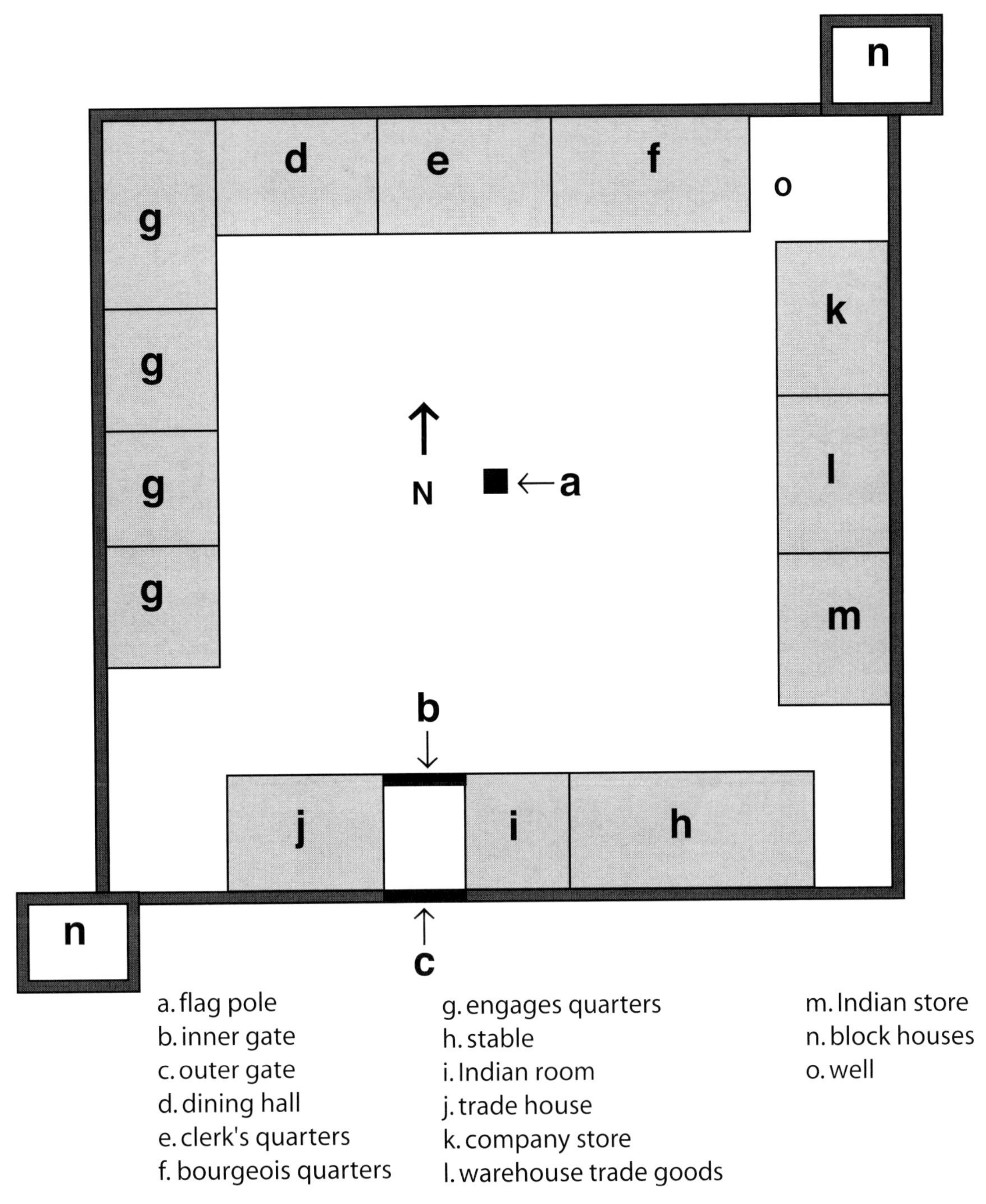

Fort MacKenzie floor plan 1833

Schwinden Library, Fort Benton

Fort Cass at the confluence of the Yellowstone and Bighorn Rivers was built by Kenneth MacKenzie to serve the Crow and the mountain men.

Building Fort MacKenzie

David Mitchell became a new partner in 1830 and was sent up river to take charge in spring of 1832. Before arriving above the Musselshell, his keelboat *Flora* was swept away by a storm. It hit a snag and sank with $30,000 worth of trade goods and two men drowned. Undaunted, Mitchell headed back to Fort Union to replace his losses.

Mitchell sent a pack train ahead to keep the Blackfoot happy until he arrived, loaded a new boat with supplies and trade goods and left Fort Union again in June. When they arrived at the mouth of Maria's River, Fort Piegan was in ruins. The Indians had burned the post shortly after Kipp left. Mitchell continued upstream about six miles to a wide bottom on the north side of the Missouri. Across from the bottom were high shale bluffs so eroded along their face that they fell almost perpendicularly to the river's edge.

Building the post in 1832 was one of the stirring stories of the Blackfoot fur trade. Shortly after Mitchell chose the site several bands of Blackfoot arrived and set up camp, ready to trade. The traders, who lived on the keelboat during the fort's construction, were in constant peril. The Indians were hostile but anxious to trade so no open conflicts broke out. Mitchell's tact - and his gifts - kept the volatile situation peaceful until his men completed the palisades.

Once the stockade was erected, the men felt safe and the Company was back in business. Interior work on storerooms and shelters continued while Mitchell, his clerks and traders were engaged in trade. The post was named for the king of the Upper Missouri fur trade at Fort Union, Kenneth MacKenzie. For the next dozen years Fort MacKenzie was a permanent foothold in Blackfoot Country and the largest contributor of furs to the Upper Missouri Outfit.

Schwinden Library, Fort Benton

Present site of Fort MacKenzie with the high shale bluffs across the river from the fort. The bluffs became a problem when Indians fired down into the fort. The white outline traces the fort's location.

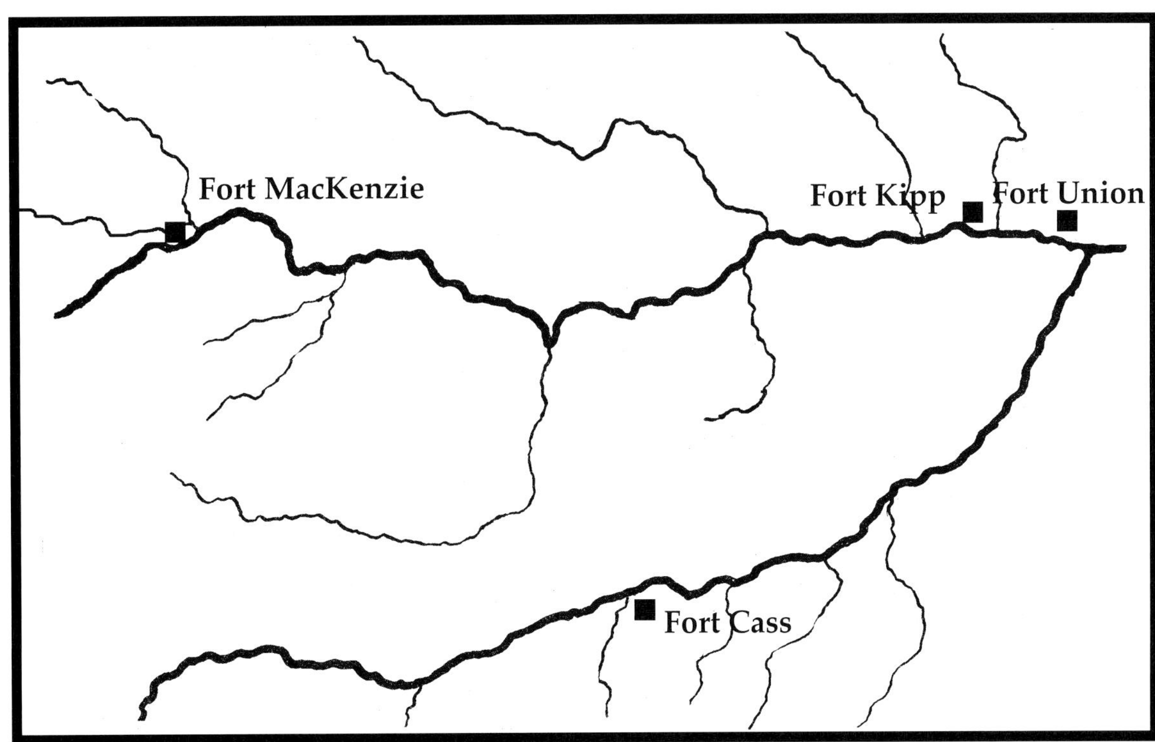

Forts built on the Missouri and the Yellowstone in the 1830's by Kenneth MacKenzie and the American Fur Company for trade with the Blackfoot, Crow, Atsina and the free trappers

Consolidation of the Upper Missouri

At the end of 1832 the Upper Missouri Outfit sat astride all fur trade on the upper river. It operated from its base at Fort Union at the confluence of the Missouri and Yellowstone and had two outposts. One was above Maria's River on the Missouri at Fort MacKenzie and Fort Cass was at the mouth of the Bighorn on the Yellowstone. The two posts were in the heart of the best beaver country in North America and monopolized the Blackfoot and Crow trade.

The steamboat's arrival on the upper river opened wide the buffalo robe trade. The bulky heavy packs of hides could be moved in volume to markets in St. Louis from the upper river. The small fur business of beaver and muskrat declined in both American and European markets and was replaced by the robe trade. Buffalo robes were bought from the natives by the Americans at higher prices. Their edge in transportation just about put the Hudson Bay Co. out of business.

The First Opposition

The only cloud on the horizon for the American Fur Company was organized opposition developing in St. Louis. It was mounted by a partnership formed by William Sublette and Robert Campbell. William Ashley, an old friend from the earlier Rocky Mountain fur trade, was a silent backer and financial partner who had retired to the friendly surroundings of St. Louis. Jim Bridger also joined the partnership. The new firm, organized late in 1832, was sometimes called the Rocky Mountain Fur Company because of the partners' earlier affiliations. At the end of the 1830 rendezvous the three partners of the mountain trade - Jedediah Smith, David Jackson and Wm. Sublette - sold out to Jim Bridger, Tom Fitzpatrick, Milton Sublette, Henry Fraeb and Jean Baptiste Gervais. They had also called themselves the Rocky Mountain Fur Co.

Artist David Parchen

A likeness of William Sublette, owner/trader and a tough competitor of the American Fur Company during the mountain trade.

New Competition on Two Fronts

Campbell and Sublette's plan was to challenge MacKenzie not only at the rendezvous but also with forts on the Upper Missouri and on the Yellowstone. Early in 1833 Samuel Tulloch, in charge of Fort Cass, sent a message with Hugh Glass to MacKenzie at Fort Union concerning a threat from the opposition. Glass, who had been hired as a hunter by MacKenzie in 1828, Edward Rose and a third companion were to deliver the message. When the trio crossed the Yellowstone on the ice near Fort Union, a war party of thirty Arikaras shot, scalped and stripped all three. Ol' Glass who had survived a grizzly attack and many other wounds "met his maker" and the fur trade lost another of its legendary figures.

The summer campaign of 1833 was a two-pronged effort. Campbell took a party into the mountains to the Green River rendezvous. He returned to the confluence of the Yellowstone and the Missouri where he met Sublette. Somewhere on the upper river, Sublette abandoned the steamboat *Otto*, sent it back downstream, and came to the mouth of the Yellowstone by keelboat. The partners built a post on the north bank directly across from the mouth of the Yellowstone and about three miles downstream from Fort Union. They christened their new post Fort William in honor of Sublette and perhaps their silent partner Ashley. Campbell was left in charge of the new post for the winter trade and Sublette returned to St. Louis.

According to Larpenteur who was employed by the opposition, the Indians had little confidence in the new company and the

Schwinden Library, Fort Benton

Jim Bridger was one of the most famous mountain men and a partner in the Rocky Mountain Fur Company.

Schwinden Library, Fort Benton

Robert Campbell was a long-time nemesis of the American Fur Company. His opposition began during the rendezvous period in the Central Rockies.

bulk of the trade that winter was still at Fort Union.

An exception was Gauche, the Assiniboine chief who abandoned trade at Fort Union in favor of the opposition at Fort William. Larpenteur reports, "It was not until night that we all got ready to trade. It must be remembered that liquor, at that early day, was the principal and most profitable article of trade, although strictly prohibited by law . . . The liquor trade started at dark, and soon the singing and yelling commenced. The Indians were all locked up in the fort, for fear that some might go to Fort Union, which was about two and a half miles distant. Imagine the noise – upward of five hundred Indians, with their squaws, all drunk as they could be, locked up in the small space. The old devil Gauche (Left Hand) had provided himself with a pint tin cup, which I know he did not let go during the whole spree…This was a great night, but I wish that the old rascal and his band had gone to the big fort. At last daylight came and the spree abated." The next day the real trade for goods continued into the evening and by the next morning the Indians had all left the area. It was the only big trade that came to Fort William that season of 1833-34. (2)

The other new posts down river did not fare any better than Fort William in trade that winter. MacKenzie was willing to pay any price necessary for the furs and used more liquor to secure his trade. His greater resources and financial backing allowed him to absorb the losses and drive the opposition from the river.

Opposition Fails

During the winter of 1833-34, Campbell sent a small party up the Yellowstone to trade with the Crow and hoped to persuade some of the Rocky Mountain trappers to bring their winter furs to Fort William. Fitzpatrick and his trappers also joined Campbell's men at a Crow village where the Indians relieved them of their furs and horses . . . but not their lives. The Crow sold the stolen furs at Fort Cass but MacKenzie offered to sell them back to Fitzpatrick for what the American Fur Company had paid for them. The raid on the trapping parties was a tremendous loss to Sublette and Campbell and was instrumental in their offer to sell out.

At the end of the season, the opposition asked MacKenzie to buy them out but he refused. In St. Louis, however, more levelheaded members of the Company, knew of Sublette's connections to Ashley, then a Congressman, and were willing to deal. In 1834 Sublette reached an agreement with Chouteau in New York under which all equipment and goods on the river became the property of the American Fur Company. In return American Fur Company would retire from the mountain trade the next year. The agreement ended all organized opposition on the Upper Missouri for several years. When Chouteau notified MacKenzie of the settlement, "The King" was furious. He felt that he would have driven them off the river the next year with no financial loss to the Company.

Artist David Parchen

Fort William, just three miles down river from Fort Union at the mouth of the Yellowstone, was the opposition fort of the Rocky Mountain Fur Co. built by Campbell and Sublette in 1832.

Whiskey Problems

In July 1832 the federal government proposed a total ban on the use of alcohol in Indian country. All traders as well as the Company immediately opposed the proposal. The reason cited by all was that the Hudson Bay Company used whiskey in their trade. John Jacob Astor stated that because Hudson Bay Co. was involved, that was reason enough to continue its use. In spite of all the political pressures, the prohibition was passed in Congress in July 1834. In disgust, MacKenzie complained to both Chouteau, who agreed with him, and to Crooks, who violently disagreed. At Fort Leavenworth even before it became law, MacKenzie's fifty kegs of alcohol were confiscated, which constituted enforcement before passage of the law.

Under pressure from the Hudson Bay Company's use of alcohol in the north and the opposition's obtaining its alcohol up river, MacKenzie felt that it was impossible for him to compete. When further negotiations failed, a frustrated MacKenzie smuggled a distillery into Fort Union. Using Mandan corn, he made his own brew and reasoned that would not be transporting alcohol into Indian country and really would not be breaking the law.

MacKenzie loaded his collection of vats and coils on board the *Yellow Stone* then transferred it to the *Assiniboin*. The still arrived at Fort Union in the spring of 1833. In a few days MacKenzie was in the business of making his own "high wine." Chouteau and the St. Louis office were well aware of his production since his letters mentioned it. The opposition also knew; Campbell wrote in his journal, "MacKenzie gives as much whisky as the Indians can drink for nothing. Barrel after barrel he sends all around amongst the Indians and these will not trade otherwise." Some of it must have been loaded on the keelboat headed for Fort MacKenzie that spring because Prince Maximilian told how much was used in the opening of trade that August.

Production was short-lived however. When Nathaniel J. Wyeth arrived at Fort Union, MacKenzie refused him a supply of alcohol for trade. MacKenzie, always a good host, believed business was business and would give no quarter when it came to the trade. Wyeth paid full price for trade goods and got no whiskey except that served at MacKenzie's table during Wyeth's stay at Fort Union. When Wyeth and Sublette arrived down river at Fort Leavenworth, they either accidentally or on purpose mentioned the distillery. MacKenzie and the American Fur Company were in trouble.

At first Chouteau tried to discredit the accusers but before the smoke cleared,

Schwinden Library, Fort Benton

David Mitchell, a new partner in the Company, built Fort MacKenzie in 1832.

Senator Thomas Hart Benton stepped in to save the company's licenses. MacKenzie was banished for a year from the upper river. During that year he went to Europe and visited Prince Maximilan of Wied-Neu Wied who had been his guest on the upper river in 1833. He returned to the river in 1835 but stayed only until 1837 when, his effectiveness lost, he moved to St. Louis. Still associated with Pratte and Chouteau, he entered a wholesale wine and liquor business. The crown and scepter passed to Honore' Picotte and Alexander Culbertson.

Mitchell Entertains Royalty

Mitchell's first season under the bluffs at Fort MacKenzie was a success because the Blackfoot produced pelts and robes far in excess of the year before at Fort Piegan. In the spring of 1833 the keelboat and the loaded mackinaws, with Mitchell in charge, headed down river to deliver the peltries to Fort Union where he met Prince Maximilian of Wied-Neu Wied and the artist Karl Bodmer. Alexander Culbertson and Alexander Harvey, two new young traders who had joined the Company, were also there.

In February Culbertson, who had signed a three-year contract as a clerk for $2000, was assigned to learn the trade under Mitchell. Harvey, the Prince and the artist had come from St. Louis aboard the steamboat *Assiniboin* that summer. Prince Maximilian convinced Kenneth MacKenzie that he should be allowed to go with Mitchell, Harvey and Culbertson when they returned on the keelboat *Flora* taking the next year's trade goods to Fort MacKenzie.

Trip Up River

As the keelboat slowly proceeded up river, the Prince collected plants and animals and his artist Karl Bodmer recorded with his precise brush and pen the land and its natural beauty, the wildlife and the Native Americans. When they entered the White Cliffs area, Maximilian was reminded of his home and its castles along the Rhine.

At Slaughter River (today's Arrow Creek) they had an altercation with the Atsina (Gros Ventre of the Prairie). A few Indians were brought aboard, many others swam across the river and tried to climb on board. Chaos reigned as engages threw Indians back into the water. Order was eventually restored and the keelboat lost only a few items to the uninvited boarding parties.

Arrival at the Fort

Almost a month after leaving Fort Union, Mitchell and Prince Maximilian rounded the bend at Fort MacKenzie and were greeted by a magnificent scene that astonished the European visitors. On the vast open bottom near the wooded stockade several hundred tepees were pitched. From the staff in the center of the fort flew a huge American flag. Hundreds of Blackfoot were lined along the bank, many riding horses up and down accompanied by shouting, singing, rifle shots, and a cannon report announcing their arrival.

When the keelboat reached its moorings and was tied up, personnel from the fort came down to greet the returnees, surrounded on both sides by chanting and shouting Indians still randomly firing their guns into the air. It was a great occasion, reminiscent of the days on the North Saskatchewan when the Canadians returned to their distant posts and were greeted by the Blackfoot. "Let the Trade Begin."

There were twenty-seven whites and their Indian wives and children living at Fort MacKenzie. The forty-five people on the keelboat swelled the numbers at the fort and placed an additional burden on the hunters and cooks. It took two buffalo a day to feed the inhabitants; most of the engagés subsisted almost entirely on buffalo meat.

Impressions of the Fort

Maximilian's and Bodmer's reaction to Fort MacKenzie was at first one of astonishment. The post was very primitive when compared to Fort Union. The Prince made up his mind right then and there to return down river before winter closed the river.

Maximilian described the fort: "A quadrangle whose sides are 45 paces and 47 paces. Two blockhouses on opposite corners each with some piece of cannon. Dwellings are one story, most without floors, generally with an open fireplace and a chimney, wooden door, and small window with parchment instead of glass. A very flat roof covered with green sod, where inhabitants post themselves when in case of being attacked they have to fire over the high pickets which make the back wall of the dwellings. When trading the inner gate is closed. The entrance to the Indian store between the gates is then free. Guards are then posted at the store. The fort's gate is 120 paces from the river."

One of the first events witnessed by Maximilian and Bodmer upon their arrival was the ceremony of opening the fur trade. The ceremony was very elaborate and described in great detail by Prince Maximilian. The ritual was performed annually during the first few

Artist Karl Bodmer

When the keelboat arrived at the mouth of Arrow Creek, there was a large Atsina encampment along its banks. Indians swarmed into the river and tried to come aboard. The engages' pushed them back into the river to prevent them from stealing the trade goods and demanding alcohol.

Artist Karl Bodmer

Fort MacKenzie looking from the back side toward the river and the high bluffs. Notice the large American flag flying from the staff in the courtyard. At that time many Indians were camped in the vicinity and were trading at the fort when Prince Maximilian and Bodmer were there.

days of the fall trade. After it was over, the Indians packed up and left on the fall hunt.

Liquor in the Trade

When Prince Maximilian was at Fort MacKenzie, the value in trade goods between a buffalo robe and a beaver plew had changed dramatically. In the first years one beaver plew was equal to two robes; by the end it took three beaver to equal one robe.

Bartering their furs for whiskey, the Indians continued to get drunk. When their furs ran out, wives and daughters were offered in exchange for whiskey as were horses and any other tradeable item that they owned. Everyone must have gotten something to drink. Prince Maximilian said that the old and very young alike could neither walk nor stand during those days of trade.

The Prince even used "spirits" to obtain goods and clothing from the Indians. In his journal he recorded that he traded whiskey for a tame female bear. The record also showed that there were three pet bears and a fox at the fort when he arrived. Mitchell later presented him with a male bear for a mate as well as the fox.

Other groups also arrived to trade. All preferred whiskey, although other items were also traded. Most groups stayed a few days, then moved camp to other locations on the Teton River with better grass and good hunting.

In spite of confiscation by the Army at Fort Leavenworth, there was still plenty of whiskey at Fort MacKenzie in 1833. Maximilian wrote, "Our cabin was like a pigeon loft, with all of the soldiers going and coming on aboard the *Yellow Stone*." Either the army missed finding it all or it was the "wine" made by MacKenzie at Fort Union from his distillery. Having whiskey in Indian country, no matter how illegal, never seemed to be any more of a problem than it was later when the government banned it from everyone during prohibition in the 1920's.

Artist Dave Parchen

Fort Leavenworth was on the lower river where the U.S. government inspected all boats headed up river to Indian country. The troopers were looking for illegal alcohol being taken up river.

Building a New Fort

Maximilian's journal reports bringing window glass and other items for a new fort. The hickory oars of the boat were cut up to make axe handles for the workers. Trade continued while preparations were made to build a new fort at a more favorable site. Mitchell, the Prince and Bodmer ascended the hills behind the fort to visit the new site. Although no exact record of the location exists, men had already been working on foundations.

Early one morning a large group with carts went out to commence building structures at the site. Soon Mitchell and his party caught up with them on the prairie. The journal says that as they rode they could see the Teton Valley to their right. On their left was the valley of the Missouri with the Snow River (Shonkin Creek) on its south bank. They followed a path along the north bank until they could look across to the fort site on the south bank. A map of the river shows that the next bottom up river large enough to hold a fort and have ample space for Indian camps is the one on the south side just below the mouth of the Shonkin. The next one up river would be across from the present Fort Benton.

The new site was abandoned, and may have been the one used in 1846 for Harvey's Trading Post. Maximilian's journals later mention that Harvey and a building party took a pirogue up to the new site to start building the fort. Whether it was discontinued because of the pressures of trading, the stress of the Blackfoot presence, or the dangers to Fort MacKenzie is unknown; there is no further mention of building a new fort in any records until after 1835.

Soon after his arrival Prince Maximilian recorded the marriage of Alexander Culbertson to an Indian woman. He, like many of the traders, took an Indian wife to help him in his relationship within the trade. His wife was of the family of White Buffalo, a Piikani Chief. Horses, a rifle and other goods were exchanged as part of the ceremony.

Culbertson quickly became very involved in the Blackfoot trade and was an excellent trader. As he gained expertise, company executives feared that at the end of his contract they would lose him. When he had first arrived, Culbertson complained of the Company's store prices and the cost of goods to the men.

Preparations were underway to outfit a party of traders going to the Kutenai villages, a trip of several weeks across the Rocky Mountains into the western valleys. The party with Doucette and Sandoval in charge did not plan to return until spring. Somewhere on the trail several days after leaving the fort, the Kainaa overtook the traders. They shot Doucette and the expedition ended in utter failure.

The departure of Doucette's group reduced the numbers and consequently the security of the fort. More groups of Indians arrived daily to trade and often remained in the vicinity for several days. According to the journal, the main trade item was still whiskey which produced a great number of drunken, ill-tempered Indians and in turn created a tense situation, almost like a state of continual siege. Personnel became more and more edgy with the drunken war-like people in and around the fort almost daily. Nevertheless, the enormous profits on whiskey made traders willing to gamble their lives to continue the trade.

Attack of the Assiniboine

In late August after several shooting incidents in which Indians and whites alike were killed, war finally erupted. At dawn the fort was awakened by gunfire and shouting outside the walls. At first they assumed the fort was under attack, but mounting the walls they realized that the thirty Piikani lodges of Chief Lame Bull were under attack by 600 Cree and Assiniboine. The Piikani, who had come a few days earlier to trade, were in a state of hysteria as the Assiniboine came pouring down from the hills into their camp.

When the attack began, a Piikani rider rushed for help to the main Blackfoot camp up river a few miles at the Crocondunez. (3) The inhabitants of the fort joined the fight, giving the Piikani a hand by firing from the walls. Assisting the Piikani was considered good trade strategy since the Assiniboine did not trade at Fort MacKenzie.

In the excitement Price Maximilian double-loaded his shotgun and when he fired, it blew him clear across the bastion and against the wall. Unhurt, he rebounded and jumped back into the fight.

Culbertson and Mitchell rushed to open the gate allowing the Piikani to gain refuge inside the fort. With the gates open,

Artist Karl Bodmer

The early morning attack on the Piikani camp by a mixed party of Cree and Assiniboine. Once they determined that the fort was not under attack, the traders fired from the walls to aid the Blackfoot. The gates were opened to give refuge to the women and children from the war party.

Artist Karl Bodmer

The Piikani camp on the bottom just up river from Fort MacKenzie in August 1833 when Prince Maximilian and artist Karl Bodmer were visiting the fort. Theirs was a scientific expedition assisted by the American Fur Company. Those types of visitors were encouraged to visit at the Company's expense.

hand-to-hand fighting erupted nearby. Culbertson was pushed aside by an Assiniboine warrior who shouted, "Out of my way! Out of my way!" as he reached across Culbertson to attack one of the fleeing Piikani. Years later during annuity time at Fort Belknap, Lunica, chief of the upper Assiniboine, reminisced with Culbertson about the battle and the comic incident in which Lunica had pushed Culbertson out of his way.

Within an hour or so Blackfoot warriors gathered in groups near the fort. While shooting continued from the walls, the Assiniboine retreated up the hills. Wounded Piikani were gathered for treatment inside the fort. Meanwhile, the lone Assiniboine warrior killed (probably by the hunter Deschamps) was thoroughly mutilated by the Piikani.

The Prince, Mitchell, Culbertson, Harvey and some of the engages joined the forces fighting the Assiniboine. Pitched battles still raged across the bottom before the Assiniboine warriors retreated across Maria's River. As the Blackfoot and the traders chased them, the Assiniboine under Left Hand mounted a counter-attack in which the Blackfoot lost fifteen men and the entire force plunged wildly into the river to seek safety on the fort side. Fighting continued across the river. Mitchell's and Culbertson's horses were shot from under them and they retired to the fort.

By late afternoon more and more Blackfoot joined the battle until superior numbers drove the Assiniboine away. Darkness finally ended the fighting with reported estimates of six to eight Assiniboine and twenty to forty Blackfoot dead.

Under Continual Siege

After the battle, more bands arrived, each expecting and receiving a ceremonial reception of the Chiefs, and entertainment of sub-chiefs and principal warriors with tobacco and whiskey. Only the Kainaa remained across the river until their cousins the Piikani left the fort. They were a little edgy because the Kainaa had recently killed a Piikani and were afraid of reprisal.

With so many Indians around, the

fort's horses could not be pastured for fear of losing them. Mitchell sent them to Fort Union on a moonlit night under the protection of Deschamps, Papin and a few other men. Maximilian regularly spoke of their feeling like prisoners because of the incredible number of Indians at the gate clamoring to get into the fort. The entire river bottom was covered with tents and roaming Indians. The problem was undoubtedly compounded by alcohol.

By evening fort personnel were tired of physically and mentally dealing with Indians all day long. When the gates were finally closed, guards were posted all night. Food was becoming scarce, they were down to eating dried meat "as tough as leather." No hunters wanted to venture far from the fort. Finally the Atsina arrived with eighteen horse loads of buffalo meat for which the traders gave them knives, powder and ball, beads and blankets.

Some insights into the trading: Only the Piikani among the Blackfoot were good beaver trappers so the traders gave them beaver traps. The Kainaa and Siksika were continually warring and were primarily hunters so they mainly traded robes at the fort. Some Kainaa who came to trade were thrown out since they had nothing to trade.

Mitchell's friend Bull's Hide, who had once saved his life, came with his band of Kainaa to trade. He apologized for his son killing the young engages during the drunken ceremonies and wanted peace and to be able to trade at the fort. Continual begging and forced entry by dangerous men into the fort made trading a very stressful occupation.

Prince Maximilian Leaves

With tension increasing daily, Prince Maximilian asked Mitchell for a boat to take him down river. Without a boat to spare, Mitchell had his shipwright Saucier build a mackinaw in the center courtyard of the fort. It took 21 men to carry the finished boat to the river, where it was loaded with specimens collected by the Prince, and two large cages

Artist Karl Bodmer

Maximilian and his party returned down river after a month's stay at Fort MacKenzie. Above is their camp along the Missouri with his scientific collections on board including the tame bears Prince Maximilian was given at the fort; the animals were in the cage on the boat.

for the bears. Mitchell could only spare four engages to accompany Maximilian's party of three. It would be a precarious trip since none of the engages had their own rifles.

On September 14, with the mackinaw finally loaded, a cannon was brought to the dock for the send off. The seven men climbed on board. As they pushed out into the current, they were given a loud and uproarious send off with cannon salutes and the entire compliment of the fort waving and shouting as the river carried them around the bend and out of sight. Glad to be leaving the wild and inhospitable country, they reached the ruins of Fort Piegan at half past two, just an hour and a half out of Fort MacKenzie. When they pulled in to shore for the night, they were well away from the treachery of the Blackfoot.

Prince Maximilian estimated that by spring Mitchell would ship 25,000 beaver plews in 100 pounds packs, each containing about 60 skins. At $4.00 a pound, that figured to be a take of $175,000 for the season.

Schwinden Library, Fort Benton

After only one trading season, Alexander Culbertson was left in charge of Fort MacKenzie when Mitchell took the returns down river and never returned.

The Trade Continues

Trade was good throughout the winter of 1833–34. In the spring storerooms were overflowing with pelts and robes. The Blackfoot continued to express their feelings about trappers and traders. John Sanford, Asst. Superintendent of Indian Affairs on the Upper Missouri, reported in July 1833 that the Blackfoot chiefs had told him, "If you will send traders into our country we will protect them, but your trappers NEVER!"

Business justified the retention of Fort MacKenzie on the upper river. When Mitchell came down river he had aboard his keelboat and the mackinaws 2000 pounds of beaver pelts and 200 bundles of buffalo robes. For some unknown reason, he went on to St. Louis. He did not return until 1836 and then only to Fort Union as a partner in charge of the post.

In Mitchell's absence Culbertson was left in charge with only one year's experience and 20 men to help him handle the volatile situation at Fort MacKenzie. Suspecting that Mitchell might not return, Culbertson sent a letter to Kenneth MacKenzie advising him of the volatile situation on the upper river and saying that he did not feel competent to assume command of the post. MacKenzie evidently decided the young trader needed a steadying influence, so he sent his old troubleshooter, James Kipp, up river to take charge. How long Kipp was there is not reported, but he never seemed to stay long at any job. He did take the returns down river in the spring of 1835. Kipp was MacKenzie's man to step in and fill vacant positions when other traders moved or left the Company. His stays were short, probably because he was not an administrator but was an excellent trader and diplomat who could handle the Indians under volatile situations. Kipp was also a skilled fort builder. In 1836 Culbertson brought the annual returns to Fort Union, signaling Kipp's departure.

After Mitchell left in the spring of 1834 and before Kipp's arrival, a raiding party of Crow drove off 30 horses from the fort's herd. A Blackfoot woman who had escaped from the Crow brought word to the post that a large encampment of Crow was planning to destroy the fort. Her message gave Culbertson time to prepare a defense. Cannons were loaded in the bastions, firearms were put at a ready and guards were posted on the walls. A new well was dug inside the fort that hit water at ten feet. Previously all water had to be carried about 150 feet from the river. Food was in short supply, but there was neither enough time nor animals nearby to solve the problem.

A few days later the Crow suddenly appeared and set up camp behind the fort. They asked for admittance to talk about the stolen horses. After a short parlay Culbertson ordered them to leave and refused to admit them to the fort. During the next ten days not a shot was fired, but the Indians had the fort literally under siege roaming around the outside still trying to gain entrance. Food was running out, so the aggressive Alexander Harvey wanted to fire the cannon into the Crow camp. Culbertson restrained him, but knew something must be done to break the siege. Because Culbertson had stopped him, Harvey plotted with some of the other men to desert, steal a boat and head down river.

Schwinden Library, Fort Benton

James Kipp was sent to Fort MacKenzie to take charge after Mitchell failed to return. His stay was short and Culbertson was given command after he left.

Threats of mutiny forced Culbertson to issue a last warning to the Crow: Be gone the next day at noon. By noon nothing had changed so he had a cannon ball shot into the middle of the camp. The Crow began to strike their lodges and in a short time the village was on the move up the river and out of harm's way. Some of the disgruntled braves crossed the river to the high bluffs overlooking the fort and began shooting down into the stockade with little effect; they soon left. The siege ended leaving the Crow with the same problem they had before . . . there was still a trading post in Blackfoot Country.

A Cannon Report

When an altercation occurred between the traders and the Indians at any fort, the trusty brass cannon was the ultimate solution. After handling the crisis in Mitchell's absence, Culbertson did not need help in management of the fort, especially after he had subdued the terrible temper of Harvey and put down the mutiny.

Near the fort in the summer of 1834 the Atsina were attacked twice, once by the Assiniboine and later by the Crow. At Snow Mountain (Big Snowy) the Assiniboine caught up with them and killed many Atsina. That fall a smaller group of Atsina warriors fell prey to the Crow near Bec d'Otard (4) and all but one were killed.

Intertribal warfare, the whiskey trade and too few men in a fort made life at a Blackfoot post quite hazardous. Many Indians were in and around the fort except when they were in winter camp. They hampered the hunters and consequently, food was never plentiful. The main source of food for Indians and whites alike was the buffalo. Hunters had to travel greater distances to find animals to supply food so the fort regularly traded with the Indians for meat.

To the Indians, stealing horses was a routine activity, an accepted practice in the culture of all tribes. It required great skill and was the source of many stories around the campfire. Consequently the natives constantly threatened livestock at the fort. Horse Island below Fort MacKenzie was an example of how the fort protected its horses. A grassy plot in the river gave the herders a chance to protect the herd. Out on the prairie even during the day the Indians were able to get away with a few head at will. There were two methods to

Artist Karl Bodmer

Stirring Iron, an Atsina; they were uneasy allies of the Blackfoot who traded at Fort MacKenzie.

discourage such thefts: bring them inside the fort every night or refuse to trade with anyone who raided the horse herd.

During the early years in Blackfoot Country the line between war and peace was as narrow as a knife's edge. The traders had little assurance from day to day that a conflict would not break out at any moment. Tension was probably one reason that no one remained long at a Blackfoot post without becoming an alcoholic.

Culbertson Takes Over

On April 24, 1835 James Kipp arrived at Fort Union with the returns from Fort MacKenzie. A May 5 unsigned letter (5) notified Culbertson that the keelboat under J. Lafountaine was being sent up river with the next year's trade goods for the fort. The letter answered some questions about the direction of Fort MacKenzie over the next two years. In the letter Culbertson was appointed to take over management at the fort. It informed him that Kipp would not return that summer to Fort MacKenzie. The letter also notified Culbertson that Alexander Harvey had been rehired to help Culbertson with trade, and a new clerk, J. Moncrevie who had worked five years at Fort Union, was being sent to aid in the affairs at Fort MacKenzie.

The trading goods for that season were worth $11,200 and Culbertson was told to push the robe trade since robes were more valuable than beaver plews. Beaver trade had declined over the past three years. Other pelts were not worth a great deal either; muskrat were only worth 10 cents a skin.

Culbertson was also informed in the letter that the use of liquor would cause expulsion of the Company from Indian country by the government, and he was advised to be very careful. However with their own supplies low, Fort Union still sent two barrels of alcohol and six of wine accompanied by this sage piece of advice: "Do not sell a single drop of it to the men." Obviously it was to be used strictly in trade even if it was illegal. If the wine was really "high wine," each barrel would produce 200 gallons of Indian liquor, sufficient for trade during the season ahead.

The trade goods, other than liquor, that brought the Company the most profits were beads, ammunition and tobacco. The fort was deficient in white beads, which were badly needed. The steamboat at Fort Union could not go to St. Louis the previous fall because of low water. Harvey was sent with horses to Fort Union to replenish the white bead stock, but was held up and did not return until after the opening of the first trade.

the Crow siege of the fort the summer before, Culbertson was directed to not spare them "tooth or nail" if the Crow returned to harass the fort.

The final instructions in the letter concerned building a new fort; the location of the old fort had been a problem since it was first established in 1832. During the past year when the Crow had the fort under siege, they fired into it from the bluff across the river. Since the first season, fort personnel had feared the overhanging bluffs. Prince Maximilian said that while he was there in 1833 Harvey and a party of men went up river on the south bank to develop a new fort site. The Company recommended that Culbertson heed Kipp's suggestion to move back to the mouth of Maria's River where Fort Piegan was first built. The letter relays a report of abundant logs up the river as well as some 100 logs at the old site.

Culbertson did not pursue the recommendations but in the ensuing years he completely remodeled the old fort. A comparison of the 1833 diagram of Fort MacKenzie in Maximilian's journal with the 1843 description by Culbertson in Audubon's journal shows that the fort underwent many major changes while Culbertson was in charge. If Prince Maximilian had returned at the end of Culbertson's tenure, he would have never recognized the old place. (6)

In 1834 American Fur Co. bought out Rocky Mountain Fur Co. at the rendezvous. Chouteau ended the rendezvous system because it was no longer profitable to bring supplies by caravan to the mountains. The price of beaver had dropped so low in the eastern markets that it was not worthwhile to continue. The next year he did not send a caravan to the mountains for the rendezvous.

The monopoly enjoyed by the American Fur Company was coming apart at the seams. Astor wanted out. Crooks was maneuvering to take over the Northern Department but wanted nothing to do with the troubled Western Department. In the summer of 1834 he informed Chouteau that their contract with the American Fur Company was terminated. Pratte, Chouteau and Company became the new owners and operators of the Western Department and the Upper Missouri Outfit, and business continued as usual. Even the name was usually retained although the original company no longer existed.

In May 1834 Campbell abandoned Fort William at the mouth of the Yellowstone and sent the stores and furs south to a new Fort William on the Laramie River which later became Fort Laramie. Sublette had laid the foundations for the new fort earlier on his way to the rendezvous. That summer on Ham's Fork of the Green, shifty dealings by Sublette incurred the wrath of Nathaniel Wyeth who vowed, "Gentleman I will roll a stone into your garden that you will never be able to get out." He did exactly that. In the fall he built Fort Hall on the Snake and sold it to the Hudson Bay Company, which cut deeply into the American trappers' profits along the Platte.

Harvey's First

With Alexander Culbertson in charge at Fort MacKenzie, 1835 and 1836 were little

Artist Karl Bodmer

While at Fort MacKenzie, artist Bodmer did many paintings of the Blackfoot who came to trade. Above is Middle Bull, a Piikani Chief.

Schwinden Library, Fort Benton

One of the most important events of the fur trade year was taking the fur and robe returns down river to Fort Union then by steamboat to St. Louis. The trip was usually under the command of the factor in charge of the post. When he returned later in the summer, he brought the next year's supplies and trade goods for the fort.

different from the previous years: Indian fights, whiskey trading, sieges and a general state of unrest on the Upper Missouri. After Kipp's departure in the spring of 1835, the Kainaa drove off 30 of the fort's horses. Except for a policy of keeping a few animals inside the stockade at all times, the Indians would have gotten them all. When Culbertson and a few men went out to recover them, Loretto, in a foolish act of bravery, was shot and died from his wounds.

Harvey's taunting of men at the fort precipitated Loretto's death. Loretto was afraid of being accused of cowardice so he foolishly and unnecessarily risked his life.

Affairs at Fort MacKenzie constantly linked Alexander Harvey and Alexander Culbertson. Harvey was a rough, tough, absolutely fearless individual with a mean temper. He was so feared on the Upper Missouri by trader and engagé alike that no one wanted to cross him for any reason. However, a Fourth of July incident in which he saved the life of one of the men showed he was a capable and resourceful man. While firing salutes in celebration, a cannon misfired and a man was badly mangled, losing a hand and an eye. With a razor and a carpenter's saw, Harvey amputated the lower arm and treated the rest of the man's wounds. The man recovered in a few weeks and lived another thirty-five years.

Alexander Harvey joined the American Fur Company in 1831 and came to Fort Union with Culbertson and the Maximilian party in 1833. Mitchell sent him overland on horseback to Fort MacKenzie ahead of the horseback to Fort MacKenzie ahead of the keelboat. At Fort MacKenzie he was put in charge of building a new post a few miles up river because of his fearless attitude toward the hostile Indians and his ability to inspire confidence in the men while on dangerous missions. Larpenteur described him as the "boldest man that was ever on the Missouri . . . a man 6 feet tall weighing 170 pounds and inclined to do right when sober."

Intertribal Warfare

In March 1836 the Atsina were camped on the Teton back of the fort when the Crow attempted to steal their horses. The entire village caught the Crow in the act, pursued them to Maria's Ridge and killed all of them without losing a man. However the next autumn near the Sweetgrass, the North Assiniboine and Cree caught the Atsina in camp and destroyed most of the village. In January the Crow were back again to steal Atsina horses, but were discovered and pursued. The entire Crow raiding party was destroyed near the mouth of the Shonkin.

A brief recess in Indian warfare occurred in the summer of 1836 when the Crow and Piikani made peace. For several months the tribes visited and traded between the camps. Long-lasting enmity did prevail. The Crow killed two Piikani, scalped them and boldly rode into the Piikani camp. When they were discovered with the scalps, the Piikani put them to death. Open hostilities resumed. In the spring of 1836 a band of Piikani about one day's ride from Fort MacKenzie was spotted by a large Assiniboine war party. The Piikani, who were rich in robes and had many horses, were a prize target. Not wanting to face them head on, the Assiniboine waited until they went into camp near the fort. The Blackfoot headed to the fort for their free liquor so the Assiniboine waited through the night. At daylight with the whole camp drunk, they attacked and in a short time killed many who were too drunk to defend themselves. The Assiniboine captured three hundred horses and claimed many scalps. Later in the summer the Piikani sent a war party to Fort Union in search of the Assiniboine and took revenge by killing the chief just outside the fort.

Culbertson Changes Jobs

Culbertson took the annual returns to Fort Union in April 1836. He went on to Fort Pierre to talk with Honore Picotte and when he returned up river he became the bourgeois at Fort Union. MacKenzie, who had been banned from the upper river for one year because of his distillery, returned the next year but was never again the agent in charge at Fort Union. With Culbertson at Fort Union, Alexander Harvey apparently was in charge at Fort MacKenzie, although this is not recorded. However, he brought the annual returns down river from Fort MacKenzie for the next few years.

Text Notes

1. John Sunder, author of, *The Fur Trade on the Upper Missouri.*
2. Charles Larpenteur from, *40 Years as a Fur Trader*
3. In French, Crocondunez means the bridge of the nose. The name was given to the narrow ridge that separated the Teton Valley from the Missouri. The two rivers were once only a few hundred yards apart. Water flowed underground from the Teton to the Missouri and bubbled up, forming the Grog Springs of Lewis and Clark.
4. Bec d'Otard, translated to mean the bill of the field duck in French; a rock formation called the Goosebill today but also includes the landmark prairie hill north and west of Fort Benton used in early days as a reference point for travelers.
5. May 5, 1835 letter from a manuscript at the MT Historical Society and in *Not in Precious Metals Alone*. All instructions were in an unsigned letter, but most likely came from Kenneth MacKenzie before he left Fort Union.
6. *Audubon and his Journals Volume II,* Maria R. Audubon

Fort MacKenzie

1837 - 1844

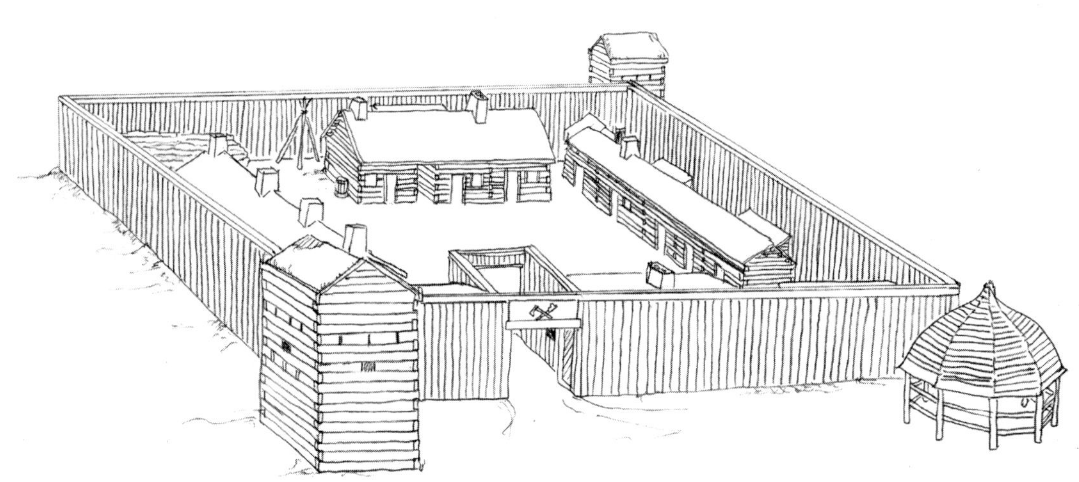

After many great years with Culbertson as factor, the Company sent him down river and the post was turned over to Francis A. Chardon. After an incident that killed several Blackfoot, the post was abandoned and burned. Chardon moved down river to safer territory at the mouth of the Judith River.

8

1836 - 1843

The Prosperous Years

Culbertson Years at Fort MacKenzie

From Beaver Plews to Buffalo Robes

Death Strikes the Upper River

In the absence of MacKenzie, Culbertson stayed on at Fort Union for the winter of 1836-37. In April Alexander Harvey took the annual returns from Fort MacKenzie down river to Fort Union. At the same time in St. Louis, death in the form of smallpox came aboard the steamboat and went up river to decimate the native population, changing the fur trade, the destiny of the land and the native populations forever.

The steamboat *St. Peter* commanded by Bernard Pratte made its way up river spreading the disease into the native people with every stop including the Blackfoot post at Fort MacKenzie. (1) Some tribes who had been exposed earlier were devastated again by the white man's disease which had stalked his civilization for centuries. Supposedly, it came aboard in the trade goods; more than likely, it was in the body of one of the passengers or crew. A few days out of St. Louis three cases broke out. (2) The steamboat continued up river with no thought of the consequences. Greed overruled good judgment.

At each stop the epidemic spread into the fur post and from there into the tribes that came to trade. After several stops at down river posts, the boat arrived at Fort Union. Harvey, who was waiting to return up river with supplies,

Schwinden Library, Fort Benton

Sometimes only the children were left when the dreaded pox swept through a village.

Artist David Parchen

Total camps and villages were wiped out by the deadly pox, only the animals survived. In 1837 the Blackfoot Confederacy lost over half of its population.

hurriedly loaded his keelboat hoping to escape the disease.

Harvey the Humanitarian

While returning up river, three cases of the pox broke out among the crew of the keelboat just three days after leaving Fort Union. When Harvey arrived at the mouth of the Judith and before he encountered any tribes in Blackfoot Country, he docked the keelboat in isolation. He sent word of his dilemma to Culbertson and waited for orders.

What transpired before a decision was made can never really be understood. Supposedly the Blackfoot were informed of the dreadful effects of smallpox but they insisted that the boat be brought to Fort MacKenzie so trade could begin. The Blackfoot made that decision without any knowledge of the disease. (3) Never in their generation had anything like the virus infected their people. Again ignorance and greed prevailed and Harvey was ordered to take the boat up river to the fort. (4)

With the three cases still on board, their arrival at the fort immediately exposed all the fort personnel and the Indians waiting to trade. Opening ceremonies for trading proceeded. After the Indians left, the disease swept through the fort and the Indian camps. Most of the 90 inhabitants at the fort came down with some degree of smallpox. The hardest hit were Indian women married to the traders. Twenty-six of them died. With few inhabitants healthy, proper burial was impossible so many of the bodies were dumped into the river. The only company person who died was Antoine Dauphin for whom the worst rapids on the upper river were named.

As the pox disappeared and people at the fort began to recover, they realized that no Indians had visited the fort for two months. Culbertson and Sandoval set out to see if they could find the Blackfoot. A recurrence of the pox forced their return but they continued the search later to the Three Forks. They approached a camp of 60 lodges where the silence was deafening. Finally at the edge of the camp they found two old women who were recovering and softly singing the songs of the

Artist, Karl Bodmer

Fort Clark was the American Fur Co. post that served the Mandans, Arikaras and Hidatsas. The smallpox epidemic was the most damaging to those people. So many died that the Mandan tribe was nearly non-existent.

dead. Throughout the camp lay dead bodies. Many had left hoping to escape the disease but only carried it to other camps or died in small groups on the prairie. Some who had watched others die committed suicide before the disease killed them. Within a few months smallpox had spread throughout the Blackfoot Nation. A disheartened Culbertson returned to the fort for a very long winter during which survivors straggled in to the fort and told their story of death and destruction in each of the villages.

Six thousand Blackfoot people perished out of an estimated population of 12,000. (5) The Assiniboine near Fort Union were even harder hit; in one village of 1200, only 80 survived. The Assiniboine lost two-thirds of their total population. The Arikara, Hidatsa and Mandans near Fort Clark were the most devastated of all. Of 600 Mandans, only 30 survived; the Arikara lost 700 out of 1000. It was the most disastrous epidemic of smallpox ever brought to the upper river . . . and would not be the last. It was the end of the Mandan people and triggered the demise of Fort Clark. Trading there was almost non-existent after the summer of 1837. The only people on the Upper Missouri who survived the epidemic without being affected were the Crow, who stayed completely away from the holocaust.

A Lively Trade

Everyone was certain that trade on the Missouri would suffer with deaths throughout so many tribes. At Fort MacKenzie, that did not happen. In 1838 they took in 10,000 robes, more than the previous season. Many speculated that they were robes of the dead and some worried that the dreaded disease would be spread into the white settlements down river by the infected robes. However, there were no outbreaks in St. Louis or other places that handled the robes that season. The robe trade grew through the next years and by 1841 had increased to 21,000 robes.

While the robe trade increased, the beaver trade was dying. The tribes gained far more in trade for robes with less labor. Hunting

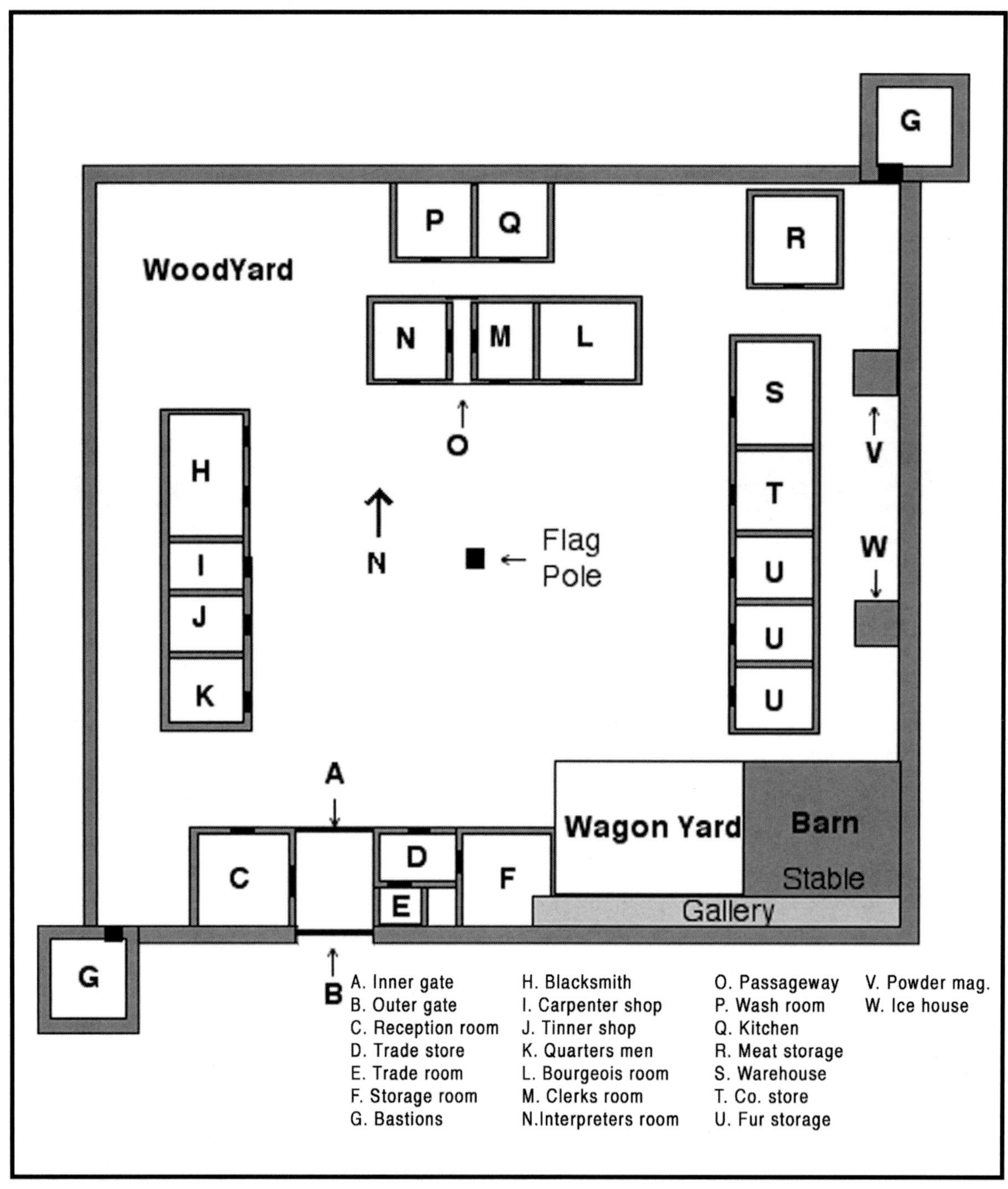

Floor plan of Fort MacKenzie in 1842 after it had been remodeled by Alexander Culbertson. The drawing is from John Audubon's journal after he had talked with Culbertson at Fort Union.

buffalo was easier than trapping beaver but not for women, whose work increased considerably. They spent the winter preparing and tanning robes. One woman averaged about twenty robes a season. Polygamy increased during those years so each family would have more trading stock.

Schwinden Library, Fort Benton

Alexander Culbertson took over as the chief factor at Fort MacKenzie after James Kipp left. Under his guidance the fort was the most profitable one on the upper river.

Remodeling

After the epidemic the Blackfoot were never as powerful or as strong as they had been. The feeling of being besieged by the Indians diminished and living in Blackfoot Country was never again such a threatening environment. Bands of Blackfoot continued to create problems for American trappers to the south. In both 1837 and 1838 at the summer rendezvous, the Blackfoot ambushed Osbourne Russell and others and made trapping in the Three Forks vicinity a hair-raising experience.

At the fort, the more relaxed conditions led to abandonment of plans to move the fort to a new location. Instead Culbertson directed improvements in the isolated settlement so living conditions were more comfortable. New quarters away from the outside walls had adobe fireplaces so some warmth was maintained during the cold Upper Missouri winters. An icehouse, meat house and a kitchen were constructed so food for the men improved. A barn and corral were built for better care of the livestock.

Big Road

In the spring of 1839 Alexander Harvey went with Culbertson and the annual returns to Fort Union and went back to Fort MacKenzie with trade goods for the next season. A small party of Kainaa joined them during the trip to Fort MacKenzie. Like many Kainaa, one of them Big Road was a quarrelsome, overbearing bully. He harassed the crew on the trip, threw rocks at them as they cordelled and in general was a real nuisance. Harvey restrained himself several times from killing him on the spot, but vowed to take care of the problem later.

Several weeks after their arrival at the fort, Big Road entered Culbertson's quarters one evening and attacked the Major when he returned home. Harvey and Sandoval heard the scuffle from the next room and rushed to Culbertson's aid. They grabbed Big Road and forced him out of the room. In the process Harvey made good his vow and shot Big Road. The Indian paid with his life as did most of Harvey's enemies. He was dumped out the front gate and all of the gates were closed to await the reaction from the Kainaa camp nearby.

Some of the young warriors drove off the horse herd and wanted to attack the fort immediately. Cooler heads prevailed the next morning and a meeting within the fort was arranged with Culbertson. An easy settlement was reached when the circumstances were explained, and the bullying nature of the man with his own people was acknowledged. The council decided his killing was justified but Culbertson had to compensate Big Road's two brothers. Culbertson insisted that without the return of the horse herd it would be impossible for him to repay the brothers. The horses were returned and each brother was given a horse and other trade goods. The council ended to everyone's satisfaction, but the two brothers still carried hatred in their hearts for

Artist David Parchen

Mackinaws from Fort MacKenzie took the annual returns down river to Fort Union where they were loaded aboard steamboats and transported to Company warehouses in St. Louis.

Culbertson. They continued to stalk him but never got a chance to attack him. The tense situation ended the next year when they were both killed in a horse raid against the Crow.

Same Company New Name

In the spring of 1839 Alexander Culbertson accompanied Harvey with the returns to Fort Union where he loaded eight mackinaws with 300 packs of robes each and took them down river. In St. Louis many changes greeted Culbertson. In new company offices the entire business was reorganizing. He had been made a partner and went back up river to take charge of Fort Union.

Since 1834 when Ramsey Crooks sold the Western Department of the American Fur Company to Pratte, Chouteau and Company, Pierre Chouteau Jr. had been in command of the Company's fortunes. Crooks was glad to get rid of the troublesome Western Department and its manager who he felt was

Schwinden Library, Fort Benton

Ramsey Crooks rid himself of troublesome Company men in the Western Department by selling it to Pratte and Chouteau.

Schwinden Library, Fort Benton

After buying the Western Department, Pierre Chouteau Jr. was the sole owner when his relative and partner Bernard Pratte died.

an unpredictable liberal and would eventually bankrupt the Company. Many incidents involving whiskey in the trade and the use of steamboats exasperated Crooks. Chouteau had expanded the business in spite of Crook's pressures, made himself the richest man in St. Louis and the Company was the most profitable.

When Bernard Pratte Sr. died in 1836, his son Bernard Jr. became a partner in the Company. Like most of the partners, he was a close relative of Chouteau but had little taste for the business. Young Pratte was extremely interested in politics, won a seat in the Missouri Assembly in 1839, and dropped his active participation in the Company. The firm reorganized once again. Chouteau increased his share of the business and changed the name of the company to the Pierre Chouteau Jr. and Co. In early fall 1840 Chouteau ended his partnership with Pratte and his business relations with Kenneth MacKenzie, who two years later bought back into the Company but only as a minor stockholder, not a voting partner.

MacKenzie's forced retirement in 1834 left upper river management in a muddle. Positions changed rapidly. Mitchell came down river in 1835, became a partner and took charge of Fort Union in 1837. He only stayed two years. Like MacKenzie, he spent the rest of his time mainly in St. Louis and had little to do with affairs of the Company on the upper river.

Culbertson was a greenhorn in 1834 when Mitchell left Fort MacKenzie. He worked under James Kipp, became a partner and took command at Fort Union. Culbertson became the Company's number two man under Honoré Picotte, the Agent in Charge for the Upper Missouri Outfit.

On his return to Fort Union in 1839 Culbertson brought with him a new young trader in the person of Malcolm Clarke. Clarke

Artist David Parchen

Young Malcolm Clarke made his first trip into Blackfoot Country with Alexander Culbertson in 1839 to work for the American Fur Co.

Schwinden Library, Fort Benton

Aerial view of the Fort MacKenzie site shows the outline of the fort in the white rectangle, the high bluffs to the left across the river and the Highwood Mountains in the upper skyline.

figured prominently in affairs of the Blackfoot posts over the next few years.

Long Winter Trek

Harvey was left in charge of Fort MacKenzie during the winter of 1839-40. With his volatile personality, he was a hard man to work for. Problems continued to build until by Christmas time word came up river that he had been fired from the Company because of complaints from the other traders. When he was ordered to report to St. Louis, Harvey immediately shouldered his rifle, loaded his pack on his trusty dog and took off for St. Louis across the plains on foot. He arrived in mid-March at Chouteau's office having walked the entire distance. His lonely and matchless winter journey so impressed Pierre Chouteau Jr. that instead of dismissing him, he rehired him and sent him back up river to Fort MacKenzie. It

Artist David Parchen

An unbelieveable trip was made by Harvey from Fort MacKenzie to St. Louis, on foot with his dog in mid-winter 1839-40.

was bad news for his enemies who had caused that winter trek.

Revenge

The first steamboat to go up river in the spring of 1840 was the *Trapper* commanded by Captain Sire. Harvey and Charles Larpenteur, who was on his first trip to the upper river to work for the Company, were on board. Harvey remarked to Larpenteur, "I have several settlements to make with those gentlemen who caused me last winter's tramp. I never forget or forgive; it may not be for ten years but they all will have to catch it." At the Fort Clark levee he found one of his adversaries, gave him a terrible beating and remarked as he reboarded the steamboat, "That's No. 1." At each succeeding post he took time to kick the hell out of any antagonist he could find. His reputation preceded him; most who had opposed him hid or got out of his way. When the *Trapper* docked at Fort Union on June 27 many of his

Schwinden Library, Fort Benton

Capt. Joseph Sire of the steamboat Trapper that brought Harvey up river in 1840

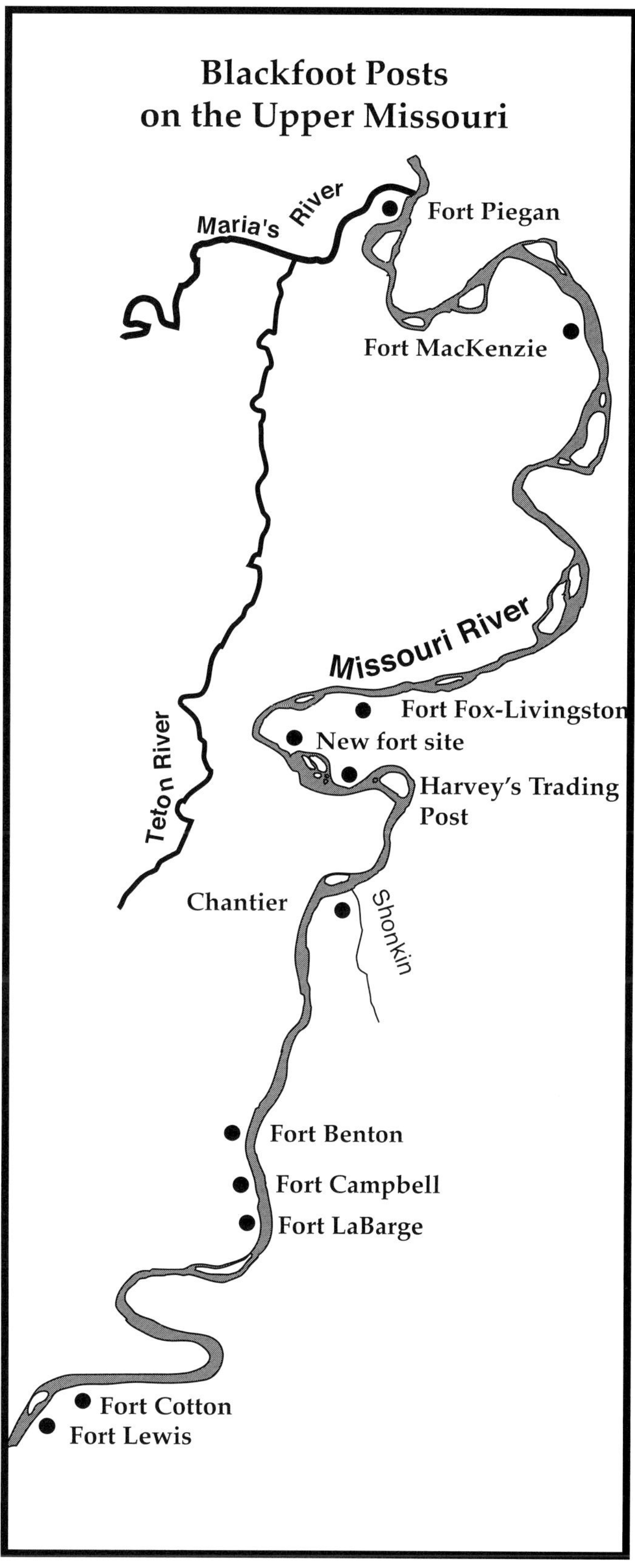

Schwinden Library, Fort Benton

Missouri Senator Thomas Hart Benton, long-time political friend of the American Fur Company. Besides helping with political appointments, he saved their license to trade on the upper river.

adversaries, who never expected that Harvey would return, had come down to the river. Surprised and afraid for their lives, most ran. The vendetta continued for years as Harvey caught them one by one and administered whatever punishment he felt they had coming. Larpenteur said whiskey had nothing to do with Harvey's vengeance; he was completely sober and gained revenge very methodically.

The Last Rendezvous

With Harvey down river that spring, Culbertson retrieved the returns from Fort MacKenzie and built five mackinaws to take 2100 packs of robes and 4 packs of beaver down river. Trade had been good, the best ever, and without competition in Blackfoot Country, the profits were tremendous.

However, two St. Louis businessmen, Wayman Crow and Robert Taylor, were quietly supporting the start of an opposition company headed by John Ebbetts. At first the company was only a threat on the lower river, but it soon expanded into Blackfoot Country.

The last rendezvous in the Rockies was in the summer of 1840. Free trappers then went to the fur posts to trade. They were at the mercy of the Company who paid what it wanted for their winter's work.

The national election in 1840 dealt a hard blow to the Jacksonian Democrats and subsequently to the American Fur Company. The Whig's old warhorse, William Henry Harrison, defeated Van Buren who had long been a friend of the Company. His defeat forced Chouteau and his St. Louis office to mend their political fences. Indian agents exercised enough authority to make doing business on the upper river easy or difficult, depending upon the agent's feelings about the traders. With the

Schwinden Library, Fort Benton

Natawista, pictured with one of her children, was a sister of the Kainaa Chief, Seen From Afar. She married Alexander Culbertson and was a great help in his dealings with the Blackfoot.

Schwinden Library, Fort Benton

Jerry Potts, a hero of the North West Mounted Police, was orphaned at age one when his father was shot at Fort MacKenzie. He was raised by Alexander Harvey and Andrew Dawson.

help of Senator Thomas Hart Benton, Chouteau maneuvered the new administration into appointing David D. Mitchell, an old partner in the Company, as the new Indian agent. His appointment meant business as usual.

Natawista

Alexander Culbertson was the most skilled trader for the Company, due in no small part to his second wife Natawista. (6) When Culbertson first arrived on the upper river, he married an Indian woman but sent her back to her people for some unknown reason. Natawista his second wife was a Kainaa woman and sister of Seen From Afar, the most powerful chief of the Kainaa.

She was a remarkable woman. Her presence at Culbertson's side created trust and good will among the bands of Blackfoot who came to trade. She was a wise counsel for the trader in his dealings with her people. They were married at Fort Union in 1841. She adopted his children from the first marriage and had a second family with Culbertson.

When Culbertson retired to Peoria, Natawista and the family went with him. Usually when traders in a mixed marriage retired and went back to the States, they left their Indian wives and children behind. Exceptions, like the Culbertsons, were rare. Sometimes traders, like Andrew Dawson, brought their siblings to raise and be educated in the "white man's society."

Natawista adapted to many of the "white man's ways" but retained much of her native heritage and religion. For example, while in Peoria she lived in a tepee on the lawn in the summer but went back to the manor house for winter. Like many Native American women, she enjoyed the clothing of the white women. In all of the photos, with the exception of Father Point's drawing, she is wearing flowing long skirts and dresses.

When the Culbertson family left Peoria, Natawista and the children came back to the river with him. His drinking and unemployment led to her leaving him and returning to her people. She lived on the Blood Reserve in Canada for 23 years. Natawista died in 1891, many years after Culbertson's death.

Killing Andrew Potts

Culbertson spent most of the winter of 1840-1841 between Fort MacKenzie and Fort Union. In mid-winter he brought a hundred horses to Fort Union for trade. They needed more so he sent Sandoval back to Harvey at Fort MacKenzie for fifty more horses. When Sandoval returned to Fort Union, he reported the death of Andrew R. Potts, the young Scottish clerk at Fort MacKenzie. Potts, a Scot born in the old country, migrated to the U.S. and went to work for the American Fur Co. in 1836. He spent one season at Fort Union then went up river to Fort MacKenzie as a trader. There he married Namo pisi (Crooked Back), a member of the Black Elk band of the Kainaa. To them was born a son they named Jerry who became a legend in Blackfoot Country.

One day a troublesome Piikani known

Artist David Parchen

Harvey, never a gentle man, would not back away from any challenge. Fearless and unforgiving, he carried a grudge until he had gained retribution. In response to Sandoval's threat at Fort Union, Harvey killed him over the trade counter with a bullet to his head.

as One White Eye (Ah-poh) was thrown out of the fort by a voyageur named Mercure'. One White Eye knew Mercure' commanded the fort's trading wicket at night. (7) Waiting one evening until no one was present, he knocked at the wicket. When the wicket door slid upward, One White Eye poked the barrel of his flintlock through the opening and fired. The blast struck young Potts who was substituting for Mercure' in the face. Year-old Jerry was an orphan since his mother immediately returned to her band leaving young Jerry behind for Alexander Harvey to raise.

Jerry Potts

As was the custom, Harvey adopted the boy into his family. For the next five years young Potts was tended by Harvey and learned the basic instincts of survival on the frontier. Harvey was a good father to his adopted children as well as his own children by an Indian woman.

When Harvey was discharged by the American Fur Co., he left young Potts at the up river forts. Potts was later adopted by the gentle Scotsman Andrew Dawson, a clerk for the Company, who was raising an Indian family of his own. Dawson was a respected trader by the Company and by the Blackfoot. He eventually became the bourgeois at Fort

Benton. Under his patient guidance young Potts learned about the white man's society and the trading business. He also spent time with his Blackfoot family and learned about their culture. Potts was proficient in his mother's tongue and other native dialects and was fluent in both French and English. With his vast knowledge of both cultures, he was an outstanding scout and advisor for the North West Mounted Police and a folk hero in the Canadian West.

The Spaniard

By the spring of 1841 the personnel at Fort MacKenzie had more than they could stand of Harvey. They plotted to kill him on the trip to Fort Union that spring. However, during the trip no one stepped forward to do the deed. When they arrived at Fort Union, Isodoro Sandoval (called The Spaniard) decided to confront him. A feud had been brewing for years between Harvey and The Spaniard; both had served at Fort MacKenzie since 1833. With whiskey courage, Sandoval brandished his rifle in the courtyard at Fort Union and boasted that he was going to kill Harvey and rid the upper river of the vermin. Cooler heads persuaded Harvey to stay away that time, but the next day the dispute erupted again at the trade store. Harvey and Culbertson were making final preparations for the return up river with trade goods for the next season. Sandoval, then sober, was behind the counter. Harvey accosted The Spaniard, called him a coward and invited him into the courtyard to fight like a man.

Schwinden Library, Fort Benton

Alexander Culbertson, Natawista and son Joseph were an important family on the upper river, dealing with all tribes at Fort MacKenzie and Fort Union. Culbertson was the most experienced American Fur Company trader on the upper river.

him into the courtyard to fight like a man. Sandoval's refusal to follow him so exasperated Harvey that he returned and according to Larpenteur said, "You won't fight me like a man so take this." He pulled out his pistol and shot The Spaniard between the eyes. Harvey announced the shooting to the entire fort and challenged any of Sandoval's friends to step forward and take up the fight. There were no takers.

Culbertson, who was present at the shooting, pressed no charges though The Spaniard had been a good and valuable man since his first days at Fort MacKenzie. Within a few days Harvey took the keelboat and trade goods for the Company and headed back up river.

Culbertson spent most of the 1841-42 trade season at Fort Union according to Larpenteur. The three traders there were drunk most of the time and losing profits for the Company. That winter trade at Fort MacKenzie was excellent. The experienced traders, Alexander Harvey and Malcolm Clarke, produced a record robe trade for the Company.

In the spring of 1842 Harvey and Clarke took the returns to Fort Union and both went back up river with the next year's trade goods. Both men had hair-trigger tempers. Within a few days of their arrival at Fort MacKenzie violence broke out again. An Atsina chief caused problems then rode off up river. He was overtaken near the mouth of the Shonkin by the two traders, killed and scalped. Violent acts like those of Harvey and Clarke plagued them both when the partners considered advancement in the Company.

Opposition Down River

Competition grew on the lower river in Sioux country, so Chouteau nagged at Commissioner Mitchell to appoint an agent for the upper river. Ebbetts was dealing in whiskey trade with the Sioux. The guarded use of illicit whiskey by the Company was in danger of being exposed. If trouble developed with alcohol, the opposition might sweep most of the trade away. In June 1842 Andrew Drips, a Company man through and through, was appointed to the position of Indian Agent

Schwinden Library, Fort Benton

Andrew Drips, Indian Agent on the Upper Missouri, was a friend of the Company. He never seemed to find any violations of the whiskey trade during his tenure.

and headed up river to cut down the use of whiskey by the opposition and quietly protect the interests of Chouteau and Company. He traveled for the next two years on the upper river checking for the illicit trade, but made not a single arrest. His visits were never a surprise; all was carefully hidden before his arrival only to be brought out again after he left.

Culbertson on the Platte

Culbertson brought the returns down river in the spring of 1843. In June the steamboat *Omega* arrived at Fort Union where Culbertson was introduced to John J. Audubon. It was company policy to aid all scientific expeditions; Culbertson spent most of the summer at Fort Union helping Audubon collect specimens for museums back East.

Pressed by the opposition company up the Yellowstone, late that summer Culbertson sent Larpenteur to burn Fort Van Buren and build a new fort. Called Fort Alexander in

Schwinden Library, Fort Benton

When John J. Audubon, noted wildlife artist, came to Fort Union, Culbertson helped collect the animals he painted. Later Culbertson spent some time at Audubon's home in the East.

Culbertson's honor, it was built twenty miles up river from old Fort Van Buren on the north bank opposite the mouth of the Little Bighorn River in hopes of recapturing the Crow trade.

Also on the *Omega* was Francis A. Chardon who had spent several years as a trader and clerk for the Company at Fort Clark. After putting up with three seasons of violence and the volatile personality of Alexander Harvey, Picotte decided to send Chardon to take command of Fort MacKenzie.

His appointment had also been precipitated by the decision of the St. Louis partners to send Alexander Culbertson to Fort Laramie on the Platte. Trade on the Platte the previous two seasons was a disaster for the Company. With the arrival of Captain Sire's boat in June 1843, orders arrived which sent Culbertson to Fort Laramie to straighten out the Company's business. Late that summer Culbertson went down river with Audubon aboard a mackinaw to Fort Pierre where he met with Honore' Picotte, the man in charge of the upper river. He pleaded with Picotte to leave things alone on the upper river and leave Alexander Harvey in charge. Picotte was not convinced. In November Culbertson grudgingly headed west with several wagons loaded with trade goods for Fort Laramie. Edwin T. Denig, a drunkard, was left in charge at Fort Union and Francis A. Chardon held sway at Fort MacKenzie. Chardon had a weak personality, was an inexperienced trader with the Blackfoot and had a drinking problem.

With the new opposition trading in liquor, in January 1843 Picotte wrote from Fort Pierre to Pierre Chouteau Jr. in St. Louis. The first paragraphs of the letter explain how much alcohol was available to the opposition. It continued, "Under these circumstances you see plainly that we must lose the Blackfeet and Assiniboine trade next year unless we have liquor. I therefore request you use your influence to send us some of that article next year say four or five hundred gallons ... At all events we must have it." Although government officials at Fort Leavenworth continued to search all boats heading up river, bribery, false labeling and general disregard for the Indians by most whites along the frontier allowed the whiskey to flow to the American Fur Co. posts at Fort Union and Fort MacKenzie.

During the winter of 1843 Malcolm Clarke lived and traded with the Atsina in their winter camps to thwart the opposition's attempt to trade with those bands. Having winter trading posts away from the main fort continued on the Upper Missouri until the end of the trade. Clarke, with his family in a log-trading house near the Atsina winter camps, made trade easy for the Indians. Traded robes were transported by wagon back to the fort. Trading had changed over the last decade when Kipp's men were reluctant to venture very far from the fort. They would have never considered traveling alone with the fur returns in the middle of the winter near an Indian camp.

Union Fur Company

In the summer of 1842 two New York investors replaced Ebbett's old partners. The new company opened for business at Fort George as Ebbetts, Cutting and Kelsey and Co. It gained financial support from Curtis Bolton, Samuel M. Fox, Mortimer Livingston and the ever-present nemesis from the past, Robert Campbell. The company was sometimes referred to as Fox-Livingston and Co. or the Union Fur Company in later years. That fall they rebuilt a post three miles down river from Fort Union at the mouth of the Yellowstone. They christened the post Fort Mortimer for Livingston.

The next spring in 1843 they invaded both Crow and Blackfoot Country, erecting a trading house at the mouth of the Little Bighorn near the site of old Fort Van Buren. They went up the Missouri beyond Fort MacKenzie and built Fort Cotton on the south bank of the river five miles above present-day Fort Benton. It was named for Mr. Cotton, a trader and partner for the Union Fur Company (8) The two posts were manned by the opposition for one or two years then passed on to the American Fur Company when the company failed. On his trip up river, Charles Kelsey realized that Ebbetts had sold him a bill of goods; he would be lucky to retrieve his investment from the company. The Union Fur Co. also built a small post the next year just up river from Fort

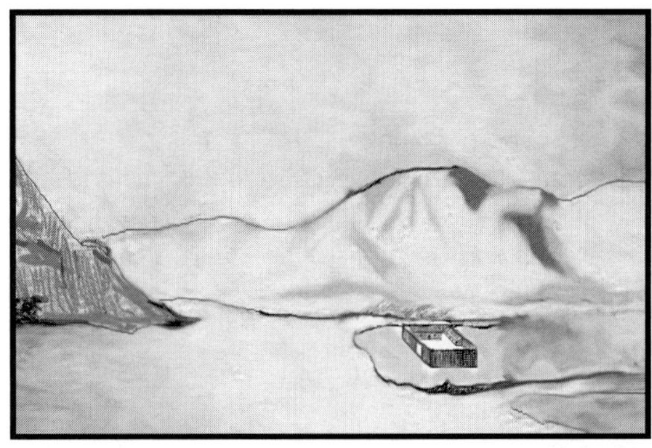

Schwinden Library, Fort Benton

A sketch from Fr. Point. Fort Fox-Livingston was on the south bank of the Missouri on the next bottom above Fort MacKenzie. It was used only in 1844-45.

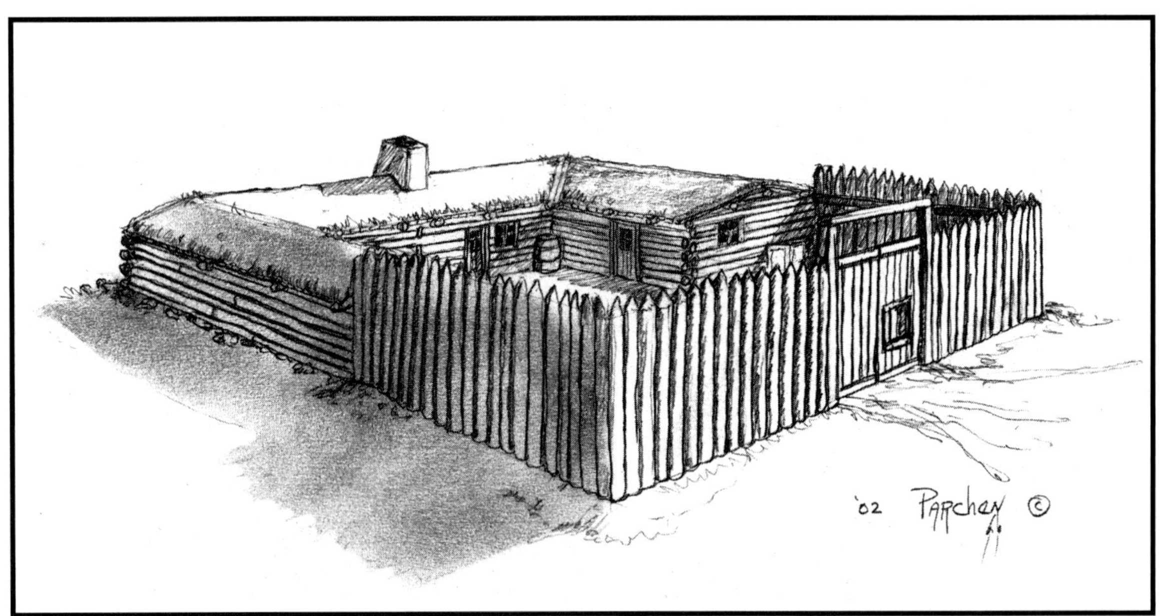

Artist David Parchen

Fort Cotton, on the second bottom above Fort Benton and about 3 miles away, was used only a short time by the Union Fur Company to challenge Fort MacKenzie of the American Fur Company.

Artist Karl Bodmer

Fort MacKenzie in 1833 at the time Prince Maximilian and Karl Bodmer visited to the post. In his paintings Bodmer recorded the Blackfoot culture before it was affected by the whites.

MacKenzie and called it Fort Fox-Livingston. (9) It probably was used the season after Fort Cotton and moved closer to Fort MacKenzie; the opposition hoped to gain more trade by being closer to the Company post.

The Demise

After two years the Union Fur Company abandoned their posts and withdrew from trade on the Upper Missouri. In May 1845 it reached an agreement with Pierre Chouteau Jr. to sell all of the company's assets to Chouteau. Total inexperience had led to the utter failure of the Union Fur Company. Several poor decisions by the leadership contributed to its demise: late annual departures of their steamboats from St. Louis; inexperienced leaders, Cutting and Ebbetts, on the upper river; and overextending their area of trade by going into both Crow and Blackfoot Country at the same time.

Again Chouteau and Company had rid themselves of competition in Blackfoot Country. The lucrative trade continued.

Artist David Parchen

Little Dog, Chief of the Piikani, was a friend of the traders who worked for peace and understanding. He had an interesting experience when he unknowlingly found gold.

Artist David Parchen

Fort Fox-Livingston was an opposition post to challenge the trade at Fort MacKenzie. It only lasted one season, 1843-44. The post was built by the Union Fur Company that was established in 1842. By 1845 the Company had put them out of business and taken over all their posts up river.

Highlight of the winter of 1843 at Fort MacKenzie was Little Dog's war party's trip into Shoshoni Country. Piikani Chief Little Dog took a war party on foot to steal horses and count coup on the Shoshoni. They went further and further south into enemy territory but found no one to attack until their trail crossed that of some mounted fur traders, possibly from Santa Fe. Hidden from the trail, the warriors swooped down on the traders and killed the entire party. They captured several horses and two burros. Tied to one of the burro's pack saddles were two extremely heavy wooden boxes. When the boxes were broken open they found them full of brass buttons. On closer examination, they discovered that the buttons had no holes. They took a few, but since they had no holes for sewing the Indians felt the buttons were of little use so they buried them near a spring. At Fort Benton several years later, Little Dog showed Andrew Dawson the "hole-less buttons." Dawson recognized the Spanish gold coins. No inducement could get the warriors to return; they believed evil spirits from the dead lurked nearby and would harm them if they returned. Even today, buried somewhere out there in Shoshoni Land, is the gold cache of Little Dog. (10)

The final chapters in the saga of Alexander Harvey were still at hand, but first to the affairs at Fort MacKenzie. In spite of the usual troubles with horse thieves and drunken Indians, things were more relaxed and trade was growing every year. The only other problem was the continual intertribal warfare between the Blackfoot, Atsina and their neighboring tribes. At the fort there no longer seemed to be the threat of siege or attack. Both sides realized that they wanted to be at peace so the trade could go on. The trader's goods were changing the Indian's culture and, like any society, as things got easier no one wanted to return to the old ways. A few distractions made life interesting for the inhabitants of the lonely fur post deep in Blackfoot Country as they made fortunes for the partners in St. Louis

.

Text Notes

1. Chittenden, quoting *Larpentuer's Journal,* dated the arrival of the steamboat *St. Peter* at Fort Union as June 17, 1837. Captain Bernard Pratte was in command and smallpox was on

board in the person of trader Halsey. Bradley in *The Affairs of Fort Benton* called the steamboat *Trapper* but says the same Captain Bernard Pratte was in command.
2. Accounts of how and where the virus got on board vary: in the trade goods, by the Indians or from the whites. Anyplace from St. Louis to Council Bluffs is named as the site.
3. Smallpox touched the Blackfoot in 1781 according to John Ewers. It came from Indians in the west through British traders. The 1873 epidemic was fifty years later; probably few were alive who remembered the earlier epidemic.
4. Accounts from each fort try to exonerate the bourgeois for the spread of the disease: Francis Chardon at Fort Clark, Edwin Denig at Fort Union and Alexander Culbertson at Fort MacKenzie.
5. Some list deaths among the Blackfoot as high as two-thirds of the population of the three tribes. Total population estimates before the epidemic ranged between 10,000 to 18,000.
6. Many Kainaa spellings of her name exist, almost as many as there are authors who write about her. This author uses the most common one. Translation of the name also varies: Medicine or Sacred or Holy Snake with or without Woman added. Here its Natawista, Holy Snake Woman.
7. A wicket is a small opening with a locked door that can be opened for trading. Usually cut in the main gate, it was used after the fort was closed for the night and to trade with individual Indians without admitting them inside the fort.
8. Larpentuer states that Mr. Cotton (no first name) who is mentioned several times at Fort Mortimer was one and the same as Fulton Cutting, one of the Company traders.
9. Fr. Point states in his journal that Fort Fox-Livingston was between Fort Piegan and Fort Clay (Benton) and existed only one spring, that of 1844.
10. From *Montana Pioneer; Jirah Isham Allen* by Mary Ellen Phinney

Schwinden Library, Fort Benton

A photo taken of Fort MacKenzie in the 1920's before the site was disturbed by farmng. Rocks from the foundations and fireplaces can be seen as well as rubble from the fire. After Fort MacKenzie was burned, the charred remains were called Brule Bottom from the French meaning burnt.

Fort Chardon

1844-45

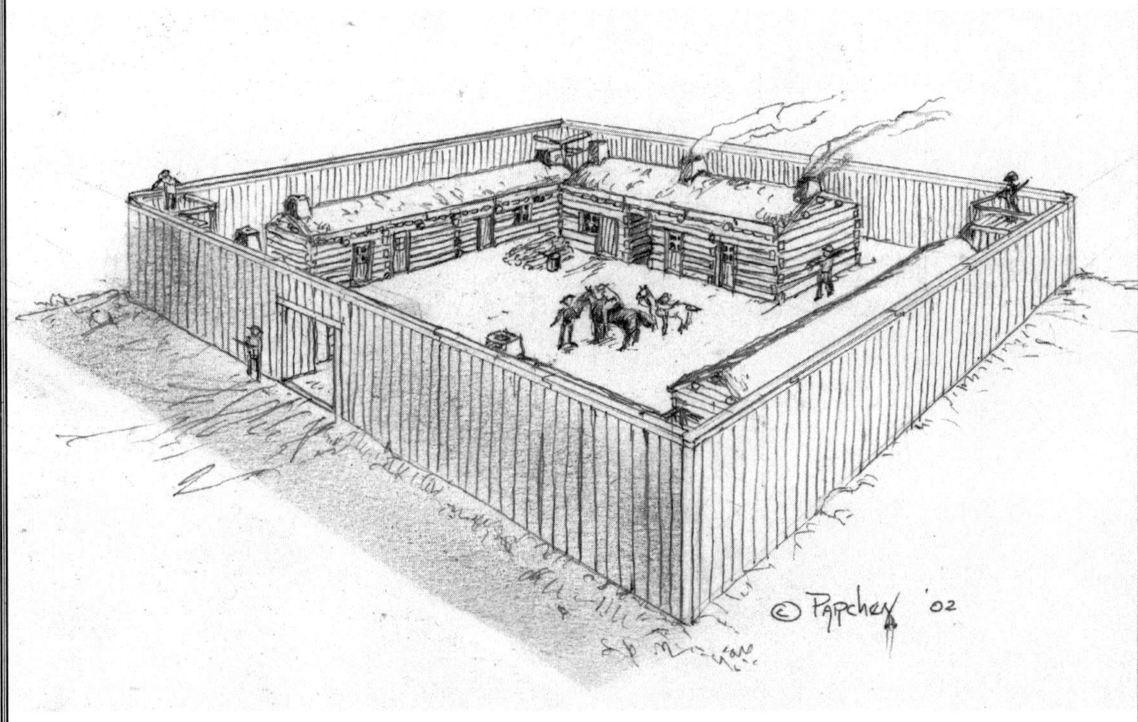

After the massacre at Fort MacKenzie by Chardon and Harvey, the traders wanted to move out of Blackfoot Country. Fort Chardon was hastily built of squared cottonwood logs by a small contingent of men at the mouth of the Judith River in March 1844. It never was successful in the trade and only survived two seasons. The post was burned by Alexander Culbertson on his way down river with the 1846 returns from Fort Lewis.

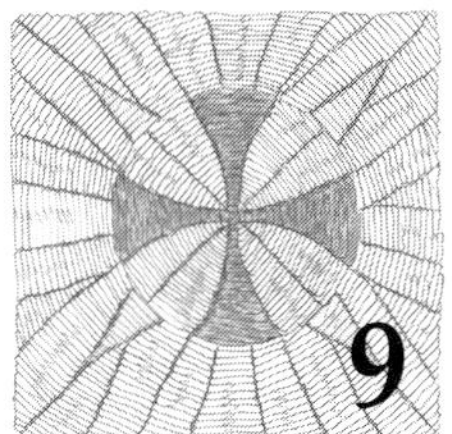
9

1843 - 1845

Death at the Gate

Last Days at Fort MacKenzie

The Chardon and Harvey Disaster

The Peace Medal

On the Lewis and Clark Expedition the two Captains carried Jefferson Presidential Medals as they crossed the continent in 1804-1806. Designed to promote peace and friendship, the medals were made in three sizes and presented by the Corps of Discovery to the tribes of Indians they met on their western adventure.

After the Expedition the medals were still used as presents from the federal government to the Indians with whom they held councils. Prized by the Indians, the medals became associated with the fur trade and symbolized an association between the federal government and the fur companies. Traders tried to persuade the government to furnish the Presidential Medals which they would present in the name of the President to secure peace, encourage friendship, and of course, promote the fur trade. When they were unsuccessful,

The obverse side of the Presidential Peace Medal carried by Lewis and Clark; trading companies copied this side for their medals.

Both sides of the Astor Medal; Astor's profile replaced the President of the United States and the American Fur Company's name went on the front. Most medals had crossed peace pipes and tomahawks, clasped hands and the words "peace and friendship" on the obverse side. The Astor Medal has the added touch of Fort Union and the initials U.M.O. for Upper Missouri Outfit.

in 1832 the companies secured permission to make their own medals.

The same year the American Fur Company produced the Astor Medal with John Jacob Astor's profile. In 1843 it produced the Chouteau Medal with President Van Buren's profile and an Upper Missouri Outfit label. Even the Union Fur Company, the opposition to the Upper Missouri Outfit, produced one of their own in 1844 with Martin Van Buren's profile and their name. A fourth medal with Washington's profile, an 1843 date but no company designation also appeared on the river. All of the medals copied the Jefferson Medal on the obverse side with clasped hands and crossed peace pipes and tomahawks.

The medals tended to denigrate and belittle the official government agents who complained bitterly. After extended controversy, continuing complaints and months of debate, on March 22, 1844 the Secretary of War banned the use of peace medals by anyone except official government agents.

The New Factor

Francis A. Chardon came up river in the spring of 1843 on the steamboat *Omega* accompanied by the natural history artist John J. Audubon. They arrived at Fort Union on June 12; Chardon left for his new post on the June 22 accompanied by Alexander Harvey. Audubon stayed at Fort Union where he did much of his painting of North American birds and mammals.

Chardon had been the clerk at Fort Clark but never had the responsibility of being in charge of a post. He was a very insecure person. Accompanied by an old hand like Harvey, Chardon relied on his judgement from the beginning. By fall Chardon, inexperienced in dealing with the Blackfoot and incapacitated most of the time by his drinking problem, allowed Harvey to make more and more decisions. Soon Chardon was in charge in name only. Harvey by nature was very aggressive, and probably resented Chardon's having been put in charge of the post. Harvey had commanded Fort MacKenzie off and on since

Artist David Parchen

Before the steamboat, large heavy keelboats brought trade goods and supplies to the Blackfoot posts from Fort Union and took down the returns.

1839. Culbertson always left Harvey in charge when his duties kept him down river. After MacKenzie left the upper river, his absence occurred more and more often and for longer periods of time.

The Prelude

A war party of Blackfoot, returning from a raid against the Crow, visited the fort late in the fall of 1844 and wanted to trade for knives and ammunition. As was the custom for trading parties that stopped at the fort, a good dinner was served and five rounds of ammunition were given for each rifle. The Indians wanted more ammunition and left very disgruntled when they did not get it. As they departed, they killed or drove off animals belonging to the fort. (1) A group of men including the black Tom Reese was sent out to retrieve the livestock. In the skirmish with the Indians, Reese was killed. (2) When the party returned to the fort with Reese's body, Chardon decided that the Indians should be taught a lesson. He was agitated by the death of Reese and probably encouraged by Harvey. Chardon and Harvey plotted their revenge against the next Blackfoot trading party who came to the fort.

According to their plan, the cannon in the blockhouse that commanded the front gate would be charged with a full compliment of lead musket balls, an early form of shrapnel. Harvey would be on the second-story platform in the blockhouse when the Indians gathered at the gate for trade. Chardon would admit the chiefs through the gate and kill them while they were inside the fort. Harvey would massacre the party left outside the walls with a cannon blast from the blockhouse.

The Killing

In mid-winter the arrival of a small trading party of Siksika set the stage for the revenge of Reese. (3) When three chiefs were admitted, Chardon prematurely tried to kill one of them. Hearing the shot, the Indians outside the gate began to flee. Harvey discharged the cannon, killed five or six and wounded many more. (4) The remaining chiefs escaped. The result of their plot was not nearly as disastrous as planned. The large number killed as reported in later journals and accounts was never close to the actual dead.

Artist C.M. Russell

Some of the Siksika were away from the cannon blast and escaped with their lives and some of their robes.

Artist David Parchen

As the trading party of Siksika approached the gate at Fort MacKenzie, Chardon tried to kill the chiefs in the inner trading space. Harvey unleashed the cannon from the blockhouse, killing several and wounding many more who were subsequently scalped alive.

The robes and furs of the Indians, abandoned during their hasty retreat, were collected by fort personnel along with scalps from the dead. Harvey rushed out with an axe and buried it in the heads of all the fallen who were still alive. He licked the blood from the blade and swore, "I will serve all the dogs so." That night, with blood still on their hands, a grisly victory party was held inside the safe confines of Fort MacKenzie. With a scalp dance around a roaring fire, the drunken traders reveled in the slaughter. The massacre was a prelude to the finale for the fort. Fort MacKenzie was built under duress but survived twelve productive yet hazardous years in the Blackfoot fur trade.

Second Thoughts

The next morning a sober Chardon realized what he had done; Harvey probably didn't give a damn. They created a dilemma and wondered what to do next. For many days after the incident, no Indians appeared at the fort. Harvey and Chardon, afraid of attack or realizing that the Indians would no longer come to the fort (or both), set about moving the fort to a new location. They picked a site down river at the mouth of the Judith River in the land of the Atsina. It was hoped that they might regain a portion of trade that was lost that winter by trading with the Atsina. The move out of Blackfoot territory and closer to the Atsina lessened the chance of retribution by the Piikani, Siksika and Kainaa.

One wintry day five or six brave men went to the mouth of the Judith where they hurriedly constructed a fort on the north bank across from the mouth of the river. Records show that construction took less than a month. Personnel and goods were moved to the new fort, named Fort Francis A. Chardon abbreviated Fort F.A.C., in late March or early April 1844.

In a recently-found American Fur Co. record is an inventory dated March 19, 1844. It is titled "The Stock of Property of Missouri Outfit on hand at Fort MacKenzie and delivered to Fort F.A.C." (5) By early spring the fort that had established the lucrative Blackfoot trade had been abandoned. A tremendous trade deficit developed which lasted for the next two years.

After Fort MacKenzie was abandoned, the Indians probably burned it. The site became known as Brule Bottom or old Fort Brule (6). When the Blackfoot discovered that the Company had built a post in the territory of the Atsina, they were enraged. They started harassing the traders, stealing horses and trying to catch lone people away from the safe confines of the fort so they could avenge the killings.

The New Fort

If only six men constructed Fort Chardon in a month, they probably completed only the palisades before the rest of the personnel arrived. They cut and half-split enough logs 8 to 12 inches in diameter and 15 to 20 feet long to build an enclosure 140 feet square. They dug a trench two to three feet deep, placed the logs upright around the perimeter and then back-filled. The limited study of the site shows two blockhouses on opposite corners and buildings inside the enclosure. Fort Chardon was probably a typical American Fur Company trading post, very similar in structure to earlier posts. The remains indicate that it was later burned. Further details of its structure will have to wait for further archeological excavations of the site. (7)

Artist David Parchen

Building trading posts of logs usually meant squaring the four sides of the logs with a broad axe so they would fit tightly together in the palisades and walls.

In the spring of 1844 Chardon took the reduced returns down river and reported on the conditions in Blackfoot Country. Even with the new fort, few Indians had come to trade that spring. Company officials down river were greatly concerned with the state of affairs at Fort Chardon. During that spring Culbertson and Honore Picotte, manager of the upper river, held long discussions at Fort Pierre about the Fort MacKenzie incident. Culbertson had come overland to deliver the returns of the season from Fort Laramie and to pick up trade goods for the next season. No action was taken in the Fort Chardon situation. Culbertson was still upset that the Company had not heeded his advice about the Blackfoot trade and had moved him to Fort Laramie. He refused Picotte's request that he return to Blackfoot Country. Chardon headed back up river, probably promising the partners better returns the coming season.

Another Terrible Trading Season

Overcoming the problems just was not in the cards for Francis Chardon. Few Indians came to trade during the winter of 1844-45, one of the coldest ever on the upper river with little snow. The buffalo migrated eastward into the land of the Assiniboine and Sioux making for poor hunting on the upper river. Even the few Indians who did come had a minimal number of robes to trade. Another major problem was the fort's location, far from the traditional winter camps of both the Blackfoot and the Atsina. The site was primarily a crossing point

Schwinden Library, Fort Benton

An artist's rendition of Fort Chardon. No known drawing exists with the exception of Fr. Point's drawing of the ruins after Culbertson burned it. One has to wonder about the elaborate bastions when it was built in such haste in the winter of 1844.

for war parties heading north or south. The inexperienced Chardon could easily have made this mistake in locating the post, but Harvey would not. He knew the country, the trade and the Indians far too well to make such a mistake. Perhaps it was Harvey's scheme to regain control and force Chardon off the upper river.

With war parties roaming the breaks, few traders ventured from the fort to visit the Indian camps. By winter the fort was cold, stressful imprisonment for the confined inhabitants. Restriction in the close quarters of any fur post created problems, but a cold Montana winter with no activity spelled additional difficulties for everyone.

By mid-winter the drunken bourgeois experienced trouble maintaining order. Weather-bound traders with their Indian women, half-breed children, yapping dogs and restless livestock had quarrels that erupted into violence. Fists, knives and bullets settled the "cabin fever" disputes. Chardon, probably in a drunken stupor most of the time, did not realize what was happening and Harvey undoubtedly encouraged as much unrest as possible. Only the coming of spring ended the mid-winter altercations among the fort's personnel.

In the early spring of 1845 Chardon took the meager returns down river to Fort Union where he was relieved of his position. He was sent down river to Fort Clark where he arrived in early May. (8) Harvey was in charge at Fort Chardon until Culbertson returned. The Blackfoot robe trade was the heart of the Company's business and after two seasons of meager returns it was imperative to get Culbertson back up river with the Blackfoot.

Return to the River

Picotte, Chouteau and the other Company partners decided to again prevail upon Alexander Culbertson to return to the upper river and reestablish trade with the Blackfoot. To induce Culbertson's return, he was invited to discuss the trading problems on the upper river with Pierre Chouteau Jr. in New York. Culbertson went from Fort Laramie to Fort Pierre in June 1845 then on to the Company offices in New York. Chouteau made a personal appeal, soothed Culbertson's

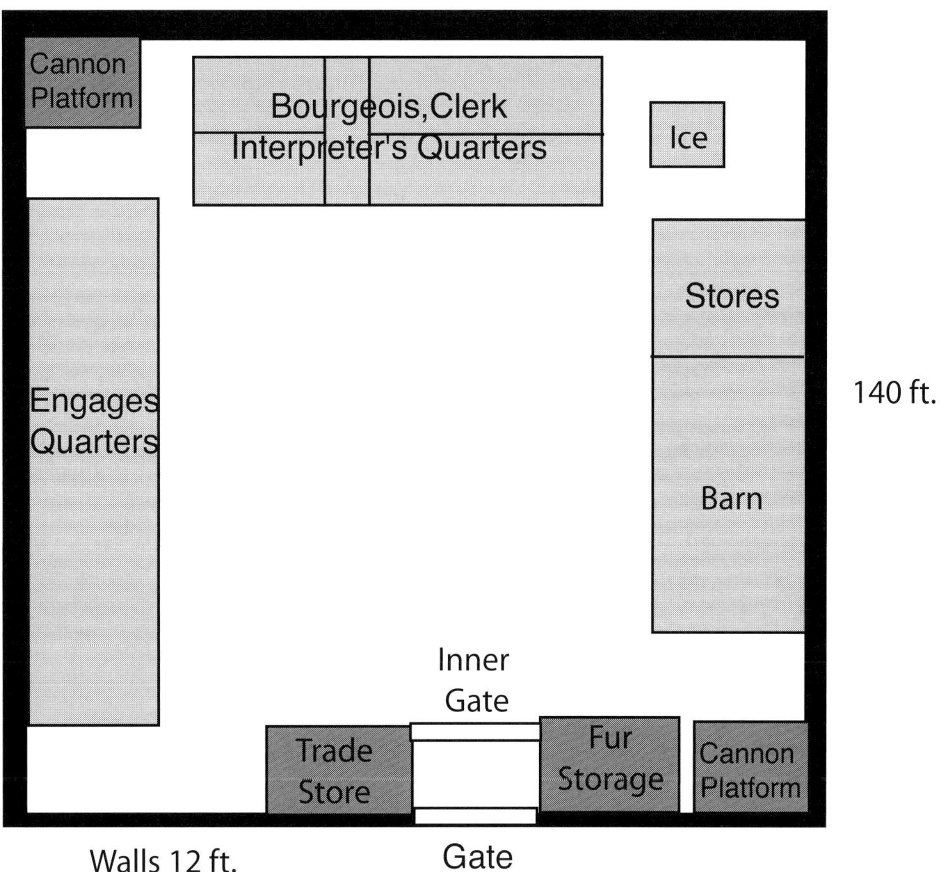

Schwinden Library, Fort Benton

Floor plan of Fort Chardon is only a guess at locations of the buildings. Since it was completed in a very short time by only a handful of men in mid-winter, there was probably no time to build blockhouses. The buildings had the palisades for their rear walls.

hurt feelings and gave him both stock and cash compensation in the Company. All Culbertson really wanted was an apology to restore his ego which Chouteau readily provided. Then a happy man, Culbertson agreed to go back up river to straighten out the Harvey and Chardon affair.

Before leaving New York, Culbertson renewed his acquaintance with John J. Audubon who was preparing his new book on the quadrupeds of North America. Specimens for the book were the ones Culbertson had helped him collect at Fort Union in 1843. Culbertson spent two pleasant weeks with the Audubon family before leaving for the upper river. (9)

A Triumphal Return

Culbertson hurried to St. Louis but missed the Company steamboat headed to Fort Union with Honore' Picotte and a host of new recruits for the Blackfoot posts. Arriving at Fort Pierre by horse, Culbertson then headed west along the Platte to Fort John (Laramie) to settle his affairs and collect his family. After

Artist Alfred Jacob Miller

Interior of Fort John (Laramie) when it served the American Fur Company on the North Platte River. Culbertson spent two seasons here.

chastising the employees for failing to get the returns to Fort Pierre that spring, he left Fort John with his family and arrived at Fort Pierre late in the summer of 1845.

Picotte was still up river at Fort Union. Culbertson took temporary charge of Fort Pierre and awaited Picotte's arrival. By the time Picotte returned, keelboats bound for the Blackfoot posts had left Fort Union. Neither of the partners knew that the up river contingent was much smaller than had been planned.

In the early spring Larpenteur, in charge at Fort Union, had a party and invited the opposition from Fort William. During the party twelve recruits were persuaded to desert Chouteau and Co. and join the opposition rather than go into Blackfoot Country and "certain death." By the time the keelboat was loaded, ten more had deserted. The frightened recruits who remained were given a gil of whiskey to fortify them and headed up river. The bungling Larpenteur was left on the bank wondering how badly he had messed up again. The opposition did not calm their fears with their parting remarks, "You are going to the butcher shop! Good bye forever."

During their meeting Culbertson and Picotte decided not to fire Alexander Harvey but to transfer him to Fort Pierre out of harm's way. Culbertson probably insisted. He and Harvey had worked together for so long that he knew Harvey was a real asset to the Company despite his volatile temper.

Harvey Attacked

When the meeting with Picotte was over, Culbertson caught up with the keelboat at the Poplar River in time to take command before they arrived at Fort Chardon. On August 16, 1845 as the keelboat approached the Judith, Harvey met them and reported to his old boss and friend. Upon boarding the boat, he was suddenly attacked by three old enemies - Jacob Berger, Malcolm Clarke and James Lee – either because of old feuds or for his part in the trade debacle with the Blackfoot at Fort MacKenzie. Before they could do him in, Culbertson stepped in and saved Harvey's life as he lay on the deck covered with blood from the many knife wounds he had received from the three assailants. Culbertson took the wounded Harvey off the keelboat and took him 15 miles overland to the fort, where he advised him to leave immediately by water and under cover of darkness. Harvey packed his gear in a canoe and drifted silently by the keelboat moored

Artist Fr. Nicolas Point

Alexander Culbertson was factor for the American Fur Company at Fort John.

Schwinden Library, Fort Benton

Honore' Picotte, chief agent for the American Fur Company on the upper river, took over from Kenneth MacKenzie.

down river, escaping death but not banishment.

Culbertson decided to abandon Fort Chardon as soon as he could build a new fort further up river in the Blackfoot winter camping grounds. He left the reliable Malcolm Clarke and five men to inventory and manage the fort at the Judith. When the new fort was completed, they were to bring the inventory up river and close Chardon's fort. In late August the decision was made to move closer to the Blackfoot camps and regain the trade of the powerful Blackfoot Confederacy.

As Harvey traveled down river, revenge was uppermost in his thoughts. Banishment to Fort Pierre away from the trade he had known so long simply was not acceptable.

Text Notes

1. Accounts of events that precipitated the demise of Fort MacKenzie do not agree. The animal was either a pig, horse or cow which was stolen, killed or driven off. The latter fits best with the rest of the story.
2. Some accounts mention only the killing of Reese, the black servant. Others say that Reese was Chardon's slave and his loss of property probably prompted Chardon's aggressive reaction.
3. The notes of Abel's *Chardon's Journal at Fort Clark 1834-1839* identify them as Northern Blackfoot (Siksika). The Indian Agent E.A.C. Hatch reported the date of the massacre as February 19, 1844. The date is confirmed in a journal written by one of the men at the fort.
4. Descriptions of killing the Siksika also vary. Some accounts place the fatalities as high as twenty to thirty. Other accounts say the cannon inside the front gate was fired when the gate was opened. That seems improbable; the delay from gate opening to powder ignition in the touch hole of the cannon would have given the Indians time to escape the blast.
5. *Inventory of Stock, 1844, Fort MacKenzie* American Fur Company, Ledger II, p. 27-32, Missouri Historical Society
6. Some historians credit Chardon and Harvey with destruction of the fort. However, smoke from the burning fort would surely have attracted nearby Indians leaving traders with no place to retreat to if they were confronted on their way to the new stockade. This does not seem to be an option.
7. Site 24CH87 Fort Francis A. Chardon, State Historic Preservation Office, Helena, MT
8. *Fort Pierre Letter Book of 1845-46* established Francis Chardon on the lower river May 2, 1845.
9. *Fort Pierre Letter Book of 1845-46*; letter of June 26, 1845 from Culbertson to LaBoue.

Fort Lewis

1845 - 1847

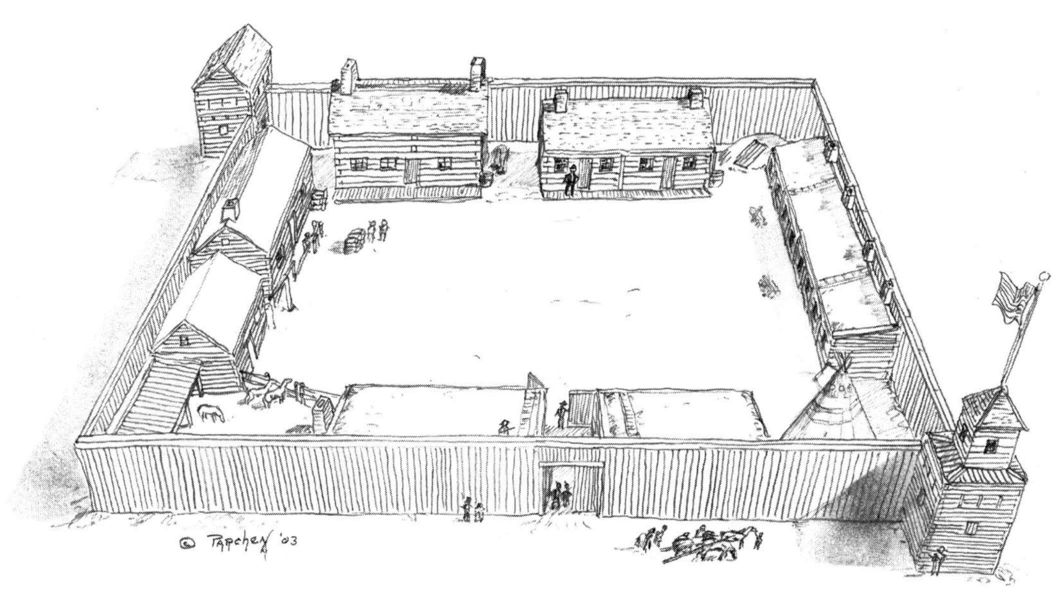

Built late in 1845 by Alexander Culbertson and named for Meriwether Lewis, Fort Lewis served only two seasons. It was on the south bank just above the old site of Fort Cotton and was difficult to reach in the winter. In the spring of 1847 it was dismantled and eventually became Fort Benton.

10

1845 - 1847

A New Start

Establishment of Fort Lewis

Reconciliation with the Blackfoot

Closing up Fort Chardon

Leaving a small compliment of men at Fort F.A.C. created a sense of security for Culbertson's party if they had to hurriedly leave the upper river. Culbertson loaded equipment, trade goods and supplies in the keelboat and went deeper into Blackfoot Country than before. His party passed through the White Cliffs, the mouth of Maria's River where the first Blackfoot post had been built, and by the burned out ruins of Fort MacKenzie. About twenty miles above the burned fort, Culbertson arrived at an expansive bottom on the south side of the Missouri where the opposition's Fort Cotton was built in 1843.

A few hundred yards up river from the Fort Cotton site he staked out the new fort. He named it in honor of Honore' Picotte, one of the Company partners. (1) The new fort's location would bring trade closer to the winter camps of the Blackfoot on Maria's and Teton Rivers.

Hurried Construction

Winter sometimes comes early on the Upper Missouri. In September there was a sense of urgency to get the stockade and quarters erected. The remains of Fort Cotton, a small log fort, had not been destroyed and became Company property in 1845. Its logs were used in construction of the new fort. Each

Artist Fr. Nicolas Point

Sketch of Fort Lewis just after it was completed in 1847 when Culbertson returned.

Schwinden Library, Fort Benton

The white rectangle marks the site of Fort Lewis, the post built by Culbertson on his return to the Upper Missouri in 1845. Sligthly to the left and at the river's edge is the site of Fort Cotton.

day the mornings were colder and ice collected on the ponds.

Another factor hastened completion. No one knew whether the Indians would accept a new post deep in their country or if they were lurking about looking for a chance to take revenge on the traders after the Chardon and Harvey disaster. Even with such motivation, the fort was not completed until January.

The new fort was 150 feet square with blockhouses on opposite corners. The bastions were two stories tall, the upper story overhanging the lower. Made of tightly-fitted four-sided squared timbers, the blockhouse had rifle and cannon ports in the upper story. Quarters and warehouses were built along the inside walls of the log stockade, much like the first construction at Fort MacKenzie. These quarters and warehouses used the stockade as their back walls.

Fort Honore' or Lewis

Culbertson wrote to Picotte asking his permission to name the new post Fort Picotte or Fort Honore'. Picotte declined and asked Culbertson to honor someone else. The post was then officially named for Meriwether Lewis, the famed explorer of the Louisiana Purchase. Lewis became Governor of Louisiana, a position he held until he took his own life on the Natchez Trace October 11, 1809.

Picotte's letter to Culbertson read, "I am flattered and thank you for your good opinion of me in giving my name to your fort, but I request you to substitute Lewis in the place of Honore' which is much more suitable and appropriate. By so doing you will oblige me." (2)

When the fort was finished in January 1846, Malcolm Clarke was ordered to abandon Fort Chardon and bring the remaining supplies to Fort Lewis. The next spring when Culbertson took the annual returns to Fort Union, he torched Fort Chardon, an act that Chardon never forgave and made Culbertson his bitter enemy.

Even before Fort Lewis was finished, Company records noted that having the fort on the south side of the river was impractical and inconvenient for trade. Most of the Indian camps were on the north side of the Missouri along the Teton and Maria's Rivers. When winter arrived and the river froze, ice flows made crossing hazardous. Winter chinooks opened and closed the river periodically. The fluctuating temperature changes doubled the trouble of crossing back and forth. In the spring of 1846 a new site on the north bank down river five miles was selected and construction began. The new fort was first called Fort Lewis then Fort Clay, and finally was officially named Fort Benton.

The New Opposition

On his journey to Fort Pierre, Harvey stopped to rest at Fort Union for two days, where he heard he would be banished permanently to Fort Pierre. Angrily, he went on down river to meet with Honore' Picotte. As soon as his canoe hit the bank, Harvey leaped out and demanded cash for his draft of five thousand dollars. Culbertson had given him a draft for wages and a letter of recommendation before he left Fort Chardon. What created and perpetuated their friendship is unknown except that they started their careers together at Fort MacKenzie. In Culbertson's opinion Harvey must have been an exceptional trader, and, though an erratic man, was worth keeping in the Company.

After listening to the unfriendly Picotte, Harvey was even more bent on revenge. He vowed to return to the upper river and start an opposition trade with the Blackfoot. At Fort Pierre, Harvey enlisted three disgruntled clerks, all life-long traders on the river, and formed a new company. Joining him in the venture were Charles Primeau, Joseph Picotte and Anthony Bouis. All vowed to destroy Chouteau and his empire.

Artist Fr. Nicolas Point

Fort Lewis at the time of Fr. Nicholas Point's visit. He baptized over 600 Blackfoot during his long winter's stay with the Culbertsons. Indians were along the river's edge where a keelboat awaited its down river trip in the spring.

Schwinden Library, Fort Benton

The landing at Fort Pierre, the main post down river for Chouteau and Company. Harvey came here after the fight at Fort Chardon and started the new opposition company after his discussions with Picotte at the fort.

Harvey, Primeau and Co.

Harvey spent several days in his canoe during the trip to St. Louis where he contemplated his next move against the Company. In St. Louis he contacted Robert Campbell and gained financial backing for his new firm which was called Harvey, Primeau and Company or the St. Louis Fur Company. In the past Campbell had joined opposition companies in losing ventures. He too may have been seeking to avenge those financial losses.

Harvey filed charges with T.H. Harvey (no relation), the Commissioner of Indian Affairs, against the three traders who attempted to kill him at the Judith. He also accused Francis Chardon and Chouteau and Company of selling liquor to the Indians at Fort MacKenzie between May 1,1843 and March 31,1844. The Commissioner directed Andrew Drips, the Indian Agent on the upper river, to send Chardon and the three traders to St. Louis to answer the accusations. Since Drips was the agent Chouteau had appointed to protect the Company's interests, nothing was done. The men never went to St. Louis, the charges were finally dropped and the accusations forgotten.

Business in St. Louis

Chardon may have been a poor trader and a drunkard, but he was very astute concerning Company politics. He reached Picotte and Chouteau first with his story and placed the entire blame on Harvey, whom he had left up river unable to defend himself. He told such a good story that he was retained as an employee and sent to work at Fort Clark, where he remained until his death in 1848. Harvey paid with banishment from the Company.

The Company had made many enemies during its years on the Upper Missouri. Some investors in St. Louis were more than willing to help Harvey. His reputation as a tough-minded trader was well known and he would undoubtedly continue to be successful. Having been beaten by the Company before did not discourage Robert Campbell, Wm. Sublette, Charles Primeau, Joseph Picotte and two new investors, Anthony Bouis and Francois Deschamps, from buying into a new firm. It was a costly mistake when Chouteau and Company dismissed the volatile Harvey; he returned up river and cut into their profits for

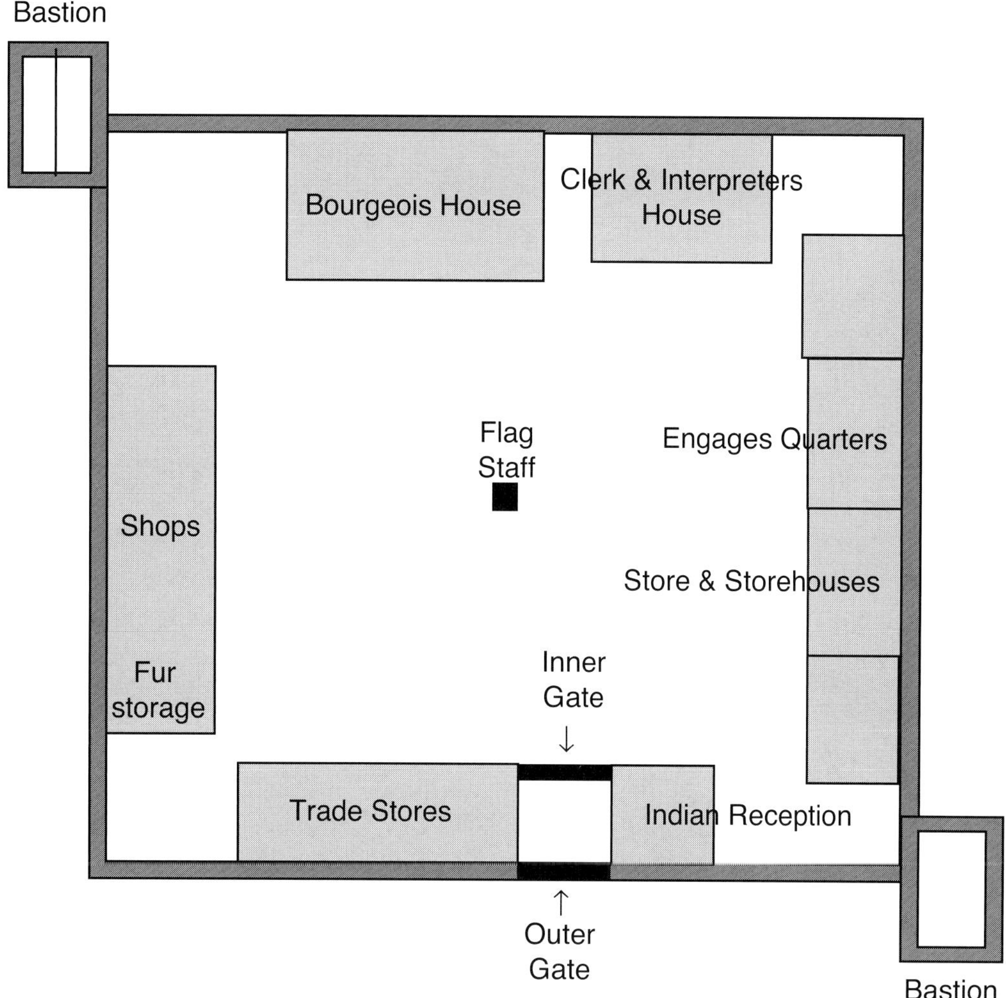

Floor plan of Fort Lewis from the drawings of Fr. Point. Notice the difference in the two blockhouses. One has a hip roof with the upper floor overhanging the first; the other has a gabled roof and straight sidewalls like Fort MacKenzie.

eight long years. As long as Alexander Harvey ran the opposition fort in Blackfoot Country, he reduced the profits of the Company until it hurt.

Affairs at Fort Lewis

Shortly after the completion of Fort Lewis, a small party of Crow drove off ten horses. The Blackfoot, who had learned that the traders were back and were building a new fort, accosted the Crow before they could ride south and recaptured the horses. The Kainaa returned them to the owners, and were the first band of Blackfoot to visit the new fort. Shortly thereafter an old Siksika warrior happened by and parlayed with Alexander Culbertson, who learned that the old man's people were camped on the Belly River. Culbertson sent him with presents of tobacco and invited his people to a council at the fort.

The Siksika accepted and about fifty returned. Culbertson met them outside the fort after they had crossed the river near the big island, and, shaking hands with them,

them into the fort. After smoking the pipe, reconciliation was accomplished and the Siksika recognized that the return of Culbertson was good. Chief Big Swan said the Blackfoot must never be the first to stain with blood. There never was bloodshed during the trade at Fort Lewis and later at Fort Benton. (3)

Schwinden Library, Fort Benton

Crow Indians were the first to discover the new fort but did not come to trade, just to steal horses. Before they got away, a band of Kainaa recaptured the horses and returned them to Culbertson at Fort Lewis.

The First Returns

Trading was brisk during the shortened season in 1846. In May Alexander Culbertson took the returns to Fort Union then went on to St. Louis to answer the charges filed by Alexander Harvey against the Company traders Culbertson, Kipp, Chardon and H. Picotte. During the previous four months, 1100 packs of buffalo robes and beaver, wolf and fox furs were taken. Everyone was satisfied that trade had been restored. In St. Louis Culbertson's stock rose mightily. Company officials could not praise him enough - or themselves - for the fruitful decisions they had made the year before.

Although the illegal whiskey charges were undoubtedly true, Company politics and Harvey's absence delayed any action. Eventually some of the charges were set aside and the fines were paid. Culbertson went up river early in October. Chouteau was embarrassed that his four top men were fined eight hundred dollars for bringing illegal whiskey into Indian Country, but the fines were paid by the Company and business went on as usual.

Culbertson probably took charge of the annual fall pack train sent to the forts with emergency supplies. In late summer when inventories at the up river forts were sent to St. Louis with the fur returns, the companies decided if additional supplies were needed. When necessary, a pack train left Independence or St. Joseph to supply the posts.

Artist Fr. Nicolas Point

Culbertson greeting the Blackfoot at the main gate at Fort Lewis; the Island of Reconciliation is in the background. The next two seasons revitalized the Company and led to fifteen peaceful and profitable years at Fort Benton.

Harvey Returns

Harvey and his partners left St. Louis in June 1846 on the steamboat *Clermont No. 2* with $50,000 worth of trade goods from Robert Campbell's trading houses in St. Louis. Campbell's business would market the robes and furs from Harvey's company. Harvey hired forty-five men in St. Louis and another fifty on his way up river to build three opposition posts near American Fur Co. forts. The crowded little steamboat left on a falling river, with stops only at Council Bluffs and Fort Pierre to be searched for liquor, and a quick stop at Vermilion to pick up Primeau's wife and two children. They proceeded to the Great Bend for a council with the Sioux, and finally reached the mouth of the Medicine River.

Harvey unloaded supplies and part of his men to build Fort Bouis or Fort Defiance. Several days later he unloaded the rest of his party and supplies just down river from Fort Union. Before heading into Blackfoot Country, Harvey constructed mackinaw boats to carry supplies up river, and made repairs to old Fort Mortimer, which Harvey renamed Fort William, to challenge the Fort Union trade.

By mackinaw, Harvey and his men continued up river past the mouth of Maria's River to the Crocondunez, about ten miles down river from Fort Lewis, where he built Harvey's Trading Post. Harvey, Primeau and Company opened trade in competition with Chouteau and Company near all three of the Company's principal up river trading posts. Each fort was operated by one of the experienced active partners; Anthony Bouis traded with the Sioux, Charles Primeau with the Assiniboine, and Alexander Harvey engaged the Blackfoot in trade.

Fort Campbell or Harvey's Post

Harvey's trading post, originally constructed of wood, was on the south side of the Missouri opposite the Crocondunez, a little above the point and 25 yards from the river. It may have been the site where Harvey had started to build a fort for David Mitchell in 1833 during Prince Maximilian's stay. In 1846 when Culbertson moved the site of Fort Lewis to the present site of Fort Benton, Harvey abandoned the first site and built a new post on the same bottom about a mile up river from Culbertson's new post. Harvey's new fort was converted to adobe starting in 1847, copying the transition of Fort Lewis (Benton) to adobe. J.B.S. Todd, Maj. D.M. Frost and Wm. Atkinson did the adobe work at the opposition fort. Perhaps Culbertson and Harvey, after settling their differences, talked about remodeling their forts. They did not live far from each other and visited on

Artist David Parchen

Reopened for a third time, Fort Mortimer of the Union Fur Company was changed back to Fort William, its original name when it was built in 1832 by Sublette and Campbell.

special occasions.

After fourteen years of opposition including eight good years of cutting heavily into the Company's profits, Fort Campbell was sold to Chouteau and Company in 1860. The clerk, Mathew Carroll, took possession from Malcolm Clarke.

The robe trade at Fort Campbell averaged over 5000 robes annually throughout its existence, but did much better during the years when Alexander Harvey was alive.

Troubles at Fort Lewis

With Culbertson in St. Louis to answer government charges and with the possibility that Malcolm Clarke may be called for his part in the Harvey affair, Honore' Picotte sent Charles Larpenteur to take command of Fort Lewis. In July Larpenteur loaded the keelboat *Bear* and headed out. In a few days the river was so low they stopped and built a small mackinaw to lighten the keelboat.

The trip to Fort Lewis took seventy days, a sure sign of Larpenteur's inability to command. He was a good clerk but hardly a bourgeois. When they arrived at Fort Lewis, Clarke refused to serve under him and the men were in open revolt. Clarke went to Fort Union where James Kipp sent him back to Fort Lewis to take command.

The feud continued. Finally in November Culbertson arrived at Fort Union with the pack train and settled the matter. Having been gone six months, he hurried to Fort Lewis and sent Larpenteur back to Fort Union, where Kipp refused to rehire him.

Schwinden Library, Fort Benton

Charles Larpenteur was an inept trader for the Company.

When Culbertson arrived at Fort Lewis in December 1846, he found a Jesuit priest visiting the fort for the winter. Fr. Pierre DeSmet and Fr. Nicolas Point had arrived from the missions in the West in September. DeSmet went down river with a disgruntled Malcolm Clarke and left Fr. Point in the hands of Larpenteur to minister to the Blackfoot and try to establish a mission.

Artist Fr. Nicolas Point

Harvey's Trading Post was built on the south side of the Missouri River near the Crocond-unez near the fort site he worked on in 1833.

A Jesuit Winter

The winter was severe but trade was brisk. Following the custom of the Company, Culbertson provided Fr. Point with quarters and a room to hold mass and educate post personnel and visiting Indians. Two incidents created conflict that winter. One Sunday with a storm

Schwinden Library, Fort Benton

Fr. Pierre DeSmet came to Fort Lewis in 1846 with Fr. Nicolas Point. He returned to St. Louis leaving Fr. Point to winter with the Blackfoot.

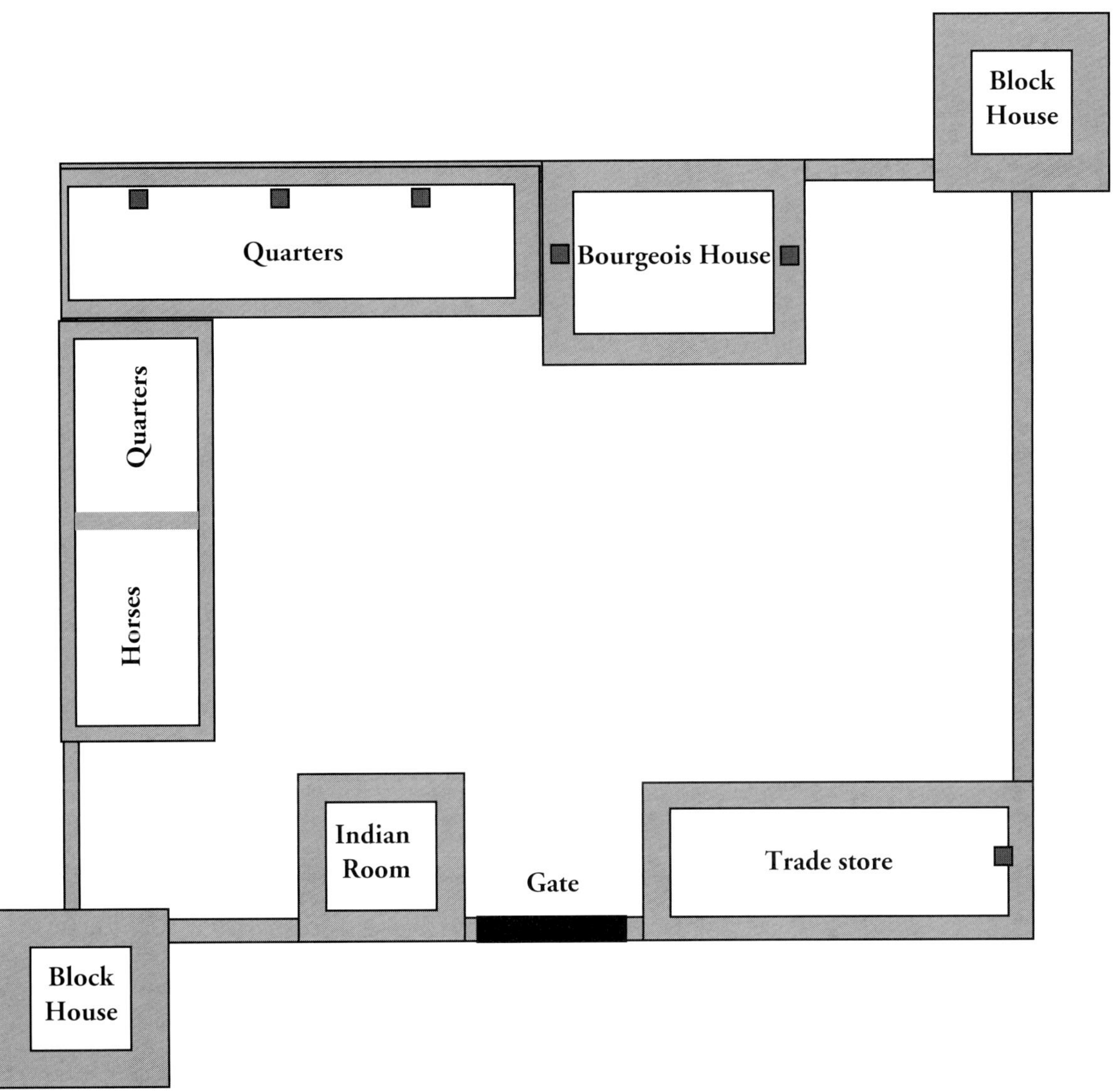

approaching, Culbertson and his men rushed to the boat dock to cover some robes; Fr. Point chastised Culbertson for working on the Sabbath. Culbertson and his men continued their labor even after several more words from the priest. Culbertson became exasperated and told the Jesuit that it was his duty to protect the property of his employer and suggested he go to his quarters and read his Bible.

The second incident occurred when Julia Culbertson became sick and the white man's medicine produced no cure. Natawista took charge. That morning at breakfast Fr. Point inquired of Culbertson about the loud chanting. Culbertson explained that it was the Kainaa medicine woman healing his daughter. The priest rushed into the room, grabbed the old woman by the neck, and threw her down. Resentful of the priest's actions, Natawista told him to mind his own business, and asked the woman to continue the steam bath and chanting. Julia recovered nicely.

Fr. Point returned from the fall hunt to the fort and began to minister Christianity to the Blackfoot throughout the winter. The camps of the Blackfoot were nearby on the Teton and Maria's Rivers; Fr. Point said he could easily walk to the eleven encampments in the immediate vicinity. During his eight-month stay at Fort Lewis, the priest baptized between 650 and 700 people, mostly children. He also married dozens of white employees to their Indian wives after first baptizing them. Fr. Nicolas Point left in the spring of 1847, and never returned to establish a mission for the Blackfoot.

Artist Fr. Nicolas Point

The burned ruins of Fort Chardon at the mouth of the Judith which Culbertson destroyed in the spring of 1846 on his trip to St. Louis with the returns.

Artist Fr. Nicolas Point

Natawista, wife of Alexander Culbertson, painted by Fr. Point while he was in residence at Fort Lewis during the winter of 1846-47. He tried to Christianize her without success.

Winter Trade

1847 was truly a vintage year. When up river returns arrived, traders and businessmen were amazed. Early returns of 750 bundles of robes and 54 of furs came from Fort Pierre. Harvey, Primeau and Company returns, 515 bundles of robes and 7 of furs, arrived by mackinaw. In July steamers carried over 1300 robe packs from the Yellowstone even though they had lost 240 bundles when one of the mackinaws sank on a snag. The largest robe shipment of the season reached St. Louis aboard the new steamboat *Martha*. Captain Joseph LaBarge had brought her to Fort Union fully loaded with trade goods in May. Accompanied by Fr. Point and Malcolm Clarke, Culbertson took the Blackfoot returns down river from Fort Lewis to St. Louis on the *Martha*. When the Company boat reached St. Louis, she unloaded 1400 bundles of robes, 280 packs of furs and 96 sacks of buffalo tongues in addition to a menagerie of live animals to be sold into private collections and traveling shows.

Some charges against the Company traders were still not settled. Jim Lee came with Culbertson to answer charges concerning the assault of Harvey. Again without Harvey

Artist Fr. Nicolas Point

Men pressing buffalo hides into bundles. The levering pole to the left was used to lift the long heavy press pole up and then with the strength of the men crushed the folded hides down before they were tied into bundles by the four men seated on the ground. They were then ready for shipment by mackinaw and steamboat to market. In front are the stacked bundles already pressed for shipment.

present, the charges were dismissed against both Lee and Clarke. Clarke returned to Fort Clay (Lewis) and Lee, "seeing the elephant," headed to the gold fields in California.

Harvey renewed his license and his small steamboat headed back up river with $45,000 in supplies. Sixty new men were aboard to trade for the opposition the next season.

Return Trip

Culbertson hurriedly finished his business in St. Louis and departed. His expertise in Company affairs necessitated several stops at other posts before he reached Fort Clay (Lewis) in October 1847.

Early in the winter of 1847, the ice broke up and tore the Company keelboat from its moorings. The men retrieved it and dragged it onto the bank for repairs. One night it caught fire and burned, an incident that Company men blamed on opposition employees. To replace it, a colossal mackinaw about 75 feet long was built that spring for transportation between Fort Lewis and Fort Union. The Company hoped to find another keelboat at Fort Union, but it was several years before that became a reality.

Forts on the Yellowstone

By late summer at Fort Union Culbertson had to press the colossus into service to take supplies and trade goods up river to the Blackfoot post. Larpenteur took the boat up river to Fort Clay (Lewis). After sending him on his way, Culbertson headed up the Yellowstone to the Crow post. Col. Alexander Redfield, Crow Indian Agent, asked that Culbertson accompanied by Robert Meldrum go up river to Fort Alexander to distribute the Crow annuities. Progress was slow and cordelling was hazardous. When a man drowned, the party became discouraged.

Artist Gustav Sohon

Kainaa warriors at Fort Benton with the American flag, chronicled by Gustav Sohon in 1855 when he was there for the treaty. The Kainaa or Bloods were the best buffalo hunters on the plains.

Redfield was sick and wanted to return to Fort Union. Culbertson sent Meldrum on to the fort and took the Indian Agent down river. After Redfield recovered, Culbertson took him overland by horse to Fort Alexander just below the mouth of the Bighorn River where they arrived in the middle of August 1847.

The Company maintained only one post on the Yellowstone to trade with the Crow. Their first was Fort Cass, 1832-1835, two miles below the mouth of the Bighorn. It was followed by Fort Van Buren (Fort Tullock), 1835-1841, located on the Bighorn River at the mouth of Rosebud Creek. Fort Alexander was

Artist David Parchen

Fort Alexander was built by Chouteau and Company on the north bank of the Yellowstone River in 1842. It was down stream from Fort Sarpy at the mouth of the Bighorn River.

built in 1842 by Charles Larpenteur and later operated by Robert Meldrum.

Fort and Boat Building

In late August Culbertson came to Fort Union, left Edwin Denig in charge and proceeded to Fort Clay (Lewis). When he arrived, he found that work had progressed as expected; James Kelly and his ten men had completed the construction. Culbertson explored the use of adobe in its reconstruction, replacing logs with adobe blocks.

Larpenteur had considerable difficulty getting the boats up river from Fort Union. The boats were overloaded with supplies and the strong, swift current of the upper river impeded their progress. The forty-day trip was perhaps due to river conditions or to Larpenteur's ineptitude.

Alexander Culbertson started his carpenter Rondin (Charles Mercier) on constructing a new keelboat, a project that continued until they ran into trouble trying to get the double curve in the bow planking. Rondin was unable to accomplish the task so the project was scrapped and the boat turned into a mackinaw. With the move to new sites by both companies, an entirely different situation was present during the last years of the Blackfoot Trade.

Text Notes

1. *Fort Pierre Letter Book 1845-46*. December 15, 1845, Culbertson to Picotte asking permission to name fort for him
2. *Fort Pierre Letter Book 1845-46*. March 12, 1846, Picotte to Culbertson
3. *Affairs at Fort Benton* by Lt. James Bradley. Reminisces with Alexander Culbertson when he returned to Fort Benton and was retired from the Company. Bradley was stationed in Fort Benton with the military. Dates are often a year or two off from those in Company records.

Harvey's Trading Post

1846 - 1847

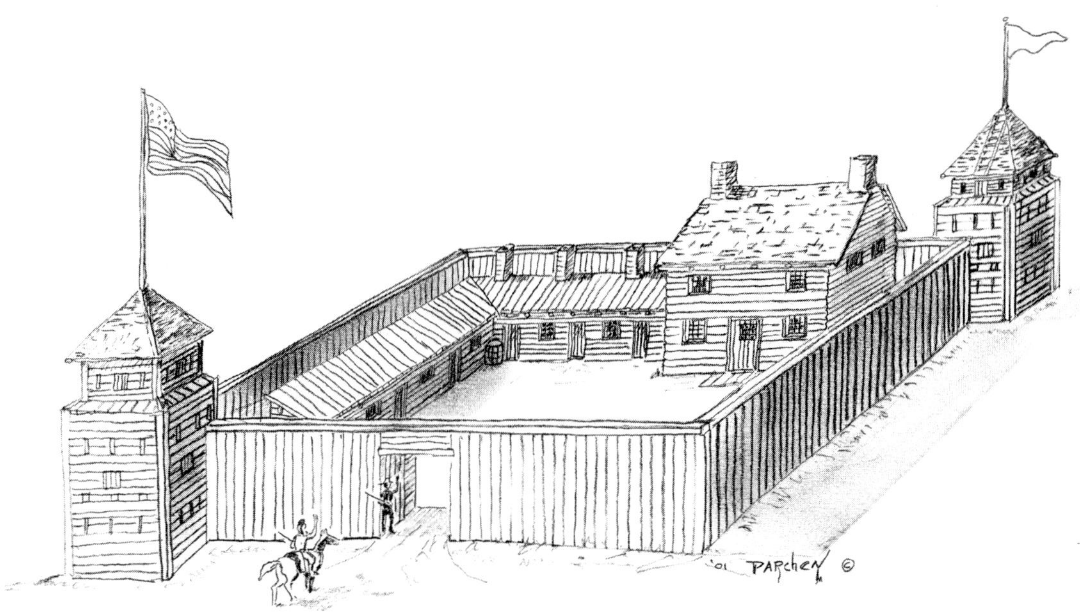

The opposition fort of Harvey, Primeau and Company built by Alexander Harvey. It was across from the Crocondunez on the south side of the Missouri River for just a single season.Harvey moved the post across and up the river to the same bottom as Fort Benton and renamed it Fort Campbell.

Part III

Fort Benton Trade

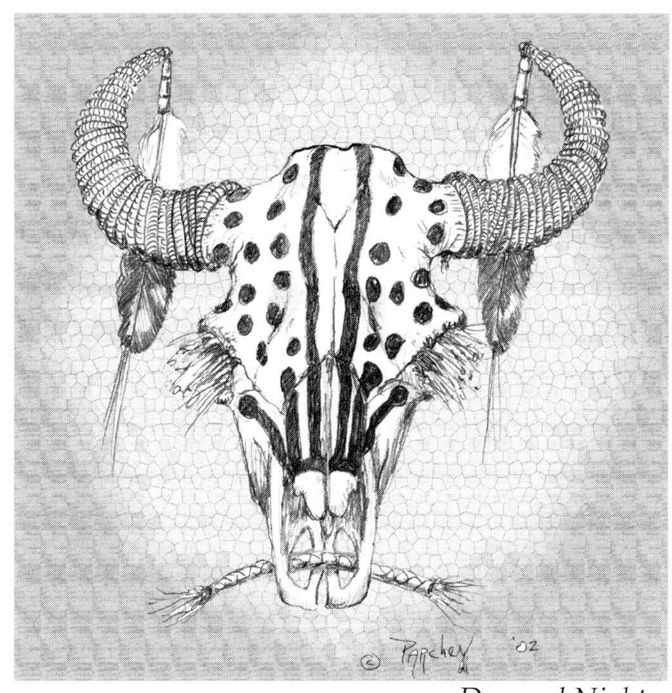

Day and Night

Fur Trade Chronology 1846-1870

Winter 1846: Harvey, Primeau and Co. established Harvey's Trading Post at Crocondunez on south bank. Fort William at mouth of Yellowstone and Fort Primeau opposite Fort Clark. Fr. Nicolas Point spent the winter at Fort Lewis; Culbertson returned in December.
Spring 1846: Culbertson took returns to Fort Union, burned Fort Chardon on the way and continued to St. Louis.
Fall 1846: Culbertson established new fort site for future Fort Benton. Fr. DeSmet and Fr. Point arrived at Fort Lewis; DeSmet went down river that fall. Harvey's Trading Post moved up river to same bottom as Chouteau and Company's fort and renamed Fort Campbell.

Spring 1847: Fr. Point went to St. Louis with Culbertson and the returns. Recorded on May 19 the demise of Fort Lewis when the last logs were floated to new site of Fort Clay (Benton).

1848: Culbertson became King of the Upper Missouri when he took over for the Company from Honore' Picotte.
Winter 1848: Culbertson spent the winter at Fort Clay (Benton) with his family.
Spring 1848: Culbertson took out returns from Fort Clay (Benton); Edwin T. Denig was the factor at Fort Union. Francis Chardon died at Fort Clark.
Fall 1848: Small outposts established away from fort to be closer to winter camps of the Blackfoot.

1850: Culbertson established Fort Sarpy on the Yellowstone River replacing Fort Alexander that was abandoned the year before.
December 1850: On Christmas Day at Fort Clay, the fort was officially renamed Fort Benton for Senator Thomas Hart Benton by Alexander Culbertson.
Spring 1850: Culbertson took returns to Fort Union.

Winter 1850-51: Culbertson spent the winter at Fort Pierre.

Fall 1851: Culbertson and DeSmet attended Laramie Treaty with Mandan, Hidatsa and Arikara. Culbertson returned to Fort Union.

1851-52: Artist Rudolph Kurz at Fort Union.

Spring 1853: Culbertson met Gov. Isaac I. Stevens in St Louis as emissary for Blackfoot.
Fall 1853: Gov. Stevens' Northern Railway Survey party arrived at Fort Benton with Culbertson. Signed an agreement (Little Dog) with Blackfoot for safe passage of government.

Spring 1854: Andrew Dawson came to Fort Benton as new factor. Clarke left Company to become independent trader.
Summer 1854: Alexander Harvey died at Fort William on July 20.
Winter 1854: Culbertson went to Washington on behalf of Stevens for the Blackfoot Treaty.

Fall 1855: Steven's treaty (Lame Bull) with Blackfoot at the mouth of Judith. Blackfoot Agency established at Fort Benton.

Fall 1856: Culbertson retired to Peoria, Illinois.

1857: Malcolm Clarke joined opposition company; name changed to Clarke, Primeau and Co.

1860: Opposition company dissolved and Fort Campbell turned over to the Company.

1861: Clarke rejoined Chouteau and Company.

1864: Andrew Dawson left upper river for his home in Scotland. Malcolm Clarke retired to ranching on the Little Prickly Pear.

Spring 1865: In May Chouteau and Co. sold out on the upper river to the Northwestern Fur Co.
Fall 1865: Fort Benton was site of Blackfoot and Atsina Treaty (Meagher) in November.

1866: Camp Cooke established, first U.S. military post in Montana.
Fall 1866: Sun River gold rush. Death of Little Dog. Piikani battle with Atsina and River Crow.
Winter 1866: John Morgan atrocities.

1867: Fort Shaw and Fort Ellis established.
Spring 1867: Meagher's million-dollar militia near Bozeman. John Bozeman killed.
Summer 1867: Gov. Thomas F. Meagher died in Fort Benton on July 1.

Fall 1868: Cullen Treaty, second Blackfoot Treaty in Fort Benton.

1869: Hudson Bay Co. turned over Rupert's Land to the Dominion of Canada. Northwest Fur Co. closed Fort Benton. U.S. Army came to Fort Benton. Blackfoot Agency moved from Fort Benton.
Spring 1869: A bankrupt Alexander Culbertson returned to Fort Benton.
Summer 1869: Malcolm Clarke killed at his ranch by Blackfoot in August.

1870: Last Blackfoot inter-tribal war with Cree and Assiniboine
Winter 1870: In January Col. Baker's command massacred Heavy Runner's band on Maria's River.

1871: Grant's new Indian policies. Loss of Blackfoot tribal sovereignty.

1878: Culbertson left the upper river for good to live at Orleans, Nebraska with his daughter Julia. Natawista returned to Blood Reserve in Canada.

1879: Alexander Culbertson died on August 27 in Orleans, Nebraska

1893: Natawista died on June 14 on the Blood Reserve.

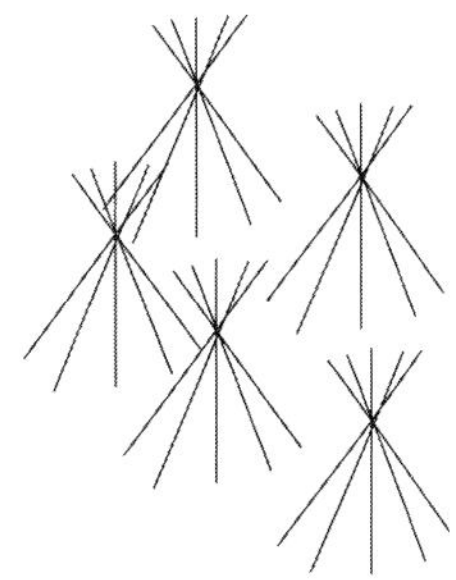

Fort Benton

1846 - 1865

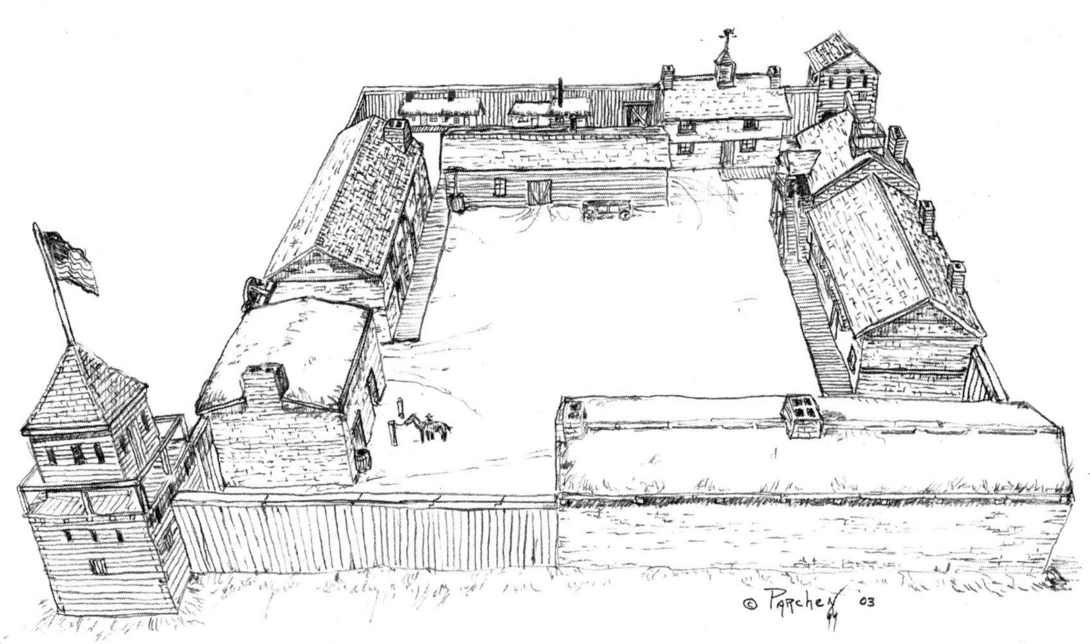

Fort Benton was established in late fall 1846; foundations were put in place before the spring move. Alexander Culbertson dismantled Fort Lewis on May 19, 1847 and floated the logs to the new site. The fort above is in transistion, before many buildings were replaced with adobe. It was officially named Fort Benton by Culbertson on Christmas Day 1850. Before that ceremony, it had been called Fort Lewis then Fort Clay.

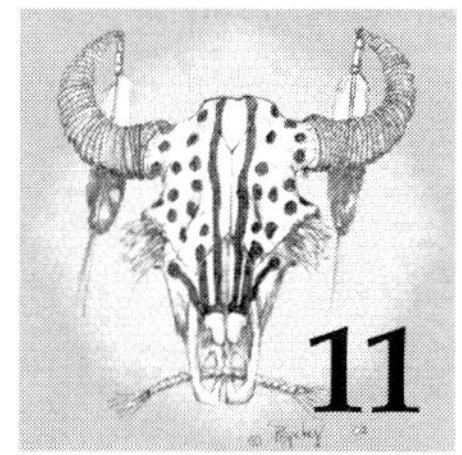

1846 - 1850

Last Blackfoot Post

Culbertson Years at Fort Benton

Fort Clay and a New Beginning

A New Star

With Culbertson' new post and excellent trade in Blackfoot Country, the next few years under the new "King of the Upper Missouri" were good ones for both the Company and the opposition. With frequent changes in fort sites, construction and names it is necessary to digress to make subsequent events more clear.

Establishment of Fort Benton

On May 19, 1847 Alexander Culbertson took the winter returns to Fort Union. He was accompanied by Fr. Nicolas Point, whose journal recorded on that date that the walls of Fort Lewis came down and were floated to the new site downstream.

Culbertson chose the new site in the fall of 1846. Construction of the fort on the bottom three miles down river and on the opposite side from Fort Lewis continued during Culbertson's long absence. This fort eventually became the premier trading post during the final years of the trade for the American Fur Company or the Upper Missouri Outfit, then officially Chouteau and Company.

After the move in 1847, the post was still called Fort Lewis then changed to Fort Clay. On Christmas Day in 1850, Alexander Culbertson officially christened it Fort Benton. (1) After the town was established and much serious discussion by the citizens, it also took the name of the fort. Some wanted to name it Benton City, others just plain Benton, but finally the majority decided there could be only one Fort Benton. In 1883 with official incorporation of city government, the town became Fort

Artist Karl Bodmer

The main reason for moving the fort in 1846-47 to the other side of the river was the perilous crossing during the winter. Ice floes discouraged the Indians to trade at the fort during that time of year.

Benton, saving the old fort's name. It is still the only town or city in the United States with that name.

The Woodcutters

During the early years of construction a party was sent out to cut logs in the Highwood Mountains. A group of six men was customarily sent to the mountains to cut logs to make sawed planks for the fort. They lived in a crude cabin while working in the mountains. Just when the men were ready to raft the logs down the river to the fort, they were attacked by a Blackfoot war party. Under siege for five days, with food gone and water running out, a brave Spaniard made several unsuccessful attempts to get water from the river. On one of his wild dashes, he shot an Indian and before others could attack, he got a bucket of water back to the cabin. The woodcutters soaked their moccasins in the water and ate them during the siege. After beating off several more attacks, one evening in a blinding rainstorm they slipped into the river. Each man hid beneath a log and managed to float down river and escape to the fort. (2)

Reconstruction

Before Alexander Culbertson left for Fort Union in the spring of 1847, he initiated reconstruction of the fort with dried earthen bricks. On his trips along the Platte, Culbertson had seen adobe buildings and decided to rebuild the fort in adobe. At Fort Laramie he noticed that adobe bricks were much more suitable than logs. Cooler in summer and warmer in winter, adobe also afforded greater protection from bullets and arrows and resisted fire and rot.

Winter 1847-1848

The 1847-48 winter was severe on the Upper Missouri; it was also a productive one for trade. The returns were even better than in the banner season of 1846-47. Harvey came up river to the Crocondunez and built an opposition post in 1846. When Fort Lewis was moved, Harvey almost immediately relocated his post up river to the same bottom. Harvey and Culbertson may have agreed to such a move for mutual protection much like Hudson Bay and the Nor'Westers did in Canada. By the fall of 1847 the two posts were located just a mile apart on the north bank of the Missouri.

Harvey's return in the late fall of 1847 was one of endurance; gale force winds and early snow hindered his journey from Fort Bouis. By the first week of November the river began to clog with ice, so he shifted his supplies from the keelboat to pack horses and finally arrived at Fort Campbell in early December. After a few days' rest he started back down river with three companions, another mid-winter trip through deep snow. Below the Yellowstone an Assiniboine war party robbed them of everything and left them stranded on the plains. Luckily, the Sioux and Mandan took mercy on them and gave them food and pack animals, which were of little use since the deep snow allowed only travel with snowshoes. After a long cold trip including several days without food, they reached Liberty, Missouri, boarded the steamboat *Bertrand* and arrived at St. Louis in March 1848. They told buyers in St. Louis that it was going to be another bountiful year for trade on the upper river. The national robe market was up, but there was little demand for beaver. Both Chouteau and Company and the opposition were financially prosperous as the year of 1847 ended.

New Winter Posts

With the opposition so close to Fort Clay (Lewis), Chouteau and Company wanted to assure a tighter monopoly on the trade. Under Culbertson's leadership, a system of outposts among the winter camps of the Blackfoot was developed. Because of their size and weight, buffalo hides and robes were difficult to handle and transport. During the winter months, the Indians were reluctant to leave their camps to trade their robes. After the fall hunt the bands of Blackfoot returned to the valleys of the Teton, Milk and Maria's Rivers to their winter camps.

Culbertson sent his traders from Fort Clay (Lewis) to set up seasonal trading posts near the winter camps. During the first

Schwinden Library, Fort Benton

Harvey's Trading Post was moved up river in 1847 to the same bottom as Fort Benton, which can be seen down river. Officially named Fort Campbell, the post challenged Chouteau and Company in the robe trade for several more years until Harvey's death.

Schwinden Library, Fort Benton

One of the temporary outposts built near the Blackfoot winter camps to make trading easier and to discourage contact with the opposition. They were usually manned by a trader and his family.

season, 1847-48, Augustin Hamell (Armell) and Malcolm Clarke built posts up Maria's River at Willow Rounds and Flatwood, which was thirty miles from Willow Rounds. Michel and Baptiste Champagne were dispatched to the Milk River Crossing to be closer to the Atsina trade.

The small outposts were operated by the trader with his Indian family, and usually were only a log building of two or three rooms. The small structure had room for robe storage and trade goods, and doubled as living quarters for the family. The posts provided no protection. Since Indians welcomed the trader, security was unnecessary particularly since the trader's Indian families lived there.

The system eliminated traveling long distances to Fort Benton in the cold and snowy Montana winter. During breaks in the weather, when chinooks hit the eastern slopes of the Rockies, the traders hauled the robes by wagon back to the fort. They remained in those lonely distant posts from October to March, when they returned to the fort. The posts were rebuilt frequently in different locations to provide easier access to the winter camps, which were almost never in the same location each year.

The outpost system worked only when hostilities had ceased and there was a better understanding between the traders and the Indians. The village inhabitants nearby helped guarantee protection of the traders, and their Indian wives and families were additional insurance against attack. It was a far cry from the early days when lone traders never ventured far from the walls of the fort and then only in large parties.

For security reasons, trade at the early posts was done through the wicket or between the main double gates; there was little trust on either side. Even in the first years of trade in Blackfoot Country, traders and Indians were reluctant to avenge indiscriminate killings. Neither wanted to disrupt the trade, so chiefs and bourgeois were regularly peacemakers on both sides of an uneasy truce which existed for the good of both cultures. Personal feuds remained personal; if a killing involved a white and an Indian, it was ignored by both sides.

During the winter, Culbertson traveled to the outlying areas to visit his friends. One was the camp of the Kainaa on Maria's River occupied by the band of his wife's people. His brother-in-law, Chief Seen From Afar, had a huge lodge constructed with 30 poles 35 feet long. The lodge contained two fires. (A normal lodge had 8 to 12 poles, was 15 to 25 feet long and was covered with 8 to 12 buffalo skins.) Seen From Afar was one of the greatest Blackfoot chiefs and had a strong influence over his people. He had ten wives and over 100 horses. Culbertson's connections to the chief through his wife Natawista were an added attribute to his trading prowess and increased his credibility with all of the Blackfoot tribes.

Schwinden Library, Fort Benton

Chief Seen From Afar of the Kainaa, brother of Natawista and a strong factor in Culbertson's success in the Blackfoot fur trade

A New King is Crowned

The winter was terrible on the upper river in 1847-48, but trade was the most prosperous. When spring approached, the trade goods were long gone; any other dispensable items and provisions had also been traded for furs and robes. Over 20,000 robes and many bundles of small furs were in the storerooms. With no trade goods left, Culbertson loaded the returns for an early trip in April when the ice went out. When he reached Fort Union, Culbertson learned that Chouteau and Company had once again reorganized. Honore' Picotte retired and Culbertson was appointed the Company's new Chief Agent on the upper river.

Before Culbertson left to meet the Company steamboat, he arranged for supplies to be taken up river by mackinaw under the care of Charles Larpenteur and his new partner James Bruguiere. Larpenteur, a free trader after he finished his one-year contract with the Company, was on his way up river to trade with the Salish. Larpenteur loaded his own supplies and Company goods into the large Company mackinaw. The overloaded boat against a heavy current extended the trip to 90 days. When Larpenteur arrived at Fort Clay (Lewis), Malcolm Clarke welcomed him, forgave the old feud and offered him horses to help in his new venture over the mountains. Never overly ambitious, Larpenteur made two or three futile attempts to set up trade that fall; none were successful. Disgruntled, he returned to spend the winter at Fort Clay (Lewis) with Clarke.

In the meantime, Culbertson hurried overland on horseback, stopping at Fort Berthold where he found that Francis A. Chardon had recently died. Culbertson took his body to Fort Pierre for burial. Just below

Schwinden Library, Fort Benton

Alexander Culbertson was the new agent in charge of the upper river in 1848.

Artist William Cary

Fort Berthold where Francis A. Chardon died; Culbertson took his body to Fort Pierre for burial.

Fort Pierre, he met the steamboat *Martha* and went up river with Indian Agent Gideon Matlock to distribute annuities. During the distribution, Culbertson, who was observing from the steamboat, was nearly shot in the head by a disgruntled Sioux. After that hair-raising experience, he resumed his trip to St. Louis to carry on the Company's business.

On his return that fall, Culbertson took a side excursion to his old post at Fort Laramie. As he traveled along the Platte River, he became ill and was delayed in Nebraska. By the time Culbertson arrived at Fort Union, winter had set in; his trip onward to Fort Clay (Lewis) was cold and through deep snow. Along the overland trip, he visited several outposts; near the Milk River he suffered a relapse and collapsed, forcing his return to Fort Union to spend the rest of the winter recuperating.

After a good season in the spring of 1849 Malcolm Clarke brought the returns to Fort Union. Culbertson had already left for Fort Pierre, where he spent the summer and fall before returning to the East. His new position allowed him time away from the upper river during the trading season and the opportunity to visit his family in Pennsylvania.

Malcolm Clarke, the acting agent in charge at Fort Clay (Lewis), had not seen his boss for over a year so in November he wrote him the following letter which provides an excellent picture of conditions at the post in 1849.

Schwinden Library, Fort Benton

Company boat Martha used by Culbertson on his river trips in 1848-49 and where he was almost shot by the Sioux.

A Status Report

Fort Benton 5 November 1849 (3)

Alex Culbertson Esq.
Fort Pierre
Dear Sir –

A voyage of 57 days (Including 5 days delay at Amelia Island to build a boat) brot our equipment safely to Fort Benton. Harvey who had the start of me some three days & no boat to build, running very light, arrived exactly the day before me. Am sorry to tell you that trade so far has been extremely dull. We have on hand only 50 packs. And have been living from hand to mouth since my arrival no buf (buffalo) to be found short of 6 or 7 days and

Schwinden Library, Fort Benton

Blackfoot encampment near Fort Benton where most bands spent the winter on Maria's River or the Teton River after the fall buffalo hunt

the Indians not having given us more than 1500 lbs. of food including everything eatable since the arrival of equipment. Nine of Harvey's men have left him from want of food. I furnished with a skiff to reach Ft Union expecting they might be needed in some of our lower posts. The majorities of our Indians are on this side and are encamped on or near the Marias and Teton Rivers. The past summer the Piegans met and traded with the Flatheads a row ensued and the Co. lost two good traders Vin Sefris to Cuz and L Enfant Pouis the younger the former I regret much. On my arrival found Old Depouis and Grand Daddy. Equipped them both gave the former horse and they started with the Collier J. E. Youfe the only blood Indian of which I have yet seen. Most of the Piegans and Gros Ventres have been in once. By the by E should your brother in law give his spotted horse up. I shall take him down in the boat. You never told me what to do with him. I understand our traders are among the buffalo but several days travel by horseback from us. If I can so arrange it without interfering with the trade shall endeavor to build a keelboat. Am burning coal and getting in fuel for the winter. David Martin is with the Indians but his place is well supplied. I have a good carpenter independent of Rondin. As soon as I can see the leading men of our traders I shall have a talk with them and unless circumstances are very adverse shall build one or more trading posts at the most suitable points. Old Monroe leaves for camp. Engaged to neither fort he has been living with me up to date. The season has been as (crossed out 2 misspelled words) singularly mild as it was severe the past year. Should buffalo be plentiful both forts will make a trade. Harvey has a nice assorted equipment. Our guns of this year you will see in my remarks in the requisition are faulty. The stocks being too straight, but every way superior to the last years article. Our colored blankets are the most indifferent and inferior.

However it is not to lament deficiency in general but to mainly inform you of our chances of opposition but we will try to do all for the best. At present I am pushed hard to find my people. The Indians have never heretofore been as backward to come in the distance and scarcity of buffalo in our neighborhood is the reason. A party of

Blackfoot returning home the other day have since learned that they broke some poor white mans leg at the Crow Post.
It is to be lamented that we are unable to put a stop to such outrages. You will see on requisition the same quantities of powder but more balls for the last two years. We have had on hand the former and deficient in the latter article. For plaid linsey I substitute bed tick and hickory stripe some suitable article in the place of backing would be also better as the above tho showy but soon loses color and the Indians are tiring of it. Hope I shall not be disappointed in requisition this winter both rose & yellow buttons
For the safety of the equipment I write for two cordels similar to those of 48 being somewhat stronger than those of 49 Coming up last summer we came near losing the boat on several occasions the cordel breaking at times in the worst parts of the river. In addition to the requisition for the trade you will see several articles to my order also to Armell Champaigne & Berger. If they are filled wholeful much obliged. You will see in my general requisition I am not guided by any expected deficiency of any article now on hand, it mainly is a specific caution of wants for the trade, should you own prefer to curtail or add to same. I hope you will so do. As it is impossible to form any accurate account of the returns of this post. Being totally ignorant of what goods will be remaining on hand next spring. I start 4 men with the accompanying papers tomorrow morning. Pascal and Vincent Dateau wish to keep on to St Louis, the latter deserted from me on the way up tho he was much insubordinate I took him back charging him 15c for his voluntary absence without leave. In conclusion the conversation we had on board the St(steam) boat Martha led me to suppose that you would not be with us the coming winter. I need not say that nothing would afford me greater satisfaction if your mind should have changed on that subject. Agreeably to your promises I shall go down with the boats. till I meet you next spring. Wish to visit the U States. Be kind enough to remember me to Mr. Hodgkiss and inform me of your latest commands.

Schwinden Library, Fort Benton

The reliable Malcolm Clarke, acting agent in charge at Fort Benton while Culbertson was down river on Company business

I am sir respectfully your obdt(obedient) servant and friend.

Mal (Malcolm) Clarke (4)

1850 Crow Posts

In early spring 1850 Alexander Culbertson returned to St. Louis from his winter in the East. His younger half-brother Thaddeus accompanied him from Pennsylvania. Thaddeus was a student who came to collect scientific specimens along the Upper Missouri. They proceeded overland from St. Joseph along the river to Fort Pierre, then traveled westward in March into the Badlands for three weeks of collecting. When

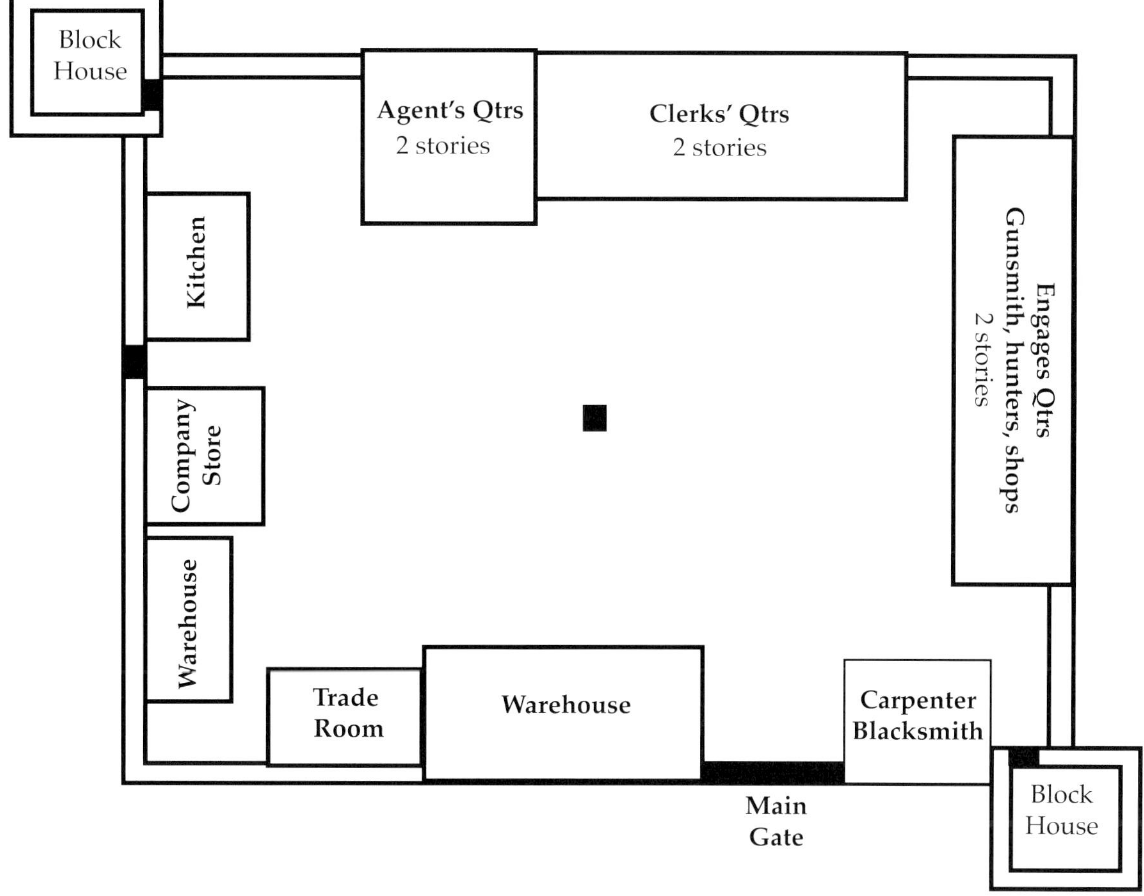

Plan by William Jackson, Indian scout whose father was the tailor at the fort before all of the buildings were reconstructed in adobe.

they then came back to the river, they boarded the steamboat *El Paso* to Fort Union where Culbertson met Malcolm Clarke who had come from Fort Clay (Lewis) with the returns.

Culbertson also received a report of conditions on the upper river. With high water the steamboat continued up the Missouri as far as the mouth of the Milk River, where they unloaded freight, trade goods and annuities that were carried by keelboat the rest of the way to Fort Clay (Lewis). Thaddeus, hating to leave his brother, returned to St. Louis in July 1850 and went on to Chambersburg where he died several months later from tuberculosis.

Before going to Fort Clay (Lewis), Culbertson went up the Yellowstone to five miles below the mouth of the Rosebud and established Fort Sarpy. It replaced Fort Alexander which had been abandoned the previous year. Robert Meldrum was left in charge of the new post which operated in Crow Country until 1855.

Schwinden Library, Fort Benton

Natawista, wife of Alexander Culbertson and one of the reasons he enjoyed such great success as a trader among the Blackfoot

Forts were difficult to maintain on the Yellowstone with constant war between the Blackfoot and the Crow, and the killing of Company men who lived with the Crow. Meldrum and many before him adapted to the Crow culture, often leading to mistaken identity by the Blackfoot when they attacked and killed traders. (5) The situation made it difficult to engage men to serve at the Yellowstone posts. Lack of personnel was the main reason that Fort Sarpy closed and Chouteau and Company left the Yellowstone. With free trappers gone, there was no competition and the Crow were forced to go to Fort Union to trade.

In earlier times the Crow were usually supplied by free traders who went to their camps in the summer to trade for furs. The traders returned as a group to Fort Union, similar to a rendezvous. At Fort Union fur bundles were sold to the Company; then the party began. After much gaiety and brawling, the traders returned to the mountains for another winter of trapping. Before they left the fort, they purchased a small stock of goods to barter with the Crow. In later years when the price of beaver declined, the free traders gradually disappeared from Yellowstone country. The Crow could trade only at the Company fort. Although irritated that there were no fur posts in their country, the Crow still made the long trek to Fort Union. They had become so accustomed to the white man's goods that they were not willing to live without them.

Furthermore, trade had changed from beaver to buffalo robes. The Crow were better trappers of beaver skins, but the Blackfoot provided far more and better-prepared robes to the traders. When the demand changed, Fort Benton became the premier fur post for Chouteau and Company among the predominant posts on the Upper Missouri.

During the last 15 years of the Company's existence, Fort Union was merely a transfer point on the upper river. Buffalo robe bundles came to Fort Union by mackinaw and were off-loaded to steamboats, a far safer and much faster mode of transport to St. Louis.

Another event in 1850 had a significant effect on the upper river. Young Charles Chouteau returned from three years' work in the Company offices in London, and started training to take over the Company from his father.

Culbertson went to Fort Union from Crow Country and by fall was headed back to the Blackfoot trade. Since he had not been home for over two years, he was glad to be there for Christmas in 1850.

Daily Life at the Post

The bourgeois or factor and the clerks formed the upper echelon in the hierarchy of a fur fort. With help from the clerks, the factor controlled salaries, prices, goods and charges. At meals they and their guests sat at the first table; in some forts they were served the best food in their own quarters inside the Bourgeois House. If available, wines and other delicacies were usually part of their meal. They also lived in the best quarters. In Fort Benton that was a two-story apartment with porches in front and a widow's walk on top. Next door on the second floor were the clerks' quarters with an outside walkway along the front. They were paid from $800 to $2000 annually based upon their years with the Company and a share of the profits according to the amount of stock they held in the Company.

Hunters and craftsmen ate at the second table in the Company mess where their fare was much poorer than the first table's. A hunter's annual salary was around $400; craftsmen such as blacksmiths and carpenters were paid from $200 to $250 a year. The men lived in communal quarters with their wives and children. They were somewhat better off than the engages and boatmen who drew $100 to $150 annually. They were at the bottom of the social ladder and literally ate from the pot, which was usually set in the center of the third table. The hot pot came off the stove usually filled with buffalo meat from poorer cuts that was boiled in a bouillon, and sometimes three or four days old. "It was everyone for himself." A pecking order probably existed with the bullies getting first choice. Their quarters were upstairs over the warehouse, usually unheated with an outside ladder up the wall to reach a bed of buffalo robes thrown on the floor. (6)

Most employees were constantly in debt to the Company with their purchases from the Company store. Liquor, a valuable trade item, was available to the employees only during celebrations and holidays. Items for sale in the store were expensive considering the men's wages. Coffee, sugar and soap sold for a dollar a pound, biscuits were seven for a dollar, and calico for shirts was a dollar a yard. Most employees usually ended the year with their wages entirely spent and in debt, so they signed on for another year. With no stake in the Company and little chance of promotion, engages and boatmen were not very efficient or enthusiastic, and avoided as much work as possible. The system was very loose; traders and clerks usually drank heavily so it was difficult to run a very efficient post, especially when the bourgeois was often absent on Company business or was drinking in his quarters.

Post life was dreary, routine and monotonous, a situation intensified by flies and mosquitoes in summer, fleas the year round, nagging Indian wives, and yelling half-breed children everywhere. Cholera and smallpox were just a breath away. Needless to say, it drove many a good man to drink. Drunken agents were the rule rather than the exception. When they failed their watch, the Company lost money through theft of merchandise, Company furnishings and livestock. A good

Schwinden Library, Fort Benton

Bourgeois House at Fort Union was the headquarters of the American Fur Company for many years. By 1850 it was only a transfer and loading site for steamboats.

sober man was hard to find after they spent a few long winters on the Upper Missouri. There were some who amassed a small fortune like Alexander Culbertson, who retired to a country house in Peoria, Illinois. (Unfortunately he was a generous man who mismanaged his fortune as a country gentleman; when he reached old age, he came back to the river penniless and lived the lonely life of a drunkard.)

Boats and the River

An early innovation at Fort Benton was the chantier or boat yard like the one at Fort Union, where artisans not only repaired Company boats but also constructed new ones in late winter. For years Rondin (Charles Mercier) was the head carpenter at Fort Benton. A second chantier was located 3 miles down river at the mouth of Shonkin Creek where wood was more plentiful.

The new craft, called a mackinaw, was usually 50 to 60 feet long and 20 feet wide with a flat bottom shaped to a point at each end. It had two compartments to hold the bundles of robes which were lashed down and covered for the trip down river. The boat had two seats amidships for four oarsmen. In the rear was a raised deck from which the sweep man operated the large square sweep used to guide the boat. The area under the deck served as quarters for passengers or shelter for the crew. The mackinaw was usually manned by five or six men. It was very susceptible to snags and sinking which resulted in total loss of the goods. Instability of the mackinaw was the major reason for steamboats to come to the upper river. Other boats manufactured in the chantiers were dugout canoes and square-ended flat-bottom barges.

The use of mackinaws continued into the gold rush period after Fort Benton was established as the head of steamboat navigation in 1860. Steamboats could not operate in the low water of late summer and fall. Miners returning to the States to avoid the dreaded cold weather of a Montana winter went by mackinaw and barge down river to catch a steamboat at a lower landing. (7)

As 1850 ended, prosperity lay ahead for the new fort of Chouteau and Company. It handled over a million robes during its trade years.

Schwinden Library, Fort Benton

Near the fort where a supply of logs was available, the boat builders had a chantier or boat yard. Mackinaws were built each year to take the returns to Fort Union. The chantier that served Fort Benton was at the mouth of Shonkin Creek down river from the fort.

FORT CAMPBELL 1860

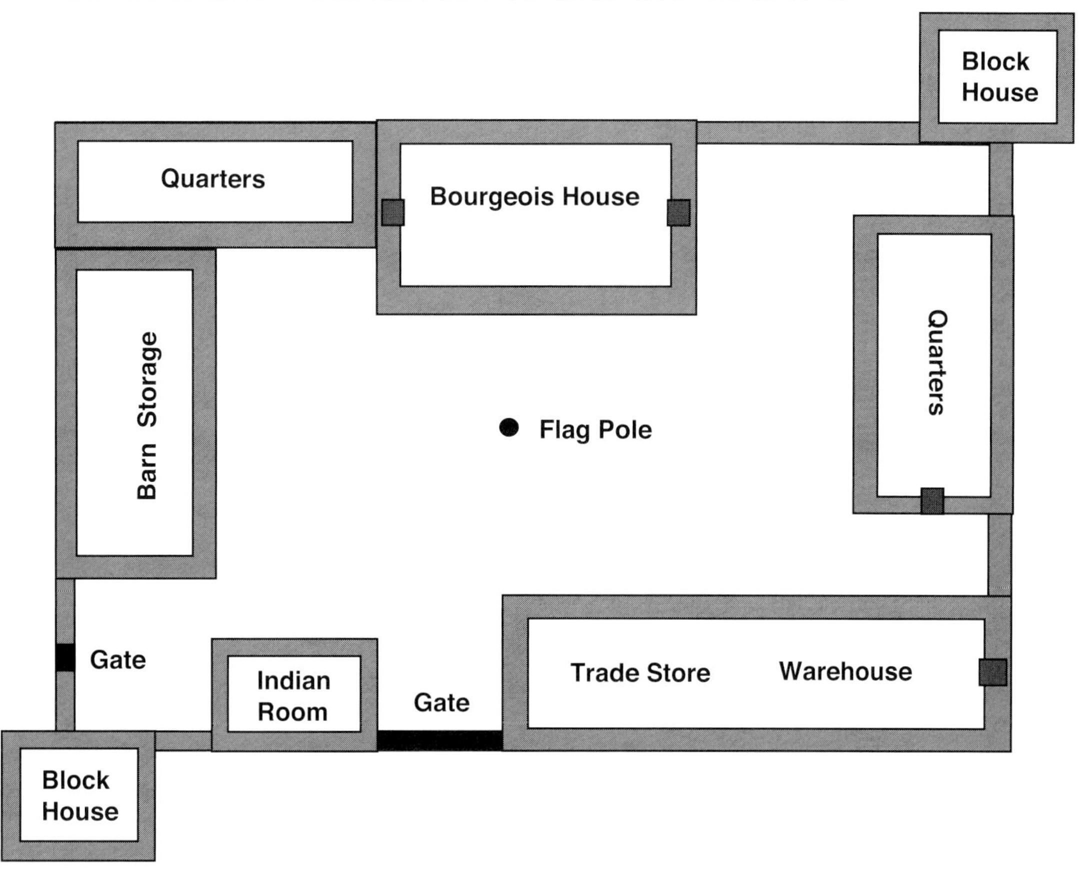

Fort Campbell was smaller than its counterpart Fort Benton. It also was rebuilt in adobe on the same floor plan that Harvey had seen during his years with the American Fur Company.

Text Notes

1. *Affairs at Fort Benton*, Lt. James Bradley, Volume III
2. *Not From Precious Metals Alone*
3. Notice in the heading, they were calling the new post on the upper river Fort Benton even before its official christening on Christmas Day 1850.
4. The hand-written letter is difficult to transcribe, particularly the names of employees. Where doubt exists, words are underlined. Misspellings and abbreviations are retained and some explanatory material is added in parenthesis.
5. The underlying reason was that the Blackfoot did not want their enemies the Crow to have a trading post in their territory; attacks on the traders drove them off and closed the post.
6. *Audubon Journals*, II, p. 185-190
7. *Montana Pioneer: Jirah Isham Allen* by Mary Ellen Phinney

Fort Campbell

1847 - 1859

Fort Campbell, the opposition post, was built a mile up river on the same bottom as Fort Benton and named for the St. Louis financier who backed Harvey, Primeau and Company, Robert Campbell. It was first built of logs from Harvey's Post down river but gradually converted to adobe buildings like Fort Benton.

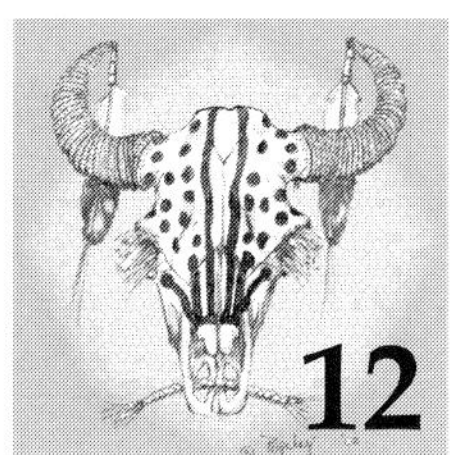

1850 - 1854

Built in Adobe

Culbertson and Clarke Years at Fort Benton

New Capital of the Fur Trade

A Christmas Party

Upon Culbertson's return in the fall of 1850, he began to rebuild his own quarters of adobe to provide Natawista with a better home, one more like what she had at Fort Union. The log building at the back of the fort was dismantled and construction of a new two-story Bourgeois House began. After two severe winters, the fall of 1850 was very open and warm as it sometimes is along the east slopes of the Rockies. During the long building season the engages' made bricks when they were not involved in trade. As the weather grew colder, the walls grew higher and higher. Before the house was finished in early December, the adobe started to freeze before it was dry, but it did not seem to weaken the walls. By the time the roof went on and the windows and doors were in place, it was almost Christmas.

Culbertson decided to celebrate the occasion by having a grand ball in the new quarters on Christmas night. To the music of several fiddles the voyageurs danced with their wives, their Indian sweethearts and with each other all night. When most were exhausted or had partaken too heavily of the spirits, Culbertson called a halt to the festivities for an important proclamation. He proposed that the fort be officially renamed for a good friend of the Company, Senator Thomas Hart

Artist David Parchen

Culbertson toasted the official naming of Fort Benton with Natawista, Seen From Afar, Malcolm Clarke and Alexander Harvey.

Beineke Library, Yale

Fort Benton in July 1860 before completion of the trade store in adobe. Not only was the fort completely reconstructed that year, but the year also heralded the arrival of the first steamboats and opening the Mullan Road, the first government road in the Northwest.

Benton, who had saved the Company from ruin by mitigating a suit against it in Congress. The announcement was received with wild acclimation and loud cheering by the entire assembly. Company records show that it was called Benton before this occasion so perhaps the partners had decided on the name long before the Christmas celebration.

Reconstruction

Directed by Malcolm Clarke and Andrew Dawson, the change from log to adobe continued over the next ten years. The last building was the trade store in 1860. J. M. Hutton took the earliest known photo of Fort Benton in July 1860. He was the photographer and topographer for Capt. William F. Raynolds Yellowstone Survey Expedition which visited the fort that year. Hutton's photo shows the entire front exposure from the river; the buildings are all finished except the trade store, which is missing above the wall in the southeast corner of the quadrangle. The photo shows that the old store had been removed, but no roof is present on the new one.

Records of the rebuilding are sketchy but the journals of 1854-56 regularly mention the making of "dobes," the brick used in reconstruction. The journals also mention construction of the kitchen and a bastion. When Culbertson returned in September 1852, the northeast side of the fort and a bastion were finished. The craft shops and engages' quarters, a two-story building holding four shops on the first floor and four apartments on the second had been rebuilt of adobe. That building had outside stairways and two double fireplaces on

Schwinden Library, Fort Benton

Skilled craftsmen worked as blacksmiths, carpenters and boat builders.Their shop was next to the main gate.

Schwinden Library, Fort Benton

Bourgeois House at Fort Benton with Indian rooms on the first floor and the clerks and interpreters quarters on the second level. The Bourgeois and his family lived in the quarters with the porch and widow's walk; the office of the agent-in-charge was below.

the center wall, both upstairs and downstairs, and a double hearth on one end wall.

Schwinden Library, Fort Benton

Charles Mercier, "Rondin," boat builder and carpenter at Fort Benton during most of the fur fort's existence.

Charles Mercier, who was at the fort during most of the rebuilding, said that one bastion was built in 1855-56 and the other in 1859. He confirmed that the trade store was the last to be built of adobe in 1860, substantiated by the 1860 photo, but leaving a question about the bastions.

Building notes from the Fort Benton Journals dated September 28, 1854 to November 20, 1856 mention several new buildings at the fort. On October 14, 1854 construction of the kitchen began; the walls were up by the Oct. 28 and the gabled ends finished by November 4. By December 8 the roof was finished. Other entries allude to putting down the floors and the finish work, with the last date December 20. In November 1855 work on the bastion began. The walls did not reach their 21-foot height until July of the next year. The roof was finished September 6, 1856 after which rebuilding the south wall began.

Throughout the period the journals mention the problems builders had with the wind, the biggest hazard. It got so strong that it blew down the pickets along the south wall, perhaps prompting construction of the new adobe wall in 1856. Which bastion was built first is a matter of conjecture. No reports clearly answer the question. Probably the one next to

Schwinden Library, Fort Benton

The warehouse and tradestore were along the front exposure of the fort. Quarters for single engages were above the warehouse portion of the building. The door opening into the wicket was on the front side and allowed the trader access to the store rather than through an opening in the main gate.

the river protecting the front gate was the first reconstructed blockhouse. (1)

Records indicate that the first adobe structure constructed was the Bourgeois Quarters in 1850. The warehouse, used to store robes and furs, was completed by December 1851, the engages' quarters by the fall of 1852 and the kitchen in 1854. Bastions were finished in 1852 or 1855-56, or even 1859. The southwest wall was done in 1856 and the last building, the trade store, in 1860. Sometime in that ten-year period the blacksmith-carpenter shop and the quarters for the trading room clerk and the interpreter's quarters were finished; no known record of the dates exists.

Animals at the Fort

In the spring of 1851 Culbertson left Fort Benton via Fort Union to Fort Pierre with 30 horses. Livestock at the forts were the forerunners of the livestock industry on the Northern Plains. An 1851 Fort Benton inventory listed horses, mules, cattle, oxen, pigs and even a cat. Cats were important since rats were aboard the Company boats and shared employees' quarters and food. One of the fort's journals listed the number of rats killed

Artist David Parchen

A valuable domestic animal, the cat was the nemesis of abundant rats that plagued all posts, coming in by boat and infesting the fort's food.

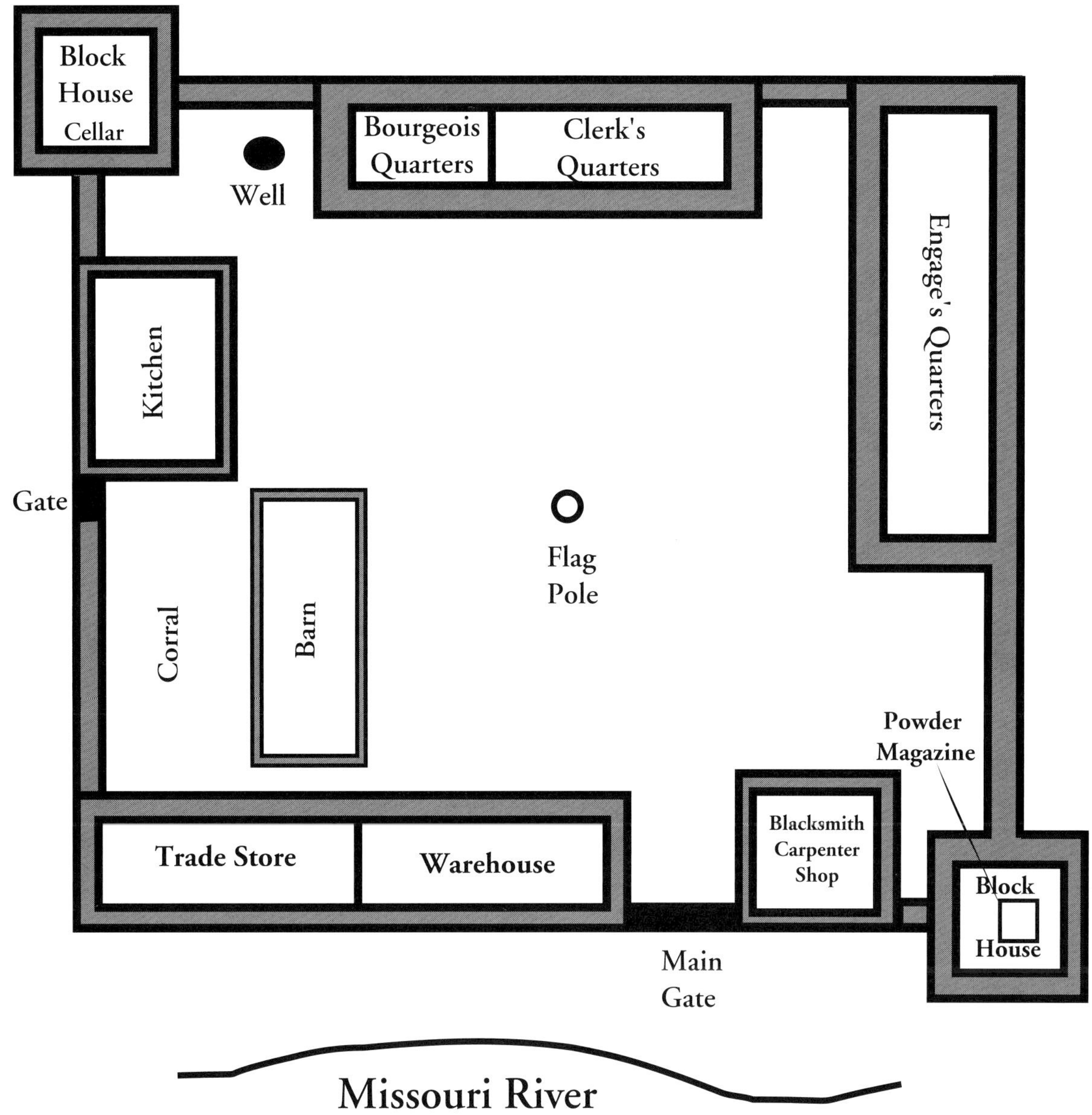

1855 floor plan of Fort Benton in the middle of reconstruction to adobe during the busiest years of the robe trade.

monthly. The hunting prowess of domestic cats definitely promoted a more comfortable life style at the fur posts.

Cholera

In 1851 at Fort Pierre Culbertson met Honore' Picotte, the retired Company official who had come up river to visit his old home post. They boarded a mackinaw and met the Company boat coming up from St. Louis. They reached St. Joseph early and decided to wait there for the boat's arrival. The *St. Ange* soon came into sight but completely ignored Culbertson and Picotte who were trying to hail them from the bank. Culbertson took

Schwinden Library, Fort Benton

The cholera boat that brought Fr. DeSmet up river and where Culbertson ministered to the sick on board; the water-borne disease did not spread to the Indian population.

after the steamboat on horseback and Picotte followed in a wagon with their supplies and belongings. Culbertson caught up with the boat about thirty miles upstream . . . and learned that the *St. Ange* had a cholera epidemic on board. Thirty people had died so they avoided the stop at St. Joseph. Fr. Pierre DeSmet, who was returning to his mountain missions, was on board ministering to the sick and dying. One of the dead was Fr. Hecken who was accompanying Fr. DeSmet. Picotte and Culbertson boarded the boat and cared for the sick as the outbreak infected passengers and crew; fortunately neither trader was stricken. By the time they reached Bellevue the disease had abated. Culbertson credited it to the "clean, fresh prairie air." During the winter smallpox again hit the Sioux and the bands scattered for protection, causing a great loss in the robe trade below the Big Bend.

Alexander Harvey and a few of his traders came to St. Louis in May and reported that after a mild winter the buffalo were so scarce that some of the Crow and Blackfoot were starving. The Missouri River above the Platte was so low that steamboat navigation was going to be very difficult. On July 1 in spite of the river condition, Harvey was aboard the steamboat *Robert Campbell* with 100 new employees and two hundred tons of freight. He boasted that they were headed to a landing above the Milk River and challenged the Company to follow.

Fort Laramie

After the *St. Ange* left Bellevue, a second outbreak of cholera was blamed by the uninformed on the liberal consumption of intoxicants while in port. Culbertson decided to travel overland from Bellevue to Fort Pierre. A rider caught up with him with a message from the U.S. Government Agent for Indian Affairs,

Schwinden Library, Fort Benton

Tribes gathering at Fort Laramie in 1851 for the first treaty with the Plains tribes and the federal government. Culbertson represented the Blackfoot; Mandan, Arikara, Hidatsa and Assiniboine chiefs signed the treaty that divided land in the west among the tribes.

David Mitchell. Culbertson was ordered to collect a delegation of chiefs from all the tribes on the Upper Missouri and bring them to a grand council in August at Fort Laramie.

It was too late for him to reach the Atsina and the Blackfoot, but he did find chiefs from thirty other tribes that were closer to Fort Pierre and Fort Union. The chiefs were Four Bear from the Hidatsa; Iron Bear, Arikara; White Wolf, Mandan; and Fool Bear, Assiniboine. Culbertson represented Blackfoot interests at the treaty. They left from Fort Union the first of July accompanied by Fr. DeSmet. Culbertson had two ambulances and two carts for their belongings. Most of the Indians walked but some rode horseback. They went up the Yellowstone to Fort Sarpy in hopes of finding the Crow. After several days no Crow had come to the fort so the group continued south. They found Robert Meldrum at the Tongue River and sent him back to get the Crow. Meldrum brought about 40 Crow to the council, arriving a few days after the Culbertson/DeSmet party.

Non-arrival of goods for gifts delayed the council at the mouth of Horse Creek east of Fort Laramie until September 1, 1851. The council continued for the next 18 days. All principal chiefs signed the treaty, which permitted construction of forts and roads for the passage of wagons and settlers along the Oregon Trail. Other parts of the agreement assigned each tribe a certain territory. The treaty included the Blackfoot and Atsina even though they were not present to agree to the provisions. The treaty also stated that the treaty signers would receive $50,000 in annuities for 50 years as long as they remained at peace.

Schwinden Library, Fort Benton

Fr. Pierre DeSmet, a Jesuit missionary to Indians of the Northwest

The Indians left the council happy, but it was the first of many treaties where annuities from the U.S. Government blinded the chiefs to the ultimate results of the agreement. All of the treaties ended badly for the Indians and good for the whites. The treaty at Horse Creek was the first step by the federal government in appropriating Indian lands, and led to reservation life for all tribes by the turn-of-the century. Culbertson found a wagon to carry the Assiniboine's goods and sent another trader with the other tribes to Fort Berthold. When Culbertson arrived at Fort Sarpy, he transferred the Assiniboine's belongings into a mackinaw and headed down the Yellowstone. Along the way a Blackfoot war party threatened the boat from the bluffs above the river but did not attack.

Schwinden Library, Fort Benton

Robert Meldrum, trader on both the Yellowstone and the Missouri for Chouteau and Co.

A New Road

Culbertson's party got to Fort Union the middle of October, and Culbertson soon left for Fort Benton. He set out in a wagon with five men, establishing the first wagon road across northern Montana. The route paralleled the north side of the Missouri to the Milk River, around the north side of the Bears Paw Mountains, south along Sandy Creek to Maria's River and into Fort Benton. The trip took about three weeks. The route established by Culbertson is part of the highway today. At Fort Benton Culbertson found affairs had been aptly handled by Clarke. Culbertson spent the winter with his family in his new cozy quarters. The

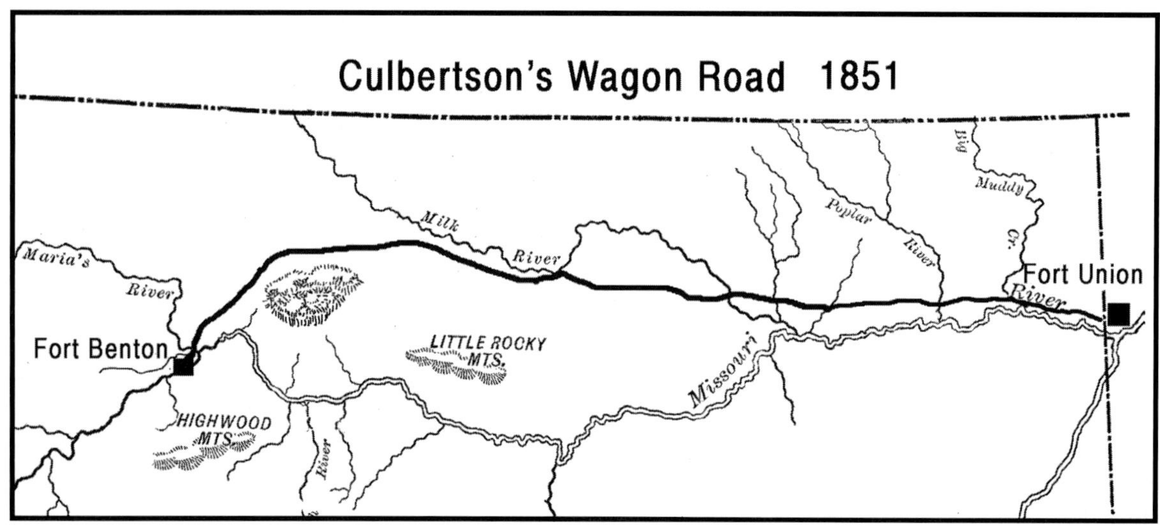

Schwinden Library, Fort Benton

Culbertson's road was along the north side of the Missouri to the Milk River Crossing, around the Bears Paw Mountains then south along Sandy Creek to the Marias and on into Fort Benton.

buffalo had returned so trading was brisk in the winter camps of the Blackfoot and the Atsina along the Teton, Maria's and Milk Rivers.

Culbertson Winters at the Fort

Trade produced great winter returns, so in May 1852 Culbertson loaded the mackinaws and took them to Fort Union where he spent the summer. Malcolm Clarke was left in charge; early rebuilding was under his direction and the success of the Chouteau and Company's summer and fall trade was in his hands. Like Culbertson, Clarke had a Blackfoot wife; she was Piikani and they had several children.

In the fall of 1852 Culbertson came back to Fort Benton overland by wagon and ambulance, accompanied by John Tevis who was a merchant from St. Louis. A friend of the Company, Tevis came to spend the winter at the fort. Culbertson again directed winter trading at the camps of the Atsina and Blackfoot bands. (2)

Northern Railway Survey

In February 1853 Culbertson was called down river; he went from Fort Benton by wagon to Fort Union. As soon as the river opened, he and Colin Campbell and their wives went by mackinaw to St. Louis where they arrived in early May. Culbertson was introduced to Isaac I. Stevens, newly-appointed Governor of the Washington Territory.

By the end of May returns from the upper river began to arrive at the St. Louis wharves. Four packets brought the early returns from the mackinaw fleet at Council Bluffs and St. Joseph. The *Highland Mary No. 1* arrived on June 8 with Alexander Harvey on board. He brought promising news of the up river trade that was contradictory to Culbertson's report.

Schwinden Library, Fort Benton

Newly-appointed Issac I. Stevens, Territorial Governor of Washington

However, Culbertson had left the upper river early when late winter trade had been excellent.

Harvey, backed by Robert Campbell, renewed his license and engaged the packet *St. Ange* for his up river trip. Leaving July 7, the *St. Ange* made a fast roundtrip. She delivered the opposition's goods to the mouth of the Yellowstone and was back in St. Louis on August 27 carrying 1300 packs of robes from the late winter trade.

Gov. Isaac I. Stevens organized a party to conduct the Northern Pacific Railway Survey as he journeyed to the Pacific to take over the Territory of Washington. His large contingent included surveyors, geologists, Army engineers and the artist John Mix Stanley. Stevens asked Culbertson to accompany his party through Blackfoot Country, from Fort Union to Fort Benton.

Lt. John Mullan, Culbertson, Lt. A.J. Donelson, Dr. John Evans and six men went by steamboat to Fort Union. Also aboard the steamer *Robert Campbell* were John B. Sarpy from the Company, John C. Tevis and Indian Agent Alfred J. Vaughan with $30,000 in Indian annuities. Gov. Stevens took the rest of his expedition up the Mississippi River to St. Paul where they started overland for Washington Territory. They stopped at Fort Abercrombie then crossed Minnesota and Dakota to Fort Union where they met the Culbertson party and proceeded along Culbertson's wagon route to Fort Benton. The group ran into two parties of Indians, one Blackfoot and the other Atsina; Stevens held a council with both. After smoking the pipe, he dispatched them peacefully with gifts. Culbertson observed that Stevens was a skilled negotiator and could handle the Indians as well as conduct the government's survey. At Milk River Crossing, Stevens dispatched Lt. Lander to explore the upper reaches of the Milk River Valley then meet him in Fort Benton. The rest of the party's trip to Fort Benton was accomplished without incident.

At Fort Benton Stevens was met by Lt. Saxton and forty men who had come overland from Fort Vancouver. Lt. Saxton had rounded the cape by sea, picked up supplies on the Columbia and carried them to Fort Owen in the Bitterroot before coming on to Fort Benton. Stevens purchased a Company keelboat for

Artist John Mix Stanley

Agent Alfred Vaughan with the Steven's party at Fort Union where he distributed annuities to the Assiniboines and waited for the rest of the Steven's party coming overland from Fort Abercrombie in Minnesota.

Artist John Mix Stanley

Stevens' survey party, with Alexander Culbertson along his wagon road to Fort Benton, counciled with the Blackfoot and with the Atsina. After smoking the pipe, gifts were exchanged and the party continued to Fort Benton.

Lt. Saxton and his company to return to the States. He appointed Alexander Culbertson as a Special Indian Agent to go with Lt. Saxton to St. Louis, then to Washington D.C. to lobby for an appropriation to facilitate a treaty with the Atsina and the Blackfoot. They left October 1, 1853, late in the season to be on the river in a mackinaw but did not encounter any ice on their trip to Fort Leavenworth. Culbertson proceeded to St. Louis on horseback and spent two weeks with the partners before heading to Washington D.C.

Lobbying Congress

Culbertson spent the entire winter of 1853-54 in the capital. When the original bill failed in Congress, his efforts finally secured its passage. $10,000 was appropriated for the treaty and for presents for the tribes. Culbertson returned to the river in the spring of 1854 accompanied by Andrew Dawson to take charge of Fort Benton. It was Dawson's first trip into Blackfoot Country. His appointment probably riled Malcolm Clarke who soon quit, became an independent trader then went to work for the opposition in 1857.

Stevens directed Culbertson to purchase $1,000 worth of goods for distribution to the Blackfoot and Atsina as an inducement to come to the treaty table. The selection of goods was left to Culbertson's discretion. He purchased mostly food - sugar, coffee, rice, flour - and some tobacco. Their share was given to the Piikani that fall when they were at the fort. Goods for the Atsina were taken to the Milk River area for distribution. The Atsina were not familiar with white man's food and not know how to prepare it. They ate too much at a time, became ill and a few even died. A free

Artist John Mix Stanley

Fort Benton in 1853, Fort Campbell is up river. Notice the wooden walls. Steven's Northern Railway Survey Party stopped in Fort Benton that year on their way to Washington Territory where Stevens would become governor.

Schwinden Library, Fort Benton

Andrew Dawson, new bourgeois at Fort Benton in 1854

trader tried to stir them into a reprisal, but their great respect for Culbertson allowed him to return peacefully to Fort Benton.

A New Bourgeois

Late in the fall of 1854 Alexander Culbertson and his wife Natawista went with three men to Fort Benton to supervise the Company's business and put Andrew Dawson in charge of the fort. (3) Culbertson staged a feast and a ball for the fort's personnel to which he also invited the opposition. Fort Benton produced the major part of the buffalo robe trade of the Company each year. The new King of the Upper Missouri spent much of his time in Fort Benton which had replaced Fort Union as the center of the Company's business. Affairs in St. Louis and on the lower river often took time away from his upper river home.

The largest concentration of buffalo left in the West was in the hunting grounds claimed by the Blackfoot, land which lay between the Missouri and the Yellowstone west of the

Musselshell. The Blackfoot jealously protected those hunting grounds, causing discontent among the western tribes which had been driven across the mountains. The Assiniboine, Sioux and Crow who invaded the area from the east and south were always at risk, fearing an attack by the "Terrible Blackfoot." The "Black Robes" and the Lame Bull Treaty of 1855 were the result of conflicts in the buffalo hunting grounds of Blackfoot Country.

Death Strikes the Opposition

In the summer of 1854 Alexander Harvey became ill at Fort Campbell and went down river to meet his partners. By the time he reached Fort William, the opposition post just down river from the mouth of the Yellowstone and Fort Union, he realized he was near death. On July 17 he wrote his last will and testament, making Robert Campbell the executor of his estate. Three days later Harvey was dead. A 47-year-old St. Louis native, Harvey had led an active life as an Upper Missouri River trader for 20 years, most of it with the Blackfoot and the Atsina. St. Louis newspapers reported his death, saying that he was the senior partner of Harvey, Primeau and Company, a very successful trader, and a man of firmness, honesty and courage. They noted that he was extremely popular with the Indians who regarded him with respect and esteem. A testament to the accolade was how deeply his opposition company had cut into the profits of Chouteau and Company. One paper ended the obituary, ". . . upon his gravestone may be fitly inscribed the epitaph, 'Here lies a brave, and honest, and kind-hearted man.' "

The will of Alexander Harvey, written as he lay dying on board a keelboat, was addressed to his financier Robert Campbell.

Traders like Sandoval, Clarke, Lee and Berger might take issue with Harvey's being "kind-hearted," but he did take good care of his Indian wife and family. He also adopted young Jerry Potts after the boy's father was killed at Fort MacKenzie in 1840. In his will, Harvey provided for two daughters by his Piikani wife; they were educated in the East. There are some final comments about the man who, next to Culbertson, was the best trader on the upper river.

It is difficult to analyze his relationship with Culbertson, since Harvey is never mentioned in Culbertson's correspondence. Evidently their friendship lasted through several strained situations. Even after Harvey joined the opposition and the two were separated only by the mile between the forts, they visited back and forth and invited each other to social events. Building both forts in adobe was probably a collaboration. Culbertson's vouchers for future services and Harvey's reassignment rather than dismissal are other indications of their friendship. Chouteau's effort in 1857 to combine the two companies also acknowledges his ability as a trader, and attests to the appropriateness of the words of the Missouri Republican on September 20, 1854: ". . . his proverbial honesty and kindness to the Indians, secured for him a degree of confidence, which has rarely been accorded to any man. The Indians loved him and his influence over them was unbounded."

Decline of the Opposition

The opposition was cutting deeply into Company profits. In the winter of 1848 Pierre Chouteau approached Harvey and Campbell about merging the two companies. The opposition declined, thinking trade could only get better for them, and they would have their revenge. Chouteau gradually got the better of them, but it was not until Harvey's sudden death that the tables really turned in Chouteau's favor. With Harvey gone, the opposition's business became disorganized. Harvey's aggressive trade policies at Fort Campbell had forced Chouteau and Company into higher expenses and reduced profits. The cost of robes was also increasing. The Company began to look for ways to put the opposition out of business.

The opposition's demise did not occur until after Harvey's death when the partners began to quarrel among themselves. Robert Campbell urged the surviving partners to reorganize as J. Picotte & Co., but after two seasons they called it quits. Campbell, unwilling to give up, formed a new partnership with Frost, Todd & Company. The firm struggled for three seasons; in the fall of 1859 they gave up and transferred their up river posts to Charles Primeau and his new partner, none other than Malcolm Clarke. After only one season Campbell realized that the new group would not be successful against Chouteau and Co., withdrew his financial support and the opposition folded. Campbell limped off licking his wounds. He never was able to best his nemesis, Pierre Chouteau Jr. With no funds, the two remaining partners sold the up river forts and went to work again for the Company.

Once the opposition was eliminated, concessions to the Indians stopped and it became a trader's market rather than one favoring the Indians. When one company went under another sprang up, financed by rival St. Louis businesses usually masterminded by Robert Campbell. With his seemingly limitless fortune, he bankrolled many ventures but always ended up with a broken company. His hatred of the Company must have been very deep for him to finance so many companies to oppose the American Fur Company, the Upper Missouri Outfit and Chouteau and Company.

Artist Gustav Sohon

After Harvey's death, Alexander Culbertson and Chouteau and Company dominated the robe trade on the Upper Missouri.

Malcolm Clarke had been a clerk at Fort Benton and was usually left in charge when Culbertson left for Company business at other posts. After Harvey's death and his demotion at Fort Benton, Clarke became a free trader. In 1859 the opposition engaged Clarke as a partner with Charles Primeau and Company. The name was changed to Clarke, Primeau and Company. After a single season followed by lack of funding, Chouteau interests took over. Clarke's ability as a trader and respect from the Indians were not nearly as great as Harvey's. The results of his leadership may have led the Company to bring in Andrew Dawson as the new factor at Fort Benton.

Schwinden Library, Fort Benton

The new adobe kitchen was the common mess for all the fort's personnel. Note the buffalo weather vane on the cupola.

Life at the Fort in 1854

In the fall of 1854 fort personnel were busy with reconstruction, trade and preparing for winter. The journals mention the routine tasks and difficulties making "dobbies." Despite the cold and rainy weather, by October 13 they had produced enough "dobbies" to build the kitchen; Dawson put all hands into its construction. Work progressed rapidly. They had the walls up by early November, the roof on and the floors laid by mid-December. Then they put away their tools for the winter.

There were almost daily comings and goings of parties doing a variety of tasks throughout the fall. Men and wagons were sent to the Highwood Mountains to cut logs for timbers, planks and shingles, to build mackinaws and most importantly as firewood for winter. Other wagons went to the Teton for firewood, lime and charcoal. Hunting parties brought in meat by the wagonload to be dried for consumption during the long Montana winter.

Winter Trading

Other parties went out to establish winter trading posts among the Blackfoot winter camps. Competent and trusted traders of the Company manned those outlying posts. The two Champagne brothers, Baptist and Michel, and Hugh Monroe spoke Blackfoot and had Piikani wives so they were assigned posts near the Piikani and Kainaa camps. Little Gray Head, a Piikani Chief who felt neglected, came to the fort and demanded a post near his camp. In response James Bird, the interpreter, set up a post provisioned with two four-mule wagons loaded with supplies.

Jacques Bercier (Jacob Berger) came from a short trade across the mountains with the Flatheads, bringing gold and beaver pelts. As soon as he could be resupplied, he returned to the Flatheads. A disappointed Dawson ended this trade abruptly when he acquired only 17 horses. Louis Rivet (Revais) came back from a 40-day hunt and was immediately sent out with a trading party to rebuild the Milk River post and get ready to trade with the Atsina who wintered along the river.

Artist David Parchen

Michel Champagne

Artist David Parchen

Baptist Champagne

The two brothers were trusted traders for the Company and worked at Blackfoot outposts during the winter trade.

Artist Gustav Sohon

Little Gray Head, Piikani Chief, wintered near Fort Benton to trade.

Under the direction of Culbertson and Dawson, the trade progressed smoothly. When word was received in the villages that Culbertson had returned, many of his Indian friends came to visit. Among the first was Little Dog, a cousin of Natawista's who was a Piikani chief and a great friend of the white traders. Chief Little Dog and his large band were very protective and loyal friends of the whites at Fort Benton. Other bands were exceedingly jealous of the relationship which later led to the death of Little Dog at the hands of his own people.

Culbertson visited various camps to renew friendships and to encourage the Blackfoot to continue their trade with the Upper Missouri Outfit. Their travels gave Natawista a chance to visit her people and maintain the ties which remained until her death. Small parties of natives came to the fort for two or three days to visit and trade. Some were war parties headed into buffalo country and the territory of their enemies, the Crow and the Sioux.

One of those parties found themselves on foot on the wrong side of the river. They borrowed horses from the fort's herd which was pastured down river, crossed the river then turned the horses loose before coming to the fort. Under the care of Alexander Rose and two other men, the herd had been brought in during early September to be checked and shod. They were then moved across and down the river to better pasture for the fall and winter. Later in 1854 the herd got too large to manage so Pierre Cadotte (Cadot) took 31 horses to Fort Union.

By the mid-1850's the Company had built and maintained a small fleet of wagons and livestock. Not only were the wagons vital for robe transport, they also hauled hay, adobe, wood for fires, and lumber for planking, buildings and mackinaws. Culbertson's new road up the Milk River made travel easier and faster between Fort Union and Fort Benton with lightly loaded wagons than going by water. The Missouri often remained frozen during the winter months. With wagons, communication between the two forts was possible all winter.

Schwinden Library, Fort Benton

Chief Little Dog of the Piikani controlled one of the largest bands of Blackfoot, the Little Robes, and was always a good friend of the traders.

Schwinden Library, Fort Benton

Fort Benton in the 1860's after it had been rebuilt of adobe. The remaining original blockhouse is in the foreground of the lithograph.

Wagons on the Plains

The number of wagons on the move that fall was astounding. Several four-yoke oxen wagons hauled logs and timbers from the Highwood Mountains. Each trading party had two or more wagons to haul supplies to their outposts. Wagons brought in firewood and meat from the hunters. The fort had at least two or three dozen wagons rolling all fall and winter. The number of mules and oxen to pull the wagons ranged between fifty and a hundred in addition to the horse herd. It was difficult to feed so many animals if the snow got too deep for grazing. Fortunately, that rarely occurred in this part of Montana with its open winters and chinook winds. Though large, the barn at the fort could not hold that many animals. The open range was the only alternative. Herders were absolutely necessary to prevent thievery. Carpenters and blacksmiths were kept busy the year round, not only with repairs but also building new wagons, carts and mackinaws.

Dawson wrote that Sunday, November 19, 1854 was the busiest day he had ever seen at the fort. As winter neared, the firewood and meat details increased in intensity. George Weippert, one of the fort's best hunters, returned after 20 days with two fully-loaded wagons of meat. During November wagons with robes came in from the outlying posts and the warehouse was filled with the returns. When ice formed on the river, the two boats were slid up on the bank until spring. Dawson reported that in December 1854 not much was going on; the fort was empty with all of the trading parties out. The journal reported that every few days throughout December wagons came in loaded with robes and returned to the post for more supplies. Early in December a wild wind struck and blew down the wood pickets along the entire southwest wall. The next days were spent putting them all back up.

Winter of 1854-55

The bands were waiting at the fort for the return of Alexander Culbertson and refused to trade until he arrived. When he was two days overdue, the fort received word to bring him three mules. His horses had been stolen while he was visiting the Indian camps. Culbertson's party along with several Indian friends finally got to the fort four or five days later. During those cold blustery days an old friend, White Calf, and a few braves came in to get warm and to trade. Word came from Michel Champagne that his camp had only a few robes left to trade, so no new supplies were sent to him. He finished his trading and returned to the fort.

During the last months of his contract, Malcolm Clarke came from Fort Union and returned a few days later with three men and 36 horses. The fort was hit by an early winter blizzard with strong winds that even shook the thick adobe walls. Again they lost all the pickets along the southwest side of the fort. The next day, December 29, was calm and clear and the temperature dropped to 5 degrees below zero. Even at that temperature a large party of Indians arrived to trade. As it got colder during the next few days, trade continued. When it became apparent that the Indians were more interested in a warm place to stay, the traders made every effort to get rid of them. Snow fell, it got even colder and they were running out of firewood. The Piikani found a lost trader who had frozen hands and arms and brought him to the fort. Wagons sent out for firewood returned empty because of the depth of the snow. A chinook finally broke the cold spell. After Christmas the Culbertson family went to Fort Union. The New Year was ushered in at Fort Benton with parties, but everyone readied themselves for more cold mid-winter days.

Schwinden Library, Fort Benton

Remains of the trade: broken-down wagons and the crumbling adobe fort

Text Notes

1. Culbertson told Bradley that when he came in 1852 the whole northeast side of the fort had been completed in adobe which would include this bastion. He also stated that the bastions had been built up one story. The journals agree with Mercier, one bastion was built in 1855 and finished in 1856, but never say which one. Mercier said it was the north bastion and that the one built in 1859 was the east one. Since directions are not precise, the construction dates of the bastions are still obscure.
2. John C. Tevis was a businessman from St. Louis who went up river for his health. His arrival at Fort Benton in September 1852 is erroneously reported, or he may have been up river on two different trips. Bradley reported the date to be during the winter of 1852-53. This is also the first mention of Tevis by Sunder.
3. The journals published in the Montana Historical Society Contributions start on September 28, 1854. They mention the arrival of Culbertson and three men on this date. It is also the first date of the journal and probably signals the take over by Andrew Dawson. On December 26,1854 the journal says that Culbertson and his wife with Mr. Tevis started for Fort Union. Dawson's day-by-day journal chronicles events at Fort Benton for the next two years, giving a clear picture of what occurred each day at the Blackfoot post.

Fort Benton

1846 - 1869

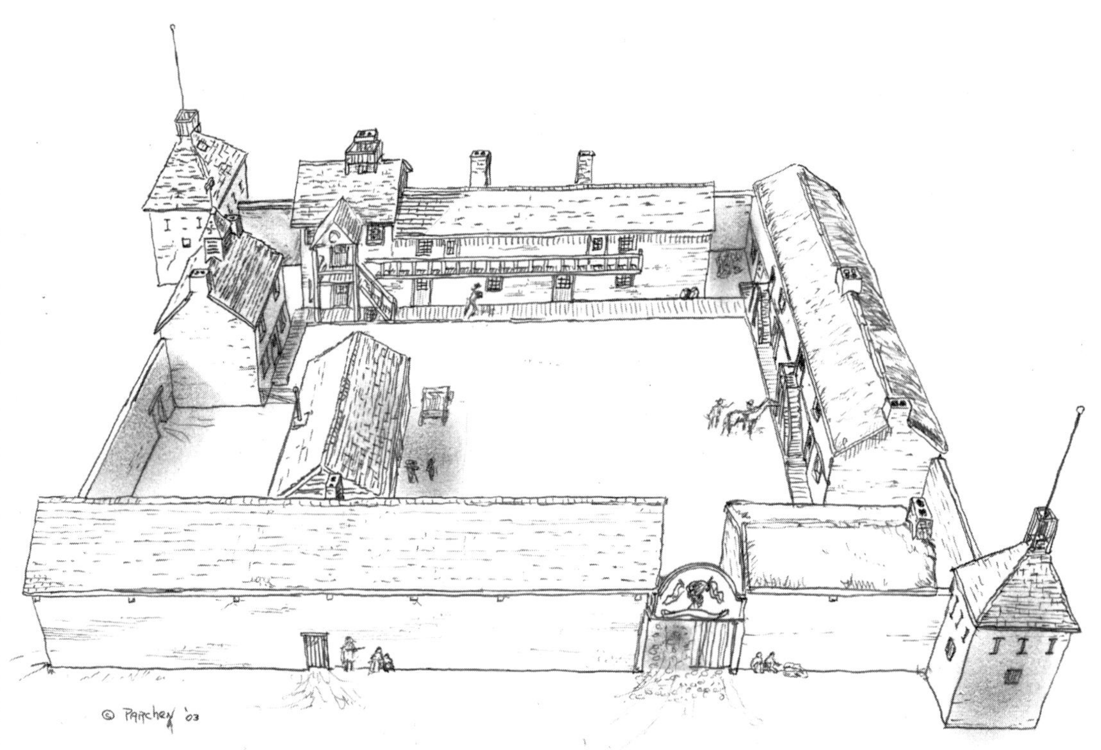

Between the years of 1847 and 1860 Fort Benton was gradually rebuilt of adobe. The trade store was the last building to be completed in 1860. The barn was the single log structure left..

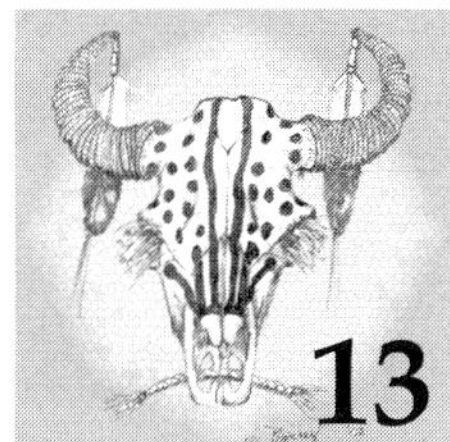

13

1854 - 1860

Robes by the Thousands

The Dawson Years at Fort Benton

Peace and a Great Trade

Winter Montana Style

The New Year of 1855 was celebrated with a feast as trade continued. Fort Campbell, the opposition fort up river, apparently was doing as well as Fort Benton. January was snowy and bitterly cold. When the chinooks blew in, they brought melting snow so trade and work went on. During one cold spell, the Indians found a frozen man coming from one of the outposts and brought him to the fort. He recovered but lost some of his toes and fingers. The temperature dropped to 26 degrees below zero; the snow was so deep that wagon travel was almost prohibitive. Trading and movement of parties in and out of the fort was impossible for several days.

A wagon loaded with robes was abandoned at the edge of Maria's River; it was frozen so deeply into the ice that it could not be retrieved and the oxen were released to wander in the deep snow. When the temperature warmed with the chinook winds, the abandoned wagon was freed, the oxen were found nearby and brought into the fort. Despite nine disabled men, most with frostbite, when the weather improved, work and trading resumed. Platform sawing began in anticipation of spring. More planks were needed for building mackinaw boats for the spring returns.

One of the men sent to the outpost for the Little Robes band to fetch horses returned without them saying he ran into a party of Crow who shot him in the thigh. Dawson suspected that the wound was self-inflicted so the man could return to the safety of the fort.

As winter dragged into February, snow, cold and tension returned. They first ran out of meat, then wood became so scarce that some of the rooms went unheated. Everyone was thankful that the Indians were also huddled around their fires so none came to the fort.

Like many a Montana winter, it warmed

Schwinden Library, Fort Benton

The Company leased the St. Mary. She was built in 1855 and made her maiden voyage to Fort Union that year. The St. Mary brought the treaty party, annuities and gifts for the council at the Judith.

up several days later, the ice jam on the river broke up and flooding was avoided when the river ran free. Several engages were still sick, or pretending to be, so work had slowed almost to a standstill. By March when the season ended, a few Indian trading parties returned their allegiance to the fort by trading with Dawson who was offering a better price than the opposition.

After Christmas Culbertson spent the winter at Fort Union then went to St. Louis where he arrived on May 18, 1855. Along with returns from up river came the news of Indian unrest. Traders told the press that the Crow and Blackfoot had fought each other all winter long, and that the Sioux had attacked a party of traders between Fort Union and Fort Sarpy. The party was left with two wounded and were robbed of all gear including clothing. It was a freezing, quick trip back to Fort Sarpy for those traders.

With Harvey dead, the spring of 1855 saw a change in the opposition strategy in St. Louis. The number of traders was cut to fourteen and the goods were sent overland by mule rather than up river by packet. The death of Harvey was already affecting the company.

The Treaty Party

The Company hired the packet *St. Mary,* in the capable hands of Captain Joseph LaBarge, for the up river trip. Culbertson accompanied the Superintendent of Indian Affairs, Alfred Cummings, up river for the treaty council of 1855. Along with Gov. Isaac Stevens, he had been appointed as a commissioner to negotiate the Blackfoot Treaty. Thanks to Culbertson, Chouteau and Company supplied presents and annuities for the Indians and he was responsible for transporting them to the treaty site. The *St. Mary* brought Charles Chouteau, Culbertson, Cummings and two Indian Agents - Alfred J. Vaughan for the Upper Missouri and Edwin A. C. Hatch for the Blackfoot – up the river. When the steamboat reached Fort Union on July 17, the goods and treaty party were transferred to two keelboats. Agent Hatch was in charge of the treaty goods for the slow trip to Fort Benton. The keelboats under the command of Andrew Dawson were piloted by Michel Champagne and Paul Polach. Alfred Vaughan stayed at Fort Union to distribute annuities to the tribes there and to the Crow on the Yellowstone.

Overland Trip

At Fort Union, Culbertson convinced Cummings that he would be more comfortable and would arrive more quickly at Fort Benton if he transferred to an ambulance and

Schwinden Library, Fort Benton

Fort Union passed the power of the Company up the river to Fort Benton.

completed the trip overland. The over-weight and pompous Cummings delayed the trip, complaining about almost everything and slowing their travel at every turn in the road.

In the meantime, Governor Isaac Stevens arrived in Fort Benton on July 26 after consulting with the western tribes along the way. Growing impatient, he traveled up the Culbertson Road toward Fort Union and found Cumming's party on August 15 camped at the Milk River Crossing. They had been camped there for two days so Cummings could rest. One probably could not have found two people with any larger egos than those of the two appointed commissioners. From the very beginning, arrangements could not have been worse. Both wanted to be number one and to call all the shots. Because of Cumming's position as Superintendent of Indian Affairs, Stevens reluctantly yielded to him but took issue with him every step of the way. By the time Culbertson got them to Fort Benton, they were barely speaking. The animosity was so great that when Cummings chose to reside

Artist Gustav Sohon

Superintendent of Indian Affairs Alfred Cummings brought gifts up river then went to Fort Benton over Culbertson's new road.

Schwinden Library, Fort Benton

Distributing government annuities to the Atsina along the Milk River with Agent Alfred Vaughan in charge.

in the fort, Stevens refused to stay there and camped in a tent outside the walls. The goods had not arrived and the impatient Indians were ready to leave on the fall hunt.

Leaving the two problem children at Fort Benton, Culbertson went down river to find the boats. The river was extremely low and their progress slow. Culbertson got back to Fort Benton on September 10 and convinced the two prima donnas to move the treaty site to the mouth of the Judith River. They needed to get started because they were losing Indians daily to the hunt. Finally, on October 16, 1855 the first treaty negotiations began between the U.S. government and the Blackfoot and the Atsina. The council grounds were in a grove of cottonwoods about three miles below the mouth of the Judith on the north side of the Missouri. A young artist Gustav Sohon drew excellent portraits of both whites and Indians. His detailed sketch of the council site preserved the event for posterity. Sohon's work depicts the participants in concentric arcs around a canvas shelter reserved for the treaty commission.

Schwinden Library, Fort Benton

Isaac I. Stevens, Governor of Washington Territory and Indian Commissioner, came in 1855 to negotiate the treaty with the Blackfoot.

The Lame Bull Treaty 1855

The Great Council was an attempt to establish peaceful relations between the Blackfoot Confederacy and the western tribes - Nez Perce, Salish, Pend d'Oreille and Kootenai - who had come out on the plains into Blackfoot Country for years to hunt buffalo. They were always harassed and driven back into the mountains by the Blackfoot.

Schwinden Library, Fort Benton

Blackfoot hunting buffalo in the Sweetgrass Hills. The major problem addressed by the treaty was allowing western tribes to hunt in Blackfoot Country.

In 1840 the tribes appealed to the Jesuits for their "Sacred Medicine" to help them in those encounters with the Blackfoot. In 1841 the Jesuits established St. Mary's Mission in the Bitterroot Valley, in what was eventually western Montana. The Jesuits also tried to Christianize the Blackfoot but had little success until after 1870. Their program with western tribes met with questionable success and the mission was closed in 1848. When Steven's Northern Railway Survey Expedition arrived in western Montana in 1853, he too heard of the troubles in meetings and councils with the western tribes he held along the route. It was hoped that the treaty would bring the tribes west of the mountains to a council with the Blackfoot and the Atsina to stop intertribal warfare and permit peaceful hunting.

Schwinden Library, Fort Benton

Treaty site near the mouth of the Judith River. Government dignitaries are beneath the canopy; Cummings is seated with Gov. Stevens who is addressing the council. The chiefs are seated in rows listening to the terms that would permit western tribes to hunt in the fall in Blackfoot Country.

The Council

The council was scheduled for early August but Cumming's trip up river with the treaty goods and presents dragged on into October. It was estimated that there would be 12,000 Indians, but delays and a change in site considerably reduced participation. On October 16, 1855 after the keelboats arrived with the goods, the proceedings began. At about 1 p.m. the Indians gathered in large semicircles around the tent cover of the commission and were addressed by "The Great Soldier Chief," Governor Stevens.

The first order of business was assigning interpreters for the tribes. The three for the Blackfoot were James Bird, the half-breed son of an English trader and a Piikani mother; Alexander Culbertson, Chouteau and Company's head trader on the Missouri River; and Benjamin DeRoche, a private in Steven's party. For the Nez Perce there were William Craig, an old trader with Wm. Sublette; and

Artist Gustav Sohon

Lame Bull, head chief of the Piikani and principal Blackfoot at the treaty on the Judith

Delaware Jim, one of the Indians with Fremont in 1843 and with Stevens in 1853. The Salish interpreter was Ben Kiser, a half-breed Shawnee who lived with the Salish.

Commissioner Cummings, indicating that he came from "The Great Father in the East," said that if they signed a treaty to live in peace and friendship, presents would be given and each year goods would be sent to the people if they honored the treaty. The government would send people to show them how to farm so they would always have plenty to eat. In his remarks Governor Stevens added several tribes to the treaty in absentia: the Crow, Assiniboine, Cree, and Shoshoni. In addition to the tribes at the council, they were also to be left alone and at peace with the Blackfoot and Atsina. Stevens assured the Indians that peace with the whites would continue.

The Indians were told that the buffalo would not last forever, but their lands would not be taken away (Indian Agent James Doty). The white men wanted to set up ranches, farms, mill and shops for them. Hunting grounds for the western tribes would be established along the Musselshell and Yellowstone where they could come through Big Hole Pass, Medicine Rock Pass and others farther south. A single dispute arose over hunting around the Three Buttes (Sweetgrass Hills). Alexander of the Pend d'Oreille complained that this was where his people wanted to hunt. The tribes were told that Blackfoot Territory was set by the Laramie Treaty of 1851; the western tribes received smaller parcels because they were only one-fourth the size of the Blackfoot.

At noon on October 17 the meeting reconvened and the dispute over Three Buttes was settled. The Blackfoot allowed the Pend d'Oreille to hunt on their way through the northern passes to the hunting grounds. It was stipulated that there would be no permanent settlements in Indian lands for 97 years. Annuities were settled and would be distributed the next day. The Blackfoot would receive their annuities at Fort Benton. Three goals of the treaty were emphasized: the desire to teach the Indians the ways of the white man, the cessation of horse stealing, and the end of the war with the Crow even though they were not present at the council. At four o'clock in the afternoon the council was adjourned after all the chiefs signed the treaty. The major Blackfoot chiefs from the Piikani were Low Horn, Lame Bull and Little Gray Head; from the Kainaa were Seen From Afar and Calf Shirt; representing the Siksika were Three Bulls and Old Kootenai. (1)

Artist Gustav Sohon

Low Horn was one of the principal Piikani chiefs who signed the Lame Bull Treaty of 1855.

Annuities

Ten years of annuities were granted by the 1855 Blackfoot Treaty. The 1858 payment given to 3500 Piikani was as follows:

10,000# flour
5700# rice
7600# sugar
7400# pilot bread (hardtack)
802 blankets
2280 yards calico
3000 yards gaudy cloth
128# black and white beads
843 red and blue beads
576 squaw awls
25# thread
108 tin cups

300 2 qt. pans
119# brass kettles
432 butcher knives
1650 frying pans
200# vermilion
108 NW trade guns
1300 gun flints
16 kegs gun powder
29 bags of balls
400# hoop iron (for arrowheads)
1 ton tobacco
12 gross fishhooks and lines

Treaty Signers

Three Bulls, Siksika

Calf Shirt, Kainaa Chief

Aftermath

There were several unforeseen consequences of the treaty. The large reservation setup on the north side of the Missouri included Fort Benton. A federal law passed in 1834 made the reservation Indian Territory and forbid the sale of liquor. It was illegal for Indians to bring liquor into their territory. None of the above was ever enforced.

Because Culbertson and Cummings had traveled together that summer and fall, Governor Stevens accused them of conspiring against him. Culbertson withdrew as an interpreter for the treaty and James Bird, the mixed-blood, was his substitute. The two later reconciled their differences and parted as friends.

Alfred Cummings loaded his ambulance aboard a mackinaw and headed down river with three of his party, and Professor Hayden and Culbertson. By the time they reached Fort Pierre, the river had iced up so they had to wait for the overland party which arrived on foot many days later. They had lost their mules to the Sioux. Commissioner Cummings went begging but old General Harney was in no mood to loan that treaty-maker anything. Harney told Cummings that he did have mules but none were for him. He said he only regretted that the Sioux hadn't taken his scalp as well as his mules. Culbertson, perhaps to be rid of Cummings, prevailed upon Charles Galpin who was in charge of Fort Pierre, to give Cummings eight mules to pull the ambulance and wagons. The party returned to St. Louis where Culbertson spent the winter.

Schwinden Library, Fort Benton

Gen. Wm. S. Harney, military commander at Fort Pierre

Boats Finally Arrive

When the treaty concluded on October 17, Governor Stevens and his party went to Fort Benton with the new bourgeois, Andrew Dawson, before returning to the Washington Territory. The Dawson party remained at the council site for a few days; Indians attending the treaty wanted to trade. On the first of November E.A.C. Hatch, the Blackfoot Indian Agent, arrived in Fort Benton after leaving his boats down river with annuities. On November 5 the boats finally arrived after 112 days from Fort Union, the longest trip ever.

The big keelboat could not be pulled over a ford so they dropped back down and unloaded her, bringing the cargo by wagon to the fort. The newly-made mackinaw was lighter; with her shallow draft she crossed the ford and unloaded at the landing. The trip included an eleven-day stop to build the mackinaw and a fourteen-day stop at the council grounds. Light trading began after the hunt; the Company men continued to split their duties: rebuilding with adobe, trading and bringing wood from the mountains.

On November 14, 1856 Malcolm Clarke with his trading party and 13 carts arrived to give Fort Benton more opposition for the robe trade. He moved his goods to the Teton and

Schwinden Library, Fort Benton

Andrew Dawson was the new bourgeois at Fort Benton in 1854 and chief fur trader for Chouteau and Co. until the end of the era.

Schwinden Library, Fort Benton

Inside a Blackfoot lodge at their encampment near Fort Benton

built near the winter camps of the Indians. Since Fort Benton was the new Blackfoot Agency, Dawson and Major Edwin Hatch selected a location on the bottom for the new headquarters.

Trade was brisk by the beginning of December when the weather turned cold and snowy. Dawson remarked in his journal that they had fifteen lodges inside the fort for a few days, quite different from the tight security of previous seasons. The holidays brought two celebrations and feasts: one on Christmas given by Indian Agent Hatch for personnel of both forts and a second hosted by Dawson on New Year Day's. The bands of Lame Bull, Little Dog, Two Elk and Calf Robe had all been in to trade. In December, Little Antelope died along the trail; at his request his companions brought him for burial at the fort's cemetery, which was outside the stockade behind and up river from its walls.

January and February, though cold and snowy, were excellent for trade at both forts. Near the end of January, a special guest, Seen From Afar, chief of the Kainaa and Culbertson's brother-in-law, came to the fort to trade. A Siksika group - Old Sun, Big Sun and Bull Sitting Down – appeared at the fort, their first return to American traders since the cannon had been turned on them. By the end of February trade goods were getting low. They had already traded for 5586 robes. Mountain Chief and Seen From Afar returned to trade a second time and depleted the store's supply of blankets.

FORT CAMPBELL 1860

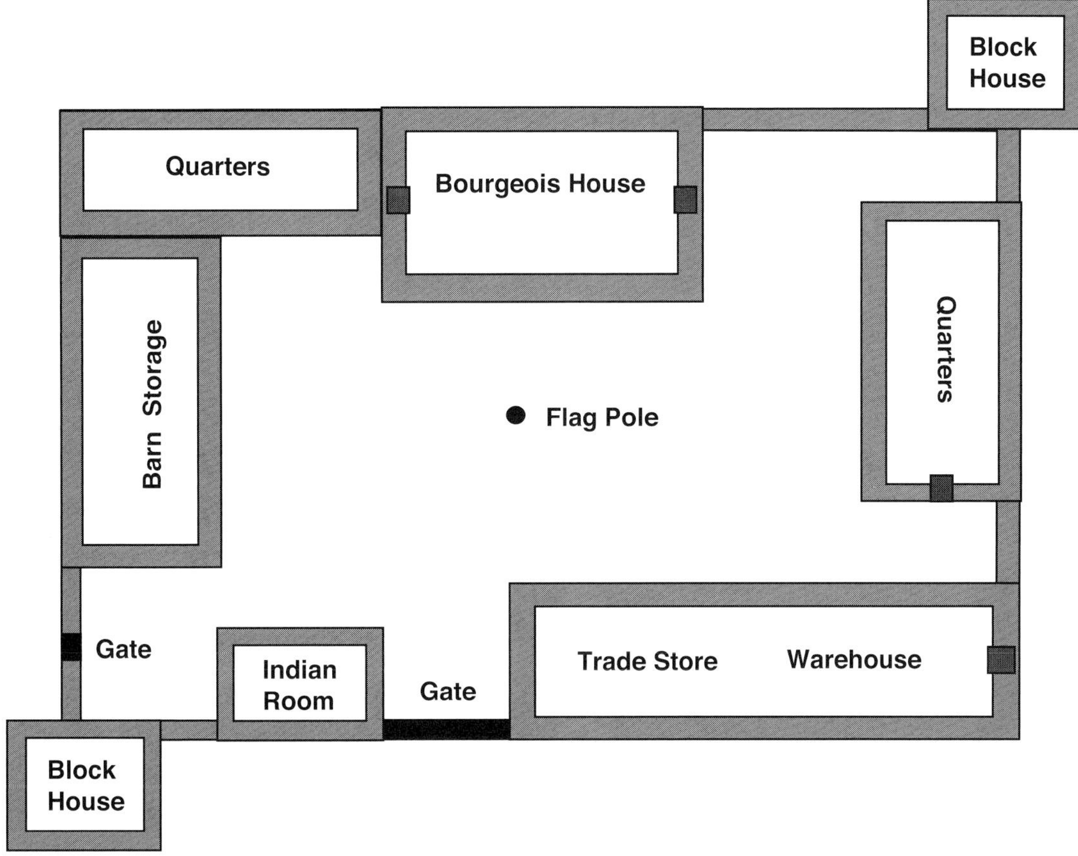

On March 6, Agent Hatch went to Fort Union to catch the Company steamboat back to St. Louis. Clarke, who did not have a good season, sold out to the opposition at Fort Campbell and left. The next year he joined Primeau and Company, replacing DeRoche at Fort Campbell. Mr. Wray had been the express man between Fort Benton and Fort Union all winter, carrying messages between the Company men. The last express of the season was on March 15. When the ice left the river, Revais and Wray went to St. Louis with the season's trade report. Other events included John Owen from the Bitterroot's stop for supplies for Fort Owen and the men constructing a new robe press outside the walls to make bundling easier.

In March and April the major activities were pressing robes into bundles and making the mackinaws ready to take the furs to Fort Union. Everyone knew that the big new keelboat had too deep a draft for the river, a fact acknowledged by those who had to cordelle her to Fort Benton. With the spring rise they managed to get her up to the landing so they could caulk her bottom. The 1856 returns were so large that a third boat had to be built to carry the extra bundles of robes. She was 85 feet by 12 1/2 feet, the largest mackinaw ever built in the chantier. The three boats hauled 1540 packs of robes with 12 to 15 robes per pack; 1581 sacks of tongues; and hundreds of packs of small furs to market. After being delayed by rain, on May 12 the small fleet under the command of Andrew Dawson left for Fort Union to meet the steamboat *St. Mary*.

Schwinden Library, Fort Benton

John Owen built Fort Owen in 1850 after purchasing the buildings abandoned by the Jesuits in 1848 at St. Mary's Mission.

Up River Above Fort Union

Piloted by John LaBarge, the steamboat *St. Mary* left the levee at St. Louis on June 7, 1856 riding a swollen river. Chouteau and Co. had secured the annuities contract and outfitted her for the trip up river. Commanding the group was Charles Chouteau; Alexander Culbertson and Indian Agents Alfred Vaughan and E.A.C. Hatch were on board. At Fort Pierre Lieutenant Gouverneur K. Warren, his two assistants and Professor Ferdinand Hayden with a Smithsonian Institute expedition joined the group. Lt. Warren was with the U.S. Army Engineers on his way to the Yellowstone to do a topographic survey. As soon as they docked at Fort Union, Lt. Warren and his detachment set out to explore the Yellowstone Valley. Professor Hayden, the geologist, came back to the river every year from 1857 to 1860 with Captain Raynolds to explore Yellowstone country and the Blackfoot lands.

After several stops down river for Commissioner of Indian Affairs Vaughan, who attended Indian councils and distributed annuities, the *St. Mary* docked at Fort Union on July 10. The Assiniboine annuities were

Artist David Parchen

The new fur press at Fort Benton made the work easier, but it still took a great deal of labor to fold and press the hides into bundles of 12 to 15 that weighed approximately 200 pounds.

unloaded for distribution and the *St. Mary* went on up river to just below the mouth of the Milk River at El Paso Point. (2) She off-loaded more annuities then turned around because the river was falling rapidly. Her cargo of Blackfoot trade goods and annuities was left in charge of E.A.C. Hatch, the Indian Agent. Chouteau immediately ordered the construction of mackinaws to cordelle the goods to Fort Benton. The *St. Mary* hurriedly loaded the returns at Fort Union and arrived in St. Louis on July 29, 1856.

Pierre Chouteau was gradually retiring and turning the business over to his son Charles, who followed in his father's footsteps as a patron of the sciences. He and fourteen others founded the Academy of Science of St. Louis. Charles brought many specimens aboard the *St. Mary* to start the collections for the Academy.

Schwinden Library, Fort Benton

Capt. Wm. F. Raynolds, head of the military expedition to explore and map a road between the Yellowstone and Fort Benton from 1856-60

Smallpox Again on the River

An opposition's boat, the *Clara,* left St. Louis on July 14, 1856 with freight for the upper river. Shortly after her departure, small pox broke out on board. Captain John Shaw refused to land the victims down river and brought the dreaded pox to the upper river. It infected the Arikaras, Mandans, Hidatsas and Assiniboines that summer and spread to the Crow and Blackfoot during the next winter. Kipp reported that by January 1857 over three hundred Assiniboine had perished from the disease near Fort Union.

The Protestant Missionary

July 1, 1856 was a memorable date. It brought Rev. Elkanah D. Mackey and his wife Sarah of the Presbyterian Church to Blackfoot Country on a steamboat. Although Catholic Jesuits periodically visited Fort Benton, held services and baptized children, they were the first Protestant missionaries to come to the region. Culbertson provided for their safety in Indian country and encouraged their missionary work. Andrew Dawson and Natawista warmly welcomed the Mackeys aboard the steamer. Dawson was pleased to see Presbyterians coming to do missionary work. Dawson and Culbertson had supplies and annuities on board to deliver in Fort Benton; they sent word overland to build a boat and send it down to them. The new boat was finished quickly and with F. Wray in charge was sent to Fort Union. When the steamer arrived at Fort Union, the minister held his first Protestant service on August 17. They boarded the new boat with the Company traders bound for the Judith to distribute annuities to the Blackfoot.

While Agent Hatch distributed the annuities, Mackey received permission from Chief Lame Bull and other chiefs to found a mission in their country. However, his pregnant wife fell ill and they had to return to the East before winter set in. Although he volunteered to return the next year, the church council denied his request. Another attempt to Christianize the Blackfoot failed.

Dawson's Trading

Years later Many Tail Feathers described the trading at Fort Benton under Andrew Dawson to James Willard Schultz:

We had many buffalo robes to trade so we came to the Teton River where we made a great camp. Andrew Dawson the factor at Fort Benton sent the chiefs presents of tobacco, coffee, hard bread, and sugar. The chiefs invited the minor chiefs in to smoke and have a feast. Next day we packed our horses and travois with buffalo robes, furs, dried meat, and skins. As the chiefs approached the fort, the men inside rolled the cannon out and brought out their flag. Then one of the white men invited Many Horses, head chief and the minor chiefs to come forward. Our head chief was taking a present for Dawson who was coming outside. When the two men shook hands, the cannon was fired in a friendly salute. Then the men at the fort brought a huge copper kettle of whiskey outside the gate and passed cups of it to the circle of chiefs. Afterwards, the chiefs were invited inside where the factor dressed them all in fine clothes and gave them each a gallon of whiskey. When this ceremony was over, a few of us were allowed at a time (to) go inside to trade. We bought guns, ammunition and tobacco mostly. We gave 10 robes for a flintlock gun, eight robes for a No. 10 size keg of powder and a sack of balls, and four robes for four plugs of tobacco. A knife was worth one robe and we gave four robes for a gallon of whiskey. We could have all the whiskey we were able to buy but only the old, mature people drank. They dressed up in their full outfits, started to drink, and went around singing and dancing.

Hunter or Killer

A sidelight to 1856-1857 was a foreign visitor to the Upper Missouri, Sir St. George Gore. He was an Englishman who ascended the river with a hunting party of 43 intent on killing everything that moved. Sir Gore had equipped the party with a train of wagons and secured Jim Bridger as his guide. The venture probably rivaled any of the famous expeditions of royalty from Europe who came to North America to hunt and return with trophies. Sir Gore's party came up the Platte River in 1854 then crossed over into the Tongue River drainage, killing everything they could.

Schwinden Library, Fort Benton

Coat of Arms of Sir St. George Gore who carried on a wholesale slaughter of animals on the Upper Missouri in 1856-57.

At the mouth of the Tongue, he constructed a fortification, and for nine months pursued hunting on a grand scale. The killing was so excessive that it incited the Crow to steal most of his horses and chase him out of the country. A letter to St. Louis said that by 1856 he had already killed 2000 buffalo in addition to elk and deer. The slaughter left hundreds of carcasses to rot on the prairie, all in the name of sport.

Sir St. George wintered in 1856-57 below Fort Union while building a plush mackinaw to descend the river. At Fort Union he tried to sell his wagons but at far too high a price. In

Schwinden Library, Fort Benton

Chouteau's large boat the Spread Eagle was used for several years to make the spring run from St. Louis with goods and annuities to Fort Union and to bring robes and furs back down river.

a rage, he had them all destroyed. During the following months the Sioux and Assiniboine followed the example set by the Crow and stole the remainder of his horse herd before he reached St. Louis.

Partial Retirement

The winter of 1856-1857 was another cold one on the river but trading was excellent. Reconstruction of the fort in adobe was ongoing. The smallpox epidemic spread from the Crow and Assiniboine to the Blackfoot. Fortunately it was not wide-spread among the bands because they had separated for the winter. In late fall Culbertson left Fort Benton to spend the winter in the East, partly in Washington, D.C. The urge for retirement in the East to spend more time with his family grew with each passing season.

1857 saw some very drastic changes in the fur companies of the upper river. In April, a discouraged Joseph Picotte came down river. Alexander Culbertson was negotiating a partial retirement so that he could move his family to Peoria in the winter. John Sarpy died in April, and the next month John F. Sanford was also gone. Chouteau lost two major partners and was forced to reorganize the company. In anticipation of a more formidable opposition, the Company got on the river early that spring. Captain John LaBarge brought the steamer *Spread Eagle* with Culbertson and Charles Chouteau up river three weeks ahead of the *Twilight.* The *Spread Eagle* carried Company supplies for the upper forts, army freight and passengers; she returned from Fort Union with five thousand packs of robes and furs for St. Louis delivery.

The New Opposition

When Joseph Picotte returned from Fort Campbell to St. Louis in the spring of 1857, he was disenchanted with his partners and wanted Harvey, Primeau and Company dissolved. Picotte led the opposition at Fort William in 1854 after Harvey's death then

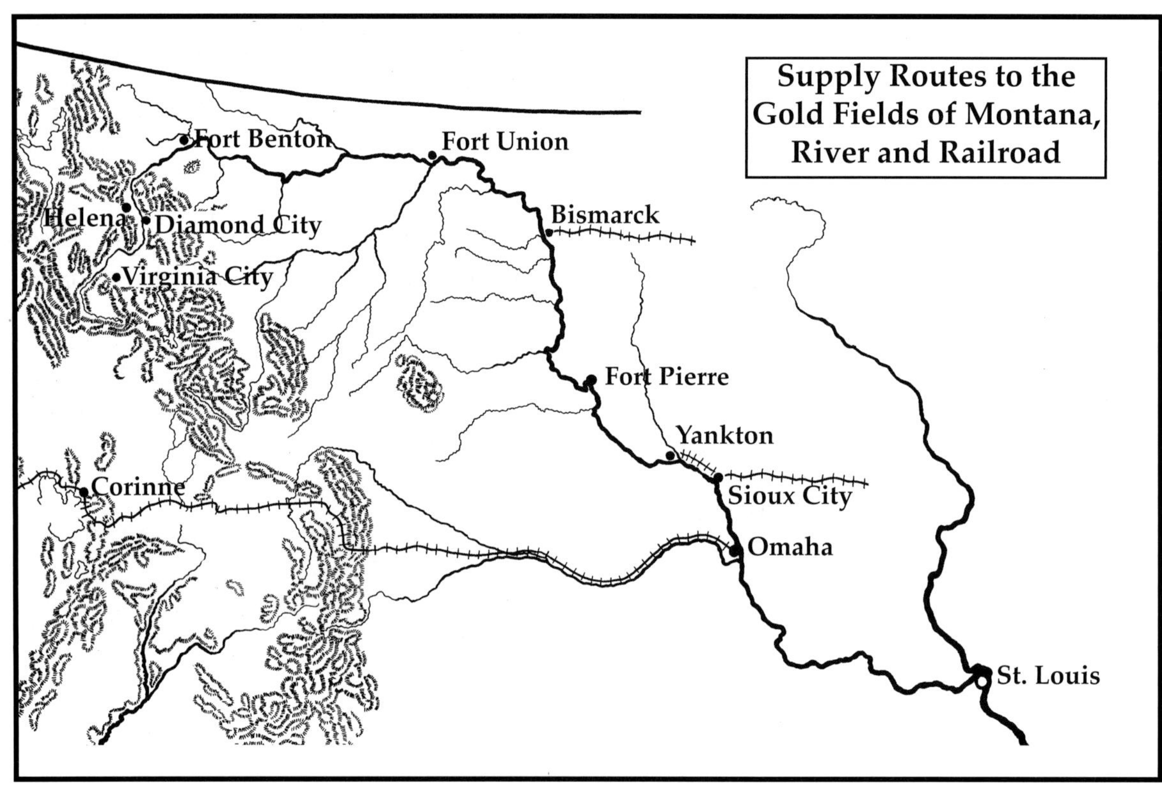

moved to Fort Campbell in April of 1856. The lack of other opposition was short-lived. Robert Campbell organized and financed another company to compete on the upper river with Chouteau and Company. Campbell's outfit was named Campbell, Frost, Todd and Company of St. Louis; Picotte agreed to manage the upper river business for the new company for one year.

In May 1857 they chartered the side-wheeler *Twilight* to carry their outfit to the upper river. The new company had underbid Chouteau for the Indian annuities, and agents Vaughan and A.H. Redfield boarded the *Twilight* at Fort Randall where she had unloaded Army freight. On July 5 the *Twilight* reached Fort William, near Fort Union, where Redfield stayed to deliver annuities to the Crow on the Yellowstone. The *Twilight* went on up river to the mouth of Poplar Creek where supplies for Fort Campbell and the Blackfoot annuities were unloaded in the care of Alfred Vaughan.

In early August Malcolm Clarke took command of Fort Campbell for the opposition. Charles Primeau went back to Fort William and the firm was called Clarke, Primeau and Company. It competed with Chouteau and Company at the two up river forts until 1860.

Trade Statistics from Chouteau and Company

1856: Buffalo robes - price range, $3.25 to $5.50
August robe prices: No. 1, $5.50; No. 2, $5.00; No. 3, $3.25
Beaver were graded Nos. 1, 2 and 3 from $.75 to $1.00

August 22, 1856: 34,243 buffalo robes at $4.50; 671 beaver at $.80
August 15, 1857; 30,047 buffalo robes at $4.00; 1,511 beaver at $.75
Kinds of skins shipped to St. Louis from the Upper Missouri: buffalo, opossum, raccoon, skunk, gray deer, badger, elk, beaver, prairie wolf, dog, otter, mink, fox and wildcat.

A Change of Administration

With the election of James Buchanan as U.S. President, a reshuffling of Indian Agents occurred in May 1857. A.H. Redfield was the new Commissioner and Alfred Vaughan took over the Blackfoot Agency from Hatch. In October 1857 Culbertson arrived at Fort Benton just in time to negotiate the first sale of goods for Montana gold dust. John Silverthorne brought in a pouch of dust he had found in a creek west of the mountains. Unwilling to divulge the exact location, he traded with Culbertson for a supply of horses, blankets, arms, tobacco and food. When the dust was evaluated, Culbertson came out on the long end of the exchange.

In another three years that transaction prompted a gold rush that brought hordes of miners into the territory. A late summer panic that year caused a tightening of the purse strings by St. Louis owners, but it had little effect on Fort Benton and Fort Campbell. The robe trade for 1857-58 grossed $300,000 for the Company. The Upper Missouri was still a lucrative venture regardless of the economy in the rest of the country.

Peoria

Alexander Culbertson took advantage of the reorganization of Chouteau and Company to reconsider his life in the fur trade. He spent the winter of 1857-58 in Peoria, Illinois with his family. The large fortune he had accumulated during the previous decade triggered his partial retirement from the upper river. He had obtained a land grant in 1825 on a piece of property near Peoria and had purchased a second piece of land in town in 1845. In the fall of 1857 he bought additional acreage outside Peoria and built the manor house he called Locust Grove where he stayed with his family during the winter of 1857-58. He had to make some concessions to Natawista to persuade her to live away from her people; one was in having a tepee on the front lawn during the summer. Until 1861 he still returned annually to the upper river to manage affairs for the Company.

Artist David Parchen

Malcolm Clarke became a free trader then went to work for the opposition during the last years of the trade.

In May 1858 after discussing business in the Company offices in St. Louis with the two Chouteaus, Culbertson went up river with James Kipp and Andrew Dawson. The *Spread Eagle* was commanded by Charles Chouteau and piloted by John LaBarge. She was loaded to capacity with the passengers; each paid $150 for the trip. She made good time up river, arriving at Fort Union on June 10.

From Fort Union, the *Spread Eagle* continued on up river pulling two mackinaws, one on each side. Just below the mouth of the Milk River she was stopped by low water after smashing one of the mackinaws into the bank. Her freight for Fort Benton was unloaded onto the other mackinaw called the *Black Feet Star.* On her return to St. Louis, the *Spread Eagle* carried only 1700 bundles of robes from Fort Union; the season had just been average. She was back in port on June 28.

Fort Stewart

Fully loaded, on May 23 the opposition's boat, the *Twilight*, left St. Louis to waving crowds on its journey to Fort William. On board was Swiss artist Karl Wimar, who painted scenes of the Upper Missouri much as Karl Bodmer had in 1833. Because of the Sioux menace, Redfield took the annuities to Fort Union for the Assiniboine and made arrangements with Culbertson to take the Crow annuities up the Yellowstone.

Malcolm Clarke came down the river that spring to talk with Campbell and his partners about the next year's trade. He returned on the *Twilight* and closed Fort William on the Yellowstone as ordered. Supplies from the fort were loaded on the *Twilight* and moved up river near the mouth of Big Muddy Creek. Clarke unloaded and started building a new post on June 25. The post was named Fort Stewart (Stuart) for his partner. Vaughan took the Blackfoot Nation annuities and headed overland to distribute them to bands along the upper river.

It was the last winter that Alexander Culbertson spent at Fort Union. His family may have been with him, but probably they were at the manor house in Peoria. Little record of the fall and winter of 1858-59 at either Fort Union or Fort Benton exists, but early in the spring of 1859 Culbertson came overland to Fort Benton and helped ready the returns for down river.

In St. Louis there was a great deal of speculation about taking a steamboat all the way to Fort Benton to distribute the annuities and freight from government contracts and to bring the returns down river. Charles Chouteau was determined not to allow someone else to reach the head of navigation before he did. Throughout the winter he planned a light draft boat to make the trip.

Schwinden Library, Fort Benton

Fort Benton in 1860 showing arrival of the first steamboats. The military detachment on board was to travel over the new wagon road into Washington Territory.

Beinecke Library, Yale

Captain Raynolds Survey Party in 1860 mapped a possible road between the Yellowstone and the Missouri.

Fort Benton or Bust

In 1859 the Indian annuity contract, for two years instead of one, was awarded to Chouteau and Company. The other two bidders complained that Chouteau had manipulated the contract but when it came to the bottom line, Chouteau and Company still had the lowest bid. Charles Chouteau intended to win the war of the Upper Missouri. Like his competitors, he intended to send a steamboat all the way up the river to Fort Benton to deliver the Blackfoot annuities.

The returns for 1858-59 increased to such an extent that there was the threat of a surplus of robes in St. Louis. However, if the Company boat could deliver supplies to Fort Benton for the Indian Service, the Army and private businesses, revenues would improve and the Company could be the first to deliver robes in St. Louis. These advantages, plus passenger fares, could easily turn a profit for the Company. Chouteau found the ideal boat, the *Chippewa*. She was a sternwheeler 165 feet long drafting only two feet of water when loaded. She would accompany the side-wheeler *Spread Eagle* on the up river trip in 1859.

With several invited dignitaries, including the artist Wimar and Indian Agents Vaughan and Bernard S. Schoonover (the replacement for Redfield) on board, the cabins at $150 each were full. At St. Joseph Captain William F. Raynolds with the Topographic

Schwinden Library, Fort Benton

Charles Chouteau took over from his father and pioneered steamboat travel from St.Louis up the Missouri to Fort Benton.

Engineers party boarded. He was to mount an expedition into Yellowstone Country to explore a possible wagon route to Fort Benton and across the Rockies to the coast.

Lt. Henry E. Maynadier, second in command, came aboard with mules and supplies at Fort Leavenworth accompanied by Indian scout Jim Bridger. His army command disembarked at Fort Pierre and headed overland on their explorations. On June 30 the two steamers landed at Fort Union. As he had previously agreed, M.H. Crapster sold the *Chippewa* to Charles Chouteau and returned down river.

Fort Kipp

Chouteau loaded the *Chippewa* with 160 tons of freight and tied on two mackinaws, one to each side. On July 3 he ordered Captain John LaBarge to take her up river headed to Fort Benton. On the Fourth of July they celebrated the day by firing their cannon as they passed Fort Kipp. The new fort had been built for the Assiniboine trade a few miles above Big Muddy Creek right next door to the opposition's Fort Stewart. They encountered little trouble until they reached Dauphin Rapids, where they had some problems crossing through them. They released the two mackinaws and proceeded without trouble to Brule' Bottom (Rowe's Landing) where the channel grew shallow and they ran out of wood.

Chouteau unloaded his freight at the landing, only a dozen miles from his destination, and went overland to Fort Benton. He made arrangements at the fort for a supply of cordwood for their return. Chouteau also made plans to have more wood on hand the next season so the boat could come all the way to Fort Benton to establish a new head of navigation on the Missouri River. He returned to the *Chippewa* with Alexander Culbertson and the two went to St. Louis. Culbertson spent the winter in Peoria with his family.

That season the opposition sent the steamboat *Florence* up river with Malcolm Clarke on board and reached Fort Stewart in 23 days. When the *Florence* returned with meager yearly returns, Campbell, Frost, Todd and Company withdrew from trade leaving Clarke, Primeau and Company on their own.

Dawson Injured

In the summer of 1858 Andrew Dawson, who like many traders was a heavy drinker, fell into the cellar at the fort and seriously injured his back. His condition worsened and he gradually lost the use of his lower limbs. In 1864 he was forced to retire and returned with two of his mixed-blood sons to his native Scotland.

The winter of 1859 was unusually mild in Montana. Large herds of buffalo surrounded Fort Benton and made the Blackfoot hunt extraordinarily large. The robe business for the season had an estimated sales of $340,000. The fur trade still commanded its place in the business houses of St. Louis and other down river ports.

When the ice cleared the river in 1860, Charles Chouteau readied three steamboats

Schwinden Library, Fort Benton

Steamboats Chippewa and the Key West were the first steamers to make it to the levee in Fort Benton, and established the city as the head of navigation on the Missouri River and the gateway to Montana's gold fields.

for the annual up river trip: the *Spread Eagle*, a large side-wheeler and two stern-wheel mountain boats, the *Chippewa* and the *Key West 2*, which could handle the channel above Fort Union. The *Key West* drew 30 inches of water when fully loaded with 180 tons of freight. It became a model for future mountain boats.

On May 3 after the presentation of flags to Charles Chouteau (one carried the motto "For Fort Benton or Bust") to the roar of cannon and cheers of the crowds, the little flotilla headed up river into history.

Aboard was a contingent of military under the command of Major Blake, whose

Schwinden Library, Fort Benton

The Key West, at the levee in Fort Benton, made several trips during the fur trade era to Fort Benton. She was much luckier than her sister ship the Chippewa who blew up on her second trip to Fort Benton.

wagons were the first across the Mullan Road from Fort Benton to Fort Walla Walla. On June 15 the boats reached Fort Union, unloaded annuities for the Assiniboine and Crow tribes and started for their destination at Fort Benton. The *Spread Eagle* made it to El Paso Point where Captain John LaBarge took over command of the *Key West* for the ten-day trip to Fort Benton. On July 2, 1860 the two boats tied up to the levee at Fort Benton establishing it as the world's innermost port, 3485 miles from the Gulf of Mexico. On board was the founder of Fort Benton; Alexander Culbertson was about to end his career with Chouteau and Company and retire to Peoria.

Steamboats ended the grueling chore of bringing keelboats and mackinaws from Fort Union by cordelling through the Badlands and the White Cliffs with Company supplies and annuities for the Blackfoot. They eliminated the precarious trip down river with the annual returns. This momentous occasion was the beginning of change in this isolated Blackfoot fur post near the headwaters of the Missouri.

Text Notes

1. Artist Gustav Sohon was a young private in Army service who recorded the treaty site and many of the important chiefs of the Northwest on his trip with Gov. Stevens.
2. A point on the river reached by the Steamboat *El Paso* in 1850; at that time it was the most distant up river site reached by a steamboat.

Upper Missouri Steamboats

1860 - 1887

Deer Lodge

Red Cloud

Benton and Helena

1861 - 1865

Steamboats and Trade

Last Years of Fort Benton

Baker and Northwestern Fur Co.

Demise of the Opposition

The arrival of the first steamboats at Fort Benton was probably the most important event on the upper river. Other events in 1860 also caused changes up and down the river. By July when the *Chippewa* and the *Key West* reached port in Montana, the opposition had not dispatched a boat from St. Louis to the upper river. After the return of the *Florence* the previous season, Robert Campbell and his partners evaluated their fur and robe returns. By fall Frost and Todd concluded that their future was better served by politics and the Dakota land business, so on November 4 the company was dissolved by mutual consent of the partners, except the up river business of their subsidiary Clarke, Primeau and Company.

In the spring of 1860 Clarke and Primeau came down river to outfit their company not knowing about the dissolved partnership. Robert Campbell was unwilling to finance them so the opposition was virtually dead. Chouteau and Company immediately saw a way to end all opposition and offered the traders a job with the Company. When both accepted, they were sent upriver, Primeau to Fort Pierre and Clarke to Fort Union.

Schwinden Library, Fort Benton

Daniel Frost was one of the partners who financed the opposition and decided to quit in 1860.

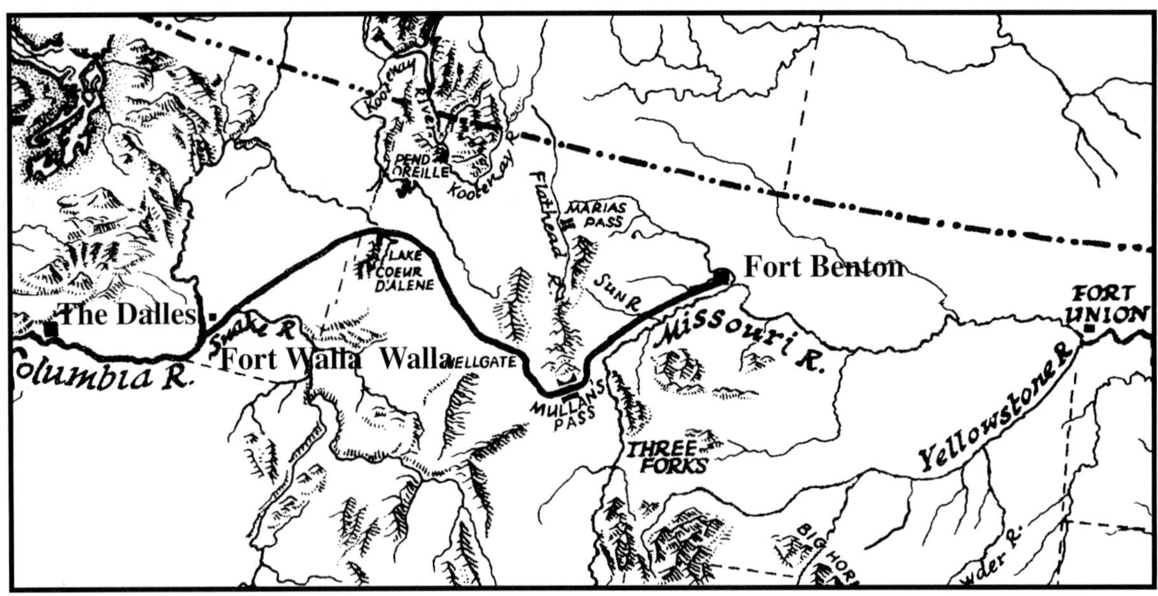

The Mullan Road was the first government road in the Northwest. It connected Fort Walla Walla at the head of navigation on the Columbia River, to Fort Benton, the head of navigation on the Missouri River, and created the first practical passage across the continent of North America.

Fort Closures

Then in complete control, the Company made drastic changes to the trading posts on the Missouri; the Indians did not like it. The first closure, Fort Sarpy II on the Yellowstone, had been hard to maintain from the start. The Crow were forced to come to Fort Union to trade. Down river, Fort Clark was abandoned as were Fort Kipp and Fort Stewart near Big Muddy Creek. The disgusted Indians immediately burned the two forts. Fort Campbell, the main opposition post, suffered an even greater disgrace when it was turned over to the Jesuits as a mission. How could any "reputable" fur post endure such humiliation?

Dawson reported that life was peaceful at Fort Benton after the celebration for the arrival of the Company's first steamboats. Annuities that came with the boats were distributed by the agency and fort personnel were working on the trade store, the last building of the fort to be rebuilt of adobe. On his first assignment since being rehired, Clarke took over Fort Union late that summer, just in time to be in the middle of a Sioux uprising.

The Military Arrives

In the summer of 1860 Andrew Dawson extended the hospitality of the fort to three military parties. The first to arrive by steamboat was Major George Blake and his contingent. Later Captain William F. Raynolds came with a government topographic party of 38 men. Captain John Mullan returned with his road building detachment, pack train and wagon.

Schwinden Library, Fort Benton

In 1860 Capt. John Mullan built a military road that connected the waters of the Columbia and the Missouri.

On August 1 Capt. Mullan came to Fort Benton, completing his road from Fort Walla Walla on the Columbia River. He had finished work on the Clark's Fork and made final changes from the Continental Divide across the prairie to Fort Benton. Waiting for him in Fort Benton were Major George Blake and his 300 raw recruits who were ready start their trek to Washington Territory with pack mules and wagons. They were the first train over the new road. Captain Raynolds built mackinaws to go down river to Fort Union. There he met the rest of his party under Lt. Maynadier who had traveled to the mouth of the Yellowstone.

The robe trade at Fort Benton still produced 20,000 to 30,000 robes each season. In spite of his bad back, Andrew Dawson operated the fur post for Chouteau and Company with skill and efficiency between bouts with the bottle. Culbertson, who was semi-retired, spent more and more time down river and in Peoria. In 1861 he left the Company for good. Still drawn to the upper river, he and Natawista returned to Montana the next year and spent the summer with Rev. A.S. Reed at his trading post at the Blackfoot farm on Sun River.

Schwinden Library, Fort Benton

Wagons and mule teams loaded and ready to travel the Mullan Wagon Road to Fort Walla Walla in Washington Territory

Improvements in transportation on the trails, roads and river came just in time for the discovery of gold in Montana, only two years away. Neither Indians nor whites who lived

Schwinden Library, Fort Benton

Major Blake and his contingent of men and wagons were encamped just down river from the fort awaiting the arrival Captain Mullan and his road building party who were completing the road from Fort Walla Walla.

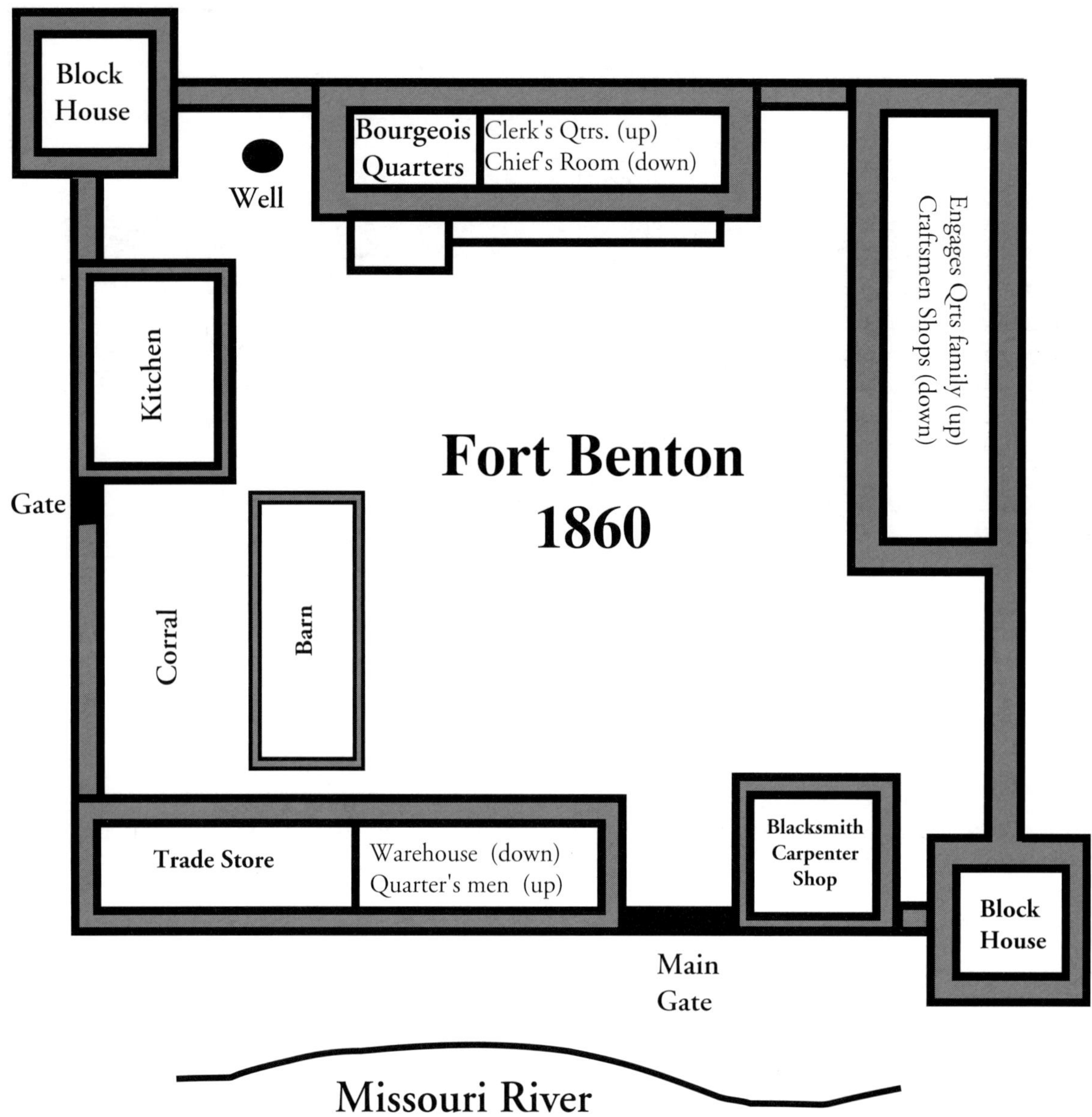

together in the fur trading era were ready for the transition. The amicable mixed culture was soon destroyed and the country was changed forever.

Civil War

When Lincoln was elected President, the country was thrust into secession and Civil War. Transportation on the rivers, particularly on the Mississippi below St. Louis, had considerable effect on moving robes and furs to market. The war had little effect on upper river traffic on the Missouri. Gold seekers headed to the Idaho diggings and military troops and supplies came up the river, and the fur trade boats continued without interruption. Many river captains and pilots were Southern sympathizers but their bosses were not. Trade went on with little obstruction. Chouteau

Schwinden Library, Fort Benton

The Chippewa, the first boat to Fort Benton, exploded the next season on the Missouri River in Montana after she caught fire.

family members, confirmed Democrats and slaveholders, kept a tight lip and the Company gave no aid or comfort to the Confederacy. Charles Chouteau even took an oath of loyalty to the Union. It's amazing what money can do.

The Republican administration brought a new group of politically appointed Indian Agents to the area who were not any worse than the previous ones, except Gad E. Upson. As a group they showed considerable hostility toward Chouteau and Company because of their Southern sympathies. Samuel N. Latta, the Upper Missouri Commissioner, believed the whole system, especially the Company, were rotten through and through.

Destiny at Disaster Bend

In the spring of 1861 Charles Chouteau, Captains John LaBarge and William Humphreys came up river with the *Spread Eagle* and the *Chippewa*. Aboard were three young New Yorkers, one of whom was William de la Montaigne Cary, an artist who made sketches of the river and later turned them into oil paintings.

On June 15, 1861 the first steamers bound for Fort Benton arrived at Fort Union; the *Spread Eagle* unloaded her freight and annuities and transferred her passengers to the *Chippewa*. She loaded tons of robes and furs and headed back to St. Louis on June 23. Meanwhile, the over-loaded and crowded *Chippewa* started up river to Fort Benton and her date with destiny. A few miles below Poplar Creek late one afternoon she caught fire. A considerable cargo of gunpowder was on board; crew and passengers were in a panic to abandon ship. Before they could jump into the river, the boat veered toward the bank and a line was tied. Amid the melee of pushing and shoving, everyone made it to the bank and safety. When the hawser gave way, the boat drifted onto a sandbar, burned to the water line and exploded. Cargo was thrown in all directions. The night sky looked like the Fourth of July in St. Louis. The next morning revealed an amazing scene: a mass of humanity rushing up and down the banks collecting anything within reach. Not far from the explosion was a camp of River Crow who joined men from a woodcutter's yard, the passengers, the crew

Montana Historical Society, Helena

After Culbertson retired, Charles Chouteau (seated) and Andrew Dawson ran the fur trade for Chouteau and Company during the last years of its existence. The levee at Fort Benton with the fort and steamboats is in the background.

and the Company men in the game of "Steal What You Can." When order was restored, Chouteau sent Andrew Dawson post haste to Fort Benton for wagons while he went up river to the Company post at Poplar Creek for mackinaws. Chouteau loaded the cabin passengers and what little freight had been retrieved and floated to Fort Union. The gleeful Crow danced all night with their newfound booty, particularly relishing the Blackfoot annuities they had stolen.

It took Dawson six weeks to bring his oxen-pulled wagon train to Fort Union to pick up supplies needed at Fort Benton to survive the winter. Cary and his party joined the wagon train and spent time some with Dawson at the fort before going across the Mullan Road to Fort Walla Walla and down the Columbia to the coast.

After taking care of the freight and passengers at Fort Union, Chouteau hurried down river to report the disaster to the Indian

Artist David Parchen

Fort LaBarge was built up river above Fort Benton and Fort Campbell by Joseph LaBarge and James Harkness. It was an open set of buildings and warehouses built in 1862.

office and to the insurance company since the annuities were insured. He offered to furnish annuities to the Blackfoot the following spring from the Company store at Fort Benton, an offer readily accepted but not quite at the rate Chouteau expected. Agent Latta continued his unrelenting indictments against the Company and made the Indian annuities quite an issue. Latta claimed Chouteau and Company took Crow and Assiniboine annuities for their own use then claimed they were lost on the *Chippewa*. He believed the annuities had already been unloaded at Fort Union and the Indians were told they had been lost. Whether Agent Schoonover sold them to the Company or they were used to replace the lost Blackfoot goods remains unclear. At any rate, Latta's charges got no more attention from federal officials than any of the others.

During the winter of 1861-62 Charles Chouteau appointed Andrew Dawson as the new "King." Charles Galpin deserted the Company and joined the last opposition on the upper river.

Fort LaBarge

In 1862 the Stuart Brothers found gold on Gold Creek near Deer Lodge, a discovery which started the gold rush. Gold fever in Idaho Territory spilled over into what became Montana in 1864. An opposition company to take advantage of the wealth of the gold rush was formed in St. Louis. The LaBarge brothers, James Harkness, Charles Galpin and Eugene Jaccard invested in the new venture. They were joined by the Company's old nemesis Robert Campbell, who agreed to market their robes, and Charles Larpenteur who the Company was probably glad to see join the opposition. The LaBarges, Joseph and John, captained the two steamboats, *Shreveport* and *Emilie*, and demonstrated that they were the best pilots on the river. They beat the Company boats to the Fort Benton levee by three days, arriving on June 17. They brought a crowd of miners for the Idaho gold fields, the first steam sawmill and tons of trade goods.

James Harkness came with them to take charge of the goods and start a store in Deer Lodge. Harkness hated life on the frontier so much that before the season was over he booked passage back to St. Louis and never returned.

Schwinden Library, Fort Benton

Granville Stuart and his brother made the first gold strike at Gold Creek in Montana.

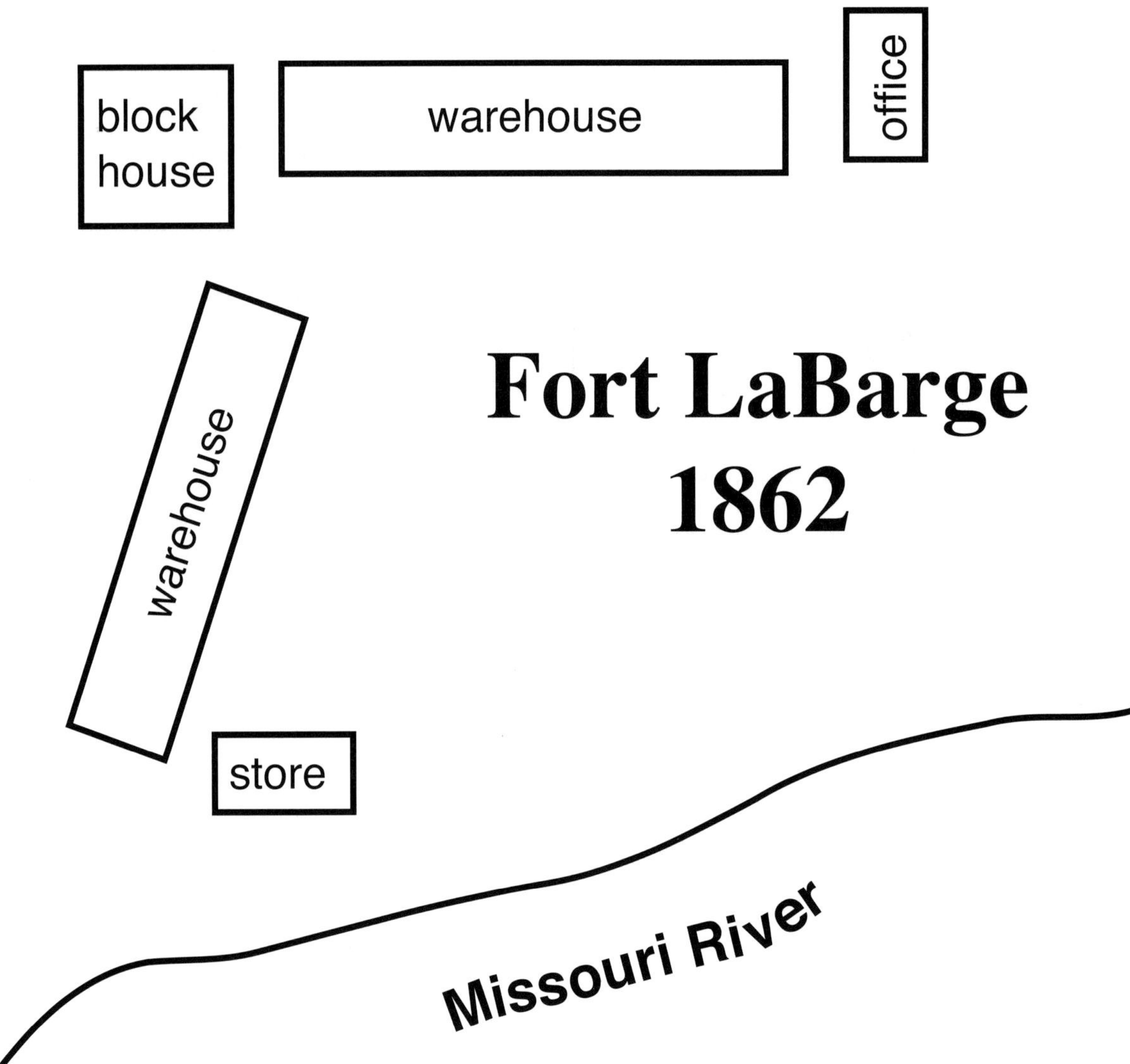

Young Joseph Picotte was left in charge of their up river interests.

The sawmill was first used to cut timbers for the buildings at Fort LaBarge. Since there was little or no Indian threat, the new fort had no palisades. The buildings consisted of low warehouses, quarters and a store built in the shape of a U with the open side facing the river.

LaBarge, Harkness and Co. intended to oppose Chouteau and Company all the way up the river. In addition to Fort LaBarge, in 1862-63, they built Fort Galpin at the Milk River, Owen MacKenzie's Post near old Fort Stewart and Fort Kipp, which lasted only a year. Other posts were constructed down river below Fort Union. Chouteau and Company resumed building in 1862 with the construction of Fort Andrew, 15 miles above the mouth of the Musselshell River on the Missouri. It was built by carpenters from Fort Benton and named for Andrew Dawson who supervised its construction; it also survived only one season.

Boats and Wagons

Company boats that came up river again in 1862 were the side-wheeler *Spread Eagle* and a new smaller sternwheeler. The *Key West* was a better boat for the upper river. They carried Father DeSmet, the Culbertsons, Andrew Dawson and Agent Latta with the Indian annuities. Latta had been assured of safe delivery of the annuities by the Company. When they reached Fort Union, Charles Chouteau decided to take the *Spread Eagle* on up river with the *Key West* because of the high water. The river was so high and so swift that when the boats crossed the Old Indian Ford, four of the crew drowned before reaching reached the levee at Fort Benton. The boats spent only four days in port, hurriedly unloaded the supplies and reloaded the robe returns. They were back in St. Louis on July 7. The last word concerning the trip was written by Lewis Henry Morgan who really enjoyed his round trip to Fort Benton ". . . and the bar keeper is an original genius."

A major event that season was arrival of the Fiske Wagon Train loaded with gold seekers from Minnesota. The train carried 150 people from Fort Abercrombie west across Minnesota and Dakota to Fort Union then on to Fort Benton. It left St. Paul on May 16 and arrived at Fort Benton on September 6 following Culbertson's road between the two Montana forts. The wagons traveled the Mullan Road to the gold fields of Virginia City and Bannack.

1862 was a high water year. In June the Fort Benton bottom on both sides of the river was inundated. Sitting on high ground, the fort had water lapping at the edge of its gates but none came inside the buildings or courtyard. Deterioration along the lower courses of bricks in the south wall caused it to lean; that summer the wall between the kitchen and trade store fell over.

Fort Benton had gold fever. A package from a man named LaRue was delivered to Andrew Dawson at the fort. It contained gold dust that supposedly had come from the breaks north of Fort Benton. Excitement reigned at the fort and a party of gold seekers was organized. LaRue volunteered to guide the group but never showed up. The party of Matt Carroll, James Arnoux, James Brown, Dr. Monroe Atkinson, Hugh Monroe and other Bentonites started north and prospected at every stream along the east slopes of the Rockies up to the Willows just south of Fort Edmonton. They found color in several places but not enough to stake a claim. By fall they returned disillusioned to Fort Benton, realizing they had been victims of a hoax. They sought revenge upon LaRue who left the country rather quickly.

Schwinden Library, Fort Benton

George Steell (left) and Mathew Carroll (right), clerks for Chouteau and Company, built their own mercantile enterprise, the first business outside the forts.

Culbertson's Return

By late summer 1862, Culbertson had enjoyed his first year of retirement by spending a relaxed summer in Montana and was ready to return to Peoria with his family. He hooked up with a group of Missourians to return to St. Louis. They bought a fifty-foot mackinaw for $100 and set off for home on September 10. Big Head with a band of Assiniboine warriors waited at the mouth of the Milk River to prey upon any boat that passed. They stopped Culbertson's boat, but when the warriors recognized him the group passed without incident. A day later another small boat behind the Culbertson party was stopped, plundered and stripped of literally everything. When they caught up with Culbertson's boat the next day, they had nothing left except a few clothes to hide their nakedness.

Low Water

In 1863, Clement Cornoyer erected the first building outside the forts. His building symbolized the changing times. There were more Indian problems, the gold rush, increased population, killing more buffalo, and eventually the end of the St. Louis robe trade. Two former Chouteau and Company clerks went up the levee and built Fort Benton's first commercial enterprise in 1864. Matt Carroll and George Steell entered the mercantile business and became wealthy businessmen in the Montana Territory.

The water was low in the spring of 1863 and no boats reached Fort Benton. Both companies outfitted boats bound for the upper river. Besides low water, the boats faced Sioux hostilities in Dakota before they reached the mouth of the Yellowstone. Again the opposition was first on the river that season with the refitted *Shreveport* and the larger *Robert Campbell*. The *Shreveport* left St. Louis April 20 while the other boat waited for the Indian annuities to arrive from the East. LaBarge, Harkness and Company had underbid Chouteau for the annuities contract and was also furnishing transportation for the Culbertson family to return up river.

The *Shreveport* got above the Yellowstone at MacKenzie's Post before Captain LaBarge evacuated the personnel. They fought off the Sioux during the winter but lost their livestock and two traders were killed. Captain John LaBarge took the personnel up river to Fort Galpin before he went to Snake Point, where he again ran out of water and unloaded the freight. He retreated down river to help the larger *Robert Campbell*. He met the Chouteau boats struggling up river just above the Yellowstone, and found his brother Joseph and the *Robert Campbell* with the Culbertson family on board just below Heart River. Three of the crew had been killed when they encountered the Sioux while distributing annuities. Below Fort Union the river was so low that the smaller boat had to carry the

Schwinden Library, Fort Benton

Low water in 1863 did not allow boats to reach Fort Benton. The unusual circumstances created financial difficulties that put the last opposition company out of business.

annuities across the bars to the fort's landing. The Blackfoot annuities were stored at Fort Union by Agent Reed to await more favorable river conditions.

Robert LeMond, the new agent for LaBarge, Harkness and Company, left the boat at Snake Point and came overland to Fort Benton to relieve Joseph Picotte as the agent at Fort LaBarge. Picotte had been a poor choice when Harkness left the year before. The inexperienced Picotte was usually drunk and did little to move freight up river that fall. In his drunken neglect, he turned to Dawson to bring cargo up the river. Dawson, having no loyalty to the opposition, brought all his own freight up before moving any for LaBarge, Harkness and Co. Most of their freight was on consignment for John F. Roe and Company and their agent Nicholas Wall. Roe and Co. sued LaBarge, Harkness and Company for late delivery.

When LeMond arrived at Fort Benton, he discovered that his freight was still at Snake Point and had to be brought to Fort Benton. He hired King and Gillette to haul it to Bannack for 25 cents a pound, which used up most of the profit before the freight was even sold.

Schwinden Library, Fort Benton

After the first load of freight was left at Cow Island in 1864, a road was built along the north side of the river to Fort Benton. Cow Island became an established low water landing for Fort Benton freight.

Those heavy losses and Captain Wall's winning judgment against the company forced LaBarge, Harkness and Company into receivership. Fort LaBarge was sold at a Sheriff's sale in 1864 ending the company holdings on the upper river. Chouteau and Company bought Fort LaBarge for its goods and sold the sawmill which was taken to Helena. The Company had put another opposition firm out of business, that one to mismanagement, and maintained their near-monopoly in Blackfoot Country.

The End Draws Near

Chouteau and Company boats waited until May 1863 but still had to leave in low water that was falling daily. The *Alone* and *Nellie Rogers* were loaded with mining supplies and their cabins and decks were full of gold seekers. As the boats passed through Sioux country, Indians firing from the bank harassed the travelers and slowed the boat's progress. The *Nellie Rogers* reached the mouth of the Milk River in late June and unloaded her passengers and freight, which were taken overland to Fort Benton. The *Alone* only reached the reopened Fort Charles. Chouteau had ordered Robert Meldrum to reopen the post to compete with the opposition nearby. Both boats dropped down river to Roulette's Post. The *Nellie Rogers* got there first, loaded furs and robes, and smuggled Roulette on board out of harm's way and the Assiniboine who were camped close by and threatening the post. Coming in later, the *Alone* took on some cargo before dark and tied up for the night. The Assiniboine attacked the post that night, killing all seven of the traders and burning it to the ground. Both boats turned tail for St. Louis, but it was late November before the *Alone* finally came into port.

When the *Nellie Rogers* unloaded at the Milk River Landing, she took on a new passenger, Owen MacKenzie, who had just come from his abandoned post. The son of Kenneth MacKenzie, he had lived on the upper river most of his life. Malcolm Clarke was also

Schwinden Library, Fort Benton

Steamboat Yellowstone, one of the last Chouteau and Company boats that came to Fort Benton

on board. MacKenzie and Clarke had "bad blood" from many years earlier at Fort Union. The two quarreled again in the main cabin of the steamer. Clarke, taking no chances with the accomplished frontiersman, bushwhacked and killed him in the hallway, claimed self-defense then immediately fled overland to Fort Benton to avoid retaliation by MacKenzie's friends. The boat dropped down river to Fort Union to bury young MacKenzie then went on to St. Louis with a full load of robes for the Chouteau warehouses.

Cow Island Landing

By 1864 the robe trade of Chouteau and Company was in severe distress. The rush of the gold seekers, the uncertainty of transportation on the lower river because of the Civil War and Indian uprisings in Sioux country all created major problems for the Company.

Charles Chouteau was ordered to use his boats to transport the U.S. Army in their campaign against the Indians on the Missouri. Throughout most of the season Company steamboats helped General Sully with his operations against the Sioux. Chouteau had the annuities contract for the Blackfoot and for the Salish west of the mountains. On April 16 Chouteau and Fr. DeSmet aboard the new steamboat *Yellowstone* left St. Louis with a full complement of passengers, freight and annuities. The *Yellowstone* did not get to Fort Benton until June 13. Struggling up river, when she reached Cow Island Chouteau realized they could go no further and unloaded at the landing. The stop established the low water landing for Fort Benton during the years ahead. Word was sent to Dawson who dispatched William Gladstone by boat to return with the goods and annuities to Fort Benton. After they moved the freight from the island to the north bank, Gladstone and some of his party blazed a new trail up Cow Creek and met the wagons from Fort Benton. It took two months to transport four hundred tons of freight overland to Fort Benton. It was the first freight taken over the Cow Island Trail, which was continually improved and become the main overland route in low water years.

On the way to Cow Island Gladstone's party met the steamboat *Benton* headed up river with a double load of passengers, her own and those from the *Yellowstone*. On the *Benton's* return trip, Agent Gad Upson stopped at Cow Island to disperse some of the annuities rather than transport them back to Fort Benton. He sent word to the Atsina to come to Cow Island. Within a week, 700 Atsina lodges appeared to claim their goods then left on the fall hunt. The Upson trading party went to Fort Benton with the rest of the annuities.

Although LaBarge, Harkness and Company was almost finished, Captain Joseph LaBarge and the *Effie Deans* came up river in 1864. He met the Chouteau boat returning to St. Louis. LaBarge and Chouteau discussed the annuity problem from the previous year, but no agreement was reached. To prove a point, an irritated LaBarge continued up river to Cow Island where he picked up some of Chouteau's freight and took it to the mouth of the Marias, just 12 miles below Fort Benton.

Dawson Goes Home

With his bad back and partially paralyzed legs, Andrew Dawson was forced into retirement in 1864. Coming in on the

Benton was Isaac G. Baker, the new factor, who took over the Company's operations. Dawson passed the command, boarded the *Benton* with his two Indian sons and went home to Edinburgh, Scotland where he died in 1871. Baker was the last bourgeois for Chouteau and Company, for only a single year.

Schwinden Library, Fort Benton

I. G. Baker was the last factor at Fort Benton and was only there for one season before he started his own mercantile business.

Two clerks, George Steell and Mathew Carroll, quit the Company late that summer. When Baker arrived, they moved down town and built the first commercial business outside the fort.

In late fall 1864 Gladstone returned to Fort Benton from Cow Island with the last of the freight. During the few months that he had been gone, the town had grown from one building to six saloons, a blacksmith shop, a large store and several log houses. Upson again hired Gladstone to help distribute annuities to the Blackfoot. About two weeks after the word went out, the tribes began to come into Fort Benton. The first were 400 lodges of Piikani who set up next to the fort. 600 lodges of the Kainaa and 900 lodges of Siksika soon came for the festivities of dispersing the annuities in Fort Benton.

Gladstone said it was common knowledge that the agent took a large rake off from the annuities for himself. He forced his employees to sign vouchers saying that all goods had been distributed before he would pay their salaries. Actually only about half of the merchandise was given to the native people. The Blackfoot knew they were being cheated and were very resentful, a situation which led to trouble in the years ahead.

The Chouteau empire was crumbling even if the trading season was successful. Most of the returns went down river by mackinaw due to low water. Isolation of the posts disappeared that summer when buildings sprang up like mushrooms on the flats surrounding the forts. The wilderness also disappeared with the influx of people. The old American Fur Company (Chouteau and Company) after a long reign was in its last year in Blackfoot Country.

Civil War Ends

By the end of the Civil War, Fort Benton was the leading up river outfitting point for military personnel and for gold seekers in the Northern Rockies. In spite of the new business, the Company sold all interests on the Upper Missouri and went to St. Louis in the spring of 1865. The buyer was the Northwestern Fur Co. whose partners were James Hubbell, Alpheus Hawley, Francis Bates and James A. Smith. Charles Chouteau and I.G. Baker came up river on the *Yellowstone* to Fort Benton and relinquished Company property to two of the new partners who accompanied them, Hubbell and Hawley.

I. G. Baker started his own commercial business in Fort Benton and built it into the largest mercantile in Montana. In those first years his trade was in buffalo robes and whiskey. As civilization crept into the Northern Plains, it turned more to commercial goods. Fort Benton changed from a trading post in the wilderness to a steamboat and wagon transportation

Schwinden Library, Fort Benton

Sheriff Wm. T. Hamilton was sent to bring the tribes to Fort Benton for the treaty of 1865.

center serving the Northwest and Canada.

The buffalo lasted for another decade but they too disappeared from the plains. The Indians who were so dependent upon them faced starvation then went to reservations. Killing the buffalo and smallpox contributed more to the demise of the Blackfoot than any regiment of infantry or cavalry that served the U.S. government on the high plains.

The Blackfoot agency stayed in Fort Benton until 1868 when Indian lands were confiscated by the U.S. government and the borders of the reservations were moved. The Agency was relocated to Old Agency near the present town of Choteau.

One More Treaty, 1865

In most cases throughout history treaties ended wars, but the Blackfoot Treaty of 1865 started a five-year conflict between the whites and the Indians in Montana. The savage encounters were usually precipitated by white aggression followed by retaliatory measures from the Blackfoot. In 1868 a second attempt at a treaty to end the hostilities was unsuccessful and resulted in the most disgraceful action by the military during all of the Indian Wars. No treaty was possible after Heavy Runner's band was massacred during the winter of 1870. The two treaties were exercises in futility. They were never ratified and led to many needless conflicts on both sides.

Treaty Time

One of the last hurrahs between the Blackfoot and Fort Benton was the treaty engineered by Acting Governor Thomas Francis Meagher, Judge L.E. Munson and E.W. Carpenter. Arrangements were in the hands of Gad E. Upson, the Indian agent. Upson dispatched Wm. T. Hamilton, the newly-appointed Sheriff of Chouteau County and Marshal of Fort Benton, to locate the Indians and advise them to come to Fort Benton for the treaty with the promise of annuities and presents. To be included were the three tribes of the Blackfoot, their sometimes-allies the Atsina, and their eternal enemies the Crow.

The Lame Bull Treaty of 1855 was to have made peace among the Blackfoot, the tribes west of the mountains and the whites. It was short-lived. The Piikani never stopped killing isolated parties of whites, nor did the citizens of Fort Benton ever quit killing Indians on Front Street and tossing them into the river.

The latest incidents occurred in the spring of 1865 when three or four Indians were killed on the streets of Fort Benton by Henry Bostwick and Joseph Spearson. Some escaped and went back to the Kainaa. Their reprisal was the formation of a large war party of over a hundred warriors led by Calf Shirt. They were sidetracked before they could "Hoorah" Fort Benton; the party killed ten woodhawks who were cutting logs for cabins to build the new town of Ophir at the mouth of Maria's River. The Ophir Massacre certainly stopped

Artist David Parchen

Just a village in 1865 at the time of the treaty, Fort Benton grew as steamboats brought gold seekers headed to the placers in the mountains of the south and west. As the white population increased, more and more incidents occurred with the Indians.

development of a river town to rival Fort Benton. Calf Shirt did Fort Benton a big favor while seeking revenge. Some Bentonites even cheered at the news! (2)

Schwinden Library, Fort Benton

Mountain Chief, Piikani chief and an antagonist of the whites, "Hoorayed" Fort Benton during the treaty of 1865.

Coming to Fort Benton

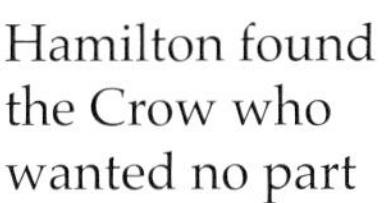

Hamilton found the Crow who wanted no part of a meeting with the Blackfoot. They said they would go to Fort Union to receive their annuities. On the north slopes of the Bear's Paw Mountains, Hamilton located the Atsina under Farmasee and lesser chiefs Star Robe and Bear Wolf. After a council the Atsina agreed to attend the treaty council with the Blackfoot.

The steamboat carrying the annuities docked at the levee in Fort Benton in the middle of September. The Indians came in until there were well over 4000 Native Americans encamped on the bottom: 350 lodges of Piikani and Kainaa and 500 lodges of Siksika. The Blackfoot were well represented. The Atsina moved in and camped by themselves on the up river side of the fort, well away from the big encampment of the Blackfoot which was down river from the fort. The Atsina, sometimes allied with the Blackfoot, had been warring with the Blackfoot during the past several years.

Treaty Terms

In the log council chamber built for the agency by Upson, the unarmed Blackfoot chiefs sat down but the Atsina chiefs were afraid and refused to enter. Marshal Hamilton convinced them to come to the agency for the reading of the treaty. Like most government agencies, their agents had no idea of the practicalities of such encounters. The lengthy document had to be read in English, translated into Blackfoot then translated again for the Atsina. The Indians did not understand the legal jargon of the government. As slowly as the first reading progressed, they were going to be in council for months. Hamilton said, "the commissioners knew as little on how to proceed in making those Indians understand their meaning as an Apache would know of Latin."

Finally the clerk, who had extensive experience with the Indians, condensed the forty-plus pages down to one for the next day's meeting. They agreed that the Blackfoot would cede all land south and east of the Missouri and the land south of the Teton to the mountains to the U.S. government in exchange for annuity payments over the next twenty years. Land to the north and west of the Teton was set up as a reserve for both the Piikani and Kainaa. Warring among the tribes was to cease as well as their attacks on the whites. By afternoon all seemed to understand, but many did not agree. Nevertheless, the negotiations ended. The Indians and whites signed the document but the U.S. Senate in its ultimate wisdom never ratified the treaty.

When a two-day distribution of goods was finished, the commissioners and Gad E. Upson left for Helena. In parting, Hamilton made another accurate observation: "He (Upson) knew as much about Indians as I did about the inhabitants of Jupiter." Gad Upson, Indian Agent Extraordinaire, never returned to Fort Benton. He died a few months later in Helena.

Schwinden Library, Fort Benton

Little Dog, Chief of the Piikani, saved the day by preventing a bloody fight between the Blackfoot and the Atsina.

Hot Time in the Old Town

After the commission departed, Little Dog rode into town from his camp on the Teton to warn the whites. He said that Mountain Chief and his North Piikani band, along with the Kainaa and Siksika, had obtained some whiskey to celebrate. They threatened to attack the Atsina and Fort Benton. When the news spread, the town prepared by digging rifle pits along the street; the Atsina did the same in their village. People at the fort locked the gate and prepared for the worst. All in all, possibly a hundred whites could shoulder a rifle. Fortunately, Little Dog said he would help with his 250 warriors.

Efforts to defuse the explosive situation may have helped, but around noon five hundred warriors, painted and on their best ponies, rode pell mell across the bottom by the fort and town and circled the Atsina camp. No shots were fired but insults and challenges were exchanged while they rode around and around the camp. As the wild threatening scene unfolded, the town's inhabitants cowered in their rifle pits, wondering what would happen next. With only verbal abuse exchanged, Mountain Chief and his warriors, with the South Piikani and Little Dog watching from a distance, rode back through the town, yelling and firing their rifles into the air and frightening everyone into their cellars. Five hundred painted savages on horseback running full speed with guns firing, yelling and whooping with clouds of dust rolling up the street was a terrifying experience for people of the little frontier town.

The warriors formed a half-circle facing Front Street. A few chiefs rode forward still threatening and calling names, but the possibility of Little Dog entering the fight was a deterrent to open hostilities. They eventually rode back to their villages still yelling threats and insults, but for the time being calm descended over the bottom. Later that afternoon with bolts of calico tied to their horse's tails, the warriors rode at full speed across the bottom with the calico flying, again yelling and shooting their rifles into the air. Most of the whites scurried for cover to avoid stray bullets and wild horses. Hordes of Indians rode in every direction among the buildings and kept the population cowering throughout the night. Such an exciting event was called "treeing the town." It was not the last time it happened to Fort Benton.

The uproar continued all night; it was morning before the people reclaimed their town. When the sun rose across the river and light of the new day streaked across the bottom, the Atsina village melted away. Not wanting the Blackfoot to have any second thoughts about attacking them, they disappeared across the river. With heads heavy from alcohol, occupants of the other Indian camps slowly packed up and headed north. Little Dog and his band remained another day before leaving for the buffalo hunt.

Treaty with the Blackfeet

The Montana Post reported on the treaty: (3)

"The terms of the treaty of October 17, 1855 between the Blackfoot Nation and the U. S. Government negotiated by Alfred Cummings and Isaac Stevens acting for the U. S. needed to be changed, because the gold discoveries created valuable assets which should be taken from the Indians. The Post decried the 1855 treaty; ". . . by which nearly the whole of what is now Montana was given over to the exclusive use, the northern portion for a dwelling place and the part south of the Muscle-Shell River for a hunting grounds. The government thought itself perpetuating a master stroke of policy when it appropriated to the Indians land that it seemed would never be good for anything to the whites. No one needs to be told that it has become desirable to extinguish the Indian title to these lands, since fifty thousand whites have settled upon them, attracted hither by the magnetic influence of the precious metals."

Yielding to the demands of settlers and miners, the federal government empowered the infamous Gad E. Upson to organize another treaty with the Indians and wrest those lands away from them.

Dateline Fort Benton November 17, 1865

The account of the treaty by the Post's special correspondent presents an interesting comparison with what Wm. T. Hamilton reported in his book My 60 Years on the Frontier.

"Arriving here the day before the ceremonies I found the place all alive with preparation for the morrow, the whites getting in readiness to astonish the natives and the Indians back in their camps upon the Teton and Missouri fully expecting to surprise the whites.

The morrow came and with it a bright bracing day and to the Council House about noon went forty-three chiefs and head men, with their wild retinues, delegates being present from the Piegan, Gros Ventres, Bloods and Blackfeet. All embraced under the general name of the Blackfoot Nation. With regard to the Bloods, it must be noticed that the hostile band by whom the murder of the eleven whites was perpetrated last spring, on the Marias River, was not represented, these savages ever since the murder having outlawed themselves beyond the British line. The Gros Ventres came into the place in fine style, the chiefs prancing along at the head of quite a troop of young warriors drawn out in a line who chanted a song of peace as they advanced. The room selected for the holding of the council had been finely decorated, the whole interior of the building being lined with cotton cloth, the white ground work upon which were festooned the long strips of red and blue flannel, producing, with fine effect, the national colors wherever the eye wandered. The four pillars in the center of the room served as emblematic columns upon which to arrange the insignia of both war and peace - the rifle, the bow, the tomahawk; and as the opposite of all these, the only olive branch to be obtained in these regions, the evergreen bough.

Upon the blanket-covered seats the red delegates seated themselves; and upon the platform at the head of the room, and in front of the beautiful national decorations, were seated the Commissioner, Major Upson, and by his side General Thomas Francis Meagher, as Superintendent of Indian Affairs for the territory; United States Judge L.E. Munson as legal council for the government. The interpreters, and other whites having influence among the natives also occupied seats on the platform.

As the artillery firing ceased on the outside, the parley commenced within. The pipe of peace was passed and was received with thanks. Perfect harmony seemed to prevail, both the pipe bearer and the pipe being stroked affectionately, some of the chiefs even going so far as patting each other on the head in token of amity.

The talk which was carried on through

Schwinden Library, Fort Benton

"Meagher of the Sword," Acting Governor of Montana Thomas Francis Meagher came to Fort Benton to make peace with the Blackfoot.

the means of a French and Blackfoot interpreter as necessarily somewhat tedious and cannot be repeated at length. The Indians were assured that we desired a permanent peace and that we wished peaceful relations to exist between the various tribes. The treaty was then read by Judge Munson and interpreted. Its principal provision and the one which will most interest your readers is contained in Article III which provides for a cession of all lands heretofore claimed by the Blackfeet excepting those lying north of the 48 degrees north latitude - the Teton, Marias and Missouri Rivers as far east at the Milk River - the Indians agreeing that other tribes may be settled in this reservation. This article is somewhat modified by the next which allows the government to build roads and telegraphs, establish military posts, agencies, mission schools, etc., in the reserve territory, and permits the whites free privilege to travel across it; but whites are prohibited from making settlements or trading (unless specially licensed), within the limits of the reservation; and intoxicating liquors, and all persons in them are to be strictly debarred entrance thereon.

They and their obligation to obey the laws thereof and they agree to exert themselves to the utmost of their ability for the purpose of enforcing them promising to deliver all offenders to the proper authorities whenever called upon so to do. As recompense for the lands ceded the United States agreed to expend for the Blackfoot Nation in addition to the goods distributed at the time of signing the treaty, $50,000 annually for twenty years. Such portion of this money as may be deemed proper by the President to be used in promoting civilization among the Blackfeet."

Quotes from the speeches of the Indian Chiefs were printed in The Montana Post.

Little Dog, Head Chief of the Piikani: "We are pleased with what we have heard today. One reason why I am glad to hear what you have had to say is because there are three nations here to listen. With regard to the Indians, the words are strong that you have told us. The land here belongs to us; we were raised upon it; we are glad to give a portion to the United States, for we get something for it. We don't intend to put aside the whites who have married in the nation; we want to give the half-breeds a share of our annuities. They own the land as much as ourselves, and we want them to get their portion of what they receive for it. I am very glad that you have told us today that you are going to send mechanics, physicians and teachers among us. Everything told us today we are willing to agree to; we see nothing bad in the treaty. Whatever we Piegans have promised, we shall try to perform; so that the Great Father below will be pleased."

Schwinden Library, Fort Benton

Bull Back Fat, Kainaa Chief and one of the principals at the 1865 treaty in Fort Benton.

Bull Back Fat spoke to the same effect on behalf of the Bloods (Kainaa).

Farmasee (Sitting Squaw), head chief of the Gros Ventres (Atsina), said: "We have been at war with the Piegans and

Schwinden Library, Fort Benton

During the treaty, one of the events to impress the Indians was when they fired a cannon off the back of the mule. The mule kicked and turned; the Indians stood stoically by but the whites ran for cover. Luckily no one was hurt except the sign over the gate at the fort.

Bloods and the nations all around; but today my heart swells up; it is as glad as the earth is big on account of the peace. For our part we are done going to war; we want to be at peace with all nations and all be brothers."

Fish Child, Blackfoot, agreed in sentiment with Little Dog and the others.

The Montana Post continued:" . . . and so was concluded a treaty in the highest degree advantageous to the whites which gives over to us all the vast extent of country between two and three hundred thousand square miles in which are situated our largest towns: Helena, Virginia City, Bannack, etc. and containing all our rich mines, our best agricultural land, some of our largest rivers, and in fact all those portions of our territory that have been proven to be of any worth. Too much commendation cannot be bestowed upon Major Upson, the Commissioner who had the treaty matter in charge, not only for the perseverance with which he has striven to effect it, but also for the thorough manner in which his work has finally been accomplished."

The Montana Post wrote about Thomas Francis Meagher's role in the treaty: "The general, the governor, the secretary, his Excellency, the Honorable Thomas Francis Meagher has not only with his many titles served to add dignity to all the treaty ceremonies, but, as Superintendent of Indian Affairs for the territory, has materially assisted in the work by his prompt decision and ready counsel."

The Cannon and the Mule

Some attribute the legend to the Fourth of July, but it probably occurred at the opening of festivities during the late October treaty. Gladstone's diary set the stage by remarking that the last wagon train out of Cow Island that year carried an old four-pounder that was being taken to Helena. The 1884 account of the incident in the River Press mentioned that a Diamond R freight train had arrived from Cow Island and the travelers camped on the flats. The barrel of a four-pounder was strapped to the back of one of the mules. Some thought it might be a good idea to show the Indians the strength of the "little gun" by discharging it while strapped to the back of the mule.

Most of the townspeople and many chiefs from the encampments were present. Near the main entrance to the fort, the mule was led to the bank of the river. The muzzle of the cannon was pointed toward the mule's tail and the cannon loaded with grapeshot. The appointed officer, none other than X Beidler, inserted a fuse and touched it off. When the quiet mule heard the sizzling just back of its ears, it turned its head to investigate. The River Press continued: "As he did so his body turned and the howitzer began to take in other points of the compass. The mule became more excited as his curiosity became more and more intense, and in a few seconds he either had his four feet in a bunch, making more revolutions a minute than the bystanders dared count, with the howitzer threatening destruction to everybody within a radius of a quarter of a mile, or he suddenly would try standing on his head with his heels and howitzer at a remarkable angle in the air."

The whites and Indians scattered in all directions. Col. Broadwater, Mose Solomon, H.A. Kennerly and Joe Healy dove over the river bank to a wet landing. Matt Carroll, George Steell and James Arnoux sprinted up the street and Hi Upham, Bill Hamilton and Johnny Healy sought shelter on the ground. I.G. Baker and two of the peace commissioners ran for the fort. The Indians sort of stood around, wondering what all the excitement was about. With a sudden puff of smoke the cannon discharged and grape shot headed toward the fort.

According to the paper, the mule "with his heels in mid-air, was shaken with the most violent agitation ... oh where was he? Ask of the wind, for no soul saw him, and they will tell you a lonely, forlorn mule might have been seen turning over and over until he tumbled over the bank with the howitzer and cast anchor in the river." The shot hit the buffalo painted over the main gate which was well perforated. With tongue in cheek the River Press said it was X. Beidler's first buffalo. The

Schwinden Library, Fort Benton

X. Beidler, the Vigilante hangman, was a U.S. Deputy Marshal and the brunt of the joke when the cannon was fired from the mule's back during treaty ceremonies at Fort Benton in 1865.

Indians departed, still wondering about the crazy antics of the Bentonites.

An Approaching Disaster

Again the Indians were left disgusted with the terms they were forced to accept. The annuities promised for the next twenty years were never delivered and in the next twenty years the buffalo disappeared. The Blackfoot were forced to smaller and smaller reservations and became wards of the U.S. government.

The end of trade was near. For 35 years two giants, the American Fur Company and the Hudson Bay Company, dominated the fur trade. Chouteau left the upper river and

Schwinden Library, Fort Benton

Trade was about over when Chouteau and Company left Blackfoot Country. The peaceful co-existence of two cultures changed to hostilities and degredation when uncontrolled whiskey trade reared its ugly head.

The Bay gave up its crown and monopoly in Canada. Both compromised the liquor trade with twice-a-year festivities to promote their business, and it was a lucrative business. Moral issues never stood in the way of profit.

The new traders were a different breed who did not restrict their use of liquor. For the next few years liquor was the main item of trade, with disastrous effect upon the Blackfoot culture. The trade was in shambles except for huge profits carried away by the free traders and mercantile companies of Fort Benton.

At the end of 1865 Blackfoot Country saw the departure of Chouteau and Company after participating in the fur trade since 1830. An omen of the finality was the death of its architect Pierre Chouteau Jr., who passed away on September 6, 1865

Text Notes

1. In the early history of Fort Benton, Chouteau was misspelled as Choteau. The Choteau House Hotel and the county were spelled incorrectly. In 1913 the family requested the Legislature and the County to correct the spelling of the family name. Since then, Chouteau County has been spelled correctly but confusion remains. The town of Choteau originally spelled it correctly but when the county name was corrected, they changed to without the "U" to be different.
2. Some believe that the attack was staged by whites dressed as Indians to stop building a town that would compete with Fort Benton as a river port. No historical data supports this theory.
3. Montana Post, Dec. 9. 1865. This was a Virginia City newspaper until 1868 when it moved to Helena. Fort Benton did not have a newspaper until 1875.

1866

Fort Benton 1866-68

1868

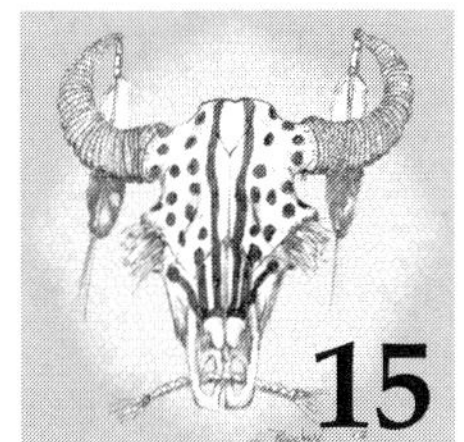

15

1866 - 1868

War and Peace

Continuing Troubles

Guerilla War and One Last Treaty

Democrats and Republicans

The Treaty of 1865 and the departure of the American Fur Company (Chouteau and Company) from the Upper Missouri that year ended stability in the Blackfoot fur trade. Many problems undermining the trade after the Civil War resulted from establishment of the Montana Territory in 1864. The Republicans were in power in Washington so all federal appointments went to the party faithful. By a wide majority, Confederate veterans, Irish Americans and pro-Confederate Northerners were welded into the Democratic party of Montana.

In the first Territorial election the Democrats elected all but one of their candidates to the legislature and sent a Representative to the U.S. Congress. Attempts by federally-appointed officials to enforce federal laws were always opposed by the Democratic majority.

Almost overnight, the big gold strike in Montana at Bannack in 1862 increased and changed the white population so drastically that nothing would ever be the same. The gold rush brought a whole new group of people to Montana who had never done business with

Schwinden Library, Fort Benton

Main street of Virginia City that saw ten thousand people at the height of the boom.

the Indians. They had no compunction about trespassing on Blackfoot lands, and considered the Indians only a menace who stole their horses, interfered with their claims, and confronted them on the trails. They caused death and disruption and, according to the settlers, the only good Indian was a dead one.

Schwinden Library, Fort Benton

In early Montana politics there was always conflict between appointed Republican officials and elected Democrats like James Cavanaugh, the Territory's Representative to Congress.

Placers Explode

Mining towns sprang up in the mountains at Virginia City, Helena and Diamond City. All were served by the transportation center at Fort Benton. The towns had streets of saloons and dance halls where liquor flowed like the water in their sluice boxes. Fort Benton was not only the center of Blackfoot trade, but it was also the liquor distribution center for the mining frontier. The two did not mix, and violent confrontations were often the norm. The rough mining frontier had a whole new mixture. It was a male gold-seeking population who had "seen the elephant" and a free-enterprise collection of whiskey-trading whites. Horse-stealing Indians were upset because the whites encroached on

Schwinden Library, Fort Benton

Diamond City, another large Eldorado where thousands mined the placers until the dust ran out.

their hunting grounds. In 1865 the pot finally boiled over. A series of ugly incidents during the next five years was politely called the Blackfoot War.

Gold Rush to the Sun

After the Indian incidents of 1865, January 1866 brought more of the same. The Montana Post reported a gold stampede to Sun River that emptied Helena, and was a false alarm. Winter hit with a fury; a blizzard claimed several lives. Indians were blamed for several deaths, but Little Dog and his band saved many gold seekers during the cold winter. Gold brought many miners to the Sun River where they had contact with the Blackfoot. A new government farm was being setup to teach agriculture to the natives.

In February 1866 officials in Helena reported more Indian outrages at Fort Benton, though the locals had noted none at all. In the same issue of the Post, Acting Governor Thomas Francis Meagher issued a proclamation calling for 500 volunteers to go to Fort Benton and punish the Piikani. The article cited a letter from Hi Upham, Assistant Indian Agent, to his old friend Gad Upson. The Post concluded, "We trust that an efficient force will be organized, and that these red ruffians will be pacified with lead and steel wherever they are found." (1)

The call for action was triggered by a party of Piikani who caught a group of Atsina trading with two whiskey traders, Hunicke and Legis from Fort Benton. They killed both traders and several Atsina. The populace of Fort Benton wanted to send a petition to the Territorial Governor demanding a force of 500 men to avenge the killings. The government was unable to recruit the force immediately, so the Bentonites led by Frank (Joe) Spearson, took the law into their own hands and killed the first Indian who came to town. It happened to be the Kainaa chief Sitting on Eagle. According to reports, he was killed and shoved under the ice where his feet stuck out for several days.

Indian Militia

Absent in the Helena article was the Governor's desire to return to the "glory days" of the Civil War. It would boost his ego up to an acceptable level for such a fine Irish patriot or Fenian. His eloquent tongue had little effect on Montanans, and the activity to raise an army fell far short. When a small contingent of militia under John B. Morgan finally arrived in Fort Benton, action was limited since no Indians were seen. The townspeople soon tired of Morgan appropriating supplies and promising

Schwinden Library, Fort Benton

As war continued, peaceful Indians painted their lodges to represent the American flag and camped near the trading posts.

payment from the government. When no money was forthcoming, the merchants stopped his credit and the force melted away with the spring snow.

Morgan would not be forgotten; he was a violent Indian hater. The same winter of 1865-66 on the Sun River, Morgan had invited four Piikani into his home with the promise of whiskey. Brave miner friends brutally hanged three in his home and shot the fourth while he was trying to escape. The hangings were observed by several other Indians who rode off to tell their people. The Kainaa responded by raiding a horse herd in the Sun River Valley and stealing all the horses and mules from a wagon train headed to Fort Benton. Chief Bull Head and his North Piikani also returned the favor in April 1866 with an attack on the government farm at Sun River. They burned buildings and killed Cass Tuff, one of the employees. Morgan and his family sought shelter with the Jesuits at Saint Peter's Mission; the raiding party killed his livestock, took his horses and followed his trail to the mission.

At the Mission the Indians slaughtered the cattle herd and killed the young herder, John Fitzgerald, before they continued south. That was enough; the Jesuits gave up trying to pacify the Blackfoot, closed the mission and went west of the mountains the next spring. The Piikani went to the Dearborn, burned a ranch, killed Charles Carson and drove off the horse herd before going back to their winter camp. John Morgan escaped to Helena and later became sheriff of Choteau County.

In retaliation, late in 1866 a group of ruffians attacked a small band of Piikani who were crossing at the ford just below the fort. They killed and scalped one, the rest fled down river. The next day they found another band on the Teton, killed six and returned to Fort Benton to do a scalp dance on Front Street.

Besides whiskey trading, another illegal activity was trafficking Indian annuities by the agents. In December 1866 a local

Schwinden Library, Fort Benton

St. Peter's Mission was founded by the Jesuits to minister Christianity to the Blackfoot. They also had a boarding school for Indian boys and girls. During the Blackfoot War the mission was often besieged until the Jesuits closed it and went west of the mountains. (inset - The Mission Church is still standing.)

resident reported that Blackfoot Agent Major George B. Wright furnished Old Bill Hamilton and Captain Nels with about $2,500 worth of annuities that were traded to the Indians for about four wagonloads of buffalo robes. About 100 robes were counted out for the agent. A Negro employed by Wright sold his share of the robes to the I.G. Baker Co. Promised annuities eventually got to the Blackfoot, but not until the Indians paid for them in trade and lined the pockets of agents and traders in Fort Benton. Annuities like whiskey were stored in warehouses along the levee where access was easy because the merchants owned them all.

Northwestern Fur Company

In the spring of 1865 James Boyd Hubbell and Alpheus F. Hawley formed a business called the Northwestern Fur Co. They bought the Upper Missouri posts of Chouteau and Company. The deal was consummated when Hubbell met with Pierre Chouteau in Washington, D.C. Hubbell sold a half interest to his partner Hawley after he returned to Minnesota. Hubbell and Hawley took in Francis Bates and J.A. Smith as partners to form the new company. Their contract was for four years, but at the end of the year they all agreed to dissolve the company. Their survival on the upper river was short-lived. By 1869 they had sold the posts below Fort Union to Durfee and Peck and retired from the upper river.

When the company first came up river, I.G. Baker was offered a position but he turned it down. He recognized the big profits available in the mercantile and whiskey trade particularly since Chouteau and Company was gone. Baker employed William Gladstone to build his store during the winter of 1865-66 and went down river to acquire his first cargo of

Schwinden Library, Fort Benton

James B. Hubbell, major partner of the Northwestern Fur Company that bought out Chouteau and Company and took over the upper river

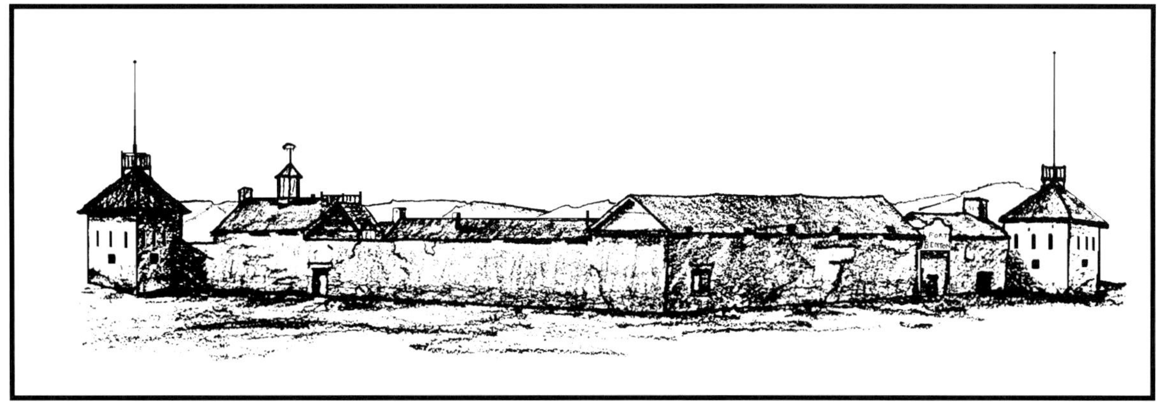

Schwinden Library, Fort Benton

Fort Benton, as seen by Granville Stuart in 1866, at the time of the takeover by the Northwestern Fur Company; the military arrived in 1869.

Schwinden Library, Fort Benton

Fort Benton was growing in 1866. There were many buildings outside the fort and steamboats brought more and more miners to the placers. Up river are the two abandoned opposition forts; one became a Jesuit mission, the other was just left vacant.

goods. The next year the Northwestern Fur Co. met his competition by building Fort Hawley in Atsina Country to be closer to the winter camps. A Baker post followed at the Milk River Crossing the next year. (2)

The dissolution of the Northwestern Fur Company in 1869 left the upper river trading to a group of Fort Benton merchants intent on getting rich quickly; greed was their only master. The company had entered the fur trade at the worst possible time. The western tribes were in turmoil, wars were breaking out in all sectors along the Missouri River, the Sioux below Fort Union were making life difficult as were the Blackfoot in Montana. The abandoned buildings at Fort Benton were taken over by the military who stayed until 1881.

Hubbell reported that the first year of business was good and the furs would repay their investment. In 1866 Hawley was trading at Fort Sully and J.A. Smith and David Pease were at Fort Benton. The take at Fort Sully was reported at 4,000 to 5,000 robes and 15,000 robes came from Fort Benton; the total robes amounted to over 25,000 for the Upper Missouri plus the small furs. It was the only year that the company made money. In the future, whiskey traders and merchants in Fort Benton cut deeply into the robe trade.

Military Fort Benton

In 1867 trouble with the Sioux erupted down river. They besieged the military at Fort Buford below Fort Union and destroyed Hubbell's post on the Niobrara River during the winter. His wagon supply trains were considerably more susceptible to raids by Indians than the boats had been. Hubbell's greatest loss that year occurred when he supplied the military at Fort Buford, but never collected from the U.S. government. Guerilla warfare went on around Fort Benton in 1867 and 1868. Blackfoot raiding parties attacked wagons and besieged lone traders away from their posts. The new

Schwinden Library, Fort Benton

"Old Glad," William Gladstone, carpenter and builder in Fort Benton

company did not have another successful year on the Upper Missouri. In 1869 they closed the stores in Fort Benton.

The U.S. government established a military reservation across the lower end of the Fort Benton bottom adjoining the townsite. The reservation extended over the hill to the northwest and encompassed part of the Teton River valley. The army moved into the old fur post and turned it into a military establishment to protect government freight at the levee. They built a new headquarters building outside the fort by dismantling the southeast wall and kitchen, using the adobe block for the new structure. Military supplies were shipped by steamboat to Fort Benton and taken by wagon train to other military establishments in Montana Territory.

The old fort was in such a state of disrepair that the troops were quartered in downtown Fort Benton. Adobe did not last as well as it did in the Southwest; maintenance hardly existed during the years of Chouteau and Company. With little or no care, the buildings were sagging, walls were falling down and when the military left in 1881 the fort was in ruins.

Fort Benton Cannons of the Fur Trade

Chouteau and Company sold Fort Benton in 1865. With that date as a reference, a story of two cannons from Fort Benton, now owned by the museums at Fort Macleod and Lethbridge, tells how they made the long trip up the Whoop-Up Trail and now reside in Canada.

In 1832 the West Point Foundry in New York cast the older of the two cannons. It has a three-pound cast-iron barrel mounted on a naval-style carriage. Made for the American Fur Company, it was shipped to Fort Union in 1833 probably on the steamboat *Yellow Stone*. The cannon was moved to Fort Benton after it became an important post in Indian country. When the fort closed, the cannon was sold to free trader John J. Healy and taken to Fort Hamilton in Canada during the whiskey trade era 1869-1874. Today the cannon is at reconstructed Fort Macleod in Alberta. An identical cannon, probably from Fort Union, is owned by the North Dakota Historical Society in Bismarck.

Horace E. Dimmick and Co. in St. Louis cast the second cannon in 1865. It has a one-pound, lathe-turned steel barrel originally mounted on a light prairie carriage. The cannon was made for the Northwestern Fur Company and shipped to Fort Benton the same year aboard the steamboat *Yellowstone*. (This is not the same steamboat as the one that came in 1833). This cannon is now the property of the City of Lethbridge. The barrel is mounted on a reproduction of the carriage and is displayed in reconstructed Fort Whoop-Up (Fort Hamilton). The original carriage is in the Galt Museum in Lethbridge.

Fort Benton residents John J. Healy and A.B. Hamilton probably purchased the two cannons sometime in 1869. They owned Fort Whoop-Up which was built in 1869; the two cannons were taken to Canada to protect the fort. One is mentioned in the Spitzee Cavalry incident at Fort Hamilton.

In 1890 J.D. Higginbotham purchased the one-pound cannon from Dave Akers, a trader at Fort Whoop-Up. Ownership then passed to the City of Lethbridge. The three-pound cannon was probably purchased from Fort Whoop-Up by the North West Mounted Police and later acquired by the Fort Macleod Historical Society.

Schwinden Library, Fort Benton

The Fort Benton cannon inside Fort Hamilton (Whoop-Up). It was taken to Canada by the trader John J. Healy.

Schwinden Library, Fort Benton

A.B. Hamilton, one of the partners in the whiskey trading venture at Fort Hamilton in the Canadian West after the Hudson Bay Co. gave up their charter

Schwinden Library, Fort Benton

John J. Healy, the other partner, started trading at Sun River but went to Canada to trade for T. C. Power at Fort Hamilton near Lethbridge.

Intertribal War

Although they continued the guerilla war with the whites who were invading their land in ever growing numbers, the Piikani still had time to attack the Atsina. The tribes sat in peace in the treaty house in Fort Benton in 1865, and called each other brothers, but the disruption in town after the treaty was a better indication of how they felt about one another. The Blackfoot had not forgiven the Atsina for the attack in 1861, when a raiding party of Pend d'Oreille stole horses from the Atsina along the Missouri River. They left some of the Atsina horses with the horse herd of the Piikani in their fall camp on the Marias. Without asking questions, when the Atsina found their horses with the Piikani herd, they mounted a surprise attack on the Piikani camp and killed a few before the Piikani recovered. Allies immediately became enemies. An effort to start a major war and wipe out the Atsina failed, so the Piikani contented themselves with small raids.

Late in the summer of 1866 the Atsina formed an alliance with the River Crow and continued the war. They attacked a large Piikani encampment near the Cypress Hills under the leadership of Many Horses. The Piikani were forewarned of impending danger. During the heat of the battle, the Piikani received word that Many Horses had been ambushed and killed. The infuriated Piikani deserted their distant battle line and mounted a charge on the Atsina and the Crow. (Most Indian battles were fought at the maximum distance, either the range a rifle could shoot or the flight an arrow would travel. There usually were few casualties.) The unusual tactic of the Piikani charge turned the tide and the enemy broke and ran. Mounted Piikani warriors drove their enemy like buffalo for miles, killing them in a mad chase across the prairie, like wildfire through grass, until the few survivors sought refuge in trees along a creek bank. The battleground looked much like a buffalo kill except that 300 human bodies were scattered across the bloody field instead of the hairy beasts. To the relief of their enemy, the Piikani decided that was enough and returned to the field to claim the spoils of war. It was a devastating defeat. Women and children were taken prisoners along with horses, guns and many sacred articles.

Again, the Blackfoot demonstrated their superiority over the neighboring tribes and perpetuated the universal fear that made them legendary on the plains. The next year Indian Agent Augustus Chapman exclaimed, "Acting Governor Meagher's Indian War in Montana . . . the biggest humbug of the age." He also said that "civilian travel on the Benton to Helena Road had not been impeded, and those citizens were not in any more danger from hostile Indians than they would be in Washington City."

More Whiskey

By 1867 the whiskey trade had spread to all the stopping points for steamboats. Indian Agent Nathaniel Pope complained that wood hawks supplemented their income by trading whiskey for robes. They obtained the whiskey from captains and crews of the boats that stopped at the yards to wood up.

Because trade was primarily for whiskey, guns, and ammunition in exchange for buffalo robes, assaults by the "red devils" on the citizens of Montana went on. Senseless killings and reprisals were frequent. A freighter named Lowe was robbed and killed; he was literally shot full of holes with six in his chest and shoulders and one between the eyes. The newspapers complained about war parties along the Benton-Helena road that managed to scalp up to a dozen innocent people each spring and fall.

Another giant Fort Benton firm, T.C. Power and Bro., was mixed up with Indian Agent Wright in an annuities scam. It involved a personal debt which was settled by giving the firm several cases of Indian goods. Back door trading and illegal trafficking in whiskey by Fort Benton's two large mercantile firms was not only overlooked by authorities, it was brazenly done in broad daylight for anyone to see.

Schwinden Library, Fort Benton

T.C. Power and Bro. was one of the large mercantile businesses of Fort Benton engaged in Indian annuities and the whiskey trade.

Meagher's Militia

In April 1867 a war party of Blackfoot killed John Bozeman. Isolated ranches were attacked and the settlers were killed. The Sioux raids along the Bozeman Road brought a cry for protection from the settlers and miners. Acting Governor Meagher again answered the call; he asked for and received authority to raise a federal militia. With money in hand and the political hangers-on waiting for the government dole, "Meagher of the Sword" accumulated an army of 600 including several of his Irish friends from Fort Benton. One of his lieutenants was Johnny Evans, a saloon owner and one of the many Fenians in the river town. They camped in the Bozeman Valley, but spent little time looking for Indians. On the contrary, they did nothing but party and run up a horrendous bill for supplies.

Meagher went to Fort Benton to pick up an arms shipment and to meet his wife who was coming up river on the *G.A. Thomson*. On July 1, 1867 the ex-general and Acting Governor ate his last meal in Fort Benton, then went to his demise in the Big Muddy. His body was

Schwinden Library, Fort Benton

Acting Governor Thomas Francis Meagher formed a militia to fight the Indians. He came to Fort Benton to pick up arms for his volunteers and lost his life in the Missouri.

never seen again. Drunk, shot, thrown, pushed, jumped or fell? Who knows? Who cares?

By the time Meagher's Militia disbanded, the troops had run up a million-dollar bill for Uncle Sam who refused to pay the debt until it was settled for half that amount. Most of the men went home unhappy that they could not stay longer; they enjoyed the easy duty on the government payroll. Meagher was a hero in his Irish homeland and to thousands of Fenian supporters in Montana who raised his equestrian statue on the Capitol lawn.

Killings of and by Indians finally brought a real military presence to Montana. The first military post, Camp Cooke, was established at the mouth of the Judith River in May 1866. It was built in such an isolated area, away from the main trails and roads used by both whites and Indians, that it survived only four years. Rats took over the supplies and the men went AWOL in such numbers to the gold fields that the army couldn't catch them all.

The next summer in 1867 the military established two major posts: Fort Ellis near the town of Bozeman and Fort Shaw at Sun River Crossing. Fort Shaw became the regimental headquarters for the newly-formed Military District of Montana. Strategically located on the main road half-way between Fort Benton and Helena, it protected the masses of miners headed to and from the gold fields. With four companies of infantry, it had an excellent command of Blackfoot Country and the mining district, but achieved only more Indian resentment by its presence.

Annuities promised by the 1865 Treaty had never been delivered and no one bothered to explain to the Blackfoot the technicalities of ratification. The Secretary of Interior in his ultimate wisdom believed neither party would observe the treaty, so he failed to submit it to the Senate. The Blackfoot gave up their lands as expected by the government and the whites, but delivery on the part of the government was not forthcoming due to technicalities. Things never seem to change when it comes to U.S. government Indian policies.

Little Dog

One of the most shameful deaths to occur during the period was that of Little Dog, an Indian who stood for peace and good will. The chief of the Piikani, Little Dog probably

Schwinden Library, Fort Benton

Camp Cooke, Montana's first military establishment at the confluence of the Judith and Missouri Rivers

an Indian who stood for peace and good will. The chief of the Piikani, Little Dog probably did more than any other leader to preserve peace, not only between the whites and Indians but also among the tribes themselves. He was a Good Samaritan during the bad winter in 1865, helping feed beleaguered miners who were starving to death in winter storms. Unappreciated by both sides, he met his death at the hands of his own people.

Little Dog was a good friend of the traders at Fort Benton. He punished the horse thieves in his tribe, even going so far as to kill members of his tribe if they did not obey his demands to return the horses. His great loyalty to the whites led to his death. A contributing cause was failure of the government to make good on their promises of annuities from the Treaty of 1865, promises that Little Dog had praised and supported just one year before.

The Piikani were camped on the Teton. Little Dog, his son and their wives went to Fort Benton to trade one day in 1866. When they returned to camp, six young braves led by Cipino executed the chief. When his son Fringe found his father dead, he set out to avenge his death but he too was ambushed by the young hot bloods and died of his wounds. Both the chief and his son were held in high esteem. They had asked to be and were buried in the cemetery at Fort Benton. (3)

Schwinden Library, Fort Benton

Chief Little Dog of the Piikani, always a friend of the whites, was ambushed and killed by his own people.

Spring Brings War

When spring came in 1868, activity at the mining camps grew. Blackfoot attacks and horse raids increased in the gold rush towns and newspapers complained about the vicious attacks. Bentonites topped the grisliness of any attack when they chased down and killed three Piikani warriors and came home with the skin from the head of one warrior. The streets of Fort Benton, which for several years had not been a safe place for Indians, erupted again. A group of Indians was shot and chased to the island before the whites killed them all except one old woman.

The Mountain Chief incident was next. He came to Fort Benton to request that the Commissioner ban certain whites from Indian country and was chased out by the townspeople. When the Indian Agent tried to have them arrested, the judge and sheriff resigned rather than make an arrest or press charges.

Reprisals were not always taken against perpetrators, sometimes almost anyone on the other side would do. Indians ran off 80 horses from Confederate Gulch and Diamond City and escaped to the north. An eye for an eye policy was followed when a posse near Sun River took twenty young Piikani boys as prisoners because they couldn't catch anyone else. They were turned over to the military at Fort Shaw as hostages for the horses. After some bargaining, half of the horses were returned and the hostages were released. Still resentful, both Indians and whites got into a scuffle before the army took over and escorted the Indian youths back to their camps.

Schwinden Library, Fort Benton

Alexander Culbertson moved back to the river after filing for bankruptcy.

Charges Leveled

In March 1868 with spring coming on, the whiskey trade began in earnest. Charges and counter charges flew to and from the Commissioner of Indian Affairs. The last factor of Fort Benton was I.G. Baker, who went into business for himself after Chouteau and Company left, was right in the middle of the whiskey trade. In March 1868 J.B. Hubbell, a partner in the new company at the fort, complained to Indian Agent George Wright that Baker was taking wagons loaded with whiskey to the Indian camps. No real attempt was made to stop him although on one occasion, while on the trail, he was stopped by Deputy Marshall Hard who found a cache of whiskey and made him return to Fort Benton. In the same letter Hubbell complained, "Parties go out to meet the Indians on their way in to trade and of course the Indians will give them the blankets off their backs for a half pint of diluted alcohol and no effort made by the agent to stop it." Wright declared himself powerless because he had no cooperation from the U.S. Marshall who operated a saloon of his own. Furthermore, elected officers were receiving whiskey by the keg throughout the winter via Wells Fargo, and he did not know if they were trading it to the Indians.

Schwinden Library, Fort Benton

U.S. Deputy Marshal Charles Hard and X Beidler were the only lawmen in northern Montana to control the whiskey trade.

The King Returns

In the summer of 1868 Alexander Culbertson, Natawista, Fannie and Joe came back to the upper river, their first trip since 1864. He was immediately contracted to help with a new treaty between the Atsina and their new-found friends the River Crow. The treaty took place at Fort Hawley, 25 miles above the mouth of the Musselshell. Culbertson and Alfred Vaughan, the old Indian Agent, were hired by the commissioner as interpreters. A boyhood prank by Joe Culbertson almost upset the negotiations. The two tribes were given the easternmost portion of the Blackfoot reservation and again promised yearly annuities.

A New Town

When the council was finished, Culbertson was quite amazed when he arrived at the bustling boomtown of Fort Benton. When he left in 1864, there were only the first signs of buildings outside the fort. As the steamer rounded Signal Point, he saw a levee crowded with cargo and freight trains loading up to take to the trails out of town. Front Street was a mass of tents and wooden false-fronted buildings strung out for a mile along the levee. Even the streets toward the hills were lined with many new structures in various stages of construction. Scattered among the merchant businesses were 20 or more saloons and brothels, with two or three billiard and dance halls mixed in. All were open twenty-four hours a day and were willing to relieve any man of his poke at the drop of a hat or the turn of a card.

William Gladstone provided a picturesque view of life in Fort Benton during that period: "One could never tell

Schwinden Library, Fort Benton

Placers in the mountains yielded millions in gold and Fort Benton was a growing town in 1869. Local establisments operated 24-7 with little or no law and order to hamper anyone doing business as they pleased.

when Sunday came around as there was no distinction made between that day and any other. Drinking and gambling and whiskey selling went on just the same. On my first Sunday there I went to hunt up some friends and opening the door . . . Found four eager-eyed gamblers hard at work. Each had a bag of gold dust and pistol on the table before him. One of the men . . . 'Stranger do you indulge?' he hospitably asked. Upon admitting that now and again on rare occasions, I was known to do so, he pointed to a bucket and told me that I would find some Knock-me-down in there. I dipped some of the liquid fire out of the bucket and asking for water was directed to another bucket which I found contained whiskey too. They all laughed at me and asked if they drank water where I came from as the water in Benton was never used for that purpose." Gladstone continued, "Oh those were great days in Benton. Shooting and stabbing and rows of all kinds were daily occurrences it was a wonder to me more men were not killed." (4)

The Last Treaty 1868

Confusion of the treaty terms by Indians and whites alike and frequent Indian attacks which had not abated since 1865 finally forced the government to try to clear up the misunderstandings from the treaty of 1865. The Culbertson family spent the summer in Fort Benton and that fall he was asked to stay and help with the new Blackfoot treaty.

William J. Cullen was the commissioner in charge for the treaty with the Blackfoot and Atsina. On September 1, 1868 the Blackfoot tribes came together at Fort Benton for a second treaty. The Atsina and River Crow, not wanting to be mistreated by the Blackfoot, refused to come to the table. The new agreement was to explain the first one. Few details about the events of the day are available; the treaty terms were basically the same as those in 1865.

Land given up by the Indians was the same. The Atsina and River Crow had all they wanted of life near the Blackfoot after their defeat near the Cypress Hills the year before. The negotiators gave them the far eastern portion of the reservation and the Blackfoot were ordered to stay away. An omission in the new treaty was the provision for annuities to the individual chiefs, which upset all the chiefs and caused hostilities after the council. (5)

Mountain Chief, Chief of the Piikani; Calf Shirt, Chief of the Kainaa; and Three Bulls for the Siksika signed the treaty. Other sub-chiefs also signed but it mattered not. This treaty ended exactly as the one three years earlier; it was never ratified. Warfare went on for two more years culminating in the tragedy of 1870, the massacre of Heavy Runner's band.

Artist Gustav Sohon

The three Blackfoot Chiefs who signed the treaty at Fort Benton in 1868. L to R: Calf Shirt of the Kainaa, Three Bulls of the Siksika and Mountain Chief of the Piikani

Another Treaty Story

Henry Kennerly, who observed the treaty of 1855 as a clerk, married a Blackfoot woman. In 1913 he signed a deposition in Glacier County about the Treaty of 1868 at Fort Benton. Kennerly said that he was in the butcher business in Fort Benton in 1868. The deposition indicated that Commissioner Cullen came to Fort Benton and established a camp four miles northwest of Fort Benton on the Teton River for several weeks that summer. He attempted to assemble the Blackfoot at a general council for making a treaty. Conflicts with the whites occurred and the Indians would not come to meet him. Kennerly stated that he observed the camp almost daily and never saw any Blackfoot in Cullen's camp. On one of his visits to the commissioner's camp Kennerly found the Commissioner, Alexander Culbertson and J.D. Beidler (X Beidler?) all drunk. Cullen wanted Kennerly and Beidler to sign the treaty as witnesses. Kennerly declined, saying that he saw no Indians to make a treaty. "Old Man" Culbertson broke out into a loud guffaw of laughter and said, "By God we can make treaties without Indians." Kennerly wrote that at no time did Indians come to the fort. If they had, he would have known; it was customary for the Indians to visit his house. Yet according to the newspaper and other accounts, the treaty really happened . . . (6)

Whiskey was always available in Fort Benton for any white or Indian to celebrate almost anything. According to W.S. Stocking, one occasion was not much of a "treeing of the town" since the saloon crowd paid little attention to the several hundred Indians riding up and down the streets shouting and shooting their guns all night long. Perhaps it wasn't much different than any other night along Front Street during the freighting season. Most people took to their homes or cellars until after sunrise when the "threat" returned to their tepees to sleep off the night air.

Law Enforcement

The Intercourse Law of Prohibition, which had been basically ignored since its passage in 1834, was still in effect. In 1868 it was brought back by Territorial Governor Clay Smith who declared it was still the law and would be enforced as amended in 1862. Any boat, wagon or other conveyance could be searched without warrant in Indian country, and if liquor was found, the vehicle, horse and goods could be seized.

In addition the culprit's license could be jerked, his liquor destroyed, and Indians could serve as witnesses against him in court. After publicizing the law, the Governor wanted immediate action, especially around Fort Benton. Of course no local support existed, bribery immediately reared its ugly head, and animosity toward the Blackfoot grew. Enforcement never came because too much money could be made.

Village Trading

Later in 1868 I.G. Baker sent his teamster Jake LaMott with a freight wagon north of Fort Benton to find Charles Conrad who was trading with the Piikani. At Captain Nels Leavings on the Teton, LaMott ran into a band of Indians who harassed him for food and whiskey.

When LaMott found Conrad that evening, they tried to slip away in the middle of the night. Around dawn the Indians overtook them and tried to persuade them to come to their camp. They finally parted company at Dead Indian Coulee, where Conrad and LaMott went on to the Marias. They found the villages full of Fort Benton traders selling whiskey to the Blackfoot. Agents of Carroll & Steell, Northwestern Fur Co. and T.C. Power and Bro. were all there.

The Piikani chiefs were so upset with all the drunkenness that they chased off the traders, including Captain Nels and Charlie Duvall who had just shown up as free traders. They almost killed Joe Spearson who worked for the Northwestern Fur Co. before they packed up their camp and left. Conrad's wagons were the last to leave. An angry group of young warriors in Full Bear's camp sent them on their way and told them not to stop until they reached Fort Benton.(7)

The Blackfoot complained bitterly about the rush of company and free traders to the Indian camps to trade whiskey. They sent this message to the commissioner: "We want the new traders to act like the old men who traded long ago when there was nothing but peace and quiet." Mountain Chief reiterated the message, "We do not wish these pale faces to come to our villages. If we desire to trade we will go into their forts, dispose of our robes and leave. There is nothing in common between us."

Continuation of Trouble

Roaming war parties created incidents along trails and around mining camps during the winter of 1868. A Blackfoot raiding party took the life of Charles Scott, tried to steal the Wells Fargo livestock but was driven off by gunfire from Scott's companions. A few weeks later the Piikani caught a woodhawk away from his shelter on the Missouri and killed him. They held a scalp dance in full view of Camp Cooke to frighten the new recruits. As a parting gesture they stole over two dozen mules and horses and headed north to the border.

A final event closed the season of 1868. One of the terms of the treaty was removal of the Blackfoot Agency from Fort Benton to within the new boundaries of the reservation, seventy-five miles northwest of Fort Benton.

Text Notes

1. Montana Post, April 28, 1866, Helena. Letter May 19, 1866. Report Hiram D. Upham, April 20, 1866; MHS SC 895
2. Northwestern Fur Co., Minnesota History, Winter 1955. Also called Northwest or North West, Hubbell used Northwestern.
3. Montana Magazine of Western History, Vol. 14, No. 2
4. Gladstone's Diary from Lethbridge Herald Oct. 21, 1958 to Nov. 26 1958
5. Treaty Terms 1868; Montana Historical Society manuscript collections
6. Copy of Certificate, Glacier County by Henry A. Kennerly on the Blackfoot Treaty of 1868, dated 1913, Montana Historical Society
7. Sun River Sun, Dec. 25, 1864

Fort Shaw

1867 - 1891

Fort Shaw was built by the U.S.Army on the Sun River where the Benton to Helena Wagon Road crossed. It controlled attacks by the Blackfoot on travelers to and from the gold fields and was the base from where the military came who massacred Heavy Runner's band in January 1870. The post served during the Indian Wars then was abandoned in 1891.

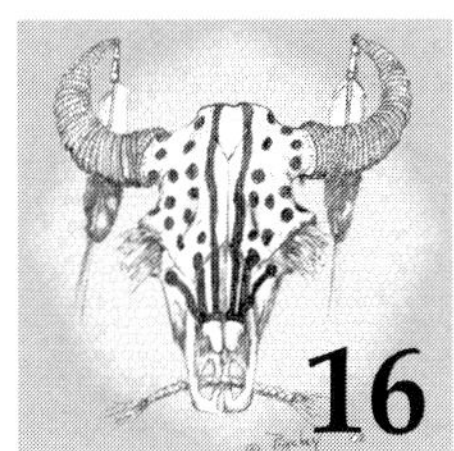

16

1869 - 1870

Final Pages

Death to Heavy Runner

End of a Free Life and Banishment to the Reservation

Agency is Moved

Early in 1869 the Blackfoot Indian Agency was moved to a site on the Teton River about seventy-five miles northwest of Fort Benton. Away from the environs of a growing hostile population in Fort Benton, the new agent hoped to be his own master. The inhabitants of Fort Benton were extremely antagonistic toward the Indians. The transient population of Civil War veterans, merchants and itinerate miners tried to dictate Indian policy by their actions and with political pressure. All the townspeople wanted were the Indian lands, huge profits from the annuities, the opportunity to trade whiskey for robes and the right to shoot and ask questions later. In other words, theirs was another white solution to solve the "Indian problem" in the West. The Commissioner believed that the move would reduce the number of Indians on the streets of Fort Benton where they were fair game if any citizen decided to shoot them and pitch their bodies in the river or down a well. During the years of the gold bonanza in Fort Benton, when the Indians were more peaceful, another needless shooting along Front Street renewed hostilities.

Fort Conrad

By the end of 1868 the Northwestern Fur Co., merchants and free traders cruised at will on and off the reservation, trading whiskey for robes. The federal government finally had to take steps to clean up the mess. They decided to issue only two permits to trade on the Blackfoot Reservation and hoped the Blackfoot would trade only at the two posts; if liquor was found, the permit would be revoked. I G. Baker and

Co. was issued a permit for a post on Maria's River just down from Willow Rounds which would be called Fort Conrad. The other permit went to the Northwestern Fur Co. to build a post on the Teton near Old Agency and the present town of Choteau. John Riplinger and James Hubbell built and took charge of the one on the Teton, 75 miles from Fort Benton. Baker was granted a permit to trade on the Milk River with the Atsina and Assiniboine, and T.C. Power went south to trade with the Crow.

S.C. Ashby, Baker's cousin, was hired by the Conrads to build the post on Maria's River about 100 miles northwest of Fort Benton. A work party of twenty-five men constructed the post and in a short time the buildings and stockade were finished. The post immediately became popular with all tribes of the Blackfoot because it shortened the trip for the northern bands who went there instead of Rocky Mountain House or Fort Edmonton. Soon all Blackfoot bands north of the border were trading at the new post. Ashby assisted Roche de Rouche once construction was done. Trade was so brisk that winter that William Conrad, a partner in the I.G. Baker Company, came to manage the business. At the end of the season, Ashby claimed that $40,000 worth of trade occurred without selling whiskey.

Trading as Usual

As soon as the locations of the two posts were known, free traders congregated within a few miles of the posts and began selling whiskey from their wagons. Drunken Indians were again a nuisance at the posts. In one incident, Calf Shirt and his Kainaa followers threatened Father Imoda, who would have been killed had it not been for Wm. Conrad's presence of mind.

In the winter of 1868-69, a decree came from Washington ordering the army to seize all liquor in the hands of Fort Benton merchants.

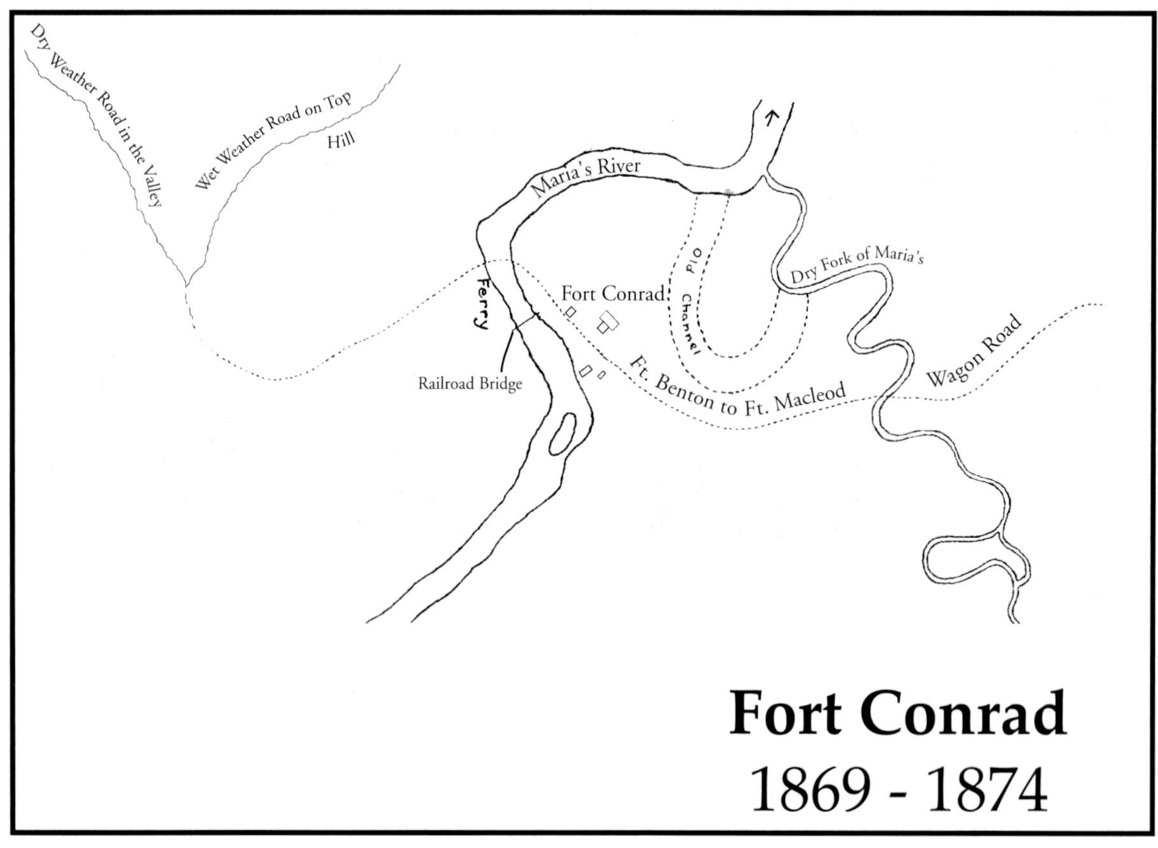

Schwinden Library, Fort Benton

William G. Conrad, one of two brothers who ran the I.G. Baker Co. in the West from their headquarters in Fort Benton

A technicality in the Treaty of 1855, when the Missouri River became the southern boundary of the Blackfoot Reserve, legalized the action. Located on the north bank, Fort Benton was on the Reservation where no liquor was allowed. Confiscation of the large stocks that belonged to I.G. Baker, T.C. Power, Carroll and Steell and W.S. Wetzel caused a protest heard across the territory. Another technicality was found and the confiscated liquor was returned. For some reason, none of it had been destroyed.

Desperate to gain control of the whiskey trade, in 1869 Washington dismissed Indian Agent Wright and replaced him with Nathaniel Pope. The job of Superintendent of Indian Affairs was removed from the governor's office and given to W. J. Cullen. U.S. Marshal Howie was removed in favor of W.T. Wheeler. None of the changes affected the whiskey trade at Sun River and Fort Benton, where merchants just moved north of the border since the Hudson Bay Company had given up Rupert's Land to the Dominion.

Hudson Bay Co. Leaves

In 1869 the Hudson Bay Company gave up their sovereignty over lands north of the Montana border to the Dominion Government of Canada. The door was open to Fort Benton merchants, whiskey traders and outlaws to move their operations north of the "Medicine Line," away from U.S. Marshals and off the reservations into a virtually lawless land. Incidents along the Whoop-Up Trail in what is now southern Alberta are legends in themselves. Lawlessness was the norm until 1874 when the North West Mounted Police brought law and order to both sides of the border.

During the entire trade period, the Blackfoot Nation's culture was degraded. Whiskey provided a fortune in buffalo robes for those involved in the trade. The five years from 1869 to 1874 were black years for the fur trade between the Blackfoot and the Americans. Few whites had any feelings for the Indians they were exploiting. Congeniality, family relationships, compassion between trader and Indian, and reliance on one another in the wilderness disappeared. Big business, "make a profit regardless of the land or the people you destroy," ruled the day. The attitude has not changed much over the last hundred years.

At War Again

Peace sought by the Treaty of 1868 did not happen. Beginning in 1869, a series of hostile actions on both sides led to pitched battles. Malcolm Clarke was killed in August. In January a war party attacked a party of hunters on the Dearborn and a few were wounded. Seven Piikani chased a Diamond R train on the Benton-Helena Road in April. In a wild gun battle an Indian was killed and the wagon master Watkins was wounded. That night on the streets of Fort Benton a drunken crowd retaliated by killing two Indians and throwing them into the river.

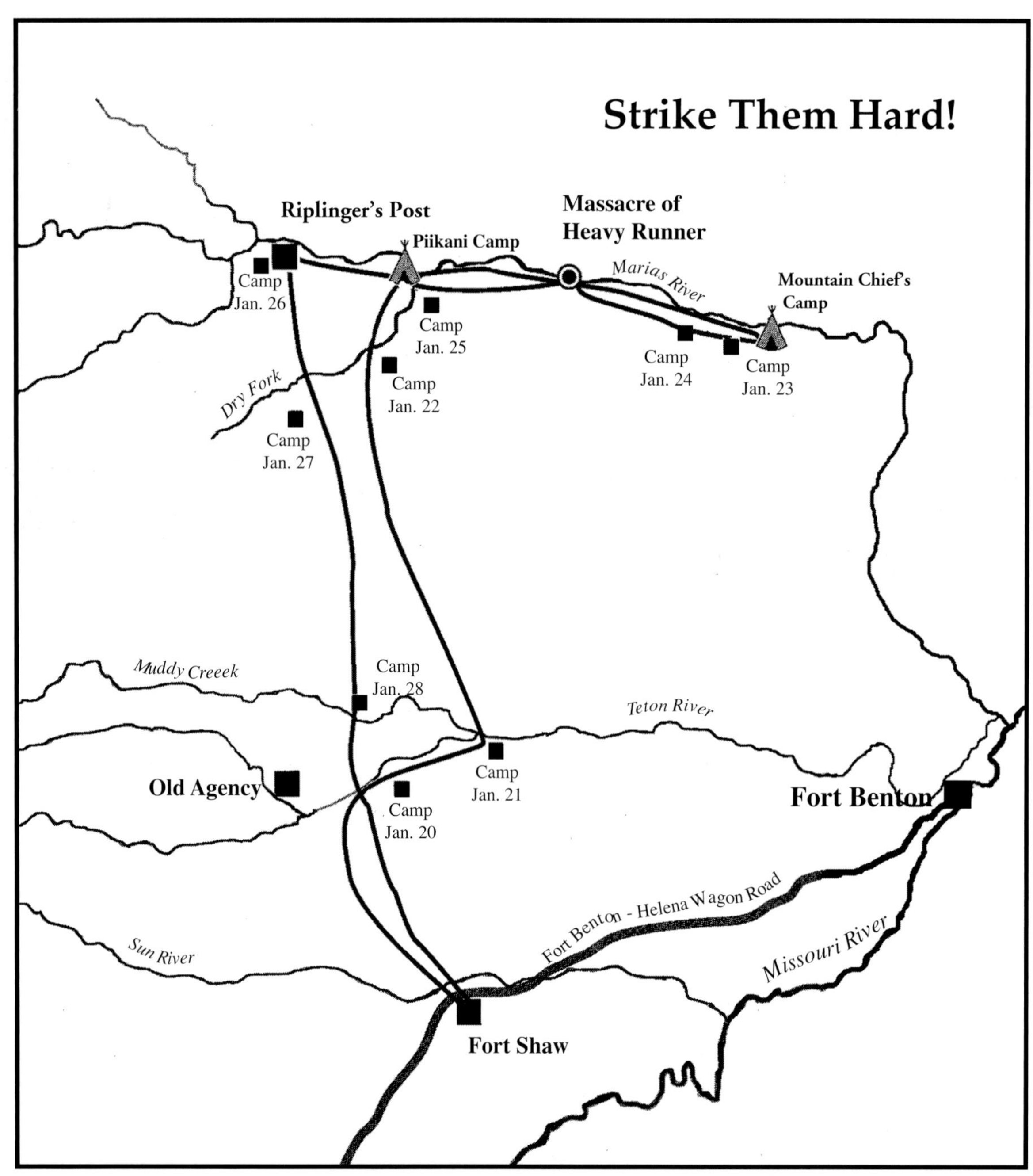

Baker's 1870 Ride into Infamy

Massacre of the Blackfoot on Maria's River in the Winter of 1870

In the summer a roving Crow war party stole horses from a wagon train and killed two herders. Fort Bentonites vowed to get even. When one of the dying herders was brought to Fort Benton, Henry Kennerly, Houk and Lukins cried for blood. Two Piikani were dragged out of Gladstone's home and killed in the street; they seized three perfectly innocent Blackfoot and hanged them. They were left hanging for a few days with a note on the bodies, "There are three good Indians." Two of the murdered Indians were relatives of Mountain Chief. A few weeks later Mountain Chief's brother and a companion were shot down in the middle of the day on Front Street, no reason and no questions asked. The killers were known to all, but were not arrested for killing an Indian or two in Fort Benton.

General Alfred Sully, recently-appointed Superintendent of Indian Affairs for Montana, wanted to take action but felt it was useless. He said, "I think I can arrest the murderers but doubt very much if I can convict them in any court." Even keeping them jailed in Fort Benton would have been a problem. General Sully added, "Nothing can be done to insure peace and order till there is a military force here strong enough to clear out the roughs and whiskey-sellers in the country."

Schwinden Library, Fort Benton

General Alfred Sully, Indian fighter and the Superintendent of Indian Affairs in Montana

Schwinden Library, Fort Benton

Some of Fort Benton's independent whiskey traders: (LtoR) Mose Solomon, Joe Kipp, Bob Mills, Henry Kennerly and John Largent

Mountain Chief, then head chief of the Piikani, was a far different and less tolerant leader than Little Dog. The previous year Fort Benton citizens had insulted and abused him because of his demands to enforce the treaty he had signed. Of course he had no way of knowing that the treaty had met the same fate as the Treaty of 1865. Killings escalated the hostilities and he and his Piikani sought revenge.

In early August a large war party of Piikani found a government wagon train at Eagle Creek; after a three-hour gun battle the

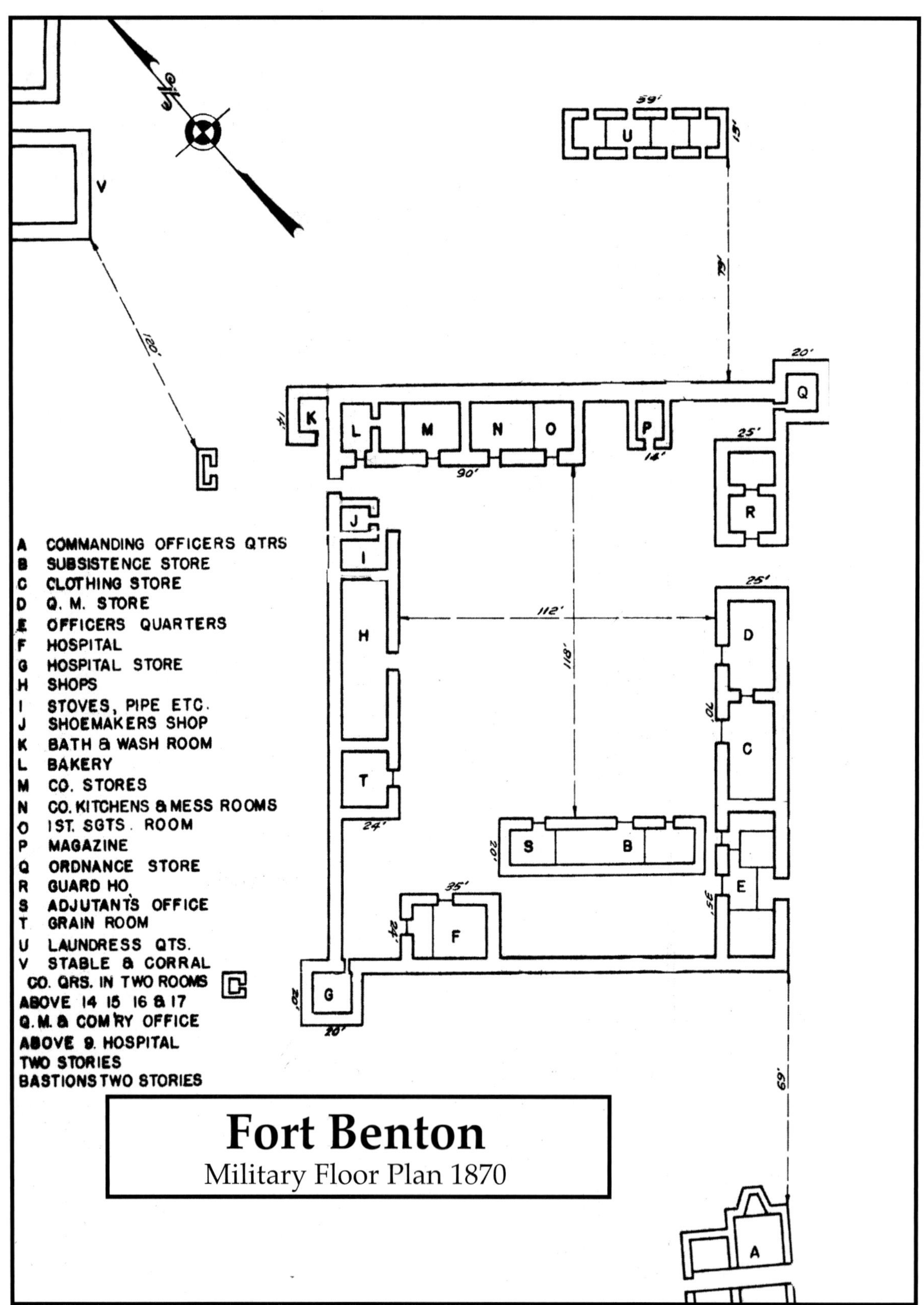

Fort Benton

Military Floor Plan 1870

Indians had killed most of the oxen. Another unsuspecting train came along the trail and it too was attacked. A young bullwhacker tried to negotiate a peaceful settlement but was shot in the process. After several hours, the freighters were able to drive off the Piikani. Only one teamster was wounded. In the Indian party, two were wounded and four were killed.

Attacks along the Benton-Helena Road went on until winter. Blackfoot raids generally disrupted travel along the road. The Indians made off with livestock and shot isolated ranchers and freighters. Thirty-seven horses were stolen on the Benton to Helena route. A haying party from Fort Shaw was attacked but no one was injured. As life on the Montana frontier headed into the "Dog Days of August," a mighty uproar came from her citizens demanding more protection from the army. The climax of the guerilla war was the death of Malcolm Clarke and the wounding of his son at their ranch in August.

Malcolm Clarke's Death

After sitting on his hands for a month or more, General Sully decided that a state of war existed with the Blackfoot and informed higher authorities of the situation. On the night of August 17, twenty-five Piikani warriors visited Malcolm Clarke's ranch at present day Sieben on Little Prickly Pear. Clarke, an old trader for the American Fur Company, had a Piikani wife and mixed-blood children, and was a respected rancher in the white community. That night in a confrontation outside his house, Clarke was shot and killed. He had been their friend, had lived and hunted with the Piikani, but sometimes the innocent pay for the crimes of the guilty.

Schwinden Library, Fort Benton

Malcolm Clarke, long-time fur trader for the American Fur Co., became a rancher and was killed by his wife's people.

Among the buildings on the ranch on a little knoll above the creek is a black wrought iron fence surrounding Clarke's grave. It is a lonely tribute to one of the many martyrs of the Blackfoot Wars.

The Last Open Season

After Clarke's death, at protest meetings in Helena the people wanted to equip a volunteer force to hunt down the Indians and pay a bounty for each one killed. A grand jury met and after much "saber rattling," matters were turned over to the military. Still . . . whiskey continued to flow like water on the Montana frontier.

As the winter trading season of 1869-70 got underway, John Riplinger wrote a letter in December to the Commissioner of Indian Affairs stating that his business would be a lost cause with all the free traders in Indian country. "To my certain knowledge there has been brot here from Benton & Sun River more than 60 Gals whiskey. The Indians are going & coming from here and other camps below to Benton all the time. They don't go into town for it, they are met out on the Teton by the Bentonites and there get what they want, the same at Sun River . . . There is no use talking to them. They are nothing but a lot of unreasonable dogs; they have no sense; they don't want to understand what is good for them."

Riplinger's lengthy report provided the details about several incidents involving the use of whiskey. A month later in a second letter to the Commissioner he reported that his predictions had come true; no business was transacted at the trading post because of the Fort Benton merchants. "Last night at 11 o'clock Clarke Tingley passed here with a wagon & a half Bbl. of Liquor. He is in a Blood camp about two miles above me and has Traded about 100 Robes since he arrived . . . The Indians are Drunk all the time. The camps below all have liquor traders in them. We are doing nothing here; all Indians that don't trade their Robes for Liquor here in Camp go to Benton to Bakers

Schwinden Library, Fort Benton

General Phil H. Sheridan, commander of the armies in the West

& Powers as they report that Baker trades Liquor to them after dark."

In hopes of improving his business, Riplinger moved his post further north and down river and hired William Gladstone to construct the new post. Moving the post closer to Canada was a harbinger of things to come. Everyone would soon cross the border where it was safe to trade whiskey to the Blackfoot. Riplinger hired Tom Healy, Lee Keiser and the old American Fur Co. trader Alexander Culbertson, then down on his luck, to trade at the new post for the Northwestern Fur Company. In the last years of his life Culbertson was drinking heavily and was in poor financial condition. This was probably his last trading experience, quite a come-down from his years as "King of the Upper Missouri."

A King Abdicates

When Alexander Culbertson learned of the events in 1870, he was mystified. His whole world was coming apart. Natawista had left him that year for John Riplinger then returned to her Kainaa people in Canada. His once powerful Indian friends were subdued and subjected to life on the reservation. When his attempts to get his wife back failed, and he refused to go north of the border to live, Culbertson left Fort Benton. A lonely old man, he went to Orleans, Nebraska and spent his last years with his daughter Julia. During his final years in Fort Benton, Culbertson told his story of the Blackfoot trade to Lt. James Bradley who was stationed at the garrison in Fort Benton. Culbertson died August 27, 1879 and is buried in Orleans, Nebraska.

A Court Battle

Clarke's death and several other incidents precipitated the final act of the war. In October a grand jury convened to indict five Piikani warriors who had been recognized by Clarke's children. In his deposition U.S. Marshal Wheeler named 56 whites who had been killed and noted that over a thousand horses had been stolen. Warrants were issued and given to General Sully to make the arrests.

Reports of conditions in Montana encouraged General Philip H. Sheridan, in charge of the Military Division of Missouri, to formulate a winter campaign that would teach the hostiles a lesson. An aggressive man, General Sheridan believed in total war against the Indians to make them pay for their predations on the whites. A winter campaign plan, so successful on the southern plains, was approved by General Sherman, Chief of Staff in Washington, and sent to Montana to put into action.

One person who was not caught up in the hysteria was the Commandant at Fort Shaw, General Philip de Trobriand, who reported to General Greene in November 1869: "I do not see so far an opportunity for striking a successful blow. The only Indians within reach are friendly, and nothing could be worse, I think, than to chastise them for offenses of which they are not

Schwinden Library, Fort Benton

Alexander Culbertson's monument in the cemetery at Orleans, Nebraska

guilty. I speak not only with a view to justice and humanity but for the best interests of the Territory. " General de Trobriand was aware that the hostiles under indictment were camped near the border and would cross over the "Medicine Line" as soon as they were pursued by the troops.

Government Investigation

General Sully, the Superintendent of Indian Affairs in Helena, violently disagreed and urged a firm military policy. Agitation in Montana and conflicting reports from his commanders in the field caused General Sheridan to send General James A. Hardie to Montana to investigate. He reported to General Sheridan that the troubles were merely isolated incidents created by young hot-blooded braves in reprisal for killing Indians and the chiefs could not control them. There surely was no general uprising of the Blackfoot. General Sully admitted earlier that he could arrest the guilty parties for the Piikani deaths in Fort Benton, but it would be futile since no court in Montana would convict a white man of killing an Indian.

Schwinden Library, Fort Benton

Officers' Row at regimental headquarters in Fort Shaw, Montana Territory

Schwinden Library, Fort Benton

General Philip de Trobriand, Commandant at Fort Shaw in 1870. He sent Baker on the winter campaign against the Blackfoot.

Adding to the tension was a council on New Year's Day 1870. General Sully and U.S. Marshal W.F. Wheeler met with several of the chiefs at the Teton agency. General Sully and Wheeler demanded that the murderers of Malcolm Clarke be turned over to the authorities. They informed the chiefs that the government would make war to protect the lives and property of the whites, and bluffed that the Army would pursue the hostiles across the Canadian border. The friendly chiefs, one of whom was Heavy Runner, promised to bring in the guilty and return the stolen horses, even if there was little chance to deliver on their promises. The whites were not willing to allow them much time to fulfill their promises either. General Sully had little faith in the chiefs and recommended that the army strike soon. Even General de Trobriand lost his cool when he heard that Mountain Chief and his band had crossed the line and were in their winter camp on the Marias. The army believed that he was harboring the murderers so the general proposed an attack on Mountain Chief's winter camp as an example to the rest of the hostiles.

The chiefs were given two weeks, in the middle of winter, to find and kill the perpetrators, to round up the stolen horses and

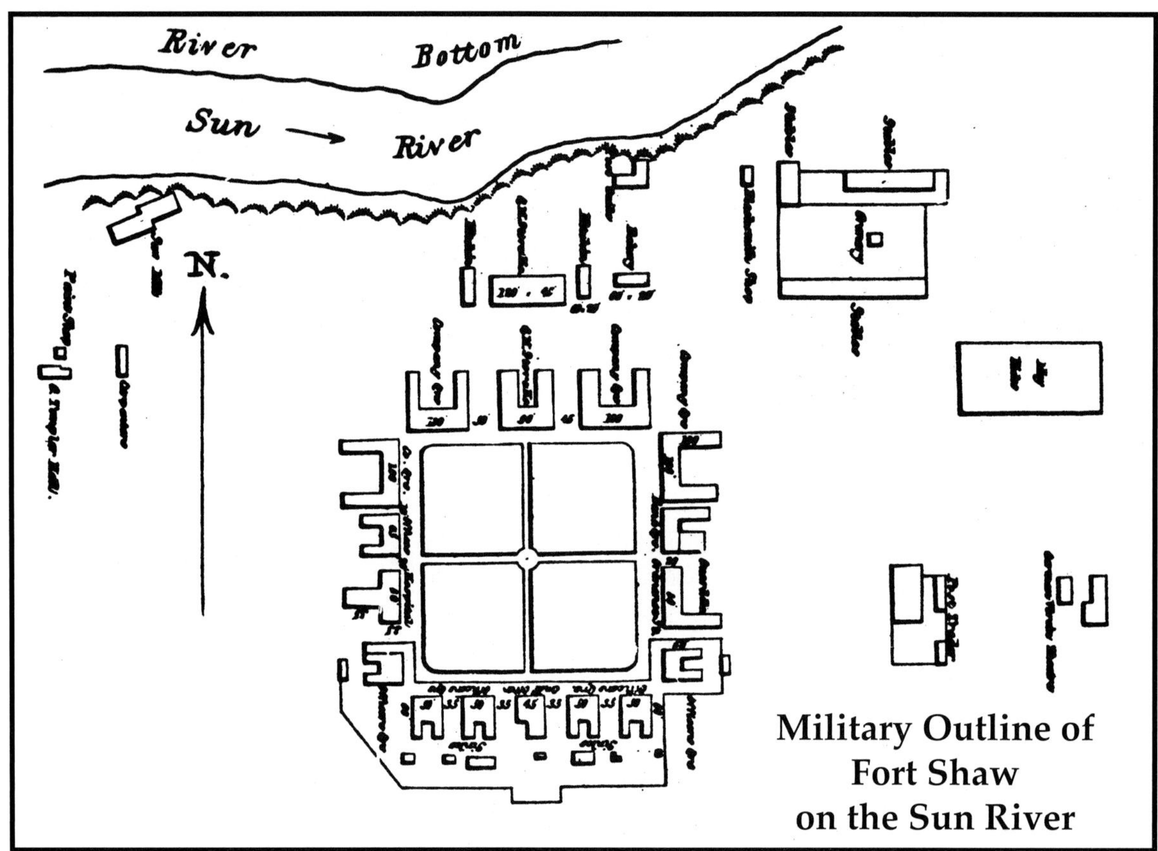

Military Outline of Fort Shaw on the Sun River

bring them to the agency, a next to impossible task. The whites really wanted blood and did not care from which Indians it was taken. In the final irony, General Sully had a change of heart and wrote in January to General Hardie, "No blood should be shed, if it is possible to avoid it."

The Massacre

When the deadline passed, and with de Trobriand's encouragement, General Sheridan sent a telegram ordering the attack. The last words were, "Tell Baker to strike them hard."

In mid-January the plains of Montana were gripped by the worst weather in years. Lands along the east slopes of the Rockies experienced not only blizzards and -30 to -40 temperatures, but also "chinooks," when warm southwest winds raise temperatures from well below zero to 40 above in a few hours.

During those inclement conditions, in anticipation of the impending action Major Eugene M. Baker moved four companies of the 2nd Cavalry from Fort Ellis to Fort Shaw in the heart of Blackfoot Country. The troops were given a few days of rest while they huddled close to the fires inside the adobe walls of the barracks; the temperature dropped well below zero every night. The clear dry air carried sound for miles; even walking in the deep snow sounded across the prairie like a trip hammer.

When General de Trobriand gave Baker his marching orders, the weather changed from bad to worse. On January 19 Baker and four companies of cavalry, one of infantry and 55 mounted infantry left the warm confines of Fort Shaw and headed north into blizzard conditions. Wrapped tightly in buffalo robes over their government-issue wool hats and coats, they traveled only at night. They wanted to surprise the Indians before they could retreat

Schwinden Library, Fort Benton

Joe Kipp, fur trader, military scout and son of James Kipp, was employed by the American Fur Company for many years.

across the international border.

Joe Kipp, a scout who could surely distinguish Mountain Chief's camp from those of friendly bands, was their guide. He had traded among the Blackfoot for years, had a Blackfoot wife, and probably knew them as well as any white man in Montana . . . but not as well as he should have.

A Montana blizzard roared in on a north wind, snow was whipped up so intensely that it was almost impossible to see one's hand in front of his face. The chill factor was intolerable. Waiting for a break in the weather, Heavy Runner's band was hunkered down in their camp at the big bend on Maria's River. The military column traveled for four nights to avoid detection. The men kept their fires small and were allowed out of the saddle only long enough to keep their hands and feet from freezing. The storm abated as they approached the Marias, where they found the small Piikani camp of six lodges belonging to Gray Wolf.

Gray Wolf told the soldiers there was a large camp six or seven miles down stream. Colonel Baker detached a small party to go upstream and protect the trading post near Willow Rounds. He left the wagon train and the company of infantry on the flats above Gray Wolf's camp to prevent them from warning any

Schwinden Library, Fort Benton

Fort Ellis was the post from where the four companies of the 2nd Cavlary went to Fort Shaw to participate in the 1870 campaign against the Blackfoot in northern Montana.

Schwinden Library, Fort Benton

Enlisted men's barracks at Fort Shaw where troopers huddled around their fires trying to stay warm before the winter campaign against the Blackfoot.

other Piikani winter camps. Baker's mounted column of cavalry and mounted infantry rode down river until they found a village of thirty-seven lodges. Just before daybreak he deployed his dismounted troops in a skirmish line along the ridge above the camp. He had achieved complete surprise.

The Killing Frenzy

When day broke in the east and dawn peeked through the cold frosty air on January 23, 1870, Kipp recognized the lodge of Heavy Runner and tried to stop the attack. Old Heavy Runner rushed out of his tepee, holding his papers and his peace medal in both hands over his head. He was met with a soldier's bullet that left him face down in the snow. With rifles ready, the soldiers assumed that shot was the signal and opened fire into the silent lodges of the camp. In the ensuing melee, panic-stricken Indians ran for any cover they could find to escape the deadly hail of bullets coming from the ridge above. Volley after volley poured

Schwinden Library, Fort Benton

Major Eugene Baker commanded the winter Blackfoot campaign that destroyed the camp of the peaceful Heavy Runner band on Maria's River.

Artist Gustav Sohon

Mountain Chief's band, who were protecting the men the army was looking for, was downstream and escaped into Canada before the army arrived.

into the camp. After an hour of steady gunfire, there was no further movement. When the shooting ceased, the only sound that drifted across the cold morning air was the soft crying of wounded women and children.

Baker remounted his forces and charged down the hill into the camp of the peaceful Piikani who had long been friends of the whites. The soldiers shot into the tepees, pulling them down with ropes and set everything on fire. They killed 173 Piikani. Only fifteen or twenty of the males were warriors, the rest were boys and old men. The dead included ninety women and fifty small children. The troopers rounded up 140 prisoners, all women and children. When they saw that the prisoners were ravaged by smallpox, they turned the homeless captives loose into the Montana winter. Many had been roused from their beds and had little warm clothing. They stood forlornly in the snow and watched as their homes, possessions and supplies burned.

The soldiers rode off down river hoping to find Mountain Chief in the next camp. When they arrived, the camp had been warned and all they found were abandoned lodges. With only a single casualty, and a soldier who broke his leg when he fell off his horse, the army came through an eventful day with minimal losses.

Baker claimed that he did not know he was attacking a friendly camp. Didn't he realize that after he had committed the slaughter? Why did he abandon the innocent women and children of a friendly band? Some historians question his sobriety that morning. After four horrendous days in the field, the Montana winter may have taken a similar toll on others in his command. Was he too proud to admit his mistake . . . or too drunk? Perhaps he had "completed his mission" as most whites in Montana saw the issue. In their eyes, regardless which band of Indians was attacked, he had struck them hard and taught the Blackfoot a lesson.

Baker submitted his report two months after the massacre when he whitewashed his command saying that Mountain Chief escaped in the confusion and all the dead were able-bodied men except 53 women and children who were killed accidentally. Joe Kipp was horrified and ashamed of his part in the massacre. He adopted twelve of the orphaned children into his family, but never regained the

Schwinden Library, Fort Benton

Troopers of the 2nd Cavlary in parade dress; four companies of the regiment slaughtered Heavy Runner's band.

Schwinden Library, Fort Benton

Site of Heavy Runner's winter camp on Maria's River where in January 1870 he was attacked by troops from Fort Shaw. Many women and children were killed trying to escape the gun fire. Their lodges were burned and the refugees had to trek to Fort Benton in freezing winter weather.

trust of the Blackfoot people.

The only positive result of the massacre was the defeat of the bill to move the Indian Bureau from the Department of the Interior to the War Department. Imagine what the results may have been with Custer, Miles and Sheridan in charge of the western Indian populations.

The Blackfoot never mounted a threat against the U.S. government again; all they wanted was lasting peace. It was obvious to them that they could not stand against such a mighty force, and that "blood for blood" was no longer an option if they were to survive. Whites applauded the army's methods and believed that Major Baker had solved the problem once and for all.

The final challenge appeared in the New York Times: "The question is whether a wholesale slaughter of women and children was needed for the vindication of our arms." Under the administration of President U.S. Grant, the government decreed in 1871 that the unrealistic treaty system based upon the fiction of tribal sovereignty would be abandoned immediately.

A final account of Heavy Runner and his band, written by the Piikani, was called -

Chase Them up the Hill

> "When they were shot on Sunday January 23, 1870, south of here on the Bear River [Maria's River] one of the worst atrocities against Bear Chief's [Heavy Runner] band of more than 300 Piikani [Blackfoot] took place. Under the command of Lt. Colonel E. M. Baker, 2nd United States Calvary, 219 Piikani women, children, infants, and

Schwinden Library, Fort Benton

Dead Indian Coulee where Mountain Chief and his band were camped in the winter of 1870. They escaped into Canada before they could be attacked by troops from Fort Shaw.

elderly were massacred. This occurred while the men of the camp were away hunting. The soldiers were pursuing Pete Owl Child and five companions.

The Piikani had justifiably killed Malcolm Clarke for many inhuman acts against their people. In the early morning hours, snow and sub zero temperatures, the army came upon the camp of Heavy Runner who had made peace with the U. S. Government. As Heavy Runner went out to meet the soldiers, waving his peace agreement papers and medals, they shot and killed him and commenced firing for over an hour upon this sleeping camp. The U. S. Calvary took thousands of horses and buffalo robes, burning shelters to the ground, destroying contents, food, smothering alive by smoke and fire families of the lodges. Although 100 prisoners survived, the soldiers released them with no food, clothing or shelter after they realized that many of them were suffering from small pox epidemic. Many Piikani froze and starved to death while seeking refuge in nearby camps or Fort Benton. Few survivors and their descendants of Heavy Runner continue to tell the horror that remains indelible in the hearts of the Piikani. Amongst the survivors were two sons and two daughters of Heavy Runner. The Piikani have never received compensation for this great loss. Annually the Piikani acknowledges a memorial for Heavy Runner's Band. "

"You could shoot with your eyes shut . . ."

One of the last battles between Native American tribes was fought in the fall of 1870. After the Baker Massacre in January, most of the Kainaa and Piikani bands stayed north of the "Medicine Line" out of reach of the U.S. military. Cree and Assiniboine united into a large war party and attacked the Blackfoot

Schwinden Library, Fort Benton

Commandant's quarters at Fort Shaw where the campaign was set in motion that was the final act to end the free native culture of the Blackfoot.

bands who were weakened by that year's smallpox epidemic. After a long march west, they camped on the Little Bow River and sent out scouts who found two bands of Kainaa on the Oldman River.

They attacked in late afternoon, killing several men and women. Although greatly outnumbered, the Kainaa defended their camp valiantly and sent for help from both Fort Whoop-Up and the Piikani camped to the south. When the messenger arrived at the fort, Jerry Potts and his buddy George Star who were there drinking and carousing, immediately took up the fight and headed to the camp under cover of darkness. Circling the battlefield, Potts found the Piikani with many well-armed riders also hurrying to the rescue. He agreed to lead them into battle the next morning and the rescue force got into position to attack at dawn.

With a loud war cry, Potts led the charge at daybreak. The enemy, startled by the new forces, retreated to the banks of the Oldman and took up positions in a coulee at the river's edge. Blackfoot forces under Potts took their stand in another coulee. Shooting went on at long range with no one being hurt. To break the stalemate, Potts sent some of his marksmen to a nearby butte where they fired upon the lines of Cree and Assiniboine. In the volleys of bullets that rained down from above, many were wounded. A great charge was led by Potts and Star. The Cree and Assiniboine panicked, dropped their weapons, and dove into the Oldman, swimming for their lives.

The battle became a slaughter. Volley after volley were fired into the helpless people in the water. Potts later remarked, ". . . you could shoot with your eyes shut and kill a Cree." A few lucky ones reached safety on the other bank and took refuge in a grove of cottonwoods. The Blackfoot pursued them relentlessly and wiped out any survivors. At the end of the battle, the Blackfoot counted forty men and women dead; Cree and Assiniboine losses were over three hundred. (1)

The slaughter ended intertribal warfare for the Blackfoot Nation, just as the January slaughter south of the "Medicine Line" had ended all resistance to the whites.

End of a Great Nation

By 1880 the whites had destroyed the free society and the culture of the Blackfoot Nation. Never again would they rule all lands along the eastern front of the Rocky Mountains, from the Three Forks to the Saskatchewan, as they had for two hundred years. Their territory contained the best beaver country and the largest herds of buffalo on the continent.

The robe trade was not what it had been, a fur company at a post trading with Blackfoot trappers and hunters. It became a commercial enterprise with government and military interference. No thought was given to the native people, and little remained of the trade or the buffalo that supported them by 1880. Joseph Kipp wrote the epitaph for the fur trade, "I was born in the fur trade and expected to die in it, what do I do now?"

Text Notes

1: "Piegan Indians" House Exec. Doc. No. 269, 41st Congress 2nd Session, Washington, D. C. 1870 serial 1426

Finis

To the trade, to the fort and to the free culture of the natives

"Mark you, my son, the time is coming, is near, when alliance with Indian women, even legal marriages with them, must end. Fort Benton – not Fort Union – will be the head of steamboat navigation on the Upper Missouri. Here in this bottom a town, a city, will spring up, the country will be overrun with settlers, and the buffalo will disappear, the fur trade end."

Andrew Dawson, 1857

Bibliography

Chardon's Journal at Fort Clark, 1834 – 1839; Annie H. Abel, 1932

John James Audubon and His Journals; Marie R. Audubon/Elliott Coues, 1897

Fort Union and the Upper Missouri Fur Trade; Barton H. Barbour, 2001

A Majority of Scoundrels: An Informal History of the Rocky Mountain Fur Company; Don Berry, 1961

Among the Indians; Henry Boller and Milo Qualfe, 1959

The Hunting of the Buffalo; Douglas E. Branch, 1962

Frontiers of the Northwest: A History of the Upper Missouri Valley; Harold E. Briggs, 1940

Three Years in the Rocky Mountains; David L. Brown, 1982

The Military-Indian Frontier in Montana 1860 – 1890; Merrill G. Burlingame, 1938

A History of the American Fur Trade of the Far West; Phil E. Chappell, 1902

History of Early Steamboat Navigation on the Missouri River: Joseph LaBarge; Hiram M. Chittenden, 1903

Forty Years a Fur Trader on the Upper Missouri: The Personal Narrative of Charles Larpenteur, 1833-1872; Elliott Coues, 1898

New Light on the Early History of the Greater Northwest: The Manuscript Journals of Alexander Henry and David Thompson 1799-1814; Elliott Coues, 1897

Five Indian Tribes of the Upper Missouri; Edwin T. Denig/John Ewers, 1961

Oregon Missions and Travels over the Rocky Mountains 1845 - 1846, Vol. XXIX of Early Western Travels 1748-1846; Pierre Jean DeSmet, 1906, 1978

Across the Wide Missouri; Bernard DeVoto, 1947

The Blackfeet: Raiders on the Northwestern Plains; John C. Ewers, 1958

The First Chouteaus: River Barons of St. Louis; William E. Foley/David C. Rice, 1983

Exploration and Empire: The Explorer and Scientist in the Winning of the American West; William H. Goetzmann, 1966

The Mountain Men and the Fur Trade of the Far West; LeRoy R. Hafen, 1965-1972

Up the Missouri with Audubon; Edward Harris/John F. McDermott, 1951

A History of Steamboating on the Upper Missouri River; William E. Lass, 1962

The Life of Father DeSmet, S.J. (1801-1873); E. Laveille, 1915

The Fist in the Wilderness; David Lavender, 1964

Henry A. Boller, Missouri River Fur Trader; Ray H. Mattison, 1966

Manuel Lisa and the Opening of the Missouri Fur Trade; Richard E. Oglesby, 1963

Fort Benton World's Innermost Port; Joel Overholser, 1987

Indian and White in the Northwest; Lawrence Palladino, 1894

The Fur Trade; Paul C. Phillips, 1961

The Life of Isaac Ingalls Stevens; Hazard Stevens, 1900

Journal of the Operations of Governor Isaac Ingalls Stevens of Washington Territory in 1855; Isaac Ingalls Stevens/Edward J. Kowrach, 1978

Carl Wimar, Chronicler of the Missouri River Frontier; Rick Stewart, Joseph D. Ketner II and Angela L. Miller, 1991

Forty Years on the Frontier; James and Granville Stuart, 1925

The Fur Trade on the Upper Missouri 1840 – 1865; John E. Sunder, 1965

Artists and Illustrators of the Old West, 1850 – 1900; Robert Taft, 1953

People of the First Man; Davis Thomas and Karin Ronnefeldt, 1976

Frontier Diplomats: The Life and Times of Alexander Culbertson and Natoyist-Siksina; Lesley Wischmann, 2000

The Fur Trade of the American West, 1807-1840; David J. Wishart, 1979

The Correspondence and Journals of Captain Nathaniel J. Wyeth, 1831-1836: A Record of Two Expeditions for the Occupation of the Oregon Country; Nathaniel J. Wyeth/F.G. Young, 1899

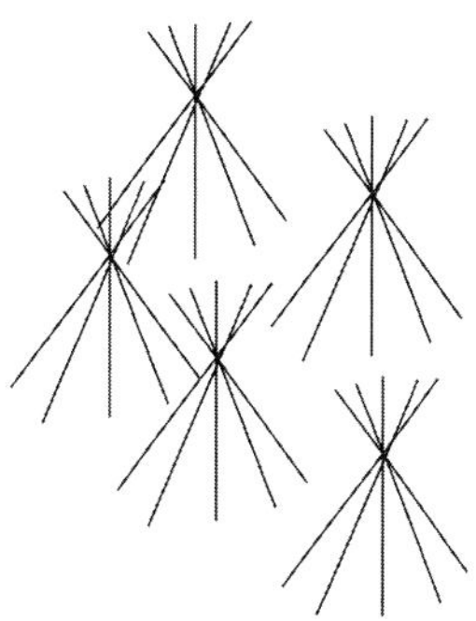

Epilogue

Into Bondage

It ended on that cold January day in 1870; the Blackfoot were beaten into submission. The Company abandoned Blackfoot Country, and the buffalo and steamboat had only a few more years before they were history. The Blackfoot fur trade was over.

Smallpox and national governments both north and south of the border had humbled the mighty Blackfoot Nation. Treaty No. 7 in Canada made the Blackfoot north of the border into reservation Indians. In 1879 the Blackfoot had their last buffalo hunt in the Judith Basin. Even before the hunt was over, the military forced them back to the reservation.

The Canadian buffalo herd moved south of the border in the winter of 1880 and never returned to Canada. 1880 annual returns showed only four thousand robes were shipped and none thereafter. In only three more killing years hunters decimated the rest of the northern herd; over 400,000 robes were shipped east in those last three years. In 1884, only four years later, only a few thousand robes went to the East. The robe trade was finished and the bison were near extinction.

Buffalo, the staff of life for the Blackfoot, had almost disappeared. In less than a dozen years the buffalo slaughter was over. In 1887 the American Museum of Natural History in New York came to Montana to collect specimens before the species was gone and they could find none. Just the year before William T. Hornaday, fearing that the National Museum in Washington D.C. would not have any specimens in its collections, traveled to Miles City and spent months along the divide between the Yellowstone and Missouri. He only collected 24 specimens for the Smithsonian.

Those plains bison were the last of the wild plains species. The mounts were exhibited at the Smithsonian for the next 70 years. Hornaday's buffalo were restored and are on display in Fort Benton, the last Blackfoot fur post. The big bull is a symbol of the federal government, adorning government seals, badges, money and stamps. Remember, this is the same government who tried to rid the plains of these animals, and force the Plains Indians onto reservations and become wards of the government. When the slaughter ceased, only few hundred animals were left in North America.

When the buffalo robe first became a marketable trade item, there were thirty million animals roaming the Great Plains. They provided a way of life for the free-roaming nomadic native people. No one could ever imagine that in thirty short years they would be near extinction. The fur companies harvested 20 to 30 thousand annually by trading with the plains tribes from the 1840's to 1865. The military and federal Indian agents eventually realized that the best method to control the tribes and place them on reservations was to remove the buffalo. That concept, and of course greed, encouraged the slaughter in earnest and by 1884 it was over.

Below are figures from several sources citing the number of buffalo robes shipped down river by steamboat from the Upper Missouri. Canadian returns were also part of the totals from Fort Benton and other up river shipping points. There were no returns from Canada after 1880. Those sent out during the last years by the Northern Pacific from Miles City and other rail stations on the line are the returns listed for 1881 to 1884.

In Thousands

1870	40 U.S.	Canada 10
1871	30 U.S.	Canada 12
1872	30 U.S.	Canada 17
1873	50 U.S.	Canada 17
1874	60 U.S.	Canada 30
1875	100 U.S.	Canada 60
1876	140 U.S.	Canada 71
1877	100 U.S.	Canada 50
1878	75 U.S.	Canada 14
1879	40 U.S.	Canada 8
1880	35 U.S.	Canada 4
1881	70 U.S.	by Train 40
1882	20 U.S.	by Train 200
1883	12 U.S.	by Train 40
1884	4 U.S.	by Train ?

The last sad chapter of the fur trade occurred in Canada from 1869 to 1874. The whiskey trade flourished in Canada until the North West Mounted Police arrived and immediately shut down the illicit trade with the Blackfoot. The five years of free traders and large companies from Fort Benton trading for whiskey, out of range of U.S. officials, decimated the Canadian Blackfoot culture, leaving them starving and ridden with small pox. Reservation life, stolen annuities, broken promises and more starvation were the final plight of the once magnificent people of the northern plains.

The fur trader was only a temporary resident of the land; he contributed little to the permanency of the region. Only his exploration was a lasting legacy. He discouraged farming, destroyed the wildlife, then abandoned the country when profits disappeared. The fur trader did very little to improve the culture of the Native Americans. He exploited them at every opportunity for the good of his company's owners in St. Louis. In a few instances he may have helped, but mostly he pillaged them with rot-gut liquor, cheated them in trade and prostituted their women. The trader brought European diseases against which the Indians had no natural resistance, diseases that depleted their population and completely wiped out some cultures.

It was a wild wasteful period in Western history and left very little to the lasting good of any society.

Appendix A

Blackfoot Treaties and Reservations

1. MacKenzie-Blackfoot Treaty, 1830-31 at Fort Union. Allowed American Fur Co. to build a trading post in Blackfoot Country and peaceful relations were established with the Assiniboine, Cree and Sioux. No Blackfoot were present at Fort Union for the treaty.

2. DeSmet Treaty, 1846. Lasted only a few months with the Flatheads, Nez Perce and three tribes of the Blackfoot Nation. It permitted Indians west of the mountains peaceful access to the buffalo range controlled by the Blackfoot once a year for a fall hunt.

3. Fort Laramie Treaty, September 1851. Blackfoot had no representatives but Alexander Culbertson was their appointed agent. The Blackfoot were assigned the land east of the divide to the Three Forks and to the Musselshell and Yellowstone.

4. Isaac Stevens Meeting, September 21, 1853 at Fort Benton. Thirty Blackfoot chiefs agreed to safe government passage through their country.

5. Lame Bull's Treaty at the mouth of the Judith River, October 17, 1855. Establishment of annuities to the Blackfoot, hunting rights for western tribes and peaceful passage for whites. Set up hunting territories for the Blackfoot: mouth of Milk River to the Musselshell in the south, to the Sun River and along the Continental Divide to Canadian border. Fort Benton became the first Blackfoot Agency for dispersal of the annuities.

6. Blackfoot Treat, November 16, 1865 at Fort Benton. Annuities promised, peace with the Atsina, boundaries established for Blackfoot. Moved south boundary from the Musselshell north to the Missouri River along the Marias and Teton Rivers to the mountains. Treaty never ratified by U.S. government.

7. Blackfoot Agency Treaty, 1868 at Fort Benton. Reaffirmation of the 1865 terms related to boundaries. Annuities reduced and changed. Again tried to establish peace with Atsina but they wanted no part of the Blackfoot and were given the eastern edge of the reserve. Treaty never ratified by U.S. government.

8. Blackfoot Agency moved to the Teton River Agency, 1869. After 1871 U.S. government refused to recognize any Indian Nation within the boundaries of the United States. There were no more treaties after this date.

9. Presidential Order and Congressional Act, 1873-74. Moved southern reservation boundary from Musselshell River to Missouri and Marias Rivers, on to Birch Creek and the Continental Divide in the west. Eastern boundary moved to mouth of Milk River. Northern boundary at Canadian border.

10. Blackfoot Agency moved from Teton River to Running Crane's place on Badger Creek, 1876.

11. Treaty No. 7 written by Canadian government September 1877 with Blackfoot bands north of the border. All Canadian Blackfoot tribes on reservations with annuities.

12. Blackfoot Agency moved 1880 downstream to what is now called Old Agency.

13. 1888 agreement. Moved reservation boundaries to today's eastern limits and to Birch Creek on the south.

14. Blackfoot Agency moved 1894-95 to more central location on Willow Creek where the town of Browning is today.

15. 1896 Agreement. Blackfoot gave up western portion of reservation from Continental Divide to present boundary between reservation and Glacier National Park.

Appendix B

Processing a Robe

Hunting cow buffalo began in November. Indian women converted the heavily furred hides into well-tanned robes. It was arduous work. The hides were fleshed, i.e. cleaned of all adhering scraps of meat and fat, then laced into lodgepole frames where they dried as stiff and firm as thin boards. Standing upon the hide, smooth side up, the tanner used an elkhorn-handled, steel-bladed instrument the shape of a hoe and chipped the hide to about one-half its original thickness. It was then rubbed with grease.

When the grease had thoroughly soaked into the hide, it was smeared with a mixture of boiled liver and brains, folded, rolled and laid away for several days so the mixture could neutralize its glue. Then came the hardest work. For an hour or so at a time, the tanner rubbed and seesawed the hide against upright, stretched thongs of rawhide until it became as soft and pliable as velvet. The result was a well-tanned cow buffalo robe which was worth five dollars in trade goods.

James Willard Schultz

Butchering Buffalo

"They cut the skin along the back and turned it down on both sides, then cut off the flesh from the hump, shoulders, and rump. When they reach the skeleton they turn the animal over and remove the contents of the cavities.

The tastiest portions of the stomach and its contents were eagerly seized and eaten raw, dipping them in the pools of blood, the marrow of the bones and the brain were also ate in the same manner. The raw liver was the delicacy of the animal and reserved for the hunter killing the animal who ate it warm as it came out of the body cavity."

A buffalo robe, hide dressed with the hair on, was the common standard of currency. It was valued at $4 in goods at the trading posts in 1858.

If you wanted to buy a horse from an Indian, his price for a buffalo horse would be 30 robes. You would pay him in goods from the trade store to the value of 30 robes. Estimate the price at $4 for each robe. The cost of the goods in St. Louis was between $30 and $40. Actual cost of the goods - four cups of sugar, coffee or tea - was equal to one robe.

1830 price of buffalo robe $4.00; 1850 price $3.00 a robe. In trade for merchandise: cost of merchandise 1.35; expenses to handle robe 1.20; total cost $2.55. Profit per robe about 45 cents

Bolle wrote his father in 1858, "Trade for a horse 30 robes at $4 a robe, in trade goods cost of trade goods would be $30 to $40 for $120 for the robe price in St. Louis."

Other furs that were traded included muskrat, badger, mink, deer, bear, fox, wolf, ermine and skunk.

Robe Trade Markets

The largest market for processed buffalo hides was for lap robes in carriages, buggies and sleighs in the populated centers of the eastern United States and western Europe. The secondary market for raw hides and semi-processed robes was also in the eastern United States where industrial machinery was powered by large steam engines. The engines were driven from a long drive shaft by systems of wheels and pulleys connected by leather belting. Buffalo hide was thicker and tougher than any other animal leather and was in constant demand during the Industrial Revolution.

Appendix C

Totals of Missouri River Fur Trade 1831 to 1858

Trade was accomplished by keelboat and mackinaw on the upper river above Fort Union until arrival of the first steamboat in 1859. Estimates are from company records and Alexander Culbertson's figures. The opposition company was about half of the American Fur Co. totals. During the early years probably the greatest concentration was in beaver pelts and other small furs rather than buffalo robes. By 1840 the trade was shifting to robes, and by the time Fort Benton was founded in 1846 most of the trade was in buffalo hides and robes. Hides were the untanned, dried and salted skins; robes were scraped and softened by tanning and were worth a great deal more.

From 1831 to 1837 freight coming to the Blackfoot posts was between 10 and 20 tons of goods and provisions. The returns went down river mainly by mackinaw. These 60-foot flat-bottomed boats made at the forts carried up to 50 tons of hides and robes. The average tonnage in those years has been estimated at 50 to 100 tons annually. There is a firm figure from Fort MacKenzie in 1837 of 6450 pounds of beaver pelts sent down and 6000 robes. 1837 was the year of the terrible smallpox epidemic that wiped out about half of the population in the Blackfoot bands and also took its toll on the fort personnel.

Even with the reduced number of Indians involved in the trade, the number of robes rose each year. More and more of the buffalo population was decimated until by 1880 there were few left on the Upper Missouri.

Estimates for the years 1831 to 1837: up trade goods, 80 tons; down tonnage, 334; robes, 25,000

Year	Tons Up	Tons Down	Robes
1838	20	127	10000
1839	20	130	10000
1840	25	135	17000
1841	40	255	20000
1842	40	290	21000
1843	42	142	13000
1844	20	100	10000
1845	10	58	5000
1846	20	220	17000
1847	25	315	20000
1848	30	350	22000
1849	30	360	24000
1850	32	320	24000
1851	35	340	23000
1852	38	350	25000
1853	35	360	28000
1854	35	320	24000
1855	40	290	18000
1856	40	275	22000
1857	42	381	27000
1858	45	326	24000
Total	**744**	**5778**	**429000**

Appendix D

Opposition Companies

Rocky Mountain Fur Company

Founded by Wm. Ashley and Andrew Henry. Was first company in the mountains.
1824, Henry withdrew from the mountains
1825, Ashley took on Jedediah Smith as his partner
1826, Ashley sold out to Jedediah Smith, David Jackson and Wm. Sublette
1830, Sold to Milton Sublette, Tom Fitzpatrick, Jim Bridger, Henry Fraeb and Jean Baptiste Gervais. Called Rocky Mountain Fur Co.
1834, Partners sold to American Fur Company at the rendezvous.
Posts: none

Sublette and Ashley

In 1832-33 Robert Campbell, Wm. Sublette and Wiliam Ashley organized to compete with American Fur Co. on the upper river.
Posts: Fort William and Fort Henry

Union Fur Co.

Also called Fox-Livingston Co. 1841-45. New York financed, based in St. Louis. Partners: Samuel Fox, Mortimer Livingston, John Ebbetts, Fulton Cutting, Charles Kelsey and Robert Campbell
Posts: Fort Mortimer, Fort Fox-Livingston, Fort Cotton and a trading house at the juncture of Little Bighorn and Yellowstone Rivers

Harvey, Primeau and Co.

Also called St. Louis Fur Company, 1845-60. Partners: Alexander Harvey, Charles Primeau, Robert Campbell, William Deschamps, Wm. Sublette, Joseph Picotte and Anthony R. Bouis.
1854, J. Picotte and Company
1856, Frost, Todd and Company backed by Robert Campbell
1859-60, a subsidiary Clarke, Primeau and Co. financed mainly by Robert Campbell
Posts: Fort Campbell, Fort William (Mortimer), Fort Bouis and Harvey's Post

LaBarge, Harkness and Co.

1861-63.
Partners: John and Joseph LaBarge, James Harkness, Eugene Jaccard and William Galpin
Posts: Fort LaBarge, Fort Galpin and Fort LaFrambois

Appendix E

American Fur Company

1784 John Jacob Astor entered the fur trade

1808 American Fur Company organized

1821 After amalgamation of Hudson Bay and North West Fur Co. in Canada, disgruntled traders formed the Columbia Fur Co. on the Upper Missouri.

1822 American Fur Co. split into two departments. Western Department managed by David Stone and Co., Northern Department managed by Ramsey Crooks.

1827 Columbia Fur Co. absorbed into Western Dept. of American Fur Co. Name changed to Upper Missouri Outfit. Bernard Pratt and Co. with Pierre Chouteau Jr. as a partner took over management.

1834 Astor sold Western Department to Pratt, Chouteau and Co.

1839 Reorganized as Pierre Chouteau Jr. and Co.

1865 Sold to Northwestern Fur Co.

Appendix F

Fort Benton Traders

From the MHS Contributions

(volume/page numbers)

Robert Campbell, 1/133,138; 8/49-60
Anthony Bouis, 4/121,213
Charles Primeau, 4/53,121; 5/71
Joseph Picotte, 4/121; 9/312
Malcolm Clarke, 1/305, 308; 2/309; 4/121-122; 8/69-72; 10/263-265
Michel and Baptiste Champagne, 10/260-261
Alexander Harvey, 4/119-123
David Mitchell, 1/149; 2/241; 4/119; 9/110
Jacob Berger, 1/107; 4/121-122; 8/71
Jim Lee, 4/121-122; 8/71
Antoine Dauphin, 10/292-298
Andrew Dawson, 10/266
Augustin Hamell (Armell), 10/261-262
James Kipp, 2/149, 205-215
Andrew Potts, 2/245
Fox-Livingston, 1/70, 302
Harvey Primeau and Co., 1/170; 4/121-122
Honore Picotte, 1/304-305; 9/310-312
George Weippert, 10/247-249
Hugh Monroe, 10/255-256
Robert Meldrum, 10/284-285
James Bird, 10/256-260
Louis Rivet, 10/250-254

Famous Visitors during the Fur Trade on the Upper Missouri

Alfred Jacob Miller 1821 Fort Union
George Catlin 1832 Fort Union
Prince Maxmilian and Karl Bodmer 1833 Fort MacKenzie
John J. Audubon 1843 Fort Union
Rudolph F. Kurz 1846-52 Fort Union
Fr. Nicolas Point 1846-47 Fort Lewis
John Mix Stanley 1853 Fort Benton
Gustav Sohon 1855-1860 Fort Benton
Karl Wimar 1858-59 Fort Benton
William Jacob Hays 1860
William Cary 1861 and 1874 Fort Benton
Granville Stuart 1865 Fort Benton
William Drummond Stewart 1866
F.J. Haynes 1880 Fort Benton
George Caleb Bingham
Seth Eastman, military artist
Henry Mollhausen
Pierre deSmet

Indian Agents

James H. Norwood - 1852; murdered year of appointment
Alfred J. Vaughan - Commissioner of Indian Affairs 1852-1857; Blackfoot Agent 1857-1861
A. H. Redfield - Commissioner of Indian Affairs 1857-1859
E. A. C. Hatch - Blackfoot Agent 1856
Bernard S. Schoonover - Commissioner of Indian Affairs 1859
Alfred Cummings - Commisioner of Indian Affairs 1855
Gad Upson - 1863-1866

Agents in Charge of Upper Missouri Outfit (Chouteau and Co.)

Kenneth Mackenzie 1828-1837
Honore Picotte 1838-1847
Alexander Culbertson 1848-1857
Andrew Dawson 1858-1862

Bourgeois of Blackfoot Posts

Fort Union
Kenneth MacKenzie 1829-1837
Alexander Culbertson 1837-1846
Edwin T. Denig 1848-1856
James Kipp/Charles Larpenteur 1854-1866

Fort MacKenzie
David Mitchell 1832-1834
James Kipp 1834-1836
Alexander Culbertson 1837-1841
Francis A. Chardon 1843-1844

Fort Benton
Alexander Culbertson 1846-1849
Malcolm Clarke 1850-1853
Andrew Dawson 1854-1862
I.G. Baker 1863-1864

Appendix G

Inventory at Fort MacKenzie, March 1844

38 prs. 3 point Hudson Bay blankets
29 1/2 3 pt. green Hudson Bay blanket
9 prs. 3 pt. white Hudson Bay blanket
2 1/2 prs. 3 1/2 pt. Dark blue Hudson Bay blanket
2 prs. 3 pt. dark blue Hudson Bay blanket

8 1/4 pieces Scarlet Saved list cloth 172 1/2 yds.
9 1/2 pieces blue Saved list cloth 162 1/2 yds.
11 1/3 pieces green Saved list cloth 98 yds.
5 pieces Blue Stroud

1 chiefs coat laced
1 green blanket capote
2 cammet vests
3 summer vests

1 doz. bennanger handkerchiefs
1/2 doz. Romell handkerchiefs
1/6 doz. yellow cotton handkerchief
1 doz. turkey red handkerchiefs
12 doz. 4/4 cotton shawls

6/4 pieces Pongee silk handkerchiefs
1 3/4 pieces black silk handkerchiefs
1 worsted shawl
1 red woolen sash
2 yds. White cotton shirting
1/4 lbs. Worsted yarn
1/4 doz. cotton suspender
2 white flannel shirts
1 white cotton shirt

1 bolt saddle webbing
37 pieces ribbon #4
2 lbs. Candlewick
2 1/2 lbs. Sewing thread
5 lbs. Holland twine
1/6 doz. chalk lines

19 lbs. gold lace
19 1/2 lbs. silver lace
3/4 doz. boxes cast balls
1 pair leather pants

191 inches wampum shell hair pipes
110 packs hawk balls
29 doz. crambo combs
3 doz. fine ivory combs
3 1/2 doz. boxwood combs

4 nests wampum moons

2 3/4 doz. roller buckles
1 1/4 doz. razors in cases
1 case razors in case (2 each)
2 M asst. sewing needles
1/4 gross Indian awls
9 sea shells abalone
1/2 doz. green goggles

1/4 doz. tin arm bands
1/2 doz. tin wrist bands
1 pair gilt bracelets
1/4 gross brass finger rings
3/4 gross brass thimbles
1/2 gross orange coat buttons
1 2/3 doz. plume sockets
1/3 doz. shaving boxes

2 prs. Stirrup irons
1/2 doz. paper covered mirrors
1/5 M pistol flints
1 1/2 M percussion caps

7/12 doz. white wool shirts
5/12 doz. black rommel shirts
1 doz. black shirts
4 boys green shirts
1 boys black shirt
43 white powder horns

112 bundles round white agate beads
13 bundles round blue beads
2 bundles round red beads
138 bundles large white R. C. beads
7 bundles blue K. beads
15 bundles blue snake beads
3 1/2 bundles large B. marble agate beads
1/2 bundle white pound beads
5 bundles Bro. Garnishing beads

1 pair mens brogans

1/2 bundle blue garnishing beads

3 doz. Britannia mirrors #4
6 1/2 doz. Britannia mirrors #3
2 2/3 doz. Britannia mirrors #2
1 1/3 doz. Britannia mirrors #1

7/12 doz. gunlocks
1/2 doz. table spoons
2 scythe stones
1 1/4 doz. sneaths
15 doz. arrow points
24 lbs. rough house bells
1 M gunflints

3 11/12 doz. Wilson butcher Knives 7 inches
4 doz. green Handle Knives
29 doz Waranteed Scalping Knives
2 doz. Commercial Scalping Knives
5 dragoon swords
1 dragoon sword
7 Indian half axes
3 tomahawks 2 thumb lancets
1 spring lancet
1 telescope
2 penknives

1/4 doz. 8 inch square file
1/2 doz. 6 inch half round cast steel files
2/3 doz. 6 inch half roundbastard files
1/4 doz. 5 inch flat files
1 7/12 doz. 5 inch hand saw files
8 1/2 doz. pit saw files
5/12 doz. 7 inch cross cut files
1 7/12 doz. nail gimlets
1 set socket chissells
1 bright auger
1/4 doz. tap borers

7 Indian battle axes
1/2 doz. cast steel axes Harris chopping
13 North West guns
135 lbs. Chinese vermillion
2 gross day pipes
13 wooden pails
512 lbs. lead in ball
839 lbs. pig lead
5 kegs gun powder 50 lbs. each
18 cartridges 50 lbs. each
2 cannister balls
32 cannon balls

2522 lbs. plug tobacco
1/2 box raisins
1 barrel flour
100 lbs. brown Havana sugar
60 lbs. coffee
3/4 bushel dried peaches
3/4 bag GA salt

2 tin kettles 3 gallon each
22 tin kettles 2 gallon
1tin kettle 1 gallon
1 Jap. Kettle 4 gallon
14 painted tin kettles #3
1 painted tin kettle #4
1 painted tin kettle #2
1 tin coffee cup
7/12 doz. tin plates #3
1/2 doz. tin plates #1
1/2 doz. pint tin cups
5/12 doz. 1/2 pint tin cups
5/12 doz. large oval tin dishes
1/12 doz. tin funnels & 1/4 doz. lanterns
1/4 doz. candlemoulds
1/4 doz. ?
1/12 doz. ?

Sundry medicines valued at
9/20 ream ruled writing paper
4/20 ream plain writing paper
1/20 ream letter writing paper
1/2 doz. black ink powder
1/6 doz. lead pencils
1/4 C quills
1 inkstand

48 beaver traps & chains
24 beaver trap springs
1 pair steelyards 180 lbs.
1 platform spring balance
2 three pound iron cannon mounted
12 North West guns
13 powder horns

American Fur Company Records, Roll 11, Ledger JJ, Missouri Historical Society

Blackfoot Fur Trade Index

A

B

C

D

E

F

G

H

I

J

K

L

M

R

S

T

U

V

W

X

Y

Z